language

 Other titles in this
series include:

language
A READER *for* WRITERS

Gita DasBender
Seton Hall University

New York   Oxford
Oxford University Press

Oxford University Press publishes works that further Oxford University's
objective of excellence in research, scholarship, and education.

Oxford   New York

Auckland   Cape Town   Dar es Salaam   Hong Kong   Karachi

Kuala Lumpur   Madrid   Melbourne   Mexico City   Nairobi

New Delhi   Shanghai   Taipei   Toronto

With offices in

Argentina   Austria   Brazil   Chile   Czech Republic   France   Greece

Guatemala   Hungary   Italy   Japan   Poland   Portugal   Singapore

South Korea   Switzerland   Thailand   Turkey   Ukraine   Vietnam

Published by Oxford University Press

198 Madison Avenue, New York, New York 10016

http://www.oup.com

Library of Congress Cataloging-in-Publication Data

DasBender, Gita.

  Language : a reader for writers / Gita DasBender. -- First Edition.

    pages cm

  Includes bibliographical references and index.

  ISBN 978-0-19-994748-5 (pbk.)

  1. College readers. 2. English language--Rhetoric. 3. Report writing. I. Title.

PE1417.D223   2013

808'.0427--dc23

                                                        2013037306

Printing number: 9 8 7 6 5 4 3 2 1

Printed in the United States of America

on acid-free paper

brief table of contents

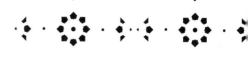

contents

3   Language & Writing   73

"Good writers do more than simply express their meaning; they pinpoint the critical differences between themselves and their reader and design their writing to reduce these differences."

"Crummy wording in instructions can mean the difference between a veteran collecting disability payments or not, or an immigrant violating visa requirements or not."

"Plain talk isn't only rewriting, it's rethinking your approach and really personalizing your message to the audience and to the reader."

"My Sergeant Martinez may be writing reports, but he's also using the alchemy of inflection to turn them into stories—narratives that believe themselves and make us believe them, too."

"Our new forms of writing—blogs, Facebook, Twitter—all have precedents, analogue analogues: a notebook, a postcard, a jotting on the back of an envelope. They are exceedingly accessible."

4   Language & Correctness   97

"Life is tricky in a world without rules. Fortunately, language does have rules, but they are more like bedrock principles than a detailed set of by-laws covering every do and don't."

"Yes, language is constantly changing, but that doesn't make grammar unimportant. Good grammar is credibility, especially on the internet."

"Managers are fighting an epidemic of grammar gaffes in the workplace. Many of them attribute slipping skills to the informality of email, texting and Twitter where slang and shortcuts are common."

"The natural evolution of language cannot and should not be used to dismiss all grammar mistakes."

"The debate about proper ways to use the English language occurs wherever English is read, written or spoken."

"Eble and some others who study the contemporary tongue do not think that bad grammar is necessarily destroying the English language."

"Acronyms have become so ubiquitous that we look for them even where they don't exist."

5   Language & Gender   127

"I hate the idea that in the United States of America, the phrase 'soccer mom' has been appropriated to mean (almost exclusively) white, middle-to-upper class, suburban women with children who may or may not play soccer."

6   Language & Race   155

8   Fighting Words   235

"I think the new definition validates what many outraged voices in blogs, on Twitter, and in the press have been saying all along: 'anchor baby' is a term that shouldn't exist but does because immigration restrictionists are really good at creating words that generate fear."

"Why have some found it vitally important to extend person to include not-exactly-human things, while others find it grotesque and overreaching?"

9 The Language of Globalization 269

"As English continues to spread, it seems like a steamroller, squashing whatever gets in its way...English seems, increasingly, to be a second first language."

"For people from affluent and developing nations alike, it is clear that the secret passwords to safety, wealth and freedom can be whispered only in English."

"The Afghan government is hard at work trying to strengthen English departments at teacher training colleges, and giving out scholarships to students to be trained as English teachers abroad."

"As opposed to physical labor, service work involves 'emotional labor', wherein workers are called on to amiably display a particular emotional repertoire. In call centers, management technologies penetrate to the very core of your identity."

"We are in danger of watering down our communication in the name of global democracy, or should that read 'in the name of Globish'?"

"'Geilivable,' a word coined from 'geili' in Chinese, a new cyber expression itself meaning 'impressive,' 'cool,' 'strong,' 'exciting.'"

10 Endangered Languages   307

"Small languages are using social media, YouTube, text messaging and various technologies to expand their voice and expand their presence."

"When languages become the preserve of the old, the knowledge systems inherent in them become endangered; for the rest of the world, this means that unique ways of adapting to the planet and responding creatively to its challenges go to the grave with the last speakers."

"Even though our language, along with other tribal tongues, suffered some losses during the course of the twentieth century, we fought hard to not lose it completely."

"The Indo-Portuguese Creole of Cochin was the mother tongue of part of the local Catholic community for over four centuries; records from the late 19th-century show that it was still vital at the time."

"Greenlandic words are too long to subtitle and to use in text messaging. Polar Eskimos tend to send text messages in Danish or English because it is easier."

"Against the erosion of language stands an ineffable quality that can't be instilled from without: someone's insistence on rapping in Aka, on singing in Tuvan, on writing in the recently orthographized Cmiique Iitom."

rhetorical contents

academic research

analogy

argument and persuasion

cause and effect analysis

comparison and contrast

definition

description

division and classification

example and illustration

narration

process analysis

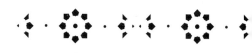

preface

As teachers of writing, we see firsthand the power and potential of language to change the lives of individual students as well as to create change in the classroom, the community, and the workplace. *Language: A Reader for Writers* attempts to capture a snapshot of the wide, almost inexhaustible, spectrum of experiences and ideas about language that shape 21st-century realities. One such reality that every writing teacher encounters today is the rapid growth of a culturally and linguistically diverse student population throughout the United States. More and more students are entering college from multiethnic backgrounds, and many come from non-English-speaking households where they are exposed to multiple languages. Yet this rich linguistic history is all but forgotten in college where language experiences that deviate from normative monolingual standards often remain unrecognized and are rarely celebrated. *Language: A Reader for Writers* mirrors the classroom community, family, and workplace in which our students often find themselves: multilingual, cosmopolitan, and tremendously exciting.

It is widely understood that language is both process and product; it provides a way of thinking, but it is also thinking made visible. Yet even as we organize thoughts, formulate sentences, and express ideas with words, we are changed by the process. We shape language but we are also shaped by it. It is this intersection of language and self that allows us to situate ourselves in a larger conversation with the world—and that invites the world to speak to us. *Language: A Reader for Writers* invites students to enter a larger conversation where they can actively participate as learners and users of language as well as develop a linguistic identity: that of competent and confident readers and writers, participants in an academic discourse that will serve them well in their college careers and beyond.

To reflect the spirit and the pedagogical intentions of the book, we have preserved the variant English spellings and conventions contained in the original readings. If our book's intention is to reflect the changing and increasingly global face of the English language, it is imperative that students intellectually, visually, and perhaps viscerally experience the rich lexical, syntactical, and rhetorical choices made by the writers represented here. Not only is such experience informative as it exposes students to the notion that linguistic variety within standardized forms is evidence that languages are flexible, their rules in perpetual flux, but it also opens up exhilarating and powerful opportunities for students to challenge established conventions and to make writerly choices that have been impossible in historically monolingual educational settings.

Language: A Reader for Writers presents a broad spectrum of writers who are researching, reflecting on, and arguing about these ideas and experiences. Some defend the status quo, and others argue for the vital force of change; some despair for what is being lost, and others celebrate the opportunities (while acknowledging the ambivalencies) of the new and different. Each chapter takes on a particularly urgent subject of contemporary conversation: the nature of language; the effects of globalization; endangered languages; multilingualism and language diversity; language, politics, and power; language and writing; language correctness; and the ways language shapes identity. Within each of these subjects, the articles embody a range of experiences, ideas, and strategies—from scientific research to poetic reflection, from powerful argument to playful celebration.

Language: A Reader for Writers is part of a series of brief single-topic readers from Oxford University Press designed for today's college writing courses. Each reader in this series approaches a topic of contemporary conversation from multiple perspectives:

- **Timely:** Most selections were originally published in 2010 or later.
- **Global:** Sources and voices from around the world are included.
- **Diverse:** Selections come from a range of nontraditional and alternate print and online media, as well as representative mainstream sources.

In addition to the rich array of perspectives on topical (even urgent) issues addressed in each reader, each volume features an abundance of different genres and styles—from the academic research paper to the pithy Twitter argument. Useful but nonintrusive pedagogy includes:

- **Chapter introductions** that provide a brief overview of the chapter's theme and a sense of how the chapter's selections relate both to the overarching theme and to each other.
- **Headnotes** introduce each reading by providing concise information about its original publication, and pose an open-ended question that encourages students to explore their prior knowledge of (or opinions about) some aspect of the selection's content.
- **"Analyze" and "Explore" questions** after each reading scaffold and support student reading for comprehension as well as rhetorical considerations, providing prompts for reflection, classroom discussion, and brief writing assignments.
- **"Forging Connections" and "Looking Further" prompts** after each chapter encourage critical thinking by asking students to compare perspectives and strategies among readings both within the chapter and with readings in other chapters, suggesting writing assignments that engage students with larger conversations in the academy, the community, and the media.
- **An appendix on "Researching and Writing About Language"** guides student inquiry and research in a digital environment. Co-authored by a research librarian and a writing program director, this appendix provides real-world, transferable strategies for locating, assessing, synthesizing, and citing sources in support of an argument. The appendix also includes a student's research paper, which models MLA style and citation conventions.

about the author

Gita DasBender is a Senior Faculty Associate and Second Language Writing Coordinator at Seton Hall University in the English Department, where she teaches first-year composition for multilingual students and other writing-intensive courses. She received her PhD in English Education with an emphasis in Composition Studies from New York University, where she taught second language writing courses and mentored other graduate assistants. She has published on reflective writing and metacognition, directed self-placement and multilingual students, critical thinking in college, and on the use of literature in a writing class. In 2011 she was awarded a five-year Fulbright Specialist grant in the field of Applied Linguistics. Her first Specialist assignment will take her to two universities in Vietnam where she will work with local faculty and students on English language development, reading and critical thinking, second language writing pedagogy, effective teaching practices, program and curriculum review, and faculty development initiatives.

acknowledgments

I wish to thank Meg Botteon, senior development editor at Oxford University Press, for giving me the creative license to imagine this book and for her incredible support throughout the process. I could not have finished this book without her insightful suggestions and encouragement. This project was completed during a sabbatical granted by Seton Hall University for which I thank Mary Balkun, Chair of English, and Provost Larry Robinson. I am deeply grateful for their support and for their unwavering commitment to faculty scholarship. My husband Dan and sons Deven and Reyen have cheered me on without complaints during this process and for this I am grateful as well. Finally, the generous and in-depth feedback, suggestions, and critique from a group of outstanding reviewers helped me make significant improvements to *Language: A Reader for Writers*. I thank Rebecca Babcock, University of Texas of the Permian Basin; Diane L. Baecker, Virginia State University; Beth Bir, Fayetteville State University; Nandan Choksi, Broward College; Kristen di Gennaro, Pace University; Rod Freeman, Estella Mountain Community College; Christopher T. Gazzara, Burlington County College; Marina Gorlach, Metropolitan State University of Denver; Charles L. Henderson, Ozarks Technical Community College; Anita Knudson, Sierra College; Carol Kushner, Dutchess Community College; Benjamin Lareau, Casper College; Majorie Lynn, University of Michigan-Dearborn; Joe Marmoud, Missouri Western State University; and Robert Mohrenne, University of Central Florida.

What Is Language For?

1

Language is the foundation of all human thought. It shapes the way we think of ourselves as well as how we interpret the world around us. Language allows us to imagine who we are, make sense of our surroundings, and participate in our culture and society. In essence, language gives meaning to our lives.

In our complex, globalized, and technology-driven world, the use of language in all its forms has been elevated to a ubiquitous activity. Every day, we text, tweet, blog, post updates on social media sites, and write e-mails—and not just in the language in which I'm writing this introduction. Yet, regardless of the language (or languages) we use, we rarely stop to wonder about how language helps us not only to express ourselves, but to create and give form to what we want to say. An inquiry into our use of language helps us develop a sense of self—a thinking self, if you will, who is eager to engage more thoughtfully and deliberately with the world.

All of the writers in this chapter are interested in exploring how, and to what extent, language shapes thought and behavior. Cognitive scientist Lera Boroditsky asks the question outright in the title of her essay, "How Does Our Language Shape the Way We Think?" She examines whether language differences naturally imply inherent differences in the way people think. Her research suggests that the distinct features of languages have a profound effect on the lives of its users. In her classic essay "Language and Thought," philosopher Susanne Langer differentiates between symbols and signs, focuses on language as symbolic expression, and argues that it is this attribute that distinguishes humans from animals. Linguist Arika Okrent takes up the fascinating subject of gesturing in "Body Language" and reveals how gestures not only complement language, but can be an enduring tool for communication. In "Alien Languages: Not Human," blogger and science fiction writer Anassa Rhenisch refers to human language patterns as a blueprint for what might seem familiar in an alien language, should we ever encounter one. Finally, in "Is Your Language Making You Broke and Fat? How Language Can Shape Thinking and Behavior (and How It Can't)," linguist and science journalist Julie Sedivy argues that language-based cultural biases say more about the culture of the speaker than the language itself. Her essay encourages us to consider the interconnections between language and culture.

Lera Boroditsky
How Does Our Language Shape the Way We Think?

Stanford University cognitive scientist Lera Boroditsky, editor-in-chief of *Frontiers in Cultural Psychology*, was named one of *Utne Reader*'s "25 Visionaries Who Are Changing Your World" for her groundbreaking work on how language shapes thought. Born in the former Soviet Union, Boroditsky explores how the language communities use can influence social policy. The following essay was published in 2009 in *Edge*, an "online salon" that brings together a community of "scientists, artists, philosophers, technologists, and entrepreneurs who are at the center of today's intellectual, technological, and scientific landscape."

A profile of Boroditsky in *Utne Reader* quoted her as observing that differences between languages can be "magical." Do you agree with this fundamentally hopeful view?

Humans communicate with one another using a dazzling array of languages, each differing from the next in innumerable ways. Do the languages we speak shape the way we see the world, the way we think, and the way we live our lives? Do people who speak different languages think differently simply because they speak different languages? Does learning new languages change the way you think? Do polyglots think differently when speaking different languages?

These questions touch on nearly all of the major controversies in the study of mind. They have engaged scores of philosophers, anthropologists, linguists, and psychologists, and they have important implications for politics, law, and religion. Yet despite nearly constant attention and debate, very little empirical work was done on these questions until recently. For a long time, the idea that language might shape thought was considered at best untestable and more often simply wrong. Research in my labs at Stanford University and at MIT has helped reopen this question. We have collected data around the world: from China, Greece, Chile, Indonesia, Russia, and Aboriginal Australia. What we have learned is that people who speak different languages do indeed think differently and that even flukes of grammar can profoundly affect how we see the world. Language is a uniquely human gift, central to our experience of being human. Appreciating its role in constructing our mental lives brings us one step closer to understanding the very nature of humanity.

I often start my undergraduate lectures by asking students the following question: which cognitive faculty would you most hate to lose? Most of them pick the sense of sight; a few pick hearing. Once in a while, a wise-cracking student might pick her sense of humor or her fashion sense. Almost never do any of them spontaneously say that the faculty they'd most hate to lose is language. Yet if you lose (or are born without) your sight or hearing, you can still have a wonderfully rich social existence. You can have friends, you can get an education, you can hold a job, you can start a family. But what would your life be like if you had never learned a language? Could you still have friends, get an education, hold a job, start a family? Language is so fundamental to our experience, so deeply a part of being human, that it's hard to imagine life without it. But are languages merely tools for expressing our thoughts, or do they actually shape our thoughts?

Most questions of whether and how language shapes thought start with the simple observation that languages differ from one another. And a lot! Let's take a (very) hypothetical example. Suppose you want to say, "Bush read Chomsky's latest book." Let's focus on just the verb, "read." To say this sentence in English, we have to mark the verb for tense; in this case, we have to pronounce it like "red" and not like "reed." In Indonesian you need not (in fact, you can't) alter the verb to mark tense. In Russian you would have to alter the verb to indicate tense and gender. So if it was Laura Bush who did the reading, you'd use a different form of the verb than if it was George. In Russian you'd also have to include in the verb information about completion. If George read only part of the book, you'd use a different form of the verb than if he'd diligently plowed through the whole thing. In Turkish you'd have to include in the verb how you acquired this information: if you had witnessed this unlikely event with your own two eyes, you'd use one verb form, but if you had simply read or heard about it, or inferred it from something Bush said, you'd use a different verb form.

> "What would your life be like if you had never learned a language?"

5   Clearly, languages require different things of their speakers. Does this mean that the speakers think differently about the world? Do English, Indonesian, Russian, and Turkish speakers end up attending to, partitioning, and remembering their experiences differently just because they speak different languages?

For some scholars, the answer to these questions has been an obvious yes. Just look at the way people talk, they might say. Certainly, speakers of different languages must attend to and encode strikingly different aspects of the world just so they can use their language properly.

Scholars on the other side of the debate don't find the differences in how people talk convincing. All our linguistic utterances are sparse, encoding only a small part of the information we have available. Just because English speakers don't include the same information in their verbs that Russian and Turkish speakers do doesn't mean that English speakers aren't paying attention to the same things; all it means is that they're not talking about them. It's possible that everyone thinks the same way, notices the same things, but just talks differently.

Believers in cross-linguistic differences counter that everyone does *not* pay attention to the same things: if everyone did, one might think it would be easy to learn to speak other languages. Unfortunately, learning a new language (especially one not closely related to those you know) is never easy; it seems to require paying attention to a new set of distinctions. Whether it's distinguishing modes of being in Spanish, evidentiality in Turkish, or aspect in Russian, learning to speak these languages requires something more than just learning vocabulary: it requires paying attention to the right things in the world so that you have the correct information to include in what you *say*.

Such a priori arguments about whether or not language shapes thought have gone in circles for centuries, with some arguing that it's impossible for language to shape thought and others arguing that it's impossible for language *not* to shape thought. Recently my group and others have figured out ways to empirically test some of the key questions in this ancient debate, with fascinating results. So instead of arguing about what must be true or what can't be true, let's find out what *is* true.

Follow me to Pormpuraaw, a small Aboriginal community on the western 10 edge of Cape York, in northern Australia. I came here because of the way the locals, the Kuuk Thaayorre, talk about space. Instead of words like "right," "left," "forward," and "back," which, as commonly used in English, define space relative to an observer, the Kuuk Thaayorre, like many other Aboriginal groups, use cardinal-direction terms—north, south, east, and west—to define space.[1] This is done at all scales, which means you have to say things like "There's an ant on your southeast leg" or "Move the cup to the north northwest a little bit." One obvious consequence of speaking such a language is that you have to stay oriented at all times, or else you cannot speak properly. The normal greeting in Kuuk Thaayorre is "Where are you going?" and the answer should be something like "South southeast, in the middle distance." If you don't know which way you're facing, you can't even get past "Hello."

The result is a profound difference in navigational ability and spatial knowledge between speakers of languages that rely primarily on absolute reference frames (like Kuuk Thaayorre) and languages that rely on relative reference frames (like English).[2] Simply put, speakers of languages like Kuuk Thaayorre are much better than English speakers at staying oriented and keeping track of where they are, even in unfamiliar landscapes or inside unfamiliar buildings. What enables them—in fact, forces them—to do this is their language. Having their attention trained in this way equips them to perform navigational feats once thought beyond human capabilities.

Because space is such a fundamental domain of thought, differences in how people think about space don't end there. People rely on their spatial knowledge to build other, more complex, more abstract representations. Representations of such things as time, number, musical pitch, kinship relations, morality, and emotions have been shown to depend on how we think about space. So if the Kuuk Thaayorre think differently about space, do they also think differently about other things, like time? This is what my collaborator Alice Gaby and I came to Pormpuraaw to find out.

To test this idea, we gave people sets of pictures that showed some kind of temporal progression (e.g., pictures of a man aging, or a crocodile growing, or a banana being eaten). Their job was to arrange the shuffled photos on the ground to show the correct temporal order. We tested each person in two separate sittings, each time facing in a different cardinal direction. If you ask English speakers to do this, they'll arrange the cards so that time proceeds from left to right. Hebrew speakers will tend to lay out the cards from right to left, showing that writing direction in a language plays a role.[3] So what about folks like the Kuuk Thaayorre, who don't use words like "left" and "right"? What will they do?

The Kuuk Thaayorre did not arrange the cards more often from left to right than from right to left, nor more toward or away from the body. But their arrangements were not random: there was a pattern, just a different one from that of English speakers. Instead of arranging time from left to right, they arranged it from east to west. That is, when they were seated facing south, the cards went left to right. When they faced north, the cards went from right to left. When they faced east, the cards came toward the body and so on. This was true even though we never told any of our subjects which direction they faced. The Kuuk Thaayorre not only knew that already (usually much better than I did), but they also spontaneously used this spatial orientation to construct their representations of time.

15   People's ideas of time differ across languages in other ways. For example, English speakers tend to talk about time using horizontal spatial metaphors

(e.g., "The best is ahead of us," "The worst is behind us"), whereas Mandarin speakers have a vertical metaphor for time (e.g., the next month is the "down month" and the last month is the "up month"). Mandarin speakers talk about time vertically more often than English speakers do, so do Mandarin speakers think about time vertically more often than English speakers do? Imagine this simple experiment. I stand next to you, point to a spot in space directly in front of you, and tell you, "This spot, here, is today. Where would you put yesterday? And where would you put tomorrow?" When English speakers are asked to do this, they nearly always point horizontally. But Mandarin speakers often point vertically, about seven or eight times more often than do English speakers.[4]

Even basic aspects of time perception can be affected by language. For example, English speakers prefer to talk about duration in terms of length (e.g., "That was a short talk," "The meeting didn't take long"), while Spanish and Greek speakers prefer to talk about time in terms of amount, relying more on words like "much," "big," and "little" rather than "short" and "long." Our research into such basic cognitive abilities as estimating duration shows that speakers of different languages differ in ways predicted by the patterns of metaphors in their language. (For example, when asked to estimate duration, English speakers are more likely to be confused by distance information, estimating that a line of greater length remains on the test screen for a longer period of time, whereas Greek speakers are more likely to be confused by amount, estimating that a container that is fuller remains longer on the screen.)[5]

An important question at this point is: Are these differences caused by language per se or by some other aspect of culture? Of course, the lives of English, Mandarin, Greek, Spanish, and Kuuk Thaayorre speakers differ in a myriad of ways. How do we know that it is language itself that creates these differences in thought and not some other aspect of their respective cultures?

One way to answer this question is to teach people new ways of talking and see if that changes the way they think. In our lab, we've taught English speakers different ways of talking about time. In one such study, English speakers were taught to use size metaphors (as in Greek) to describe duration (e.g., a movie *is larger than* a sneeze), or vertical metaphors (as in Mandarin) to describe event order. Once the English speakers had learned to talk about time in these new ways, their cognitive performance began to resemble that of Greek or Mandarin speakers. This suggests that patterns in a language can indeed play a causal role in constructing how we think.[6] In practical terms, it means that when you're learning a new language, you're not simply learning a new way of talking, you are also inadvertently learning a new way of thinking.

Beyond abstract or complex domains of thought like space and time, languages also meddle in basic aspects of visual perception—our ability to distinguish colors, for example. Different languages divide up the color continuum differently: some make many more distinctions between colors than others, and the boundaries often don't line up across languages.

20   To test whether differences in color language lead to differences in color perception, we compared Russian and English speakers' ability to discriminate shades of blue. In Russian there is no single word that covers all the colors that English speakers call "blue." Russian makes an obligatory distinction between light blue (*goluboy*) and dark blue (*siniy*). Does this distinction mean that *siniy* blues look more different from *goluboy* blues to Russian speakers? Indeed, the data say yes. Russian speakers are quicker to distinguish two shades of blue that are called by the different names in Russian (i.e., one being *siniy* and the other being *goluboy*) than if the two fall into the same category.

For English speakers, all these shades are still designated by the same word, "blue," and there are no comparable differences in reaction time.

Further, the Russian advantage disappears when subjects are asked to perform a verbal interference task (reciting a string of digits) while making color judgments but not when they're asked to perform an equally difficult spatial interference task (keeping a novel visual pattern in memory). The disappearance of the advantage when performing a verbal task shows that language is normally involved in even surprisingly basic perceptual judgments—and that it is language per se that creates this difference in perception between Russian and English speakers. When Russian speakers are blocked from their normal access to language by a verbal interference task, the differences between Russian and English speakers disappear.

Even what might be deemed frivolous aspects of language can have far-reaching subconscious effects on how we see the world. Take grammatical gender. In Spanish and other Romance languages, nouns are either masculine or feminine. In many other languages, nouns are divided into many more genders ("gender" in this context meaning class or kind). For example, some Australian Aboriginal languages have up to sixteen genders, including classes of hunting weapons, canines, things that are shiny, or, in the phrase made famous by cognitive linguist George Lakoff, "women, fire, and dangerous things."

What it means for a language to have grammatical gender is that words belonging to different genders get treated differently grammatically and words belonging to the same grammatical gender get treated the same grammatically. Languages can require speakers to change pronouns, adjective and verb endings, possessives, numerals, and so on, depending on the noun's gender. For example, to say something like "my chair was old" in Russian (*moy stul bil' stariy*), you'd need to make every word in the sentence agree in gender with "chair" (*stul*), which is masculine in Russian. So you'd use the masculine form of "my," "was," and "old." These are the same forms you'd use in speaking of a biological male, as in "my grandfather was old." If, instead of speaking of a chair, you were speaking of a bed (*krovat'*), which is feminine in Russian, or about your grandmother, you would use the feminine form of "my," "was," and "old."

Does treating chairs as masculine and beds as feminine in the grammar make Russian speakers think of chairs as being more like men and beds as more like women in some way? It turns out that it does. In one study, we asked German and Spanish speakers to describe objects having opposite gender assignment in those two languages. The descriptions they gave differed in a way predicted by grammatical gender. For example, when asked to describe a "key"—a word that is masculine in German and feminine in Spanish—the German speakers were more likely to use words like "hard," "heavy," "jagged," "metal," "serrated," and "useful," whereas Spanish speakers were more likely to say "golden," "intricate," "little," "lovely," "shiny," and "tiny." To describe a "bridge," which is feminine in German and masculine in Spanish, the German speakers said "beautiful," "elegant," "fragile," "peaceful," "pretty," and "slender," and the Spanish speakers said "big," "dangerous," "long," "strong," "sturdy," and "towering." This was true even though all testing was done in English, a language without grammatical gender. The same pattern of results also emerged in entirely nonlinguistic tasks (e.g., rating similarity between pictures). And we can also show that it is aspects of language per se that shape how people think: teaching English speakers new grammatical gender systems influences mental representations of objects in the same way it does with German and Spanish speakers. Apparently even small flukes of grammar, like the seemingly arbitrary assignment of gender to a noun, can have an effect on people's ideas of concrete objects in the world.[7]

In fact, you don't even need to go into the lab to see these effects of language; you can see them with your own eyes in an art gallery. Look at some famous examples of personification in art—the ways in which

25

abstract entities such as death, sin, victory, or time are given human form. How does an artist decide whether death, say, or time should be painted as a man or a woman? It turns out that in 85 percent of such personifications, whether a male or female figure is chosen is predicted by the grammatical gender of the word in the artist's native language. So, for example, German painters are more likely to paint death as a man, whereas Russian painters are more likely to paint death as a woman.

The fact that even quirks of grammar, such as grammatical gender, can affect our thinking is profound. Such quirks are pervasive in language; gender, for example, applies to all nouns, which means that it is affecting how people think about anything that can be designated by a noun. That's a lot of stuff!

I have described how languages shape the way we think about space, time, colors, and objects. Other studies have found effects of language on how people construe events, reason about causality, keep track of number, understand material substance, perceive and experience emotion, reason about other people's minds, choose to take risks, and even in the way they choose professions and spouses.[8] Taken together, these results show that linguistic processes are pervasive in most fundamental domains of thought, unconsciously shaping us from the nuts and bolts of cognition and perception to our loftiest abstract notions and major life decisions. Language is central to our experience of being human, and the languages we speak profoundly shape the way we think, the way we see the world, the way we live our lives.

NOTES

1 S. C. Levinson and D. P. Wilkins, eds., Grammars of Space: Explorations in Cognitive Diversity (New York: Cambridge University Press, 2006).

2 Levinson, Space in Language and Cognition: Explorations in Cognitive Diversity (New York: Cambridge University Press, 2003).

3 B. Tversky et al., "Cross-Cultural and Developmental Trends in Graphic Productions," Cognitive Psychology 23(1991): 515–7; O. Fuhrman and L. Boroditsky, "Mental Time-Lines Follow Writing Direction: Comparing English and Hebrew Speakers." Proceedings of the 29th Annual Conference of the Cognitive Science Society (2007): 1007–10.

4 L. Boroditsky, "Do English and Mandarin Speakers Think Differently About Time?" Proceedings of the 48th Annual Meeting of the Psychonomic Society (2007): 34.

5 D. Casasanto et al., "How Deep Are Effects of Language on Thought? Time Estimation in Speakers of English, Indonesian Greek, and Spanish." Proceedings of the 26th Annual Conference of the Cognitive Science Society (2004): 575–80.

6   Ibid., "How Deep Are Effects of Language on Thought? Time Estimation in Speakers of English and Greek" (in review); L. Boroditsky, "Does Language Shape Thought? English and Mandarin Speakers' Conceptions of Time." *Cognitive Psychology* 43, no. 1(2001): 1–22.

7   L. Boroditsky et al., "Sex, Syntax, and Semantics," in D. Gentner and S. Goldin-Meadow, eds., Language in Mind: Advances in the Study of Language and Cognition (Cambridge, MA: MIT Press, 2003), 61–79.

8   L. Boroditsky, "Linguistic Relativity," in L. Nadel, ed., Encyclopedia of Cognitive Science (London: Macmillan, 2003), 917–21; B. W. Pelham et al., "Why Susie Sells Seashells by the Seashore: Implicit Egotism and Major Life Decisions." Journal of Personality and Social Psychology 82, no. 4(2002): 469–86; A. Tversky and D. Kahneman, "The Framing of Decisions and the Psychology of Choice." Science 211(1981): 453–58; P. Pica et al., "Exact and Approximate Arithmetic in an Amazonian Indigene Group." Science 306(2004): 499–503; J. G. de Villiers and P. A. de Villiers, "Linguistic Determinism and False Belief," in P. Mitchell and K. Riggs, eds., Children's Reasoning and the Mind (Hove, UK: Psychology Press, in press); J. A. Lucy and S. Gaskins, "Interaction of Language Type and Referent Type in the Development of Nonverbal Classification Preferences," in Gentner and Goldin-Meadow, 465–92; L. F. Barrett et al., "Language as a Context for Emotion Perception." Trends in Cognitive Sciences 11(2007): 327–32.

Analyze

1. Why do Boroditsky's undergraduate students rarely consider the lack of language as a significant loss? For what reasons would one consider cognitive faculties such as speech and hearing more important than language?

2. Examine why the linguistic choices that affect "navigational ability and spatial knowledge" may be of greater significance to the Kuuk Thaayorre than to modern-day Americans. How does this linguistic difference influence the daily lives of the two cultures?

3. Which of Boroditsky's research experiments do you find most convincing? Why?

Explore

1. Summarize the arguments in favor of the impact of language on human thought. Consider how you think in your own language and use evidence from your experiences as you examine this view.

2. Boroditsky claims that "people's ideas of time differ across languages." As you analyze some of the author's examples, develop an argument

about how perceptions of the passage of time have real implications in the life of the language user.

3. How important is grammatical gender to language use? (For more on language and gender, see Chapter 5.) Write an essay that analyzes how the gender ascribed to certain words in a particular language has an impact on the user. Support your ideas with evidence from personal experience and carefully researched sources.

Susanne Langer
Language and Thought

American philosopher Susanne Langer grew up in a German-speaking home in New York City. She was one of the first American women to achieve wide recognition as a philosopher. Langer studied at Radcliffe College, receiving a bachelor's degree in 1920 and a doctorate in 1926. As a professor of philosophy, she taught at Columbia, Smith, and Wellesley, among other institutions. In her work, Langer explored the profoundly human trait of creating and communicating with symbols. Although in this essay (first published in *Fortune* in 1944) Langer is focused on language, in her later career she wrote extensively about the visual and performing arts.

Susanne Langer died in 1985, well before the advent of social media and widely available digital tools for creating art and music. How does your use of social media or other digital tools satisfy, as Langer might say, a basic "craving for expression"?

A symbol is not the same thing as a sign; that is a fact that psychologists and philosophers often overlook. All intelligent animals use signs; so do we. To them as well as to us sounds and smells and motions are signs of food, danger, the presence of other beings, or of rain or storm. Furthermore, some animals not only attend to signs but produce them for the benefit of others. Dogs bark at the door to be let in; rabbits thump to call each other; the cooing of doves and the growl of a wolf defending his kill are unequivocal signs of feelings and intentions to be reckoned with by other creatures.

We use signs just as animals do, though with considerably more elaboration. We stop at red lights and go on green; we answer calls and bells, watch the sky for coming storms, read trouble or promise or anger in each other's eyes. That is animal intelligence raised to the human level. Those of us who are dog lovers can probably all tell wonderful stories of how high our dogs have sometimes risen in the scale of clever sign interpretation and sign using.

A sign is anything that announces the existence or the imminence of some event, the presence of a thing or a person, or a change in the state of affairs. There are signs of the weather, signs of danger, signs of future good or evil, signs of what the past has been. In every case a sign is closely bound up with something to be noted or expected in experience. It is always a part of the situation to which it refers, though the reference may be remote in space and time. In so far as we are led to note or expect the signified event we are making correct use of a sign. This is the essence of rational behavior, which animals show in varying degrees. It is entirely realistic, being closely bound up with the actual objective course of history—learned by experience, and cashed in or voided by further experience.

If man had kept to the straight and narrow path of sign using, he would be like the other animals, though perhaps a little brighter. He would not talk, but grunt and gesticulate the point. He would make his wishes known, give warnings, perhaps develop a social system like that of bees and ants, with such a wonderful efficiency of communal enterprise that all men would have plenty to eat, warm apartments—all exactly alike and perfectly convenient—to live in, and everybody could and would sit in the sun or by the fire, as the climate demanded, not talking but just basking, with every want satisfied, most of his life. The young would romp and make love, the old would sleep, the middle-aged would do the routine work almost unconsciously and eat a great deal. But that would be the life of a social, superintelligent, purely sign-using animal.

To us who are human, it does not sound very glorious. We want to go 5 places and do things, own all sorts of gadgets that we do not absolutely need, and when we sit down to take it easy we want to talk. Rights and property, social position, special talents and virtues, and above all our ideas, are what we live for. We have gone off on a tangent that takes us far away from the mere biological cycle that animal generations accomplish; and that is because we can use not only signs but symbols. A symbol differs from a sign in that it does not announce the presence of the object, the being, condition, or whatnot, which is its meaning, but merely *brings this thing to mind*. It is not a mere "substitute sign" to which we react as though it were the object itself. The fact is that our reaction to hearing a person's name is quite different from our reaction to the person himself. There are certain rare cases where a symbol stands directly for its meaning: in religious experience, for instance, the Host is not only a symbol but a Presence. But symbols in the ordinary sense are not mystic. They are the same sort of thing that ordinary signs are; only they do not call our attention to something necessarily present or to be physically dealt with—they call up merely a conception of the thing they "mean."

The difference between a sign and a symbol is, in brief, that a sign causes us to think or act in the face of the thing signified, whereas a symbol causes us to think *about* the thing symbolized. Therein lies the great importance of symbolism for human life, its power to make this life so different from any other animal biography that generations of men have found it incredible to suppose that they were of purely zoological origin. A sign is always embedded in reality, in a present that emerges from the actual past and stretches to the future; but a symbol may be divorced from reality altogether. It may refer to what is not the case, to a mere idea, a figment, a dream. It serves, therefore, to liberate thought from the immediate stimuli of a physically present world; and that liberation marks the essential difference between human and nonhuman mentality. Animals think, but they think *of* and *at* things; men think primarily *about* things. Words, pictures, and memory images are symbols that may be combined and varied in a thousand ways. The result is a symbolic structure whose meaning is a complex of all their respective meanings, and this kaleidoscope of *ideas* is the typical product of the human brain that we call the "stream of thought."

The process of transforming all direct experience into imagery or into that supreme mode of symbolic expression, language, has so completely taken possession of the human mind that it is not only a special talent but a dominant, organic need. All our sense impressions leave their traces in our memory not only as signs disposing our practical reactions in the future but also as symbols, images representing our *ideas* of things; and the tendency to manipulate ideas, to combine and abstract, mix and extend them by playing with symbols, is man's outstanding characteristic. It seems to be what his brain most naturally and spontaneously does. Therefore his primitive mental function is not judging reality, but *dreaming his desires*.

Dreaming is apparently a basic function of human brains, for it is free and unexhausting like our metabolism, heartbeat, and breath. It is easier to dream than not to dream, as it is easier to breathe than to refrain from breathing. The symbolic character of dreams is fairly well established. Symbol mongering, on this ineffectual, uncritical level, seems to be instinctive, the fulfillment of an elementary need rather than the purposeful exercise of a high and difficult talent.

The special power of man's mind rests on the evolution of this special activity, not on any transcendently high development of animal intelligence. We are not immeasurably higher than other animals; we are different. We have a biological need and with it a biological gift that they do not share.

Because man has not only the ability but the constant need of *conceiving*   10
what has happened to him, what surrounds him, what is demanded of him—in short, of symbolizing nature, himself, and his hopes and fears—he has a constant and crying need of *expression*. What he cannot express, he cannot conceive; what he cannot conceive is chaos, and fills him with terror.

If we bear in mind this all-important craving for expression we get a new picture of man's behavior; for from this trait spring his powers and his weaknesses. The process of symbolic transformation that all our experiences undergo is nothing more nor less than the process of *conception*, underlying the human faculties of abstraction and imagination.

When we are faced with a strange or difficult situation, we cannot react directly, as other creatures do, with flight, aggression, or any such simple instinctive pattern. Our whole reaction depends on how we manage to conceive the situation—whether we cast it in a definite dramatic form, whether we see it as a disaster, a challenge, a fulfillment of doom, or a fiat of the Divine Will. In words or dreamlike images, in artistic or religious or even in cynical form, we must *construe* the events of life. There is great virtue in the figure of speech, "I can *make* nothing of it," to express a failure to understand something. Thought and memory are processes of *making* the thought content and the memory image; the pattern of our ideas is given by the symbols through which we express them. And in the course of manipulating those symbols we inevitably distort the original experience, as we abstract certain features of it, embroider and reinforce those features with other ideas, until the conception we project on the screen of memory is quite different from anything in our real history.

Conception is a necessary and elementary process; what we do with our conceptions is another story. That is the entire history of human culture—of intelligence and morality, folly and superstition, ritual, language, and the arts—all the phenomena that set man apart from, and above, the rest of the animal kingdom. As the religious mind has to make all human history a drama of sin and salvation in order to define its own moral attitudes, so a scientist wrestles with the mere presentation of "the facts" before he can reason about them. The process of *envisaging* facts, values, hopes, and fears underlies our whole behavior pattern; and this process is reflected in the evolution of an extraordinary phenomenon found always, and only, in human societies—the phenomenon of language.

Language is the highest and most amazing achievement of the symbolistic human mind. The power it bestows is almost inestimable, for without it anything properly called "thought" is impossible. The line between man and beast—between the highest ape and the lowest savage—is the language line. Whether the primitive Neanderthal man was anthropoid or human depends less on his cranial capacity, his upright posture, or even his use of tools and fire, than on one issue we shall probably never be able to settle—whether or not he spoke.

15   In all physical traits and practical responses, such as skills and visual judgments, we can find a certain continuity between animal and human mentality. Sign using is an ever evolving, ever improving function throughout the whole animal kingdom, from the lowly worm that shrinks into his hole at the sound of an approaching foot, to the dog obeying his master's command, and even to the learned scientist who watches the movements of an index needle.

The continuity of the sign-using talent has led psychologists to the belief that language is evolved from the vocal expressions, grunts and coos and cries, whereby animals vent their feelings or signal their fellows; that man has elaborated this sort of communion to the point where it makes a perfect exchange of ideas possible.

I do not believe that this doctrine of the origin of language is correct. The essence of language is symbolic, not signific; we use it first and most vitally to formulate and hold ideas in our own minds. Conception, not social control, is its first and foremost benefit.

Watch a young child that is just learning to speak play with a toy; he says the name of the object, e.g.: "Horsey! horsey! horsey!" over and over again, looks at the object, moves it, always saying the name to himself or to the world at large. It's quite a time before he talks to anyone in particular; he talks first of all to himself. This is his way of forming and fixing the *conception* of the object in his mind, and around this conception all his knowledge of it grows. *Names* are the essence of language; for the *name* is what abstracts the conception of the horse from the horse itself, and lets the mere idea recur at the speaking of the name. This permits the conception gathered from one horse experience to be exemplified again by another instance of a horse, so that the notion embodied in the name is a general notion.

To this end, the baby uses a word long before he *asks* for the object; when he wants his horsey he is likely to cry and fret, because he is reacting to an actual environment, not forming ideas. He uses the animal language of *signs* for his wants; talking is still a purely symbolic process—its practical value has not really impressed him yet.

Language need not be vocal; it may be purely visual, like written lan- 20 guage, or even tactual, like the deaf-mute system of speech; but it *must be denotative*. The sounds, intended or unintended, whereby animals communicate do not constitute a language because they are signs, not names. They never fall into an organic pattern, a meaningful syntax of even the most rudimentary sort, as all language seems to do with a sort of driving necessity. That is because signs refer to actual situations, in which things have obvious relations to each other that require only to be noted; but symbols refer to ideas, which are not physically there for inspection, so their connections and features have to be represented. This gives all true language a natural tendency toward growth and development, which seems almost like a life of its own. Languages are not invented; they grow with our need for expression.

In contrast, animal "speech" never has a structure. It is merely an emotional response. Apes may greet their ration of yams with a shout of "Nga!" But they do not say "Nga" between meals. If they could *talk about* their yams instead of just saluting them, they would be the most primitive men instead of the most anthropoid of beasts. They would have ideas, and tell each other things true and false, rational or irrational; they would make plans and invent laws and sing their own praises, as men do.

Analyze

1. Explain Langer's definition of "sign" in your own words. How convinced are you by this definition?

2. What is the distinction between "sign" and "symbol"? Use specific examples to illustrate how the properties of a symbol are different from that of a sign.
3. Consider Langer's claim that thought is impossible without language by analyzing the part of the essay where she makes this claim.

Explore

1. Langer uses words such as "conceiving," "construing," and "envisaging" to explain how the human mind works symbolically to create thought and language. Look up the definition of these words in a dictionary. What do they have in common? Write about how each term helps us imagine thoughts that can then be turned into meaningful words to convey ideas.
2. Toward the end of her essay Langer states that "*names* are the essence of language." In a brief essay, develop an argument that examines the importance of names and naming in our society. Use personal or anecdotal experience as evidence to support your ideas.
3. One of Langer's claims is that humans think and communicate symbolically while animals only use signs to communicate. Conduct research on the systems of communication in the animal world by examining how a particular creature (e.g., dog, gorilla, ants, or dolphin) communicates with others of its kind. What is special about the "language" that they use?

Arika Okrent
Body Language

American linguistic scholar Arika Okrent, who along with her native English also speaks Hungarian, Klingon, some Esperanto, and knows American Sign Language, is the author of *In the Land of Invented Languages* (2009). Okrent earned a joint PhD in the Department of Linguistics and the Department of Psychology's Cognition and Cognitive Neuroscience Program at the University of Chicago, where she worked in a gesture research lab. "Body Language," an explanation of the language of gesture, originally appeared in *Lapham's Quarterly* in 2012. Founded and edited by Lewis H. Lapham, *Lapham's Quarterly* is a magazine of history and ideas that devotes each issue to exploring a single topic (e.g., communication, family, or food) in various historical and cultural contexts.

Along with gesture, what other kinds of nonverbal language (e.g., emoticons) do you use to communicate with friends and family?

Two Jews and an Englishman are crossing the ocean on a ship. The Jews, who can't swim, start arguing with each other about what they should do if it sinks. As they argue, they gesticulate with such vigor that the Englishman backs away to avoid injury. Suddenly, the boat begins to sink. All the passengers except for the Jews, who are too wrapped up in their argument to notice, jump overboard. After a long, exhausting swim, the Englishman finally reaches the shore. He is amazed to find the two Jews there, happily waving him in. Astonished, he asks them how they got there. "We have no idea," says one of them. "We just kept on talking in the water."

A version of this joke appears in a 1941 dissertation on "the gestural behavior of eastern Jews and southern Italians in New York City, living under similar as well as different environmental conditions." The study was written by David Efron, who grew up in an orthodox Jewish home in Argentina and arrived in New York for graduate study in the 1930s. By his own account, when he spoke Spanish, he gestured with "the effervescence and fluidity of those of a good many Argentinians." When he spoke Yiddish, his gestures were more "tense, jerky, and confined." He sometimes combined the two styles, as when "discussing a Jewish matter in Spanish, and vice versa." After living in the United States for a few years, he found his gestures becoming "in general less expansive, even when speaking in his native tongue." His gestural identity was further complicated by the "symbolic Italian movements" he had picked up from Argentine-Italians and reinforced on a trip through Italy. But no matter what language he spoke, he proved to be "an adroit table-pounder."

Efron was one of the last students of the famous anthropologist Franz Boas. Boas spent his career arguing that it was culture and environment, not biological race, that accounted for differences in how groups of people behaved. Efron's study was designed as a challenge to the impressionistic explanations of gesture that the race theorists of the 1930s were passing off as science. One claimed that Jews of mixed race who no longer had other Jewish physical traits could still be identified by their gestures. Another categorized gesture by race: Nordic gestures were restrained; Mediterranean gestures were playful; the gestures of the Phalic race (as in the German region of Westphalia) reminded one of a fleeing chicken; Italian gestures were explained with reference to hot blood, light bones, and poor impulse control.

Efron observed the conversations of 1,250 Lithuanian and Polish Jews and 1,100 Italians from Naples and Sicily in and around New York City. In each group, about half were recent immigrants and half were "assimilated." They were observed in a range of settings: parks, markets, social clubs, schools, universities, Catskills resorts, Adirondack hotels, and the Saratoga racetrack. He recorded five thousand feet of film and, with an artist, produced two thousand sketches of spontaneous gestures.

5   The results paint a picture of a stereotype, but a lovingly detailed and specific one. According to Efron, Jews used a limited range of motion, mostly from the elbow. Their movements were more angular, jabbing, intricate, and vertical than those of the Italians, who used larger, smoother, more curved lateral gestures which pivoted from the shoulder. Jews tended to use one hand, Italians both. Italians touched their own bodies, Jews touched the bodies of their conversational partners. Efron describes with delight an episode he witnessed where one man grabbed the arm of his interlocutor and started gesturing with it. That man, becoming annoyed, finally grabbed the first man's wrist in retaliation and "started admonishing him back with his own . . . hand." Jews also did more gesturing with objects such as pencils or, in one case, a meatball on the end of a fork. Italians used less finger and wrist movement but more repetition. They also had a vocabulary of symbolic gestures with standard meanings—from "I know more than you think I do" to "I'll sew your lips together" to "I'll poke your eyes out"—that could be understood without any speech at all.

The main result, the one the study was designed to find, was that as the Jews and Italians assimilated, they began to gesture alike. When Efron tested a group of students at a high school in Little Italy on the meanings of the symbolic gestures used by the unassimilated Italians, less than half of their judgments were correct. He came to the anticipated conclusion: as Jews and Italians became American, so did their gestures.

The conclusion was unsurprising; it was Efron's method that made his study important. In order to make his study empirical, Efron had to develop a way to break gestures down into countable units so that he could explain differences with respect to those units. There were "emblems" that could be understood without speech, those of the Italian "I'll poke your eyes out" variety. There were also gestures that had no meaning independent from speech: "physiographics" and "kinetographics" that trace out the objects or actions under discussion, "ideographics" that trace out the metaphorical pathways of the speaker's thoughts, and "batons" that beat out the rhythm of speech.

The gestures of the subjects that Efron observed didn't differ only by the qualities of how they moved or how many hands they used or who they touched. They also seemed functionally different. Italians used emblems; Jews didn't. Italians sometimes used physiographics, depicting the size and shape of the things they talked about; Jews used ideographics, depicting features of the discourse itself. When Jews pointed a thumb toward the ground and then scooped it upward quickly, they were highlighting the crux of the discourse, physically and metaphorically digging it out for consideration. When they traced an angular zigzag with a finger, they were outlining the back and forth of an argument, linking one salient bit to the next.

After he published his study on the gestures of New York immigrants, Efron left academia for a career advocating for workers' rights at the UN's International Labor Organization. But his dissertation went on to become a foundation for the field of "gesture studies"—a label applied to the activities of various psychologists, anthropologists, and linguists who look at the things people do with their hands while they speak. Efron not only laid the groundwork for a more systematic method of studying gestures, he introduced the idea that gesture was not a companion to speaking, but a product of it.

In his *Institutes of Oratory*, the first-century rhetorician Quintilian says 10 the hands "almost equal in expression the powers of language itself," and he praises them for all the things they can do:

> With our hands we ask, promise, call persons to us and send them
> away, threaten, supplicate, intimate dislike or fear; with our hands
> we signify joy, grief, doubt, acknowledgment, penitence, and indi-
> cate measure, quantity, number, and time. Have not our hands

the power of inciting, of restraining, of beseeching, of testifying approbation, admiration, and shame? Do they not, in pointing out places and persons, discharge the duty of adverbs and pronouns? So that, amidst the great diversity of tongues pervading all nations and people, the language of the hands appears to be a language common to all men.

Quintilian implies, like many after him, that gesture is some kind of universal natural language. It was a language, however, that needed to be cultivated and practiced. Since gesture represented thoughts, or, as Cicero said, "the motions of the soul," orators had to learn how to marshal their gestures to put their thoughts in the best light. Quintilian laid out specific dos and don'ts. He tells us, for example, that when "the middle finger is drawn in toward the thumb, the other three fingers being open," this is an appropriate gesture to use during the introduction to a speech, provided it is "moderately exerted and with a gentle movement of the hand in either direction." It can add confirmation when stating the facts if the movement is "somewhat more decided," but "in invective and refutation, it must be spirited and impressive." It should never, however, be aimed sideways so that the middle finger points toward the left shoulder.

For centuries, discussion of gesture was couched in terms of what was proper or effective. There were guides for orators, preachers, and actors, and rulebooks for courtly behavior that laid down standards for gesture. In the seventeenth century there were even dictionaries of gesture: Giovanni Bonifacio's *The Art of Signs* (1616) and John Bulwer's *Chirologia and Chironomia* (1644) list hundreds of gestures, citing passages from the classics on their meanings. According to Bulwer, we know that "to smite suddenly on the left hand with the right" signifies anger because Seneca used it in a description of an angry man.

Most guides to gesture advised against mere mimicry or acting out the content of the speech they accompanied. Quintilian believed the gestures of an orator "should be suited rather to his sense than to his words." The purpose of gesture was not to repeat information, but to add it. Indeed this is how even those untrained in oratorical gesture seem to use it. We use gestures to show *how* the events we narrate happened, and to point to the particular things or people we talk about. The gestures of the Italians Efron studied added information about the physical qualities of the things they talked about as well as their attitudes toward them. The gestures of the Jews he studied illustrated the connections they were making between ideas and their relative importance. Gesture can communicate a layer of meaning missing from the speech.

But it would be wrong to say that the reason we gesture is to communicate. Almost anything can communicate—the clothes you wear, the flowers you send, the way you flutter your fan or fold your handkerchief. Gestures communicate too, but they are much more intimately tied to the act of speaking. They are not a language in themselves, but they are a complement to language, a partner with language, a byproduct of language. Subsequent research in the field that Efron founded has failed to find a culture that does not gesture during speech. Not everyone does it as colorfully as the Italians and Jews, but everyone does it, even Englishmen. While aspects of the way we do it are learned or culturally conditioned, and while some of our gestures are intentionally formed with the goal of communication in mind, imitation can't explain why congenitally blind people gesture, especially when they know they're speaking to other blind people, and communicative intent can't explain why people gesture when they're on the phone. Gesture is simply a part of language use. When we form our thoughts into speech, some of it leaks through our hands.

The sense that gesture is a language of its own is even more pronounced in those cases where it seems to replace speaking entirely. In the nineteenth century, visitors came back from Italy with news of an exotic "gesture language" that was spoken without words at all. After the discovery of the archaeological sites of Herculaneum and Pompeii in the eighteenth century, Naples had become a can't-miss stop on the grand tour. Letters home and travelogues in magazines told tales of complete conversations silently conducted between balconies, gossip and treachery performed by hand alone, and love affairs arranged without a word spoken. In one apocryphal anecdote, a young swain woos his beauty over the course of months, without discovery by her father, through gestures and looks exchanged from street to balcony. When he finally arrives at the decided meeting place to run away with her, he hears in the darkness an abrasive squawk asking, "are you there?" Realizing it's the voice of his love, which he has never heard before, he runs the other way.

For the benefit of these foreigners "who had been born in distant regions 15 and who, on account of their cool and sluggish temperament are rather unsuited to gesturing," Andrea de Jorio, an archaeologist at the Royal Borbonic Museum in Naples, produced one of the only works before Efron's to look at gestures as they were used rather than as they ought to be used, an 1832 study that catalogued hundreds of gestures used in the streets of Naples.

De Jorio provides an alphabetized index of gesture meanings for everything from "*abbondanza*" (abundance) to "*uomo panciuto*" (paunchy man). He not only describes what the gestures look like—the tips of the index finger and thumb joined together facing one another, and then separated by the index finder of the other hand means "I am not friends with you anymore"—he gives little scenarios of the gestures used in context, showing some of the varying shades of meaning they can acquire. In one example, he tells the story of "a certain count, noting that someone he did not know had joined the conversation, and who made a somewhat bad impression, asked his friends, in gesture, who this person was." The first man responded by placing the outside of his thumb at his ear, with the palm facing downward, "thus declaring him to be an ass." The second friend made the same gesture, but with both hands at his ears, "meaning the fellow was more than an ass." The third friend placed the tips of his extended thumbs on his temples with the other fingers wide open and oscillating, confirming that the poor fellow was "not just a fool, he was positively asinine."

Despite stereotypes, the Italians have never had a monopoly on the wordless gesture. Even the most sluggish-armed among us can get all kinds of messages across without saying a word: "come here," "he's crazy," "check her out," "yes," "no," "I don't know," "peace," "it's a secret," "I'm thinking," "wait a minute," "stop right there," "something stinks," "I'm not listening," "screw you," "check, please." These gestures aren't exotic to us because they're the ones we use. They seem somehow to belong to the language "common to all men" that Quintilian was talking about.

But of course, they aren't common to all men, as anyone who's ever looked at a travel guidebook can tell you. Remember to avoid the "okay" sign in Brazil, where it means "asshole." Watch out in Bulgaria, where a head nod means "no" and a head shake means "yes." Don't give the thumbs up in Iran unless you mean to say "up yours." Many of the gestures we use in place of speech aren't transparent at all. Their forms are arbitrary and need to be translated just like words.

It is in this silent use of gesture, where the gestures become like words—quotable, conventionally defined, intentionally produced, and meant to communicate—that gesture really does start to look like a language. But looked at more closely, these gestures distinguish themselves from words in interesting ways.

For one, they can be remarkably durable over time. The gestures we 20
inherited from the Greeks and Romans are much more immediately
identifiable today than are the words we inherited from them. The *digitus
impudicus* that Romans insulted each other with is the same digit we use
for that purpose today (and while the phrase "*digitus impudicus*" takes
some education and background to decipher, a display of the "impudent
finger" does not).

Also, these quotable gestures—emblems, as Efron called them—function
quite differently from words. They almost never play the role of nouns or
verbs. There are gestures that seem like adjectives—the finger twirling at
the temple for "crazy," the fingertip kiss for "delicious"—however, they act
not as descriptors, but as attitude-laden comments. Emblems don't work
like words so much as complete speech acts. They don't *say*, they *do*. They
request (come here!), admonish (shhh!), insult (up yours!), promise (cross
my heart!), and compliment (delicious!).

Only in the case of full sign languages of the deaf do gestures take on all
the properties of words. Sign languages have nouns and verbs and rules for
how they fit into sentences. Signs can say, "rosemary really brings out the
flavor in this roast" as well as "delicious!" Signs, like words, are composed
out of a finite inventory of units that are defined with discrete boundaries.
In American Sign Language, the position of the thumb in a fist—whether
it lies next to the fingers, in front of the fingers, or inside the fingers—can
make the difference between one meaning, another meaning, and nonsense, in the way that in speech, tiny alternations in vibration and airflow
can make the difference between "pine" and "mine." Gestures are wholes.
Their internal parts aren't important. When I punch my hand with a fist
to tell you that I'm going to beat you up, it hardly matters what my thumb
is doing.

The greater the burden of communication gestures have to carry, the
more languagelike they become. But if we already have a full language to
communicate, then why do we gesture? Clearly it's useful for cases where
we can't or don't want to speak. With gestures, baseball players exchange
secrets on the open field, stock traders make deals in the noisy hubbub of
the pit, scuba divers communicate through the barrier of water, and drivers
make their frustration known to other drivers through the barrier of car
windows.

These special cases don't represent the bulk of gesturing we do. Most
of our gestures happen while we can speak or are speaking. But the act

of using language is ephemeral; words disappear as they are spoken. Of course, we've had the ability to preserve the words of the past ever since the invention of writing. But the solid, linear permanence of written language encourages the illusion that language is just an object, a container for thought. In fact, language is also a behavior, a laboratory for thought creation and negotiation. Gestures are thoughts, ideas, speech acts made tangible in the air. They can even, for a moment, outlive the speaker. Death-row inmates have been executed with their middle fingers extended in a final gesture of defiance.

25   David McNeill, a psychologist who has spent his career studying gesture, first took notice of it watching two of his colleagues converse. They looked to him like "sculptors working in different media. One was always pounding and pushing some heavy blocklike stuff. I imagined that his medium was clay or marble. The other was drawing out and weaving some incredibly delicate, spidery stuff. His medium looked like strings or spider-webs." Research of the past few decades has shown that putting our thoughts in our hands can help us learn and remember better, can help us speak more fluently and find the right words.

When we speak, we shape our thoughts for language, and when we gesture, we shape them in the space in front of us. We may be different kinds of sculptors using different kinds of media, but our molding, weaving, and chiseling does us good.

Analyze

1. What are the differences in gesturing between Italians and Jews in Efron's study?
2. What method does Efron use to examine these gestures?
3. How does Okrent arrive at the idea that gestures are a complement to or by-product of language?

Explore

1. If gestures are "attitude-laden comments," write about an experience you had with gesturing that supports this point of view. What was the gesture and what sort of attitude did it communicate?
2. Examine the benefits of nonverbal cues. How can they be useful to the speaker or the listener?

3. Okrent reminds us that gestures are used for more than mere communication. Write an essay in which you develop ideas about how gesturing extends, enhances, or interferes with communication. Refer to researched sources to support your argument.

Anassa Rhenisch
Alien Languages: Not Human

Writer, blogger, and editor Anassa Rhenisch is a frequent contributor to the blog *Science In My Fiction*, where this article was published in 2010. Rhenisch, who studied linguistics and English literature in college, describes herself as an "unrepentant geek." Like her fellow contributors to *Science in My Fiction*—many of whom are scientists as well as science-fiction fans— Rhenisch is an advocate of grounding speculative fiction and fantasy in real-world science. In the following essay, she offers implicit challenges to the creativity of her fellow science-fiction writers when it comes to creating a truly "alien" language.

Do the most "believable" alien characters in science-fiction movies or books have particularly "human" traits? What role does language play in making a science-fiction or fantasy character particularly evil or frightening—or engaging and sympathetic?

Contrary to Hollywood and the majority of fictional languages, alien languages are almost certainly not going to look like human ones. They're not going to have the same sounds, the same word orders, or the same way of solving problems like time, direction, and ownership. Why? Because human DNA and culture help determine what human languages look like, and aliens will, by definition, not share that background.

That's not to say there won't be similarities, though. Because language is a communication system and therefore has to convey information efficiently, there are some facts that won't change.

On Neurobiology

The ability to use language will be coded in the aliens' genes. Either the aliens evolved language and have basic linguistic structures in their brains at birth, or every individual has to independently invent the language from scratch. With humans, we call this nativism and it applies to a whole range of mental traits, not just language.

A corollary of having language hard-wired is that other brain "structures" will affect what the language(s) look like, because everything's likely using the same neural pathways. Unfortunately, we're still trying to figure out exactly where language overlaps with other pathways in humans, so I can't give examples that aren't personal conjecture. Let's just say that if an alien fundamentally perceives the world differently, its language is going to reflect that difference.

5   A second corollary is that members of the same species can learn any language spoken by that species, because the neural pathways will be the same. (A different species, such as humans, could have tremendous, even insurmountable difficulties learning these languages, and the aliens, ours.)

A species that has multiple languages, or has had its language evolve significantly, is going to have "encoded" more linguistic structures in its brain than any one language uses. This means that languages spoken by the same species do not have to be similar, and that even related languages can have big differences because a different element of code was chosen. French, Spanish, Catalan, and Romanian were all Latin two thousand years ago.

On Organization

An alien language will be organized, because without syntax and/or word building, there's no way of knowing who did what to whom where when, meaning that communication's negated or at least significantly hindered. An efficient language is going to get the point across as simply as possible, and meaning comes across much easier if the order of information is predictable. This means there'll be rules for word order or word formation, possibly both. However, those rules may look nothing like even the least common patterns in human languages. A sentence transliterated as "the bit dog man the" could be perfectly acceptable. Ordering sounds may or may not occur. Why order sounds? Because some carry over distances better than others, and it's easier to hear soft-loud-soft or loud-loud even at close range than it is to hear soft-soft or soft-softersoft. It's also possible, but not certain, that there will be vastly different sounds in the same language (*b* vs. *ee* vs. *sh*) because again, it's easier to distinguish words when they're not all variations of *tkktt*. This is, of course, assuming that aliens will be sensitive to variations in amplitude and frequency, like humans, and that they'll use sound for communication.

There will likely be ways to combine and recombine "clauses" and "phrases" to form different patterns with different meanings—reporting speech, for instance, or passive voice. Again, this is to simplify communication. Why create an entirely new string of words or sounds when a good one's already been laid out? Does anyone *need* an entirely new string of sounds for every possible sentence?

On Culture and Language Change

On Earth, languages change over time and differ between areas. The longer a group of speakers is separated from another, or the longer they're exposed to other linguistic influences, the more distinct their speech will be from other speakers of their language. The changes are somewhat counteracted by socio-political pressures (upward mobility, government mandates, education, and so on), but dialects and new languages do develop. This will likely happen on other planets too. 10

Because language is a means of communication, it's not going to develop in places where people have no need to communicate. Lone wanderers will not create language. Tribes will.

Finally, and I know this has been said elsewhere before this: aliens will have words for concepts and objects important to them and in their world, but not for unfamiliar concepts and objects. For those, they will need to invent or borrow words.

On Differences

Humans have two kinds of language: spoken languages, which use sound waves, and gestural (sign) languages, which use light waves and images. Other species on our planet communicate through chemicals (insects, plants, fungi), though those systems aren't nearly complex enough to be called languages. Aliens also won't be limited to the same systems as we are, because they'll come from a different evolutionary path. Taste, touch, and smell are equally possible, along with systems based on abilities humans don't have, such as telepathy or electric impulses.

Some of these possible systems aren't going to allow for the same kinds of segmentation human languages enjoy. Trying to describe "speech sound" to a scent-speaker or "word" to a telepath is going to be difficult.

15   Aliens aren't going to have the same kinds of syntax, the same kinds of word structures, or the same kinds of grammatical elements (-prepositions, cases, gender . . .) as humans do. They have a different culture and biological background and can therefore develop other ways of referring to the world and indicating relationships. Perhaps it's not location that's important, but moment in time. There'd be no word for "on", but there'd be words or affixes for any time relationship you could think of.

Societies influence languages. Words, ideas, and ways of speaking can become taboo and be edited out of the language. Governments can use education and the law to enforce certain forms over others. Societies that lack moral codes or have a highly sophisticated concept of direction are going to have whole sets of words, structures, and solutions that other societies won't. Similarly, living in five dimensions is going to alter your worldview.

Summary Caveats

Sentient aliens don't *need* a language. Communication, certainly, but not a language. Civilizations will most likely have language, though, because of the distances and degree of communication required.

It's entirely possible that an alien civilization could develop with solely non-linguistic communication or a proto-language. I'm too steeped in human linguistics to see how, but I can't discount the possibility.

When I use words like "word" and "speaker", I mean the regular definition as well as the parallel meaning for languages not based on sound waves and the human brain.

Because I am taking human languages as my reference point whether   20
I like it or not, I will have introduced biases into this essay based on what's logical and definite to me. An alien (possibly another human) could read what I've written and prove me wrong.

It's my hope that by delineating what humans will recognize in alien languages, I'll inspire a completely non-human language. If we're not limiting ourselves to human-like biologies, why stick to human-like languages?

Analyze

1. Rhenisch starts out her essay by noting that alien languages can be both similar to and different from human languages. In what ways, according to Rhenisch, are they similar? In what ways different?

2. Examine Rhenisch's claim that "lone wanderers will not create language. Tribes will." Can you think of reasons why this may or may not be true?

3. Which aspect of the author's prediction about alien languages do you find most believable or compelling? Why?

Explore

1. Do you think an alien would have difficulty understanding or speaking the language that you speak? Refer to some of the points made in the article as you develop your ideas.

2. Human means of communication—language being one of them—differ from the way plants and animals communicate with each other. In a brief essay, examine the mode of communication of a particular plant or animal species and report on how it is different from human communication.

3. Alien creatures are often written about and represented in literature and in films. Select a piece of fiction, a TV show, or a movie about aliens and write about how they communicate with others, whether human or alien. What particular speech characteristics do they display? And to what extent do they confirm Rhenisch's hypotheses about alien language?

Julie Sedivy
Is Your Language Making You Broke and Fat? How Language Can Shape Thinking and Behavior (and How It Can't)

Cognitive scientist Julie Sedivy earned her PhD in linguistics at the University of Rochester, and has taught at Brown University and the University of Calgary. The author (with Greg Carlson) of *Sold on Language: How Advertisers Talk to You and What This Says About You* (2011), Sedivy is a contributor to *Discover* magazine's blog *The Crux*, where she writes about the intersections of language, culture, and society; the following article first appeared at *The Crux* in 2012.

If you could instantly learn to speak any language in the world, which language would you choose, and why? How do you imagine your life changing if you could speak, read, and write in that language?

Keith Chen, an economist from Yale, makes a startling claim in an unpublished working paper: people's fiscal responsibility and healthy lifestyle choices depend in part on the grammar of their language.

Here's the idea: Languages differ in the devices they offer to speakers who want to talk about the future. For some, like Spanish and Greek, you have to tack on a verb ending that explicitly marks future time—so, in Spanish, you would say *escribo* for the present tense (*I write* or *I'm writing*) and *escribiré* for the future tense (*I will write*). But other languages like Mandarin don't require their verbs to be escorted by grammatical markers that convey future time—time is usually obvious from something else in the context. In Mandarin, you would say the equivalent of *I write tomorrow*, using the same verb form for both present and future.

Chen's finding is that if you divide up a large number of the world's languages into those that require a grammatical marker for future time and those that don't, you see an interesting correlation: speakers of languages that force grammatical marking of the future have amassed a smaller retirement nest egg, smoke more, exercise less, and are more likely to be obese.

Why would this be? The claim is that a sharp grammatical division between the present and future encourages people to conceive of the future as somehow dramatically different from the present, making it easier to put off behaviors that benefit your future self rather than your present self.

Chen's paper has yet to be accepted for publication, but it's already generated a lot of press of the sort that's festooned with flashing lights. For example, in his popular blog, Andrew Sullivan headlined the story with the pronouncement *Why Greeks Haven't Saved for a Rainy Day*. A facetious headline, no doubt. But before someone suggests that the European Union should make bailouts of troubled countries contingent on their retiring their grammatical tense markers, it's worth taking a reality check about the ways in which language can or can't affect the thoughts and behaviors of its speakers.

Claims about the tight coupling of language and culture are incredibly   5 seductive. To many people, it's intuitively obvious that dropping consonants in pronunciation is the mark of a lazy culture, that romancing someone is easiest in a language that's intrinsically as soothing and soft as French, and that the disciplined German mind is in part a product of the strictly rigid and orderly German language. The trouble is, such intuitively obvious observations are bubbles just waiting to be burst by the sharp edges of actual linguistic evidence. As noted by Guy Deutscher, in his book *Through the Language Glass*, "the industrious Protestant Danes have dropped more consonants onto their icy, windswept soil than any indolent tropical tribe. And if Germans do have systematic minds, this is just as likely to be because their exceedingly erratic mother tongue has exhausted their brains' capacity to cope with any further irregularity."

One of the most unkillable misconceptions is that if a language has no word for a particular concept, then its speakers must have trouble conceiving of it. Is Italian culture vulnerable to corruption because there is no Italian word that directly translates as *accountability*? Not likely. English doesn't have a word for a silk green-and-pink paisley shirt, left untucked on one side, but I doubt that this makes it hard for you to picture one. Yet, this kind of thinking proves irresistible to many people—it's even been used to argue that people who speak languages without future tense marking are unable to think about the future in any meaningful way.

If this *feels* intuitively plausible to you, consider the following: In English, we mark gender on the third person pronouns *he* and *she*. But we *don't* mark gender when we use pronouns to refer to a group of men or women—we use *they* in both cases. Does this mean that we suffer confusion about people's gender as soon as they congregate in groups? Obviously not. And do languages that obsessively classify *all* nouns as gendered (as does Spanish) result in cultures that are more segregated by gender than those that don't have any such linguistic distinctions? If so, we'd expect more egalitarian cultures to spring from entirely gender-neutral languages like Dari, the variant of Persian that's spoken in Afghanistan. But as it turns out, the line between grammar and thought is simply not that direct. Languages have an enormous amount of leeway in expressing the same thoughts, and the specific methods they settle on are surprisingly arbitrary.

That's not to say that language scientists haven't found any reliable influences of language on behavior. They have. But these tend to be fairly subtle. For instance, many languages force their speakers to sort inanimate objects seemingly randomly into grammatical genders—so to Spanish speakers, a chair is marked as feminine (*la silla*) but to German speakers, it's masculine (*der Stuhl*). If you were to ask a Spanish speaker to imagine an animated chair as a cartoon character, he'd be more likely to choose a female voice for the character. But no one's ever found a clear causal link between grammatical features of a language and the sort of large-scale societal behaviors that Chen argues for in his paper. And because Chen's study simply looks for correlations, we can't be sure that grammar is *causing* the behavior. It's also possible that tense marking and live-for-the-day cultural attitudes spread together throughout populations without one causing the other. For example, I bet you'd find a correlation between tonal languages and the use of chopsticks at mealtimes, simply because both of these spread throughout a particular geographic region. But you'd be hard-pressed to tell a decent story about how the use of tone to distinguish word meanings leads to dexterity with certain dining implements.

But still, we're left with a puzzle: If language structure has quite a limited effect on the way we think and act, why then do we have these sturdy impressions that some languages are inherently more romantic, slovenly, logical, or fussy than others? The answer is that these impressions say less about the nature of those languages than they do about the strong associations we've forged between certain languages and the culture of their speakers. And these language-based associations *can* apparently trigger different behaviors.

10   A particularly nice illustration comes from a study by Dirk Akkermans and colleagues, in which bilingual Dutch subjects played a business variant of the

Prisoner's Dilemma game, intended to test the degree of cooperative versus competitive behavior. (The game is set up so that you reap the highest profits if both you and your partner choose a cooperative strategy of keeping prices for your products high, and the lowest profits if you play cooperatively but your partner chooses to undersell you.) Half of the subjects played the game in English, and half played the game in Dutch—the idea being that the English language is more closely associated with highly individualistic and competitive cultures than Dutch. The subjects who played the game in English did indeed choose a more competitive strategy than those who played it in Dutch.

But the effects of language on strategy choice really depended on how much direct exposure to Anglophone *culture* the subjects had. Among subjects who'd lived in an Anglophone country for at least three months, those who played the game in Dutch played cooperatively 51% of the time, while those who played it in English did so only 37% of the time. In contrast, among those who *hadn't* spent more than three months in an Anglophone country, the rates for cooperative behavior were 48% for Dutch, and 45% for English. Actual proficiency in English had no discernible impact. So it's not that English has any specific grammatical forms or even specific words that steer behavior in a competitive direction—it's that English *speakers* tend to subscribe to more competitive norms of behavior, norms that the Dutch subjects subconsciously adopted when speaking English. The researchers may well have gotten very similar results if, instead of varying the languages, they'd exposed subjects to national symbols such as American versus Dutch flags, or pictures of bald eagles versus tulips.

So in the end, perhaps learning to speak Mandarin *would* make Greeks somewhat more inclined to save for a rainy day. On the other hand, they just might get the same results by making a habit of eating with chopsticks.

Analyze

1. Sedivy begins the essay with a reference to an unpublished article that draws a provocative connection between language and behavior. Why does the author use this article?
2. How does Sedivy use Keith Chen's research to support her point?
3. In explaining her perspective on the effect of language on behavior, the author makes a subtle distinction between correlation and cause and effect. Explain this distinction by using one of the author's examples or one of your own.

Explore

1. To what extent does the language that you speak affect your behavior? Write about an experience you've had with language that reflects this relationship.
2. Do our beliefs and preconceptions about certain cultures really stem from linguistic biases? Examine this notion in a brief essay that uses supporting evidence from personal experience or researched sources.
3. Sedivy's article forces us to consider the impact of cultural traits, rather than language, on individual behavior. Write an essay in which you develop an extended argument that challenges or confirms this claim. Support your ideas with careful research.

Forging Connections

1. With so many different forms of communication already available to humans, why do we seem to crave the development of new communication technologies and new ways of expressing ourselves with those technologies? Drawing on at least two readings in this chapter, examine how speech and writing not only help us understand our world but also shape it, and speculate on how emerging technologies and social media might change (or are changing) the way we shape our world.
2. Despite the staggering variety of languages that exist within and across continents, human beings still find ways to communicate with each other. Why is this so? How do nonverbal signs and symbols help us convey our ideas, needs, and desires, and bridge the linguistic gap? Write an essay, or create a presentation, in which you cite at least two selections from this chapter to support your thesis.

Looking Further

1. Both Lera Boroditsky and Julie Sedivy discuss how different languages are "gendered"—how they assign masculine or feminine attributes not just to pronouns, but to inanimate objects like chairs, weapons, or "things that are shiny." Create a presentation in which you show how an object or artifact from popular or consumer culture could be perceived as either "masculine" or "feminine"—or another gender entirely—based on how it is talked about and used. Use visuals, video, audio, and any other kind of media to enhance your presentation. Be sure to cite

either Boroditsky or Sedivy (or both), as well as at least one selection from Chapter 5 ("Language and Gender"), in support of your thesis.

2. Several readings in this chapter discuss the ways in which language has been thought to create culture, or influence the way different cultures see the world. Choose one of the languages described in Chapter 10, "Endangered Languages," and research the culture of the people who still speak that language. Can you find any connections between how that culture perceives the world and their language? In an essay, describe what is unique about that culture's worldview. Use at least one selection from Chapter 1 to argue for or against the role of language in creating that worldview. If the language does disappear, will that particular worldview be lost as well?

2 Multilingualism

Whether we like it or not, the proliferation of technology has reduced the space among peoples, cultures, and languages so much so that it is now possible to instantly communicate with people all over the world in a variety of ways. We cherish the fact that mobile phones, computers, and other hand-held devices allow us to reach out across space and make a connection with those far away from us. However, the tendency to limit ourselves to one predominant language is pervasive, and in the Western world, English appears to dominate verbal and written communication. Given that knowledge of and fluency in multiple languages not only opens up new vistas for the monolingual speaker but also allows for important sociopolitical and commercial exchange, the value of multilingualism is no longer just an abstract issue. But which languages are most useful for the global citizen? What criteria should we use in selecting the foreign languages we want to learn? Why should we learn artificial and invented languages when we have at our service hundreds of natural languages connected to real people and cultures?

In his article "Which Is the Best Language to Learn?" Robert Lane Greene, an American journalist and writer, makes the case for French as the "truly global language," doubting the rise of Chinese. John McWhorter, a linguist and political commentator, makes the opposite argument in "Which Languages Should Liberal Arts Be About in 2010?" as he takes a practical look at why Chinese should replace European languages in the liberal arts curriculum. Polyglot and scholar of foreign languages Alexander Arguelles discusses his "addictive" experience with language learning in the essay "I Can Speak 50 Languages." His ambitious quest to achieve fluency in all the languages he has learned is quite admirable. Then Adam Pulford, a blogger for Oxford University Press, in his article "Words Are Wind" takes us into the realm of linguistic creativity as he analyzes the invented language used in the TV show *Game of Thrones*. Eddie Dean, another blogger, follows up with "Klingon as a Second Language." It is an essay that chronicles how Klingon, an artificial language developed for the TV show *Star Trek,* has serious followers who are intent on turning it into a real language. Finally, in her essay "Audience, Uglossia, and CONLANG: Inventing Languages on the Internet," science fiction writer Sarah L. Higley convincingly argues not only that invented languages are gaining popularity on the Internet, but also that the practice of constructing new languages is a "highly specialized and technical pursuit."

Robert Lane Greene
Which Is the Best Language to Learn?

Robert Lane Greene, a Brooklyn-based journalist and business correspondent for the British magazine *The Economist*, is fluent in five languages (German, Spanish, French, Portuguese, and Danish) and conversant in three more (Russian, Arabic, and Italian). "Which Is the Best Language to Learn?" appeared in the March/April 2012 edition of *Intelligent Life*, a bimonthly lifestyle and culture magazine published by *The Economist*. In this article Greene observes that despite the multiple advantages that come with learning a language other than English, language learning among Anglophones has declined. He also asserts that French would be the most useful language to learn given our global community.

Do you agree that interest in learning a foreign language among native speakers of English has waned?

For language lovers, the facts are grim: Anglophones simply aren't learning them anymore. In Britain, despite four decades in the European Union, the number of A-levels taken in French and German has fallen by half in the past 20 years, while what was a growing trend of Spanish-learning has stalled. In America, the numbers are equally sorry. One factor behind the 9/11 attacks was the fact that the CIA lacked the Arabic-speakers who might have translated available intelligence. But ten years on, "English only" campaigns appeal more successfully to American patriotism than campaigns that try to promote language-learning, as if the most successful language in history were threatened.

Why learn a foreign language? After all, the one you already speak if you read this magazine is the world's most useful and important language. English is not only the first language of the obvious countries, it is now the rest of the world's second language: a Japanese tourist in Sweden or a Turk landing a plane in Spain will almost always speak English.

Nonetheless, compelling reasons remain for learning other languages. They range from the intellectual to the economical to the practical. First of all, learning any foreign language helps you understand all language better—many Anglophones first encounter the words "past participle" not in an English class, but in French. Second, there is the cultural broadening. Literature is always best read in the original.

Poetry and lyrics suffer particularly badly in translation. And learning another tongue helps the student grasp another way of thinking. Though the notion that speakers of different languages think differently has been vastly exaggerated and misunderstood, there is a great deal to be learned from discovering what the different cultures call this, that or *das oder*.

5   The practical reasons are just as compelling. In business, if the team on the other side of the table knows your language but you don't know theirs, they almost certainly know more about you and your company than you do about them and theirs—a bad position to negotiate from. Many investors in China have made fatally stupid decisions about companies they could not understand. Diplomacy, war-waging and intelligence work are all weakened by a lack of capable linguists. Virtually any career, public or private, is given a boost with knowledge of a foreign language.

So which one should you, or your children, learn? If you take a glance at advertisements in New York or A-level options in Britain, an answer seems to leap out: Mandarin. China's economy continues to grow at a pace that will make it bigger than America's within two decades at most. China's political clout is growing accordingly. Its businessmen are buying up everything from American brands to African minerals to Russian oil rights. If China is the country of the future, is Chinese the language of the future?

Probably not. Remember Japan's rise? Just as spectacular as China's, if on a smaller scale, Japan's economic growth led many to think it would take over the world. It was the world's second-largest economy for decades (before falling to third, recently, behind China). So is Japanese the world's third-most useful language? Not even close. If you were to learn ten languages ranked by general usefulness, Japanese would probably not make the list. And the key reason for Japanese's limited spread will also put the brakes on Chinese.

This factor is the Chinese writing system (which Japan borrowed and adapted centuries ago). The learner needs to know at least 3,000–4,000 characters to make sense of written Chinese, and thousands more to have a real feel for it. Chinese, with all its tones, is hard enough to speak. But the mammoth feat of memory required to be literate in Mandarin is harder still. It deters most foreigners from ever mastering the system—and increasingly trips up Chinese natives.

A recent survey reported in the *People's Daily* found 84% of respondents agreeing that skill in Chinese is declining. If such gripes are common to most languages, there is something more to it in Chinese. Fewer and fewer native speakers learn to produce characters in traditional calligraphy. Instead, they write their language the same way we do—with a computer. And not only that, but they use the Roman alphabet to produce Chinese characters: type in *wo* and Chinese language-support software will offer a menu of characters pronounced wo; the user selects the one desired. (Or if the user types in *wo shi zhongguo ren*, "I am Chinese", the software detects the meaning and picks the right characters.) With less and less need to recall the characters cold, the Chinese are forgetting them. David Moser, a Sinologist, recalls asking three native Chinese graduate students at Peking University how to write "sneeze":

> To my surprise, all three of them simply shrugged in sheepish embarrassment. Not one of them could correctly produce the character. Now, Peking University is usually considered the "Harvard of China". Can you imagine three PhD students in English at Harvard forgetting how to write the English word "sneeze"? Yet this state of affairs is by no means uncommon in China.

As long as China keeps the character-based system—which will prob- 10 ably be a long time, thanks to cultural attachment and practical concerns alike—Chinese is very unlikely to become a true world language, an auxiliary language like English, the language a Brazilian chemist will publish papers in, hoping that they will be read in Finland and Canada. By all means, if China is your main interest, for business or pleasure, learn Chinese. It is fascinating, and learnable— though Moser's online essay, "Why Chinese is so damn hard," might discourage the faint of heart and the short of time.

> "If I was asked what foreign language is the most useful . . . my answer would be French."

But if I was asked what foreign language is the most useful, and given no more parameters (where? for what purpose?), my answer would be French. Whatever you think of France, the language is much less limited than many people realise.

As their empire spun off and they became a medium-sized power after the second world war, the French, hoping to maintain some distance from America and to make the most of their former possessions, established La Francophonie. This club, bringing together all the countries with a French-speaking heritage, has 56 members, almost a third of the world's countries. Hardly any of them are places where French is everyone's native language. Instead, they include countries with Francophone minorities (Switzerland, Belgium); those where French is official and widespread among elites (much of western Africa); those where it is not official but still spoken by nearly all educated people (Morocco, Lebanon); and those where

French ties remain despite the fading of the language (Vietnam, Cambodia). It even has members with few ties to French or France, like Egypt, that simply want to associate themselves with the prestige of the French-speaking world. Another 19 countries are observer members.

French ranks only 16th on the list of languages ranked by native speakers. But ranked above it are languages like Telegu and Javanese that no one would call world languages. Hindi does not even unite India. Also in the top 15 are Arabic, Spanish and Portuguese, major languages to be sure, but regionally concentrated. If your interest is the Middle East or Islam, by all means learn Arabic. If your interest is Latin America, Spanish or Portuguese is the way to go. Or both; learning one makes the second quite easy.

If your interests span the globe, and you've read this far, you already know the most useful global language. But if you want another truly global language, there are surprisingly few candidates, and for me French is unquestionably top of the list. It can enhance your enjoyment of art, history, literature and food, while giving you an important tool in business and a useful one in diplomacy. It has native speakers in every region on earth. And lest we forget its heartland itself, France attracts more tourists than any other country—76.8m in 2010, according to the World Tourism Organisation, leaving America a distant second with 59.7m. Any visit there is greatly enhanced by some grasp of the language. The French are nothing but welcoming when you show them and their country respect, and the occasional frost that can greet visitors melts when they come out with their first fully formed sentence. So although there are other great languages out there, don't forget an easy, common one, with far fewer words to learn than English, that is almost certainly taught in your town. With French, *vous ne regretterez rien*.

Analyze

1. What effect does the comment in the second paragraph that English is the "world's most useful and important language" have on you as a reader? Why?

2. Greene lists several reasons for learning a language other than English. Which of these do you find the most compelling and why?

3. Are you convinced by Greene's argument that French is possibly the most useful foreign language that one can learn? Consider some of the reasons for or against his position.

Explore

1. According to the author, there are intellectual, economical, and practical reasons for learning a new language. Reflect on a time when you had to learn a new language and describe what that experience was like.
2. Greene argues that Mandarin, the formal language of China, has little chance of becoming a popular global language. Do you agree with this point of view? Evaluate the various points provided in the essay as you develop a position of your own.
3. If you had to learn a foreign language, which language would you choose? Write an essay in which you carefully consider the advantages and disadvantages of learning this language. Refer to published sources that serve as evidence for your ideas.

John McWhorter
Which Languages Should Liberal Arts Be About in 2010?

John McWhorter, an American linguist who specializes in language change and language context, is the William T. Simon Fellow at Columbia University. He writes and comments on ethnicity and cultural issues for the Manhattan Institute, a conservative public policy think tank, and is a contributing editor to the Institute's urban policy magazine, *City Journal*. The following article was published on December 13, 2010 in *The New Republic*, a biweekly magazine and website that has been publishing continuously about politics and the arts since 1914. In this selection, McWhorter laments that universities have been forced to scale back on their language offerings, but argues that those considered most relevant to our times should remain.

Given our mid-21st-century global world, which languages do you think colleges and universities should offer?

We are to bemoan that universities across the country are eliminating or scaling back their foreign language departments. Or, what seems to arouse critics most is the disappearance of French, German, and Italian departments—what with Goethe, Balzac and Dante being pillars of a liberal arts education and so on.

Yet, former French major and great fan of foreign language learning as I am, I'm not feeling as bad about this new trend as I am supposed to. I have as deep-seated a sense as anyone that an educated person is supposed to be able to at least fake a conversation in French. But then I also have a deepseated sense that the driver's seat in a car should be on the left side. It's all I've known, but hardly the choice all humans would make if designing a car from scratch with no cultural preconceptions.

Out of the 6000 languages in the world, why is it so vital for smart people to learn the one spoken in one small European country of ever-waning influence and its former colonies? Isn't the sense of French as a keystone of an education a legacy of when few met foreigners who spoke non-European languages, French was educated Europe's lingua franca, and the elite who went to college often had plans to do the Grand Tour?

That is, is knowing French really so obviously central to engaging what we know in 2010 as the world, or is it that French is a kind of class marker? You know: two cars, a subscription to the Times, and *mais oui*, Caitlin knows some French?

5   The counterarguments are typically along the lines of this one from the Modern Language Association's executive director, Rosemary Feal: "The plans of the State University of New York at Albany to deny students access to higher learning in three modern and two classical languages are a distressing reverse to the university's recent efforts to promote global competencies. The advanced study of the languages, literatures, and cultures of the French-, Italian-, and Russian-speaking world are essential components of a liberal arts education in a university setting."

I suppose she has to say that, but if the subject is, as she claims, "global" competency then we must ask why the languages in question are spoken in Europe, geographically a mere peninsula of Asia which, if the dice were rolled again, might not even be considered a continent. Sure, Europe has been the main cradle of Western thought—but let's face it, you can be richly immersed in that via solid English translations; Nietzsche need not be read in the original. There's an awful lot of world beyond Europe; people speak some languages there too, and in our times, a liberal arts education should focus on them.

Take Chinese, which increasing numbers of students are taking. A Martian would be baffled as to why anyone would think of French, German or Italian as more important for young Americans to learn than Chinese. Or—in response to the objection that no one is saying European languages are *more* important—let's face it, the Martian wouldn't understand why *Chinese* was not thought more important.

The issue is not that China will likely surpass the U.S. economically. When that happens, the world's unofficial universal language will remain English: tradition plus the fact that English is easier for foreigners to get a grasp of and learn to read and write will make that so. However, there will still be ample use for people who can actually converse with the Chinese and read the language.

For example, it would appear that many technologies we create, such as ones to combat climate change, will increasingly be actually tested in China, whose political system is better at making real plans than ours and apparently will be for a long time. This will occasion an ever greater need for Chinese speakers for business purposes. The Chinese are also avidly interested in learning English, which will make teaching English in China as common a goal for young people as being an *au pair* girl in France used to be. China is *happening*, in a way that Italy is not.

In addition, as language goes, a solid education would expose people to   10
how different languages can be despite all of them expressing the humanity common to all of us. Because English, as a European language, is built on the same general game plan as its relatives French, German and Italian, to love languages and concentrate on the grand old staples like French, German and Italian is like being an animal lover and only engaging varieties of cat. That may come as a surprise to those exposed only to those languages, but Chinese grammar is facsinatingly unlike anything European. *Zhèi ge rén de huà shì kào bu zhù de a* means "This person's words are unreliable." Word for word in Chinese it roughly goes "This person's speech is a not-rely-hold-on-ness, you know." Plus the words also have tones; get a tone wrong and you are saying, for example, *horse* instead of *mother*.

Besides this, study Chinese and in many parts of the U.S. it will be easy to find people to practice with, as well as signs to parse and TV and radio stations to tune into. Meanwhile, how many Germans do you generally meet? Plenty, back in the day when German was America's second language the way Spanish is now. But times have changed. Chinese is, in fact, now America's third language, right after Spanish.

Or—should a modern liberal arts education cherish Italian over Arabic? More to the point, shouldn't Arabic be seen as more urgent if there has to be a choice? The scarcity of government employees truly proficient in the language is well known. We will clearly have ample need for Arabic speakers to mediate between us and its Middle Eastern speakers for generations to come.

Commonly, a school will offer years-long, stepwise training in French but only offer a year's worth of Arabic—and in that year, too often just learning how to read the script is given so much time that students barely command any grammar. Ask a student who's been taking Arabic for a semester what she's learned and you'll likely find that decoding the writing has been the main meal and that she can barely express thoughts. That won't do—and if there aren't funds for both richer Arabic training and a major's worth of the language of Stendhal, then I don't see that Stendhal is unequivocally more important here. That is, here in 2010. I love French and I've read Stendhal. But last time I checked, some interesting things had been written in Arabic, too.

Then, as European languages go, there is also an argument for sparing Russian. It is often said that Latin is useful in teaching categories of grammar in a good old-fashioned way. Well, Russian, with its multiple cases and so very much else, is structured a lot more like Latin than French is, and gives students the exact same kind of grammatical workout as Latin—but with the advantage that it is often quite easy to find people to actually speak it with. Plus, Russians, like Italians and Japanese, tend to be generous about letting people butcher their language. No Latin, no Virgil—yes; but is someone who gets to *The Brothers Karamazov* and Chekhov in the original deprived compared to someone who can decode Catullus?

15   And again, suppose there *aren't* funds for both: the issue is Chekhov or Catullus? Upon which: there was a time when the educated person was supposed to know Ancient Greek. Do we miss that, or see it as the fetish of a bygone era? Russian is a Latin you can actually speak with natives—and hear on the radio, and read on line.

There are, to be sure, western European languages more urgent to being a well-rounded modern than French and German. SUNY and other schools are sparing Spanish programs. But this is less because of a quest to inculcate young people with Cervantes than out of a demand that remains high, naturally, as Spanish is the native language of so very many people in our country. Cross-cultural communication is as important within the nation's borders as it is for students taking years abroad, after all.

Should students be able to take French, German and Italian if they want to? Of course. But should it be expected that any university worth its salt have majors in those languages? I doubt it. A university of limited resources that has majors only in Chinese and Arabic should be a perfectly normal proposition. The only reason it does not seem so now is because of noble but fraying traditions.

The world is flatter and smaller by the hour. Our sense of which foreign languages are key to a serious education cannot be founded on what made sense for characters in Henry James novels.

Analyze

1. The author asks several rhetorical questions in the third and fourth paragraphs. What is he trying to get at by asking these questions?
2. Examine the kind of tone one might detect in the sentence "There's an awful lot of world beyond Europe; people speak some languages there too." How does this understanding of tone help you understand McWhorter's overall argument in this essay?
3. Summarize the author's argument in favor of the formal study of languages such as Chinese and Arabic. Are you convinced by his argument?

Explore

1. Why would a Martian be puzzled by the value placed on European languages in American education? Reflect on an experience you've had with language learning that either illustrates or contradicts McWhorter's point.
2. If it were up to you, what language (or languages) would you learn in college? Why? Refer back to McWhorter's ideas as you write.
3. What, in your opinion, is the place of languages in a liberal arts education today? Write an essay in which you develop an argument supported by evidence both from this article and from other, researched sources.

Alexander Arguelles
Experience: I Can Speak 50 Languages

Alexander Arguelles is a foreign language specialist based in Singapore. He earned his PhD at the University of Chicago and was a professor of European languages for eight years at Handong University in South Korea. Since 2009, he has served as Language Specialist in the Training, Research, Assessment, and Consultancy Department at the Regional Language Centre of the South East Asian Ministers of Education Organization. This personal reflection appeared in the March 16, 2012, online edition of *The Guardian*, a London-based newspaper founded in 1821. Arguelles describes how learning and understanding multiple languages has enriched his life.

In what ways does the way you use language—especially if you speak more than one language—bring out different aspects of your personality?

I've been obsessed with languages for as long as I can remember. My family travelled a lot when I was young and my dad, a self-taught polyglot, would talk to everyone we met with apparent ease, confidently switching between languages. His abilities made a big impression on me, but I was intimidated by him, and he didn't encourage me to follow his lead.

I wasn't a natural language learner. Aged 11, I made slow progress with French at school and almost gave it up. But things felt different when I took on German at university—loving many German writers in translation, I wanted to read them in their native tongue, and that's been my main motivation for learning new ones since. It can be a real revelation when you start to get it. Once I got German, I was hooked; French, Latin, Greek and Sanskrit quickly followed. The idea of having an encyclopedic mind—a comprehensive overview of the world—has always fascinated me, and acquiring languages seemed a good way of achieving that. By my 20s, I'd set my heart on devoting the rest of my life to learning as many as I could.

I'm often asked what the secret is, and whether some people have an aptitude for absorbing words and phrases. The truth is, predictably, it's down to endless hours of concentration—reading, studying and practising grammar, as well as my own technique called "shadowing", which involves walking briskly outdoors while listening to a recorded language and repeating it out loud. For five or six years, before I married and had children, I would study for 16 hours a day. I'd transcribe Irish, Persian, Hindi, Turkish, Swahili. Gradually, all these wonderful languages started to swim into focus, and ever increasing numbers of great works became accessible.

It's hard, but the rewards can be thrilling. When I started studying Spanish, for example, there was a moment when the living language—which

I'd heard spoken around me when I was growing up—suddenly revealed itself to me, as if the wax was falling from my ears. That's the moment I crave—it comes to me quickly with European, Germanic or Romance languages—and it's very addictive. Something similar happened when I first went to Sweden—I'd never studied Swedish, but when I heard it spoken around me, it seemed to combine elements of languages I was familiar with. All it took was three weeks and I was able to hold my own in complex conversations. That's as much as most people would want, but as far as I'm concerned, at that stage I'm still in the foothills. Climbing the mountain—achieving native fluency—is always going to take years.

Now, I can read about three dozen languages and speak most of them 5 fluently, and I've studied many more. The more of them you know, the more you see how inter-related they are.

Exotic languages can be more of a challenge. I worked as a professor in Korea for eight years and it took almost a decade to get my Korean skills close to native level. We live in Singapore now, and at home I speak French with my sons, unless my Korean wife is there, in which case we'll use English. If we don't want the kids to understand everything we're saying, we use Korean.

I'm not a naturally forthcoming person and I used to be wary of talking to native speakers in their mother tongue. But to have the language come alive you have to speak it, to live it. Now, I find when I'm immersed in a language, I have another, more garrulous persona.

I think I'm much richer for that—it makes me more confident. If I were kidnapped tomorrow and dropped in an unknown region, I think there are only a few very remote areas I'd struggle to make myself understood.

I'm increasingly drawn to dead and endangered languages, and want to set up a polyglot academy where people with similar interests to mine can flourish. I've studied Esperanto, and although I can see the benefits of a world language, I do think the loss of so many quirks and colours would leave the world a less intriguing place. It would be like visiting a botanic garden where there was only one type of plant—that thought horrifies me.

Analyze

1. In describing his experiences with learning different languages Arguelles uses several metaphors. Select a few of these phrases and explain whether or not they are effective.

2. The author claims that one can achieve an "encyclopedic mind—a comprehensive overview of the world" by learning many languages. To what extent do you agree with this view and why?
3. What does Arguelles's anecdote about using three different languages with his family tell you about the benefits of learning multiple languages?

Explore

1. Can learning a new language really have an impact on one's personality? Reflect on a time when you engaged with an unfamiliar language and describe the effect it had on you.
2. Arguelles's essay implies that classic works of literature should preferably be read in the original. How realistic is this view? Support your argument by referring to personal experiences and other published sources.
3. Write a research paper on polyglots—those who can speak, read, and write in several languages—and consider the advantages and disadvantages of being a polyglot. What particular characteristics do they have? What makes them unique? Refer to books, journal or newspaper articles, or interviews as you write your essay.

Adam Pulford
Words Are Wind

Adam Pulford, a self-proclaimed "book geek," is an assistant marketing manager for Oxford Dictionaries at Oxford University Press. He is also a regular blogger for *OUPblog*, a space for authors, staff, and friends of Oxford University Press to contribute to "learning, understanding, and reflection . . . for the thinking world." In his article "Words Are Wind," which was published on *OUPblog* on April 16, 2012, Pulford explores the memorable languages of the fantasy series *Game of Thrones* created by George R. R. Martin. For Pulford, the archaically influenced words and expressions of the series appropriately evoke the medieval setting intended for the stories. Pulford, a fan of the series, admits to integrating the language of *Game of Thrones* into his own vernacular.

In what ways have different languages, either real or imagined, influenced your own vernacular?

Somehow *A Song of Ice and Fire*, the colossal fantasy series by George R. R. Martin, had escaped my notice until the critically acclaimed TV series hit our screens last year, prompting me to buy the first book in the series. Little did I know that a few weeks later I would spend Christmas continually ushering away family members clutching Monopoly and Cluedo boxes so that I could devour all five volumes in unhealthily close succession. The five books have now been translated into more than 20 languages and have sold over 15 million copies worldwide. As *Game of Thrones* returns to our screens for a second season, there's no better time to explore the interesting language used by its creator.

I Name You a Southron Turncloak, Ser!

The series has been labelled by many as 'medieval fantasy' and indeed much of the language is evocative of this. As well as the knightly setting of the series, vocabulary is used to add to the medieval flavour. Some are invented words—such as *turncloak*, which is Martin's archaic-sounding amendment of turncoat. But many are already-existing words with a long history. *Ser* for Sir, *Southron* for Southern, and craven meaning cowardly all date from 1451, 1488, and 1400 respectively, according to the Oxford English Dictionary. My favourite expression *mayhaps* is first cited in the OED a little later in the late 17th century, with the form *mayhap* ocurring even earlier in the mid-16th century. Aside from these inclusions I must admit that as a British reader, I found the occasional use of modern-sounding terms such as *butt* and *ass* jarring. Yet surprisingly *butt* meaning 'buttock' is first recorded in the OED in circa 1450 and *ass* is recorded as early as 1860.

To Create a Language or Not to Create a Language? That Is the Question!

It is not only the inclusion of archaic words that sets the linguistic scene of the seven kingdoms but the presence of other languages. Martin does not, however, follow in the footsteps of fantasy writers such as Tolkien and others who have fully developed fantasy languages. Martin's languages— Valyrian, the Common Tongue of Westeros; Braavosi; and Dothraki among others—are not conveyed in any great detail; instead, the tongue in which they are speaking is noted but rendered in English. The characteristics and flavour of each of the different languages in the seven kingdoms are portrayed through a number of colloquial phrases which the reader can then associate with that particular language. This can be seen in the following examples:

- Missendei, a former slave in the eastern city of Astapor, uses "this one" rather than *I* or *me*
- the Dothraki use "it is known" concerning a piece of common knowledge or folklore
- when referring to a husband who is a khal (warrior king), "my Sun and Stars" is used, again by the Dothraki

In the TV show, however, this tactic would not work and so the Dothraki language was invented based on a few snippets in Martin's first book of the series. Dothraki has now grown to a vocabulary of 3,000 words.

The Power of Proverbs

5   It is not only the eastern languages that contain these proverb-like phrases—the seven kingdoms of Westeros contain many, such as "Dark wings, dark words," spoken almost every time anyone sees a raven delivering a message. "Words are wind" is another aphorism used by the characters, meaning 'actions speak louder than words'—something particularly relevant in this land of false friends and power struggles. As in the real world, religion has an impact on proverbial sayings and 'The Seven' (the gods of the principal religion of the seven kingdoms) provide the phrase "gods be good", expressing both hope that they will bring favourable outcomes, and disbelief at the very opposite. "Seven hells" is also used as an exclamation of shock, often with humorous connotations.

Mottos and Metaphors

Each noble family has a *sigil* such as the dire wolf (this giant wolf has been extinct for around 10,000 years in our world) of the northern house of Stark, the lion of the Lannister's of Casterly Rock in the West, or the dragon of the usurped house Targaryen. This means that members of said families can be described as this animal or to have their attributes—for example Robb Stark is often referenced as "the young wolf". Furthermore each noble family has their own family motto which is indicative of their character, whether it be the foreboding "Winter is coming" of the cautious, honourable Starks or the common Lannister phrase "a Lannister always pays his debts", denoting promises of wealth, or a threat of retribution.

Here Be Monsters . . .

Martin does not only include creatures from commonly known mythology to liven up his landscape, such as dragons and giants, but moulds some creatures and objects of his own. *Shadowcat* is my favourite animal name coinage as I think the name immediately puts the idea of a stealth hunter into your mind, with an element of mystery—not a creature that you would easily catch a glimpse of. The mysterious 'Weirwood trees' are at the heart of the religion (known as 'the Old Gods') still present in the north of Westeros with their sap-bleeding faces linking them to the supernatural or religious. The *weir-* prefix could be an echo of *weirwolf* (an alternate spelling of werewolf, dating back to 1818) as indeed these trees are made into portals through which a certain *warg* can see their surrounding areas. In the seven kingdoms a *warg* describes a person who can put their consciousness into an animal's (or even another person's) body and thus control their actions. But the most menacing of Martin's creations are the *white walkers*, ominously referred to as 'The Others', and mentioned in the phrase "the others take you" and other variants when denouncing or dismissing someone.

What's in a Name?

Martin's word coinage is not limited to objects and creatures but is also evident in the names of his characters and places. One such interesting feature of these books is how the stigma of illegitimacy is displayed so prominently through a child's surname—as a bastard is not deemed worthy of a family name. Not only does this mean that one can immediately know the status of the character when they are introduced but also where they are from as their surname will reflect the area of Westeros in which they were born; those from the North would bear the name Snow, whereas those from the Riverlands would have the name Rivers, and those from the Southern areas of the Stormlands and the Reach would be Storm and Flowers respectively.

Martin's place names similarly set the scene. You can easily envisage the snowy and remote Winterfell in the North; the hot nest of vipers fighting for power in King's Landing with the grimy hustle and bustle of Flea Bottom; the swaggering Bravos (peacock-like musketeers looking for a fight) of the free city of Braavos in the East across the Narrow Sea; and the cliff-top, vertigo-inducing, unnerving heights of the aptly named Eyrie.

From Westeros to Our Own World

10 George R. R. Martin has created a legendary fantasy series which is so expansive that I would need to commandeer this blog until at least the start of the next series to do it justice. Its impact is evident not only from its dedicated fan base but how through these books, a new language has been created. Indeed the writing is so descriptive, with certain phrases recurring so frequently that somehow they have entered my vernacular. For example, my fiancée made the unlikely assurance of returning early in the morning after her sister's hen-do, to which I automatically replied "words are wind". Simultaneously, I was greeted by a baffled expression and the realization of what a book geek I can be.

Analyze

1. Pulford notes that the language used in *Game of Thrones* reflects the medieval period. Examine some of the invented words in paragraph two and write about how they reflect this period.

2. Why are proverbs used so extensively in the show? What sort of world do you think they help create?

3. What larger argument about language is Pulford trying to make in his analysis of names of creatures, characters, and places?

Explore

1. Imagine that you have been asked to invent new characters or places for *Game of Thrones*. What names would you create? Explain, like Pulford does, how the names would reflect the defining characteristics of these characters or places.

2. Watch an episode of *Game of Thrones* and pay particular attention to the language used by the characters. How similar is your observation to that of Pulford? How is it different?

3. Write an essay in which you examine whether the invention of a new language gives literature, film, or a TV show a uniqueness that known languages cannot provide. Refer to your own experiences and to other sources to support your claims.

Eddie Dean
Klingon as a Second Language

Eddie Dean is a freelance journalist based in Washington, DC. His articles have appeared in numerous periodicals, magazines, and newspapers, including *The Wall Street Journal, Harper's,* and *SPIN.* "Klingon as a Second Language" originally appeared in 1996 in *Washington City Paper,* an alternative weekly newspaper that serves the Washington, DC metropolitan area. In this profile of d'Armond Speers, a linguistics PhD candidate at Georgetown University who taught the invented language Klingon (from *Star Trek*) to his young son, Dean observes that learning to speak a second artificial language is no different than learning to speak a second legitimate language.

Do you agree that the ability to speak more than one language will improve one's ability to excel academically?

"Vavoy! Vavoy!"

The wild cries echo through the nearly empty Burger King, as 2-year-old Alec Speers calls out to his father, d'Armond, who sits wolfing down a Whopper at a table across the room. After roaming as far as the soda fountain, the tousled-haired Alec suddenly realizes the vast distance between him and his dad; tiny legs shuffling, the gleeful tot now makes his triumphant return.

"Vavoy!" he says again, pointing to his father.

The repeated word doesn't sound much like any language ever spoken in this Olney fast-food restaurant on Georgia Avenue, or any other terrestrial location for that matter. Like a Teutonic romper-room war chant or the pidgin gutter-talk of those *Clockwork Orange* punks, the mantra's enough to turn the head of a woman as Alec races by. Caught up in his infant joy, he veers past his father's outstretched arms and runs smack into the edge of the table, banging his forehead.

5   A nasty mishap, but fortunately no real disaster. D'Armond Speers cradles his bawling boy, trying to comfort him in words that sound as foreign as Alec's: "qay'be, 'yISaQQo'."

"I'm just telling him, 'It's alright, you're OK,'" explains Speers as Alec settles into a sniffling calm. The tender parenting moment for Speers doubles as another linguistic victory: He's the only person on the planet raising a child to speak Klingon.

Invented a decade ago for the Star Trek TV shows and films, Klingon is the official language of the alien warriors with the grotesque, bony foreheads. But in the past few years, the 2,000-word language has taken on a life of its own in the real world. It's now one of the fastest growing artificial, or "constructed," languages around, boasting a far-flung community of speakers, as well as a language institute, a journal, and even a poetry magazine.

Like many Klingon speakers, Speers is by no means a hard-core Trekkie, and his decision to teach Alec Klingon is as academically serious as it is unique. The 28-year-old computer programmer is pursuing his Ph.D. in linguistics at Georgetown University, and views his effort as an educational adventure. "I do have a [Klingon] forehead I've worn a few times, but my interest is primarily in the language," says Speers, an affable, witty computer geek who keeps his hair in a tight ponytail.

So far, the experiment seems to be working. Alec already speaks several Klingon words, including "vavoy," which means "daddy." "When he speaks, he tends to prefer English, although he'll use Klingon for some things," says Speers.

10   At Burger King, Alec banishes the hurt from his accident to make friends with the prize from his Kid's Meal, a toy Hunchback of Notre Dame: Right

off, he points to the Disney doll's tiny slippers and mutters, "Waq, waq." Speers smiles and says proudly, " 'Waq' means shoe." Alec knows the English word for that as well, because Speers' wife talks to Alec exclusively in English, which the boy also gets in earfuls at the day-care center.

In the Speers household, Klingon and English vie for Alec's attention, filling the town house with a wild mix of words. (Most prevalent, of course: "Don't," or "Qo" in Klingon.) Speers says his wife, though no fan of Klingon or Star Trek culture in general, fully approves of his project, as do his friends and relatives. Speers argues that raising Alec to switch glibly between English and Klingon is no less beneficial than more traditional bilingual upbringings: "My feeling is that it's good for people in general to know more than one language. You get different viewpoints and perspectives on things, and there is evidence to suggest that kids who are bilingual do better academically whether their second language is a constructed language or not."

Speers has endured onlookers' shocked disbelief and heard their snickers when he explains that he and his son are conversing in Klingon. Even in hyperpolyglot Washington, Klingon's guttural sounds really do resonate like babble from outer space: From the grocery checkout counter to the folks at the day-care center, strangers routinely stop and ask Speers what in the hell he's saying to his son. He used to simply answer "Klingon," but now he says, "constructed language," which usually stalls any further comment.

"When I say Klingon, people think of these vicious animal-like creatures they've seen on TV," he explains. "We're interested in the language. Alec hasn't even seen the show . . . and one time I dressed up [as a Klingon] it horrified him, so I've never done it again." (Even so, he adds that the Klingons have a noble culture to emulate, if not to obsess about: "We've learned that the Klingons have a society highly dedicated to the concept of honor," he says. "Even in their warlike behavior, they're very honorable.")

Speers got his first dose of Klingon as a second language not from the boob tube but from the halls of academia. Three years ago he spotted a flyer on a Georgetown campus bulletin board for the Klingon Language Institute (KLI), an organization that studies the constructed language developed by Marc Okrand. "I thought to myself, 'A new language,'" says Speers, who was getting his master's degree in theoretical linguistics. "The fact that it was a constructed language really appealed to me. It sounded like fun."

15   Artificial languages are nothing new. According to an article in the August issue of *Wired* (which features a Klingon phrase on the cover), Klingon joins a list of 700 constructed languages, from obscure medieval attempts to more recent efforts such as Esperanto. The late 19th-century invention of a Polish ophthalmologist, Esperanto remains the world's most popular artificial language. But for many, Esperanto holds no appeal because it is so abstract. "One of the problems with Esperanto is there's no binding culture behind it," says Speers.

Klingon's got culture by the gobs, and it's a smooth union of sci-fi and linguistic impulses. Even better, the Klingon image has mellowed through the years, as the fierce alien race has evolved from the intergalactic bad guys of the original *Star Trek* series to the noble, if still hot-tempered, warriors of *The Next Generation, Deep Space Nine*, and the *Star Trek* movies. In 1984, Okrand, a linguist working at the Smithsonian, was hired by Paramount to invent Klingon dialogue for *Star Trek III: The Search for Spock*. (Speers says that much of the dialogue used on the TV shows—without Okrand's aid—is bad Klingon and completely offensive to his sensitive ears.)

The following year, Okrand, inspired by his one-shot writing gig, penned *The Klingon Dictionary*, which quickly became much more than a novelty item. Now in its second printing, the dictionary has sold more than 250,000 copies and serves as the bible for the language's speakers, who take it a good deal more seriously than Okrand does. In fact, the Glover Park resident has become an elusive, legendary figure to Klingon speakers. "It's kind of like Marc Okrand is a field linguist studying the Klingon language, and as he learns things about it, he reveals it to us, the community of speakers," says Speers. "But we're not Klingons, we don't claim to have any knowledge about the language. We're just studying what little information has been available to us."

The clearinghouse for that intensive, worldwide study is the Flourtown, Pa.–based KLI, which publishes a quarterly (and quite scholarly) journal, *HolQeD* ("Language Science"), which focuses on Klingon linguistics, language, and culture, and a poetry magazine, *jatmey* ("scattered science"). The group also recently published a translation of Hamlet, and there are other projects afoot, including the Klingon Bible translation project. Meanwhile, Okrand has just released *The Klingon Way: A Warrior's Guide*, featuring a slew of Klingon proverbs: "Revenge is a dish best served cold." Not to mention his best-selling audio cassettes, *Conversational Klingon* ("Hear Klingon spoken by its creator") and *Power Klingon* ("Learn classic

Klingon jokes, insults, and toasts"). Along with the *Wired* profile, it's clear that Klingon has never been hotter.

On paper, the Klingon language, at least in its Romanized lettering, resembles the jabberings of a typewriter on the fritz, but the spatterings of capital letters in the middle of words is the key to understanding its complex system of phonetics. Making it even harder to master, verb-heavy Klingon has no tenses and no infinitives and depends entirely on context to get the speaker's point across.

Though KLI claims more than 1,000 active members, Speers estimates   20
that only about two dozen people can write and speak in Klingon. Speers communicates with fellow Klingon speakers almost daily via e-mail ("I get about 15 Klingon messages a day," he says offhandedly). Then there are the occasional phone conversations, and the annual KLI convention (at the most recent, Speers and others presented a linguistic "wish list" to special guest of honor Okrand, another of their attempts to push the language further. "He seemed really pleased," says Speers.)

But the only chance that Speers has of making the language come to life on a daily basis is with Alec.

"I've been able to say almost everything I've needed to say to Alec in Klingon," says Speers. "One of the reasons I find the Klingon language so interesting is that because the vocabulary and grammar is so limited, you really have to think to figure out how you're going to say something." Even putting Alec to bed becomes a linguistics puzzle, because there's no Klingon word for "light." "When I ask him to turn out the lights, I say the Klingon for 'make it dark,'" he explains. There's no Klingon word for "love," either (they don't have the concept), but in such situations Speers simply surrenders to English.

Ever the realist, Speers realizes that his experiment—trying to raise a Klingon warrior in the land of *Barney* and *Sesame Street*—is not only foolhardy but doomed: "There's going to come a time when he's going to stop making the effort to speak Klingon because it'll be easier for him to speak English—it's the prevalent language," sighs Speers. Until then, the father and son will continue having their own private conversation.

In the Burger King, Alec is still playing with the Hunchback, guiding him through a blood-red battle landscape of leftover french fries and ketchup.

"BIrIn'a'? bItlhutlhqa' DaneH'a'?" says Speers, adding, "I just asked him   25
if he was finished and if he wanted some more to drink." Alec shakes his

head ambiguously, and hits the straw for some soda. Apparently, even when he understands, Alec's like a lot of kids: He does what he wants.

Watching his son drink, Speers recalls the proud moment when Alec understood his first Klingon word, "HIvje," which means "vessel," Klingon's closest approximation to "milk bottle." "I was so thrilled, because it was the first time something that complex had happened," says Speers.

Outside the Burger King, in the dying twilight of a summer eve, Speers serenades his son with a rendition of the Klingon Imperial Anthem he often uses as a bed-time lullaby:

> *taHjaj wo' 'ej taHjaj voDLeHma'*
> *wItoy'mo' vaj nuquvmoHjaj ta'*
> *Dun wo'maj 'ej Qochchugh vay'*
> *vaj DaSmeymaj bIngDaq chaH DIbeQmoHchu'jay'!*
> *("May the empire endure, and may our emperor endure*
> *We serve him, so that he may honor us*
> *Our empire is wonderful, and if anyone disagrees,*
> *We will crush them beneath our boots!")*

It's a pretty little melody for a song about intergalactic domination, and the little Klingon student obviously delights in hearing it. Nestled in his father's arms, Alec whispers along to the words, even if he doesn't understand their violent underpinnings. But the anthem sure doesn't make him sleepy. He darts away from his dad, down to the sidewalk, and into the nearby parking lot, right into the path of an oncoming car:

> *"Qo'! naDev yIghoS!!!" screams Speers at the top of his lungs.*

30   Hearing the Klingon words (which translate as "Don't! Come here!"), or perhaps just the anger and fear in his father's voice, Alec wheels around away from the danger and runs back to the safety of his father.

Analyze

1. Why does Dean begin and end his article with d'Armond Speers and his son Alec's story? What impact does it have on you as a reader?

2. What are some of the advantages of learning an artificial language such as Klingon?

3. Do you agree that having the ability to switch between a real and a constructed language "is no less beneficial than more traditional

bilingual upbringings"? Is being fluent in a constructed language the same as being fluent in a natural, culturally-based language? Why or why not?

Explore

1. Watch an episode of the TV show *Star Trek* and note your observations about Klingon as a language. Do you get a "different viewpoint" from listening to the language? What is this viewpoint?

2. In his interview with the author, Speers claims that the version of Klingon used in the *Star Trek* TV series is inferior to that of the movie *Star Trek III: The Search for Spock*. Do you think the quality of a language can vary based on usage? Support your argument with personal experience or references to researched sources.

3. Examine the social and intellectual effects of being bilingual (or multilingual) by looking into sources that discuss both the advantages and disadvantages of bilingual education.

Sarah L. Higley
Audience, Uglossia, and CONLANG: Inventing Languages on the Internet

Sarah L. Higley is associate professor of English at the University of Rochester in New York, where she teaches medieval vernacular languages, literature of Northern Europe, fiction, film, and media studies. Her current interests focus on the educational possibilities of immersive environments and virtual realities. "Audience, Uglossia, and CONLANG" appeared in the March 2000 issue of *M/C Journal*, founded in 1998 as "a place of public intellectualism analysing and critiquing the meeting of media and culture." In her scholarly article, Higley questions whether invented languages, without the nuances and history of true languages but with the consumerism and participation of engaged audiences, should necessarily be deemed "impoverishments of natural languages."

Do you agree that audiences make language legitimate?

Could we also imagine a language in which a person could write down or give vocal expression to his inner experiences—his feelings, moods, and the rest—for his private use? Well, can't we do so in our ordinary language?—But that is not what I mean. The individual words of this language are to refer to what can only be known to the person speaking; to his immediate private sensations. So another person cannot understand the language.

—Ludwig Wittgenstein, Philosophical Investigations par. 243

I will be using 'audience' in two ways in the following essay: as a phenomenon that produces and is produced by media technologies (readers, hearers, viewers, Internet-users), and as something, audiens, that is essential to language itself, something without which language cannot be. I shall do so in specific references to invented languages. Who, then, are the 'consumers' of invented languages?

In referring to invented languages, I am not talking about speakers of Esperanto or Occidental; I am not concerned with the invention of international auxiliary languages. These projects, already well-debated, have roots that go back at least as far as the 17th-century language philosophers who were at pains to undo the damage of Babel and restore a common language to the world. While Esperanto never became what it intended to be, it at least has readers and speakers.

I am also not even talking about speakers of Klingon or Quenya. These privately invented languages have had the good fortune to be attached to popular invented cultures, and to media with enough money and publicity to generate a multitude of fans.

Rather, I am talking about a phenomenon on the Internet and in a well-populated listserv whereby a number of people from all over the globe have discovered each other on-line. They all have a passion for what Jeffrey Schnapp calls uglossia ('no-language', after utopia, 'no-place'). Umberto Eco calls it 'technical insanity' or glottomania. Linguist Marina Yaguello calls language inventors fous du langage ('language lunatics') in her book of the same title. Jeffrey Henning prefers the term 'model language' in his on-line newsletter: 'miniaturized versions that provide the essence of something'. On CONLANG, people call themselves conlangers (from 'constructed language') and what they do conlanging. By forming this list, they have created a media audience for themselves, in the first sense of the term, and also literally in the second sense, as a number of them are setting up soundbytes on their elaborately illustrated and explicated Webpages.

Originally devoted to advocates for international auxiliary languages, 5 CONLANG started out about eight years ago, and as members joined who were less interested in the politics than in the hobby of language invention, the list has become almost solely the domain of the latter, whereas the 'aux-langers', as they are called, have moved to another list. An important distinguishing feature of 'conlangers' is that, unlike the 'auxlangers', there is no sustained hope that their languages will have a wide-body of hearers or users. They may wish it, but they do not advocate for it, and as a consequence their languages are free to be a lot weirder, whereas the auxlangs tend to strive for regularity and useability.

CONLANG is populated by high school, college, and graduate students; linguists; computer programmers; housewives; librarians; professors; and other users worldwide. The old debate about whether the Internet has become the 'global village' that Marshall McLuhan predicted, or whether it threatens to atomise communication 'into ever smaller worlds where enthusiasms mutate into obsessions', as Jeff Salamon warns, seems especially relevant to a study of CONLANG whose members indulge in an invention that by its very nature excludes the casual listener-in.

And yet the audio-visual capacities of the Internet, along with its speed and efficiency of communication, have made it the ideal forum for conlangers. Prior to the Web, how were fellow inventors to know what others were doing—in secret? J.R.R. Tolkien has been lauded as a rare exception in the world of invention, but would his elaborate linguistic creations have become so famous had he not published *The Lord of the Rings* and its Appendix? Poignantly, he tells in "A Secret Vice" about accidentally overhearing another army recruit say aloud: 'Yes! I think I shall express the accusative by a prefix!'. Obviously, silent others besides Tolkien were inventing languages, but they did not have the means provided by the Internet to discover one another except by chance.

Tolkien speaks of the 'shyness' and 'shame' attached to this pursuit, where 'higher developments are locked in secret places'. It can win no prizes, he says, nor make birthday presents for aunts. His choice of title ("A Secret Vice") echoes a Victorian phrase for the closet, and conlangers have frequently compared conlanging to homosexuality, both being what conservative opinion expects one to grow out of after puberty. The number of gay men on the list has been wondered at as more than coincidental. In a survey I conducted in October 1998, many of the contributors to CONLANG felt that the list put them in touch with an audience that provided them with intellectual and emotional feedback. Their interests were misunderstood by parents, spouses, lovers, and employers alike, and had to be kept under wraps. Most of those I surveyed said that they had been inventing a language well before they had heard of the list; that they had conceived of what they were doing as unique or peculiar, until discovery of CONLANG; and that other people's Websites astounded them with the pervasive fascination of this pursuit.

10   There are two ways to look at it: conlanging, as Henning writes, may be as common and as humanly creative as any kind of model-making, i.e., doll-houses, model trains, role-playing, or even the constructed cultures with city plans and maps in fantasy novels such as Terry Pratchett's *Discworld*. The Web is merely a means to bring enthusiasts together. Or it may provide a site that, with the impetus of competition and showmanship, encourages inutile and obsessive activity. Take your pick. From Hildegard von Bingen's Lingua Ignota to Dante's *Inferno* and the babbling Nimrod to John Dee's Enochian and on, invented languages have smacked of religious ecstacy, necromancy, pathology, and the demonic. Twin speech, or 'pathological idioglossia', was dramatised by Jodie Foster in *Nell*. Hannah Green's 'Language of Yr' was the invention of her schizophrenic protagonist in *I Never Promised You a Rose Garden*. Language itself is the centre of furious theoretical debate. Despite the inventive 'deformities' it is put to in poetry, punning, jest, singing, and lying, human language, our most 'natural' of technologies, is a social machine, used by multitudes and expected to get things done. It is expected of language that it be understood and that it have not only hearers but also answerers. All human production is founded on this assumption. A language without an audience of other speakers is no language. 'Why aren't you concentrating on real languages?' continues to be the most stinging criticism.

Audience is essential to Wittgenstein's remark quoted at the beginning of this essay. Wittgenstein posits his 'private languages theory' as a kind of impossibility: all natural languages, because they exist by consensus, can only refer to private experience externally. Hence, a truly private language, devoted to naming 'feelings and moods' which the subject has never heard about or shared with others, is impossible among socialised speakers who are called upon to define subjective experience in public terms. His is a critique of solipsism, a charge often directed at language inventors. But very few conlangers that I have encountered are making private languages in Wittgenstein's sense, because most of them are interested in investing their private words with public meaning, even when they are doing it privately. For them, it is audience, deeply desireable, that has been impossible until now. Writing well before the development of CONLANG, Yaguello takes the stance that inventing a language is an act of madness. 'Just look at the lunatic in love with language', she writes:

> sitting in his book-lined study, he collects great piles of information, he collates and classifies it, he makes lists and fills card indexes. He is in the clutches of a denominatory delirium, of a taxonomic madness. He has to name everything, but before being able to name, he has to recognize and classify concepts, to enclose the whole Universe in a system of notation: produce enumerations, hierarchies, and paradigms.

She is of course describing John Wilkins, whose *Real Character and Universal Language* in 1668 was an attempt to make each syllable of his every invented word denote its placement in a logical scheme of classification. 'A lunatic ambition', Yaguello pronounces, because it missed the essential quality of language: that its signs are arbitrary, practical, and changeable, so as to admit neologism and cultural difference. But Yaguello denounces auxiliary language makers in general as amateurs 'in love with language and with languages, and ignorant of the science of language'. Her example of 'feminine' invention comes from Helene Smith, the medium who claimed to be channeling Martian (badly disguised French). One conlanger noted that Yaguello's chapter entitled 'In Defence of Natural Languages' reminded him of the US Federal 'Defense of Marriage Act', whereby the institution of heterosexual marriage is 'defended' from homosexual marriage. Let homosexuals marry or lunatics invent language, and both marriage and English (or French) will come crashing to the ground.

Schnapp praises Yaguello's work for being the most comprehensive examination of the phenomenon to date, but neither he nor she addresses linguist Suzette Haden Elgin's creative work on Láadan, a language designed for women, or even Quenya or Klingon—languages that have acquired at least an audience of readers. Schnapp is less condemnatory than Yaguello, and interested in seeing language inventors as the 'philologists of imaginary worlds', 'nos semblables, nos frères, nos soeurs'—after all. Like Yaguello, he is given to some generalities: imaginary languages are 'infantile': 'the result is always [my emphasis] an "impoverishment" of the natural languages in question: reduced to a limited set of open vowels [he means "open syllables"], prone to syllabic reduplication and to excessive syntactical parallelisms and symmetries'. To be sure, conlangs will never replicate the detail and history of a real language, but to call them 'impoverishments of the natural languages' seems as strange as calling dollhouses 'impoverishments of actual houses'. Why this perception of threat or diminishment? The critical, academic "audience" for language invention has come largely from non-language inventors and it is woefully uninformed. It is this audience that conlangers dislike the most: the outsiders who cannot understand what they are doing and who belittle it.

15   The field, then, is open to re-examination, and the recent phenomenon of conlanging is evidence that the art of inventing languages is neither lunatic nor infantile. But if one is not Tolkien or a linguist supported by the fans of Star Trek, how does one justify the worthwhile nature of one's art? Is it even art if it has an audience of one ... its artist?

Conlanging remains a highly specialised and technical pursuit that is, in the end, deeply subjective. Model builders and map-makers can expect their consumers to enjoy their products without having to participate in the minutia of their building. Not so the conlanger, whose consumer must internalise it, and who must understand and absorb complex linguistic concepts. It is different in the world of music. The Cocteau Twins, Bobby McFerrin in his "Circle Songs," Lisa Gerrard in Duality, and the new group Ekova in Heaven's Dust all use 'nonsense' words set to music—either to make songs that sound like exotic languages or to convey a kind of melodic glossolalia. Knowing the words is not important to their hearers, but few conlangers yet have that outlet, and must rely on text and graphs to give a sense of their language's structure. To this end, then, these are unheard, unaudienced languages, existing mostly on screen. A few conlangers have set their languages to music and recorded them. What they are doing, however, is decidedly different from the extempore of McFerrin. Their words mean something, and are carefully worked out lexically and grammatically.

So What Are These CONLANGS Like?

On CONLANG and their links to Websites you will find information on almost every kind of no-language imaginable. Some sites are text only; some are lavishly illustrated, like the pages for Denden, or they feature a huge inventory of RealAudio and MP3 files, like The Kolagian Languages, or the songs of Teonaht. Some have elaborate scripts that the newest developments in fontography have been able to showcase. Some, like Tokana and Amman-Iar, are the result of decades of work and are immensely sophisticated. Valdyan has a Website with almost as much information about the 'conculture' as the conlang. Many are a posteriori languages, that is, variations on natural languages, like Brithenig (a mixture of the features of Brythonic and Romance languages); others are a priori— starting from scratch—like Elet Anta.

Many conlangers strive to make their languages as different from European paradigms as possible. If imaginary languages are bricolages, as Schnapp writes, then conlangers are now looking to Tagalog, Basque, Georgian, Malagasay, and Aztec for ideas, instead of to Welsh, Finnish, and Hebrew, languages Tolkien drew upon for his Elvish. "Ergative" and "trigger" languages are often preferred to the "nominative" languages of Europe. Some people invent for sheer intellectual challenge; others for the beauty and sensuality of combining new and privately meaningful sounds.

There are many calls for translation exercises, one of the most popular being 'The Tower of Babel' (Genesis 10: 1–9). The most recent innovation, and one that not only showcases these languages in all their variety but provides an incentive to learn another conlanger's conlang, is the Translation Relay Game: someone writes a short poem or composition in his or her language and sends it with linguistic information to someone else, who sends a translation with directions to the next in line all the way around again, like playing 'telephone'. The permutations that the Valdyan Starling Song went through give good evidence that these languages are not just relexes, or codes, of natural languages, but have their own linguistic, cultural, and poetic parameters of expression. They differ from real languages in one important respect that has bearing on my remarks about audience: very few conlangers have mastered their languages in the way one masters a native tongue. These creations are more like artefacts (several have compared it to poetry) than they are like languages. One does not live in a dollhouse. One does not normally think or speak in one's conlang, much less speak to another, except through a laborious process of translation.

It remains to a longer cultural and sociolinguistic study (underway) to 20 tease out the possibilities and problems of conlanging: why it is done, what does it satisfy, why so few women do it, what are its demographics, or whether it can be turned to pedagogical use in a 'hands-on', high-participation study of language. In this respect, CONLANG is one of the 'coolest' of online media. Only time will show what direction conlanging and attitudes towards it will take as the Internet becomes more powerful and widely used.

Will the Internet democratise, and eventually make banal, a pursuit that has until now been painted with the romantic brush of lunacy and secrecy? (You can currently download LangMaker, invented by Jeff Henning, to help you construct your own language.) Or will it do the opposite and make language and linguistics—so often avoided by students or reduced in university programs—inventive and cutting edge? (The inventor of Tokana has used in-class language invention as a means to study language typology.) Now that we have it, the Internet at least provides conlangers with a place to hang their logodaedalic tapestries, and the technology for some of them to be heard.

References

Von Bingen, Hildegard. Lingua Ignota, or Wörterbuch der unbekannten Sprache. Eds. Marie-Louise Portmann and Alois Odermatt. Basel: Verlag Basler Hildegard-Gesellschaft, 1986.

Eco, Umberto. The Search for the Perfect Language. Trans. James Fentress. Oxford, England, and Cambridge, Mass.: Blackwell, 1995, 1997.

Elgin, Suzette Haden. A First Dictionary and Grammar of Láadan. Madison, WI: Society for the Furtherance and Study of Fantasy and Science-Fiction, 1985.

Henning, Jeffrey. Model Languages: The Newsletter Discussing Newly Imagined Words for Newly Imagined Worlds. <http://www.Langmaker.com/ml00.htm>.

Kennaway, Richard. Some Internet Resources Relating to Constructed Languages. <http://www.sys.uea.ac.uk/jrk/conlang.php>. (The most comprehensive list (with links) of invented languages on the Internet.)

Laycock, Donald C. The Complete Enochian Dictionary: A Dictionary of the Angelic Language as Revealed to Dr. John Dee and Edward Kelley. York Beach, Maine: Samuel Weiser, 1994.

McLuhan, Marshall. Understanding Media. Reprinted. Cambridge, MA: MIT P, 1994.

Salamon, Jeff. "Revenge of the Fanboys." Village Voice 13 Sep., 1994.

Schnapp, Jeffrey. "Virgin Words: Hildegard of Bingen's Lingua Ignota and the Development of Imaginary Languages Ancient and Modern." Exemplaria 3.2 (1991): 267–98.

Tolkien, J.R.R. "A Secret Vice." The Monsters and the Critics and Other Essays. Ed. Christopher Tolkien. Boston: Houghton Mifflin, 1984. 198–223.

Wilkins, John. An Essay Towards a Real Character and a Philosophical Language. Presented to the Royal Society of England in 1668.

Wittgenstein, Ludwig. Philosophical Investigations. 3rd ed. Trans. G.E.M. Anscombe. Englewood Cliffs, NJ: Prentice Hall, 1958.

Yaguello, Marina. Lunatic Lovers of Language: Imaginary Languages and Their Inventors. Trans. Catherine Slater. (Les fous du langage. 1985.) London: The Athlone Press, 1991.

Analyze

1. What, according to Higley, is the definition of CONLANG? How are conlangers different from auxlangers?
2. Conlanging is compared to building dollhouses several times in this article. Refer to these instances in the text as you examine how the image of a dollhouse helps you understand the function of conlanging.
3. What does Higley predict about the future of conlanging? Summarize her argument, with particular attention to the kinds of evidence she uses to support her claims.

Explore

1. Higley quotes the 20th-century Austrian-British philosopher Ludwig Wittgenstein to explain how the subjective nature of invented languages can limit their popularity and use. How would conlangers argue against this position? In what ways is conlanging different from other invented languages?
2. Visit the CONLANG website and write a report on what you observe there. What kinds of invented languages do you notice? What makes them unique?

3. Write an essay in response to Higley's article that investigates the current state of conlanging. Use researched sources such as scholarly articles by academics, linguists, and conlang users to examine the value of conlanging.

Forging Connections

1. Given our ever-expanding global culture, what languages seem to be on the threshold of gaining worldwide popularity and usage? Refer to and expand on the arguments of at least two selections from this chapter as you explore why certain languages might be on the rise.
2. In recent decades, popular culture, as understood through TV, films, and the Internet, has reflected a growing interest in artificial languages. Why is there such a compelling need to invent languages when there are natural languages to learn and master? Write an imaginary dialogue between the authors of two readings from this chapter who have differing positions on the natural-versus-invented language debate.

Looking Further

1. Robert Lane Greene ("Which Is the Best Language to Learn?") and John McWhorter ("Which Languages Should Liberal Arts Be About in 2010?") have different views about the value of learning French in the globalized world. Write an essay in which you discuss how the language of globalization affects the argument posed by these authors. How would Julie Traves ("The Church of Please and Thank You," Chapter 9) or Pallavi Polanki ("Operation Mind Your Language," Chapter 9) respond to their claims?
2. Even as major languages of the world such as English and Spanish become more popular and widely used, smaller tribal languages—and the cultures that support them—are vanishing. What do you make of the rise of synthetic languages like CONLANG as natural languages such as Tuvan or Aka are dying out? Are natural languages more or less valuable than CONLANG? How?

3 Language & Writing

The selections in this chapter reflect the fact that good writing is, above all, effective writing. A successful writer is not just good at conveying information but is critically aware of the conventions of the type of writing being attempted (genre), who is being addressed (audience), why the piece is being written (purpose), and how best to convince the reader (persuasion). Good writers know how to use (and, occasionally, manipulate) language to address the needs of readers. Although writers of all stripes—academics, journalists, lawyers, and bloggers—have to contend with the issues addressed by the authors of this chapter's selections, the ideas here are particularly insightful for you as a college writer. In your academic work, you are learning that the skillful use of language is essential not only for academic success but to achieve your professional goals as well.

In her essay "Writing for an Audience," Linda S. Flower, Professor of English at Carnegie Mellon University, confirms that writing is an act of communication and connection between creator and consumer—the writer and the reader. She makes us intensely aware that we are always writing in service of an audience. Emily Badger makes it clear in "Plain English Urged to Limit Federal Bureaucracy" that direct, accessible writing is not just a "civil right" but can also save the government a lot of money. In the same vein, the article "Washington State Sees Results from 'Plain Talk' Initiative" by Rachel La Corte provides compelling evidence of how use of simple and direct language can really benefit the audience targeted by bureaucrats: the public. In "The Art of the Police Report," Ellen Collett discusses how even a fact-based document such as a police report can skillfully utilize language to convey a particular—and, perhaps, biased—point of view; what might seem like neutral, impartial language on the surface can be as effective as a weapon in getting a point across. Finally, Anne Trubek strikes a hopeful note in her essay "We Are All Writers Now," observing that with the rise of nonprofessional writing in online venues, the culture of writing is thriving more than ever today.

Linda S. Flower
Writing for an Audience

Linda S. Flower is Professor of Rhetoric and Co-Director of the Center for University Outreach at Carnegie Mellon University. Her experience mentoring teenage writers led her to a deeper investigation of how writers make peace with conflicting voices and goals, and how teachers must consider and manage those struggles as a result. This work inspired Flower's research on intercultural rhetoric and education for community consequences. The following selection, "Writing for an Audience," is excerpted from her text, *Problem Solving Strategies for Writing*. In this piece, Flowers discusses the writer's goals, one of which is not to *impart* knowledge per se, but to *share* knowledge; to consider the audience in the writer–reader relationship; to persuade the reader to see things as the writer sees them, even if the reader might not necessarily agree with the writer's perspective.

To what degree do you consider your audience when you write?

The goal of the writer is to create a momentary common ground between the reader and the writer. You want the reader to share your knowledge and your attitude toward that knowledge. Even if the reader eventually disagrees, you want him or her to be able for the moment to *see things as you see them*. A good piece of writing closes the gap between you and the reader.

"Good writers do more than simply express their meaning."

Analyze Your Audience

The first step in closing that gap is to gauge the distance between the two of you. Imagine, for example, that you are a student writing your parents, who have always lived in New York City, about a wilderness survival expedition you want to go on over spring break. Sometimes obvious differences such as age or background will be important, but the critical differences for writers usually fall into three areas: the reader's *knowledge* about the topic; his or her *attitude* toward it, and his or her personal or professional *needs*. Because these differences often exist, good writers do more than simply express their meaning; they pinpoint the critical differences between themselves and their reader and design their writing to reduce these differences. Let us look at these areas in more detail.

Knowledge. This is usually the easiest difference to handle. What does your reader need to know? What are the main ideas you hope to teach? Does your reader have enough background knowledge to really understand you? If not, what would he or she have to learn?

Attitudes. When we say a person has knowledge, we usually refer to his conscious awareness of explicit facts and clearly defined concepts. This kind of knowledge can be easily written down or told to someone else. However, much of what we "know" is not held in this formal, explicit way. Instead it is held as an attitude or image—as a loose cluster of associations. For instance, my image of lakes includes associations many people would have, including fishing, water skiing, stalled outboards, and lots of kids catching night crawlers with flashlights. However, the most salient or powerful parts of my image, which strongly color my whole attitude toward lakes, are thoughts of cloudy skies, long rainy days, and feeling generally cold and damp. By contrast, one of my best friends has a very different cluster of associations: to him a lake means sun, swimming, sailing, and happily sitting on the end of a dock. Needless to say, our differing images cause us to react quite differently to a proposal that we visit a lake. Likewise, one reason people often find it difficult to discuss religion and politics is that terms such as "capitalism" conjure up radically different images.

5   As you can see, a reader's image of a subject is often the source of attitudes and feelings that are unexpected and, at times, impervious to mere facts. A simple statement that seems quite persuasive to you, such as "Lake Wampago would be a great place to locate the new music camp," could have little impact on your reader if he or she simply doesn't visualize a lake as a "great place." In fact, many people accept uncritically any statement that fits in with their own attitudes—and reject, just as uncritically, anything that does not.

Whether your purpose is to persuade or simply to present your perspective, it helps to know the image and attitudes that your reader already holds. The more these differ from your own, the more you will have to do to make him or her *see* what you mean.

Needs. When writers discover a larger gap between their own knowledge and attitudes and those of the reader, they usually try to change the reader in some way. Needs, however, are different. When you analyze a reader's needs, it is so that you, the writer, can adapt to him. If you ask a friend majoring in biology how to keep your fish tank from clouding, you don't want to hear a textbook recitation on the life processes of algae. You expect a friend to adapt his or her knowledge and tell you exactly how to solve your problem.

The ability to adapt your knowledge to the needs of the reader is often crucial to your success as a writer. This is especially true in writing done on a job. For example, as producer of a public affairs program for a television station, 80 percent of your time may be taken up planning the details of new shows, contacting guests, and scheduling the taping sessions. But when you write a program proposal to the station director, your job is to show how the program will fit into the cost guidelines, the FCC requirements for relevance, and the overall programming plan for the station. When you write that report your role in the organization changes from producer to proposal writer. Why? Because your reader needs that information in order to make a decision. He may be *interested* in your scheduling problems and the specific content of the shows, but he *reads* your report because of his own needs as station director of the organization. He has to act.

In college, where the reader is also a teacher, the reader's needs are a little less concrete but just as important. Most papers are assigned as a way to teach something. So the real purpose of a paper may be for you to make connections between historical periods, to discover for yourself the principle behind a laboratory experiment, or to develop and support your own interpretation of a novel. A good college paper doesn't just rehash the facts; it demonstrates what your reader, as a teacher, needs to know—that you are learning the thinking skills his or her course is trying to teach.

Effective writers are not simply expressing what they know, like a student madly filling up an examination bluebook. Instead they are *using* their knowledge: reorganizing, maybe even rethinking their ideas to meet the demands of an assignment or the needs of their reader. 10

Analyze

1. In the first paragraph, Flower talks about writing as an exchange between the reader and the writer. Do your own experiences as a writer support this view? Why or why not?

2. Examine Flower's point that "people accept uncritically any statement that fits in with their own attitudes—and reject, just as uncritically, anything that does not." Consider whether or not this is a valid point of view.

3. Flower states that it helps to know the "attitudes" or mental orientation of the reader. How would you go about constructing your argument if you knew your reader's attitude was very different from your own?

Explore

1. Flower notes that in college writing situations the teacher is also the reader. Can you think of other types of readers of whom the college writer needs to be aware? Explain how the needs of these readers MIGHT be different from that of the teacher.

2. As a college student, what do you think is the purpose of most academic papers? Using an example from a personal experience describe a paper you wrote recently and discuss what you learned by writing the paper.

3. Read a short article from an academic journal in the discipline or field in which you are majoring. How does the author of the article address the needs and expectations of the reader? Does he or she take the knowledge and attitudes of the audience into account? How so? In a brief essay, reflect on your observations.

Emily Badger
Plain English Urged to Limit Federal Bureaucracy

Emily Badger is a Washington, DC–based freelance journalist. Her reporting on cities, sustainability, and public policy has appeared in *SPIN*, the *New York Times International Herald Tribune,* and the *Christian Science Monitor*, among other publications. She is a regular contributor to *Pacific Standard,* a bimonthly print magazine and website published by the nonprofit Miller-McCune Center for Research, Media and Public Policy, which "strives to not just inform, but also to promote meaningful dialogue by reporting, in clear and concise language, the latest and most relevant scientific research and innovations shaping the issues of the day." The following article, which appeared in *Pacific Standard* on July 12, 2011, highlights the Plain Writing Act of 2010 and its requirement that government entities use clear and simple writing in communications to their constituents.

How important is it for the government to communicate plainly to the public?

Back when Annetta Cheek first went to work for the federal government in the 1970s, she was tasked with writing regulations for the updated Archeological Resources Protection Act, a replacement for the American Antiquities Act of 1906.

"The 1906 act was a page long, and the implementing regulations which came out a couple of weeks later were about three pages long," Cheek recalled. "I was writing a regulation that ended up being about 40 pages, implementing an act that was about 20 pages long. And it did basically the same thing."

Here's a real short version of what both bills established: You'll get in big trouble if you mess with artifacts on public land; the president gets to decide which artifacts are a big deal and merit creating historic landmarks; if you want to do research in any of these places, you need to get a permit.

Of course, no one in government put it quite that way, either in 1906 or 1979. But three pages is still less onerous than 40.

"Somehow or another, we got into a very bad place," Cheek said of Uncle 5 Sam's increasing penchant for long-winded legalese. "I really don't know how we got there, but I've thought about that a lot."

Last fall, at the prodding of Cheek and other "plain language" advocates, Congress passed a bill—the thankfully acronym-free Plain Writing Act of 2010—that aims to finally cut out all the "disallowances," "dispositions" and "probate proceedings" that stand between the American people and their government. The bill (all two-and-a-half pages of it!) required government agencies by this week to come up with plans to write all public communication from here on out in plain English so that people can actually understand it.

It doesn't sound like a very difficult mandate. In fact, you'd think it would take *more* effort—and a thesaurus, and a legal dictionary, and a lot of time—to write:

> *"If you disagree with this disallowance and believe the evidence now of record is sufficient for us to award you benefits, please refer to the enclosed VA Form 1-4107, Notice of Procedural and Appellate Rights, which explains your rights to appeal."*

instead of:

> *"If you think we shouldn't have turned down your claim, you should write and tell us. We've attached a form, which explains your rights."*

. . . to borrow from one of the examples Cheek took with her to Capitol Hill.

But it turns out writing in simple English is an actual skill—and one Cheek says most people in government don't have.

"What happens is, even when the technical people write [regulations] first, the attorneys are never happy with it. So they rewrite it," she said. "Eventually, I think people just sort of give up and say, 'Well here, you're going to end up writing it anyway, so just go ahead and write it.'"

10   Cheek thinks it takes three people to write any good regulation: a policy expert, a lawyer and a writer (no offense to the policy expert and the lawyer). The Plain Writing Act of 2010 doesn't go that far but requires agencies to train their employees on how to write in plain English and to designate senior officials to make sure they do.

As a citizen, you probably don't regularly troll through the Federal Register for arcane regulations you wish you better understood. But all of us, at some point, have to figure out how to file our taxes, enroll in Social Security, collect unemployment benefits, file for the G.I. bill or make an appointment at the VA hospital. And this is why plain language matters.

Crummy wording in instructions can mean the difference between a veteran collecting disability payments or not, or an immigrant violating visa requirements or not. The Center for Plain Language, which Cheek and several of her former government colleagues founded in 2004, even goes so far in its tagline as to call plain writing a "civil right."

"A lot of the government is about compliance with requirements—you must do this, that and the other thing," Cheek said. "We're telling people what to do all the time, but we're telling them in a way they don't understand, so we don't get compliance."

There's also one other compelling argument for simple syntax: Terrible writing (as Cheek suggests we call plain writing's opposite) is expensive. When people don't understand the letters they get in the mail or the forms they have to fill out, each case of confusion requires a bureaucrat to individually explain things, which isn't a particularly efficient use of government resources.

15   Cheek cites the example of a Veterans Benefits Administration office in Mississippi that rewrote in plain language a standard letter mailed to veterans. Confused phone calls to the local office—requiring, let's assume,

10–15 minutes each—fell from 1,200 to 200 a year, and led to more veterans taking advantage of the benefit. Similarly, an initiative in Great Britain to rewrite a customs form in plain language reduced the error rate from 55 percent to 3 percent, saving the agency about $45,000.

Cost of the redesign: $3,500.

"The government has never figured out how much poor communication costs because it doesn't admit that it communicates poorly," Cheek said. But she borrows an estimate from a British bureaucrat based on the experience there. "I think government could save 20 percent if everything it wrote was in plain language."

Analyze

1. What does Cheek mean when she says that the government has an "increasing penchant for long-winded legalese"? Why is this like being in "a bad place" for her?
2. Look at the example of legalese that Cheek brought to Capitol Hill and its simpler version. Which one would have been easier to write? Why?
3. The Center for Plain Language calls plain, direct writing "a civil right." Examine the definition of "civil rights" and explain why—or why not—you agree with Cheek that plain language is a civil right.

Explore

1. The opposite of plain language, Cheek suggests, is "terrible" language. Describe a time when you were frustrated by a formal document that was difficult to interpret. What, in particular, made it hard for you to read?
2. Do you agree that formal, legal, and governmental documents should be written in plain language? In a brief essay discuss both sides of the argument using Badger's essay and personal, anecdotal evidence.
3. Cheek states that "a policy expert, a lawyer and a writer" are needed to write good regulations. Is it possible for policy experts and lawyers to be effective writers, too? Why or why not? Refer to Badger's argument as well as other, researched sources as you develop your ideas.

Rachel La Corte
Washington State Sees Results from "Plain Talk" Initiative

Rachel La Corte is a supervisory correspondent for the Associated Press in Seattle, where she is in charge of statehouse and political coverage for the state of Washington. The following article appeared on December 10, 2006 in *The Olympian*, the daily newspaper of Washington's state capital. La Corte's article describes the state of Washington's initiative to have all its agencies use "plain talk" in their written communications to the public, and cites advocates of plain talk who urge officials to ensure that people fully understand their rights and benefits as citizens.

How well do you understand the contents of the documents you receive from your federal, state, and local governments?

OLYMPIA, Wash. (AP)—The average person may find it tough to understand state government, but Washington state officials want to deploy changes to alleviate state personnel's employment of acronyms, jargon and legalese that routinely pervade interfaces with constituents.

Or in plain speak: Talk to the public as you would talk to any other person—simply, and in plain language.

In the 18 months since Gov. Chris Gregoire ordered all state agencies to adopt "plain talk" principles, more than 2,000 state employees have attended classes on writing letters, announcements and documents in everyday language.

So words like abeyance, cease and utilize are out, replaced by suspension, stop and use.

5   "If people are able to apply for an environmental permit and get it right the first time because they were able to understand it, that's success," said Larisa Benson, director of the Government Management Accountability and Performance system.

When citizens know what the government is asking of them, there's a better chance they'll comply, officials have found.

For example, by rewriting one letter, the Department of Revenue tripled the number of businesses paying the "use tax," the widely ignored equivalent of sales tax on products purchased out of state. That meant an extra $800,000 collected over two years by the department, which had started its own plain talk initiative before the governor's order.

"Simple changes can have profound results," said Janet Shimabukuro, manager of the department's taxpayer services program. "Plain talk isn't only rewriting, it's rethinking your approach and really personalizing your message to the audience and to the reader."

Gregoire says it's "a long-overdue initiative, but it's bearing fruit."

"When we just talk in a way that takes our language, government lan-   10
guage, and throws it out, and talk in language everyone understands, we get a whole lot more done," she said.

Though other states have done some similar work, Washington state is believed to be the first to have a full-scale effort, said Thom Haller, executive director of the Center for Plain Language in Washington, D.C. The nonprofit center urges government and business officials to use clear, understandable language in laws and other public communications.

In 1997, newly elected Gov. Gary Locke issued an executive order requiring the Washington Administrative Code to be written and organized in a more simple way. In the mid-90s, some state agencies started using plain language rules for training, on Web sites and in letters to the public.

The government of the District of Columbia started a plain language initiative in 2004, and many federal agencies have plain language programs as well, Haller said.

"We're seeing them embrace it because they're recognizing that clarity in structure and language is important," he said. "It enables people to get their jobs done more efficiently."

How did state workers start speaking bureaucratic gobbledygook?   15

"It's almost as if we have hundreds of different tribes out there with different languages," said Dana Howard Botka, the plain language program coordinator for Gregoire. "Knowing the language of that tribe is essential to belonging to it. There's pride in knowing the language of your profession."

Writing consultant Sharon Bridwell, who teaches up to three classes a month for state employees, said her students just need help breaking old habits.

"It's like bursting them free to do what they really can do," she said.

At a recent class in Olympia, Bridwell used slides and easels to write out pointers such as keeping sentences short.

PLAIN TALK IN ACTION

Department of Labor and Industries

- **Before:** We have been notified that you did not receive the State of Washington warrant listed on the attached Affidavit of Lost or Destroyed Warrant Request for Replacement, form F242.
- **After:** Have you cashed your L&I check yet? The state Treasurer's Office has informed us that a check we sent you has not been cashed.

Department of Ecology

- **Before:** Specific to the CO_2 mitigation program, Ecology recommends that the reviewing authority assure compliance with the approved mitigation plan on an annual basis, unless project circumstances indicate that a more or less frequent compliance review is appropriate.
- **After:** Reviewing authorities conduct annual reviews to assure compliance with the mitigation plan.

Department of Licensing

- **Before:** If you do not wish to purchase 12 month gross weight at the time of renewal, please contact your license agent to determine the fees due for the number of months you wish to purchase. If you are not sure that purchasing 12 months is a good choice for you, please discuss the options with your license agent before purchasing your tabs.
- **After:** To license for less than 12 months, contact a vehicle licensing office to determine the amount due.
- **Before:** Per Washington state law RCW 46.12.101, this report of sale will be deemed properly filed if it includes the date of the sale or transfer, the name and address of the seller and of the buyer, the buyer's driver's license if available, a description of the vehicle, including the vehicle identification number . . .
- **After:** The Report of Sale must include:
  - Date of the sale or transfer
  - Name and address of the seller and buyer
  - Buyer's driver's license number, if available
  - Description of the vehicle, including the vehicle identification number (VIN)

Rich Coleman, a project manager with the state Employment Security   20
Department, said he'd try to be more concise in his letters to the public.
"I'm more wordy than I would like to be," said Coleman, who corre-
sponds with prisoners or their families to help them rejoin the workforce.
"It's an opportunity to see that the less I write, the more effective I am in
getting the information across."

Botka said the heart of the plain talk initiative is to change the mind-set
of state workers, to get them to think about the person who is reading the
document or the Web page before they write it.

"We're talking about people's rights and benefits," she said. "If they can't
understand them, then they really don't have access to their government."

Analyze

1. Examine the before and after examples that are provided at the beginning of the article. What effect do these examples have on you as a
   reader?
2. What differences do you notice between the original statements and
   their revisions?
3. What assumptions do state officials make about the capacity of the
   audience that reads their documents? How does the plain language
   initiative address these assumptions?

Explore

1. The author of this article calls the language that state workers use
   "bureaucratic gobbledygook." Evaluate some of the "before" examples
   and write briefly about whether they are effective or not. Do the sentences
   lose meaning or value after they are revised for simplicity? Why or why not?
2. Many pointers and suggestions for plain writing are given throughout
   this article. Write a brief essay that addresses two or three of these suggestions and explain why they are important for good writing. Refer to
   (and properly cite) additional sources to support your analysis.
3. Professional, legal, and governmental documents should be written in
   a way that conveys information simply and directly to the general population. Examine an application form, a letter, or any other formal
   document that you have had to read in the past that confused you.
   What about the language was problematic? How could the document
   be simplified for future use?

Ellen Collett
The Art of the Police Report

Prior to her transition to law enforcement and crime analysis in Los Angeles, writer Ellen Collett spent 15 years in the entertainment business. Her publications include a collection of short stories and other works that have appeared in *Writer's Chronicle* and *LOST Magazine.* "The Art of the Police Report" is excerpted from *Writer's Chronicle*, a magazine published by the Association of Writers & Writing Programs. In this selection, Collett emphasizes the importance of the precision and the persuasiveness of language within the highly specialized context of a police report. As she states, "Words committed to paper have an agenda."

How do you expect to apply the writing skills you're learning in college in your future career?

Monday through Friday, I'm enthralled by a man I've never met. His name is Martinez and he's a cop with the Los Angeles Police Department.

Martinez works in crime suppression in South Central L.A. He and his partner, Brown, patrol the streets and respond to scenes-of-crimes. Every incident they investigate generates a written account.

I know Martinez only through his incident reports, as a five-digit number on a sheet of paper. In our precinct's Crime Analysis Division, I read and code hundreds of these reports each day. They are written by every serving officer on roster, and by design most of them sound exactly alike.

Surprisingly, writing is the one constant in a cop's daily life. Whether he's assigned to vice or patrol, working bunco or undercover, every day he'll write. Most precincts have specially designated writing rooms, where the average cop hates spending time—worse than on shoot-outs, stakeouts, and court appearances put together. As with everything in the department, strict rules govern report writing, and as with any dangerous undertaking, the department will train you to do it properly. The most despised class at the police academy is the one that teaches writing. A cadet can't be sworn as a police officer without passing it.

The incident report he'll learn to write is the factual narrative account of 5
a crime—of a rape, robbery, murder, criminal threat, lewd act, vandalism,
burglary, sexual molestation, kidnapping, or assault. Every event a cop responds to generates a report.

Crime reports are written in neutral diction, and in the dispassionate
uni-voice that's testament to the academy's ability to standardize writing.
They feel generated rather than authored, the work of a single law enforcement consciousness rather than a specific human being.

So how can I identify Martinez from a single sentence? Why do his reports make me feel pity, terror, or despair? Make me want to put a bullet in
someone's brain—preferably a wife beater's or a pedophile's, but occasionally my own? How does he use words on paper to hammer at my heart? Like
all great cops, Sergeant Martinez is a sneaky fucker. He's also a master of
inflection and narrative voice.

An incident report tells only what happened: where, when, and to
whom. It offers multiple perspectives of the same event from often contradictory points of view of cop, victim, suspect, and witnesses. Even when
these accounts agree, no two people see things identically or invest their
attention in the same details. Each person's agenda is inherently personal.

An incident report lists the inventory of all physical evidence collected
and booked. Anything from shell casings and rape-kit underwear to a
three-legged dog in a custody dispute.

In structure, an incident report is a strict chronological narrative. It 10
begins with a Source of Activity section, which tees up the story. It's where
the narrator introduces himself and offers his credentials for telling this
tale: "On 4-6-10 at approx. 1922 hours, my partner Ofcr. Brown (badge
#13312) and I (Ofcr. Martinez badge #14231) were in full uniform travel-
ing westbound on Gage Avenue when we received the radio call of an
LUAC in progress at 82nd St./Central Ave."

In the investigation section that follows, the narrator tells briefly what
his investigation revealed. He lists the actions taken by himself and his
partner, and the facts of the case as discovered. The strict emphasis is on
verifiable information.

If versions of the event differ from his, these are recorded as witness
statements. These can be summaries, but quotes are often included. The
narrative voice at the center of an incident report is always emotionally neutral. He's the ultimate reliable narrator. His sole job is to convince us that
everything he tells us is the absolute truth. It all begins with diction.

Cadets are taught to write with care and deliberation, to choose each word for maximum accuracy. Precision, not firepower, is the goal; you don't use a semiautomatic at close range when you're packing a Smith & Wesson. Good cop diction means checking each word in a sentence to verify that it can mean only one thing. The officer must avoid words that carry associations, subtext, or bias.

Officers are encouraged to use action verbs in preference to *is* and *has*. *Is* and *has* speak abstractions—existence and possession, respectively—and where they go, descriptors follow. Action verbs, on the other hand, move us through time and space. "The Subject removed a hammer from the kitchen drawer and struck the Victim three times in the head and neck" is a good sentence. It tells what physically happened without embellishment.

15   Avoid modifiers, says the academy. Adverbs—words ending in *ly*—are slippery and subjective; they shade reality and opine. Any adverb can be eliminated by choosing a better verb. "The Suspect snatched the Victim's chain and fled" is a sentence without speculation. To know the manner in which the snatching or fleeing transpired would be interpretive.

The academy dislikes adjectives unless they pertain to direction, color, or amount. These are "empirical adjectives." Because they speak to precision of detail, they resist interpretation. "The black Escalade fired 12 shots into the dwelling on 865 Inglewood Avenue" can mean only one thing.

Parenthetically, the two exceptions to the "no adjectives" rule are the words *bloody* and *suspicious*, invoked to justify officer initiative in field investigations. If a suspect "fled while holding his waistband in a *suspicious* manner," it's presumptive of a concealed weapon. If an officer investigates a neighbor complaint and the victim "opened the door wearing *bloody* clothing," there's a pretext to enter and reconnoiter the premises.

These guidelines about diction and story efficiency serve a deeper purpose, which is the legitimizing of the narrative "voice." The police narrator uses neutral language and uninflected storytelling to assure us of his credibility and to win the reader's trust. He never judges.

The perpetrator in a crime report is always the "Suspect," even when 15 witnesses, half of them preachers, see him exit his car and shoot his cousin at point-blank range in a church parking lot. Until a jury reviews the evidence and pronounces, under the law, no crime took place. The police narrator is careful not to imply that he thinks otherwise.

20   The police narrator further proves his lack of bias by presenting everyone's version of the same event, giving equal space to the "truth" as reported by

victim, suspect, and witness. While he might state that DeWayne "aka Baby Insane" Johnson of the Rolling '60s Crips shot and killed J'Marcus "aka L'il Monster" Faye of Florencia Trece, he'll include Baby's explanation that he was merely examining the gun with an eye toward purchase when that muthafucker up and went off. The narrator's job isn't to judge but to relay facts to the best of his ability, and let the reader decide the truth of it.

Words committed to paper have an agenda. The purpose of a police report is to be cited in court as proof of who did what to whom. Its ultimate agenda is justice. It seeks to protect the weak and punish the guilty. Because the stakes are high—freedom, death, or life without parole—it's written with special care. Above all else, it aims to be truthful. At the same time, to do its job, it needs to be convincing. The story it tells should persuade 12 people in a jury box of something.

On the face of it, these two goals—truthful and persuasive—seem uncomfortably at odds. Shouldn't facts alone persuade? Should truth need composing? And assuming that it's possible to write toward this goal—to be truthful and persuasive at once—shouldn't all fiction writers want to learn how?

Which brings us back to that sneaky fucker, Martinez. Martinez writes incident reports that technically follow the academy's guidelines. He avoids modifiers and descriptors. He traces the physical action of an event without opining or speculating. He offers accounts that contradict his own findings. He's succinct and factual. He tells the literal and empirical truth. He writes in the dispassionate narrative uni-voice that conveys objectivity and distance. So why is Martinez instantly discernable on the page from a hundred other cops?

Despite the neutrality of his diction, Martinez's choices are idiosyncratic. Everything he sees reveals him. And syntactically, though he bends every rule to the breaking point, you can't bust him.

At a Lewd Acts on Child crime scene, Martinez's partner, Brown, writes, "The Victim sustained multiple injuries." Martinez would tell us, "The baby was bleeding from three orifices." There's a world of difference here. Brown gives us a victim; Martinez gives us a baby. Brown offers a fact; Martinez paints a picture.

Brown's statement moves us forward; Martinez makes us stop dead and envision the horrific crime that caused such injuries. Both statements are neutral on the surface, but the specificity of Martinez's language makes the reader see and feel.

At the same crime scene, Brown says, "We placed the Suspect in a felony prone position and took him into custody without incident." Martinez would write, "We cuffed the father." Martinez's version reminds us of the unnatural aspect of the crime, that a father (presumably) committed it. He edges near the academy no-fly zone with *father* in place of *suspect*, but gets away with it because the sentence describes police action—the cuffing—rather than any actions of the suspect. Also, nobody disputes the fact that the suspect *is* the father; it's the type of father he is that's at issue.

At the same crime scene, Martinez might note that there's "no food in the apartment." This is an empirical fact, so technically admissible. It doesn't speak to the specific crime of Lewd Acts on Child, but it does subtly add to the moral charges against the parents. Martinez inflects the barren apartment and makes it speak. Details bring scenes to life. Sometimes the image can tell everything.

In the witness section of the report, Brown might say, "Victim's mother gave no statement." Martinez would tell us, "Mother refused to cooperate." This carries a totally different emphasis and meaning. Martinez doesn't speculate if she's protecting her husband at the expense of her child. He doesn't need to. What kind of mother refuses to speak when her baby is bleeding from three orifices?

30   Examine these two versions of the same incident, side by side. They admit the same facts. They're both truthful. But one—Martinez's—is also persuasive. Why? It's subtly inflected in every line to signal its agenda. Though it labors under the constraints of the report format, it uses emphasis and diction to suggest how we interpret what it tells us. It may look impartial, but it's aimed like a weapon.

From a strict moral perspective or the police academy vantage point, Martinez's incident reports are flawed. They're failures of objective reportage. Though everything in them is literally true, they're technically "suspicious"; if Martinez saw a baby-raper, he's making damn sure we do too.

From a reader's perspective, Martinez's incident reports are deeply satisfying. They engage us emotionally; they vest us in the events he describes, and in the teller. They're narratives that hint at larger truths—about Martinez himself and the South Central universe he polices. They reverberate beyond the time it takes to read them. They offer a way to understand the world.

My Sergeant Martinez may be writing reports, but he's also using the alchemy of inflection to turn them into stories—narratives that believe themselves and make us believe them, too.

Martinez succeeds—or fails, if you're his supervisors—because of his commitment to what his stories mean. He continues to protect and serve because inflection isn't illegal, and you won't catch him. It's not a story, it's "just the facts, ma'am."

Like Martinez, a good story always has an agenda.   35

Like Martinez, a good story is a sneaky fucker.

Analyze

1. Why does Collett call report-writing a "dangerous undertaking" and the police academy's writing class the "most despised" class? What does this suggest to you about how policemen approach writing?
2. Collett describes some of the rules of writing that officers of the police academy have to follow. What are these rules?
3. The phrase "sneaky fucker" is used three times in the essay, each time for a different reason and with a different effect. Why does Collett use this phrase in these particular instances? What effect is she trying to convey to her readers? Do you think it is appropriate, given the overall context of her essay?

Explore

1. Collett states that "words committed to paper have an agenda." Compare Officer Brown's statements with those of Office Martinez. What agenda do their statements reflect? Is this distinction important?
2. Do you think journalists and reporters can truly engage in "objective reporting"? Why or why not?
3. The title of Collett's essay implies that police reports are not just dry, factual documents; they should actually be considered a type of "art." Do you think that legal or governmental documents (e.g., police reports) should allow for some creativity or artistry in their approach, given the subject matter? Use your library database to find two or more published accounts of the same crime or tragedy and examine the similarities and differences in how each writer composed and presented the material. Which account is most effective? Why?

Anne Trubek
We Are All Writers Now

Anne Trubek is an associate professor of rhetoric and composition and English at Oberlin College. Trubek's writing has appeared in *The New York Times*, *The Atlantic*, *The Chronicle of Higher Education*, and *Wired*. On her personal home page, she notes: "I think and write about literature, culture, and how new technologies are changing how and what we write." These sentiments are reflected in "We Are All Writers Now," which appeared in the June 2009 edition of *More Intelligent Life*, an online lifestyle and culture magazine from the British news and international affairs publication *The Economist*. In this essay, Trubek asks readers to consider the "new crop of self-possessed scribes," and the value they add to the current iteration of writers and the writing world.

Trubek considers the individual who blogs, texts, emails, or posts on online community walls a writer. What do you think of her assessment?

The chattering classes have become silent, tapping their views on increasingly smaller devices. And tapping they are: the screeds are everywhere, decrying the decline of smart writing, intelligent thought and proper grammar. Critics bemoan blogging as the province of the amateurism. Journalists rue the loose ethics and shoddy fact-checking of citizen journalists. Many save their most profound scorn for the newest forms of social media. Facebook and Twitter are heaped with derision for being insipid, time-sucking, sad testaments to our literary degradation. This view is often summed up with a disdainful question: "Do we really care about what you ate for lunch?"

Forget that most of the pundits lambasting Facebook and Twitter are familiar with these devices because they use them regularly. Forget that no one is being manacled to computers and forced to read stupid prose (instead of, say, reading Proust in bed). What many professional writers are overlooking in these laments is that the rise of amateur writers means more people are writing and reading. We are commenting on blog posts, forwarding links and composing status updates. We are seeking out communities based on written words.

Go back 20, 30 years and you will find all of us doing more talking than writing. We rued literacy levels and worried over whether all this phone-yakking and television-watching spelled the end of writing. Few make that claim today. I would hazard that, with more than 200m people on Facebook and even more with home internet access, we are all writing more than we would have ten years ago. Those who would never write letters (too slow and anachronistic) or postcards (too twee) now send missives with abandon, from long thoughtful memos to brief and clever quips about evening plans. And if we subscribe to the theory that the most effective way to improve one's writing is by practicing—by writing more, and ideally for an audience—then our writing skills must be getting better.

Take the "25 Things About Me" meme that raged around Facebook a few months ago. This time-waster, as many saw it, is precisely the kind of brainstorming exercise I used to assign to my freshman writing students decades ago. I asked undergraduates to do free-writing, as we called it, because most entered my classroom with little writing experience beyond formal, assigned essays. They only wrote when they were instructed to, and the results were often arch and unclear, with ideas kept at arm's length. Students saw writing as alien and intimidating—a source of anxiety. Few had experience with writing as a form of self-expression. So when I stood in front of a classroom and told students to write quickly about themselves, without worrying about grammar or punctuation or evaluation—"just to loosen up," I would say—I was asking them to do something new. Most found the experience refreshing, and their papers improved.

Today those freewriting exercises are redundant. After all, hundreds of thousands of people wrote "25 Things About Me" for fun. My students compose e-mails, texts, status updates and tweets "about seven hours a day," one sophomore told me. (She also says no one really talks to each other anymore.) They enter my classroom more comfortable with writing—better writers, that is—and we can skip those first steps.

My friends and I write more than we used to, often more than we talk. We correspond with each other and to colleagues, school teachers, utility companies. We send e-mails to our local newspaper reporters about their stories; we write to magazine editors to tell them what we think. And most of us do labour to write well: an e-mail to a potential romantic partner is laboriously revised and edited (no more waiting by the phone); a tweet to a prospective employer is painstakingly honed until its 140 characters convey an appropriate tone with the necessary information. A response to our supervisor's clever status update on Facebook is written carefully, so to keep the repartee going. Concision and wit are privileged in these new forms. Who would not welcome shorter, funnier prose?

The conversational arts may be suffering (despite their enduring rules), but like it or not, we are all writers now. Perhaps this explains the loud clamouring over the questionable authority of online authorship. With traditional media feeling the pain, many professional writers worry that they have become dispensable. So they unfairly degrade the prose of amateurs in order to guard the ramparts.

True, much of what is written online is quotidian, informational, ephemeral. But writing has always been so: traditional newspapers line bird-cages a day later; lab reports describe methodology in tedious detail; the founding fathers wrote what they ate for lunch. And the quality of many blogs is high, indistinguishable in eloquence and intellect from many traditionally published works.

10   Our new forms of writing—blogs, Facebook, Twitter—all have precedents, analogue analogues: a notebook, a postcard, a jotting on the back of an envelope. They are exceedingly accessible. That it is easier to cultivate a wide audience for tossed off thoughts has meant a superfluity of mundane musings, to be sure. But it has also generated a democracy of ideas and quite a few rising stars, whose work we might never have been exposed to were we limited to conventional publishing channels.

Amateurs and experts share real estate on our screens. We scroll down to add our comments; we join the written fray. The rush of prose is intense, but also exhilarating. So many hats are in the ring.

Yes, we need to darken the line between what is verifiable and what is hearsay. The financial downturn and its disastrous impact on print publishing has led some to think we can do without trained reporters and editors— professionals who know how to check facts and strip the gloss off hasty pronouncements. We need this work, perhaps now more than ever. But not at the expense of silencing the new voices—an exciting new crop of self-possessed scribes—ringing all over our screens. There may be too much, but that does not mean it is unworthy.

Analyze

1. Trubek claims that people are writing more than ever now. She states, "Go back 20, 30 years and you will find all of us doing more talking

than writing." Has the advent of the Internet really turned all of us into writers? Why or why not?

2. Freewriting, as often practiced in writing courses, can be liberating because it allows writers to express themselves freely, without concern for grammar or correctness. How does this kind of writing compare to writing on social media sites and blogs, or in emails, texts, and tweets?

3. Along with writing more, Trubek also thinks that most of us "labour to write well." Make a list of the kinds of informal, nonacademic writing you engage in regularly. Do you rethink, revise, and carefully construct these writings? Why or why not?

Explore

1. It is hard to argue against the observation that students often see writing as "alien and intimidating—a source of anxiety." Write about your own experience as a reader and writer by referring to a time when writing seemed challenging, even intimidating. How did you overcome this challenge?

2. Trubek reminds us that nonprofessional writers (e.g., bloggers) can produce high-quality writing that is not very different from published works. Conduct an online search for a personal website that contains a blog. As if you were conducting a peer review, write an email to the author in which you point out the strengths and weaknesses in two or three blog postings, and make suggestions for revising the weaknesses.

3. At the end of her essay Trubek emphasizes the need to "fact check" and verify the accuracy of ideas that are published online. Why are fact-checking and verifiability important for online writing?

Forging Connections

1. Both Flower and Collett discuss the importance of writing for an audience. Select an essay that you have written and examine whether or not you have successfully addressed your audience for the essay. Refer to Flower and Collett's principles as you review your writing and write down how you would go about revising and improving the essay.

2. Analyze a government website to see if it meets the standards for plain language described in two of the articles in this chapter. Do you find the information on the website to be easily accessible? What is your

reaction as a member of the site's intended audience? Write an email to the appropriate governmental body explaining what you think of the quality of writing on the website. If necessary, suggest changes based on plain language guidelines.

Looking Further

1. Ted Warren ("Washington State Sees Results From 'Plain Talk' Initiative") points out that the "Plain Talk" Initiative is becoming more and more popular with state agencies who are interested in delivering information to the public in plain language. Although this might be an effective way to communicate, what do you think is lost when specialized information (found in legal or medical documents, for instance) is simplified? Can you think of a situation in which plain language actually interferes with communication?

2. There is no doubt that, as Anne Trubek notes in "We Are All Writers Now," the advent of digital technology has turned us all into writers. In today's modern world, it is rare to find a person who, along with traditional forms of writing, does not also write emails, text messages, or Facebook updates. But has the quality of writing declined because of this? Would you agree with Sue Shellenbarger ("This Embarrasses You and I," Chapter 4) that digital communicators are ruining the purity of language? Look through your emails and text messages to see how these writers are constructing their sentences and ideas. Write an essay that uses evidence from these sources as you develop your argument.

4 Language & Correctness

The hallmark of any language is its inherent structure and its uniqueness. But language is not just a theoretical proposition, or only a set of rules about how it *should* work; it is a living example of how it *does* work. When we use language in speech or writing, we do so because we understand its underlying principles. We agree to play by the rules. At the same time, the particular ways we use language show that whether we are conscious of it or not, we are constantly bending, breaking, or inventing language rules and conventions. In this chapter, writers vigorously debate the issue of "correctness" and present their viewpoints on how language should be used, who gets to determine the rules of usage, and why these are pressing issues in an age of technological advancements and digital communication. They remind us that language is a dynamic phenomenon that not only changes us, but is also changed *by* us.

In his essay "On Language Nerds and Nags," Robert Lane Greene, a business correspondent for *The Economist* and author of *You Are What You Speak*, discusses the fluidity rather than rigidity of language. On the other hand, entrepreneur Kyle Wiens argues in "I Won't Hire People Who Use Poor Grammar. Here's Why." that we are what we write and that poor grammar is indicative of other flaws. Sue Shellenbarger, a columnist for the *Wall Street Journal*, reports in "This Embarrasses You and I" that there is a visible decline of proper grammar and usage in the workforce. Her position is reiterated by Alison Griswold, who invokes George Orwell to support her claims in "Your Bad Grammar at Work: What's the Problem?" Kate Dailey, a senior magazine writer for the BBC, proposes in "Are Language Cops Losing War Against 'Wrongly' Used Words?" that the problem is not just grammar but how traditional meaning of words and phrases are being transformed. In the essay "R Grammar Gaffes Ruining The Language? Maybe Not," Linton Weeks, a correspondent for digital news on National Public Radio, traces the recent upsurge in poor grammar to the rise of the digital era. Finally, in "OMG, ETC.," Robert Lane Greene shows us how acronyms, although they can appear to be silly short-cuts, are gaining wide use (and acceptance) because they perform distinct and important functions.

Robert Lane Greene
On Language Nerds and Nags

Robert Lane Greene, a Brooklyn-based journalist and business correspondent for the British magazine *The Economist,* is fluent in five languages (German, Spanish, French, Portuguese, and Danish) and conversant in three more (Russian, Arabic, and Italian). Greene is best known for his book on the politics of language, *You Are What You Speak* (Random House, 2011). His article, "On Language Nerds and Nags," appeared in *Intelligent Life,* a bimonthly lifestyle and culture magazine published by *The Economist.* A self-described "language nerd," Greene asserts that to confine the English language to strict "grammatical commandments" is to disregard the richness of the language itself.

How judgmental are you of other people's written or spoken grammar?

've long been the office language nerd. This isn't a terribly distinguished position. Every office has at least one person who proof-reads with extra zeal, striking out "between you and I" with three slashes of the pen rather than the requisite one. After establishing a reputation, this stickler becomes someone colleagues timidly ask, "Can you check this . . . ?" before sending out a note to clients. Flattered as "our office language expert" when in earshot, this chap swiftly becomes "the local grammar Nazi" when out of sight.

But I've changed over the years. The other day I was asked if a letter should read: "Staff members at the Local Planning Council, with whom we've worked for over ten years" or "Staff members at the Local Planning Council, which we have worked with for over ten years." My response was something people don't want to hear. I said that there's no clear answer. Both are correct.

"But which is more correct?" I was asked. In this case, it was a high-stakes bet between two office-mates, neither of whom cared to back down. Again, I said, both are fine. In the first version, the relative clause refers to staff members, and so it should be "whom". In the second, the relative clause refers to the council, so it should be "which". As to whether it should be "with whom we've worked" or "whom we've worked with", the answer, disappointingly, is that both are fine. The old rule against stranding a preposition at the end of a clause, like "whom we've worked with", was a peeve of the 17th-century essayist John Dryden. Over the centuries it became something every educated person "knew" was a violation. But this "rule" has been violated in common speech and in fine writing for centuries. Break it and sleep soundly.

This conundrum illustrates a common view of language rules: that there is only one right way. If X is permitted then Y must be forbidden. But this doesn't make sense: everyone knows that "it is" and "it's" are both correct English, if different in formality. But the red pen in the hands of your local Grammar Grundy has conditioned such a terror of being wrong that people fear variation itself. It's certainly easier to know one set of rigid rules than to develop a fingertip-feel for the nuances of syntax, word choice and mechanics. This is why the book *Elements of Style* is such a hit. William Strunk and E.B. White's canonised system for language use is short and sharply worded. Read, memorise and you need never think again. (*The Economist*'s in-house style guide reads much the same way.) Readers are taught any number of things, such as when to use "that" instead of "which" and how one should never begin a sentence with "However, . . .". But such guidelines should be understood as the authors' preferences, not grammatical commandments.

5   Writing in English offers far more room for manoeuvre than some may realize. In my day job writing about law for *The Economist*, I've stumbled on a useful analogy: in common-law legal systems, constitutions and statutes make up the basic set of rules, but legal opinions by judges play just as big of a role in specifying how the rules apply. The original rules allow room for interpretation, so the law can change organically with time. (Code law, by contrast, leaves less discretion to judges.)

"Writing in English offers far more room for manoeuvre than some may realize."

This kind of system requires keeping up with the times. When someone asks me, "Is such-and-such a verb?" My answer is usually, "Well, a lot of people are using it as one, including in professionally edited writing, so yes." Still nervous, they might ask, "But is it in the dictionary?" The answer is probably "not yet", but that doesn't mean much. Modern dictionary-makers are the first to explain that their job is to register the language as it is used, not to tell people how they must use it. A printed and bound dictionary starts going out of date the moment the text is sent to the typesetters. Many complained when the *Oxford English Dictionary*'s editors announced they would include such slang as "LOL" and "OMG" (online only so far, until the next printing), but this is standard dictionary practice. If tens of millions of people are using a word over a period of years, lexicographers put it in the dictionary. It's a difficult job— Joseph Pickett from *American Heritage* tells of the mistaken decision to include in one dictionary the word "beachburner", a brief-lived term for "personal watercraft (otherwise called a "Jet-Ski"). Between "LOL" (probably around to stay for a while) and "beachburner" (dead before the dictionary hit the shelves) there are tough calls to make about new words. But it isn't an option to simply not include neologisms and slang.

A lot of people don't like this fluidity. Life is tricky in a world without rules. Fortunately, language does have rules, but they are more like bedrock principles than a detailed set of by-laws covering every do and don't. A good usage dictionary should explain the principles, not simply command. Is "irregardless" acceptable? The best guides will explain that it isn't common in quality edited prose—ie, stay away. Can I split an infinitive? Again, the best usage book will show that good writers have been doing so for centuries. Use it, but brace yourself against the occasional wheedling of a misguided nag.

I still relish my job as the office language nerd. People's questions sometimes get me thinking about a problem in a different way; I'll research a thorny question and learn something new as often as not. I'm aware that I disappoint people when I send them away with some Talmudic reasoning. As Truman complained of economists, they probably wish I had just one hand, rather than always saying "on the other hand . . ." And with grammar and usage, there seems to be an added element of masochism: they want that one hand to be a hard, unforgiving one, quick to shake a finger or slap a wrist. But the English language is far too rich for such rigidity. And the study of it keeps my own two hands more than full.

Analyze

1. Why does Greene start his essay with an anecdote about being the language nerd in his office? What point does this anecdote convey?
2. Explain the legal analogy that Greene uses in the article. How does this analogy help you understand Greene's point about language use?
3. What is Greene's overall position on grammar and language rules? Do you agree with this position? Why or why not?

Explore

1. Are you a language "nerd" or a language "nag"? Write an informal response in which you explain what these two terms mean in the context of Greene's essay.
2. Write about a language rule you use regularly that you believe should not be violated. Why is this rule important to you? What happens if it is violated?
3. Given Greene's observations, it would be interesting to see what new words are entering English dictionaries today. Conduct a bit of research

and write an essay about the words that have been included in the *Oxford English Dictionary* in the past few years. What is the cultural relevance of these new terms and how widely used are they?

Kyle Wiens
I Won't Hire People Who Use Poor Grammar. Here's Why.

Kyle Wiens is CEO of iFixit, an online community that provides free online repair manuals for fixing just about anything. Wiens is also Chief Architect of Dozuki, the software that makes these online repair manuals possible. The following article was published on July 20, 2012 in the *Harvard Business Review*, a research-based magazine associated with Harvard Business School. In this controversial article, which sparked more than 3,000 comments, Wiens adamantly asserts that the use of correct grammar is essential to demonstrating one's credibility, especially when communicating online.

According to Wiens, "People judge you if you can't tell the difference between their, there, and they're." Do you agree with this assertion? Why or why not?

If you think an apostrophe was one of the 12 disciples of Jesus, you will never work for me. If you think a semicolon is a regular colon with an identity crisis, I will not hire you. If you scatter commas into a sentence with all the discrimination of a shotgun, you might make it to the foyer before we politely escort you from the building.

Some might call my approach to grammar extreme, but I prefer Lynne Truss's more cuddly phraseology: I am a grammar "stickler." And, like Truss—author of *Eats, Shoots & Leaves*—I have a "zero tolerance approach" to grammar mistakes that make people look stupid.

Now, Truss and I disagree on what it means to have "zero tolerance." She thinks that people who mix up their itses "deserve to be struck by lightning, hacked up on the spot and buried in an unmarked grave," while I just think they deserve to be passed over for a job—even if they are otherwise qualified for the position.

Everyone who applies for a position at either of my companies, iFixit or Dozuki, takes a mandatory grammar test. Extenuating circumstances aside (dyslexia, English language learners, etc.), if job hopefuls can't distinguish between "to" and "too," their applications go into the bin.

Of course, we write for a living. iFixit.com is the world's largest online 5 repair manual, and Dozuki helps companies write their own technical documentation, like paperless work instructions and step-by-step user manuals. So, it makes sense that we've made a preemptive strike against groan-worthy grammar errors.

But grammar is relevant for all companies. Yes, language is constantly changing, but that doesn't make grammar unimportant. Good grammar is credibility, especially on the internet. In blog posts, on Facebook statuses, in e-mails, and on company websites, your words are all you have. They are a projection of you in your physical absence. And, for better or worse, people judge you if you can't tell the difference between their, there, and they're.

Good grammar makes good business sense—and not just when it comes to hiring writers. Writing isn't in the official job description of most people in our office. Still, we give our grammar test to everybody, including our salespeople, our operations staff, and our programmers.

On the face of it, my zero tolerance approach to grammar errors might seem a little unfair. After all, grammar has nothing to do with job performance, or creativity, or intelligence, right?

Wrong. If it takes someone more than 20 years to notice how to properly use "it's," then that's not a learning curve I'm comfortable with. So, even in this hyper-competitive market, I will pass on a great programmer who cannot write.

Grammar signifies more than just a person's ability to remember high 10 school English. I've found that people who make fewer mistakes on a grammar test also make fewer mistakes when they are doing something completely unrelated to writing—like stocking shelves or labeling parts.

In the same vein, programmers who pay attention to how they construct written language also tend to pay a lot more attention to how they code. You see, at its core, code is prose. Great programmers are more than just code monkeys; according to Stanford programming legend Donald Knuth they are "essayists who work with traditional aesthetic and literary forms." The point: programming should be easily understood by real human beings—not just computers.

And just like good writing and good grammar, when it comes to programming, the devil's in the details. In fact, when it comes to my whole business, details are everything.

I hire people who care about those details. Applicants who don't think writing is important are likely to think lots of other (important) things also aren't important. And I guarantee that even if other companies aren't issuing grammar tests, they pay attention to sloppy mistakes on résumés. After all, sloppy is as sloppy does.

That's why I grammar test people who walk in the door looking for a job. Grammar is my litmus test. All applicants say they're detail-oriented; I just make my employees prove it.

Analyze

1. Examine the three scenarios that Wiens presents in the first paragraph of his essay. What point is he trying to make by mentioning these hypothetical situations?

2. Wiens provides several examples of what he calls "groan-worthy grammar errors." Look at each of the examples and consider why Wiens thinks they are so problematic.

3. What does Wiens mean by "sloppy is as sloppy does"? Do you agree with his point of view? Why or why not?

Explore

1. Which types of grammar errors are you most concerned about and why? Write a response in which you discuss some of these errors by referring to your own writing.

2. Wiens's argument implies that using proper grammar is related to attention to details. Write a brief essay in which you examine this view using supporting details from personal experience and other textual sources.

3. If you have already declared a major, consider the profession that you are interested in joining. Conduct research into the types of writing required by this profession and evaluate the importance of grammatically correct writing to this profession.

Sue Shellenbarger
This Embarrasses You and I

Sue Shellenbarger has been a regular contributor to the *The Wall Street Journal* since 1986. As the creator and writer of the *Journal's* "Work and Family" column, she charts the growing conflict between work and family and its implications for the workplace and society. She is author of two books, including *The Breaking Point* (Henry Holt & Co., 2005), a nonfiction work about midlife crisis in women. "This Embarrasses You and I" appeared in Shellenbarger's "Work and Family" column on June 20, 2012. Most managers, Shellenbarger notes, attribute the declining state of grammar to "the informality of email, texting and Twitter."

Does the grammar you use in informal contexts, such as in emails or text messages, differ from the grammar you use in formal contexts, such as in essays or professional correspondence?

When Caren Berg told colleagues at a recent staff meeting, "There's new people you should meet," her boss Don Silver broke in, says Ms. Berg, a senior vice president at a Fort Lauderdale, Fla., marketing and crisis-communications company.

"I cringe every time I hear" people misuse "is" for "are," Mr. Silver says. The company's chief operations officer, Mr. Silver also hammers interns to stop peppering sentences with "like." For years, he imposed a 25-cent fine on new hires for each offense. "I am losing the battle," he says.

Managers are fighting an epidemic of grammar gaffes in the workplace. Many of them attribute slipping skills to the informality of email, texting and Twitter where slang and shortcuts are common. Such looseness with language can create bad impressions with clients, ruin marketing materials and cause communications errors, many managers say.

There's no easy fix. Some bosses and co-workers step in to correct mistakes, while others consult business-grammar guides for help. In a survey conducted earlier this year, about 45% of 430 employers said they were increasing employee-training programs to improve employees' grammar and other skills, according to the Society for Human Resource Management and AARP.

5   "I'm shocked at the rampant illiteracy" on Twitter, says Bryan A. Garner, author of "Garner's Modern American Usage" and president of LawProse, a Dallas training and consulting firm. He has compiled a list of 30 examples of "uneducated English," such as saying "I could care less," instead of "I couldn't care less," or, "He expected Helen and I to help him," instead of "Helen and me."

Leslie Ferrier says she was aghast at letters employees were sending to customers at a Jersey City, N.J., hair- and skin-product marketer when she joined the firm in 2009. The letters included grammar and style mistakes and were written "as if they were speaking to a friend," says Ms. Ferrier, a human-resources executive. She had employees use templates to eliminate mistakes and started training programs in business writing.

Most participants in the Society for Human Resource Management-AARP survey blame younger workers for the skills gap. Tamara Erickson, an author and consultant on generational issues, says the problem isn't a lack of skill among 20- and 30-somethings. Accustomed to texting and social networking, "they've developed a new norm," Ms. Erickson says.

At RescueTime, for example, grammar rules have never come up. At the Seattle-based maker of personal-productivity software, most employees are in their 30s. Sincerity and clarity expressed in "140 characters and sound bytes" are seen as hallmarks of good communication—not "the king's grammar," says Jason Grimes, 38, vice president of product marketing. "Those who can be sincere, and still text and Twitter and communicate on Facebook—those are the ones who are going to succeed."

Also, some grammar rules aren't clear, leaving plenty of room for disagreement. Tom Kamenick battled fellow attorneys at a Milwaukee, Wis., public-interest law firm over use of "the Oxford comma"—an additional comma placed before the "and" or "or" in a series of nouns. Leaving it out can change the meaning of a sentence, Mr. Kamenick says: The sentence, "The greatest influences in my life are my sisters, Oprah Winfrey and Madonna," means something different from the sentence, "The greatest influences in my life are my sisters, Oprah Winfrey, and Madonna," he says. (The first sentence implies the writer has two celebrity sisters; the second says the sisters and the stars are different individuals.) After Mr. Kamenick asserted in digital edits of briefs and papers that "I was willing to go to war on that one," he says, colleagues backed down, either because they were convinced, or "for the sake of their own sanity and workplace decorum."

Patricia T. O'Conner, author of a humorous guidebook for people 10
who struggle with grammar, fields workplace disputes on a blog she co-writes, Grammarphobia. "These disagreements can get pretty contentious,"
Ms. O'Conner says. One employee complained that his boss ordered him
to make a memo read, "for John and I," rather than the correct usage, "for
John and me," Ms. O'Conner says.

Christopher Telano, chief internal auditor at the New York City Health
and Hospitals Corp., has employees circulate their reports to co-workers to
review for accuracy and grammar, he says. He coaches auditors to use action
verbs such as "verify" and "confirm" and tells them to write below a 12th-grade
reading level so it can be easily understood.

Mr. Garner, the usage expert, requires all job applicants at his nine-employee firm—including people who just want to pack boxes—to pass
spelling and grammar tests before he will hire them. And he requires
employees to have at least two other people copy-edit and make corrections
to every important email and letter that goes out.

"Twenty-five years ago it was impossible to put your hands on something
that hadn't been professionally copy-edited," Mr. Garner says. "Today, it is
actually hard to put your hands on something that has been professionally
copy-edited."

Analyze

1. Shellenbarger uses two metaphors, one of war and the other of disease,
   when she talks about "grammar gaffes." How do these metaphors help
   convey her point?
2. According to the article, what is the "new norm" that this generation
   has developed when it comes to grammar and style?
3. Is it fair to require potential employees to pass a spelling and grammar
   test before they are employed? Why or why not?

Explore

1. How have the popularity of social media (such as Twitter and Face-book) and the use of texting affected our sense of grammar and lan-guage use? Refer to your own experiences as you explain whether these
   new modes of communication have made a difference to how you use
   language.

2. Imagine that you have been asked to create a grammar rule book. Which rules would you include? Why?

3. Write a research paper that examines the prevalence of good grammar in the workplace. How often, and to what extent, do potential employers require job applicants and employees to demonstrate good grammar and language skills?

Alison Griswold
Your Bad Grammar at Work: What's the Problem?

Alison Griswold is a writer and blogger whose article, "Your Bad Grammar at Work," was published on June 22, 2012 in *Forbes* magazine, a biweekly business publication that features articles on finance, industry, investing, and marketing. In her article, which refers to Sue Shellenbarger's "This Embarrasses You and I" (in this chapter) as well as George Orwell's "Politics and the English Language" (Chapter 7), Griswold concedes that what one defines as an "error" depends largely on how one defines a "misuse." Regardless, until the "accepted misuses" are clearly and formally identified as *correct uses*, one should make the effort to follow formal grammar rules in both speech and writing.

Do you agree that frequent use of incorrect grammar validates the misuses, thus deeming them acceptable—and therefore "correct"—in all contexts?

Grammar is going all to hell, even in the office.

That's what the *Wall Street Journal* wrote on Wednesday, citing an "epidemic of grammar gaffes in the workplace" that has spread with the help of informal communications like email, texting and Twitter. Sure, this is nothing new—people were botching grammar long before the advent of social media. George Orwell lamented the deteriorating state of English in his 1946 essay "Politics and the English Language," writing that "Most people who bother with the matter at all would admit that the English language is in a bad way, but it is generally assumed that we cannot by conscious action do anything about it." Orwell felt strongly that we could and must do something about it. But what about language misuse at work today?

That's a complicated question. And it largely depends on what you define as a "misuse."

If you're anything like me, then you cringe inwardly whenever someone spurns the subjunctive by saying "I wish I was" or "if I was" instead of finishing the phrase with "were." In most of America, however, the subjunctive has already fallen out of favor, and people ignore the tense because they simply don't know any better. The same can be said of pronoun usage—some people who use "me" where they should have "I" don't intend to flout the rules of grammar. They just don't realize it's wrong. If enough of them make those errors, it means that language is evolving and they're becoming right.

It's probably less jarring to think about those shifts in terms of the creation 5 of slang or the ever-popular conversion of nouns to verbs. Google is now an accepted verb. "Can you access those records?" is by no means an uncommon phrase, though "access" originated as a noun and its first recorded use as a verb did not occur until 1962, according to the *Online Etymology Dictionary*. "Reference" falls into the same category. When people say they're "referencing" information, what they really mean is "making reference to."

"All languages change all the time—it's not just English—and people have been complaining about changes in languages for as long as they've been changing, which is forever," said Alice Harris, a professor of linguistics at the University of Massachusetts, Amherst. "When we first hear these things, we bristle, or sometimes we think they're funny. Not all of them become the norm, of course, but that's just the way language changes."

So some of these developments are natural. But today many errors that we might consider glaring—using "me" where you should have "I," or "who" instead of "whom"—have faded into gray territory. And the processes that result in additions to the dictionary can also lead to shifts in what's considered proper and acceptable grammar. Seeing this occur in the more formal settings of offices, Harris said, is another step in that progression.

"People often think that change goes from the top down, from the rich to the poor, from the formal to the informal, but it doesn't, it bubbles up from the bottom," she said. "It seems that many times things that are accepted in informal settings are then accepted in more and more formal settings. That's true of slang, and lots of things, and also grammatical changes."

Still, the natural evolution of language cannot and should not be used to dismiss all grammar mistakes. Harris says if you want to impress others, you will always try to use language correctly. Lynn Taylor, a national workplace expert, says using poor grammar reflects badly on employees at all levels. In business environments, you'll never be criticized for sending a well-written email.

10   So maybe some of these misuses—or, no, call them changes—are natural progressions in the English language. Perhaps someday it won't be frowned upon to say "me and Jim went to coffee" or "I wish I was going." But for now, here's a list of some common slip-ups that it's probably best to avoid:

It's/its. Use the apostrophe to contract "it is." No apostrophe indicates a possessive.

They're/their/there. Learn the difference.

The subjunctive. When posing a hypothetical, employ this tense. Therefore, say "If I were" and not "If I was."

Different than/different from. It's easy to remember this one if you think of "different" as "differing." You wouldn't say "differing than," so you also wouldn't say "different than."

Data. Should be used as a plural. The data show a pattern.

Between/among. The former is used with groups of two, the latter for three or more.

Who/whom. "Who" is a subjective pronoun, such as he, she, I, and acts as the subject of a clause. "Whom," on the other hand, is an objective pronoun like his, her, me, and acts as the object of a clause.

Me/I. Similar to above. These most often get confused when used in conjunction with another name or pronoun. When in doubt, just remove the other person from the equation. "Jim and me went to the store" wouldn't work, because you wouldn't say "me went to the store."

Less/fewer. Less in quantity, fewer in number. You wouldn't ask for fewer butter.

Don't end a sentence on a preposition. Unless doing so makes your writing far more awkward. That, as Winston Churchill said, is "nonsense up with which I will not put."

And finally, it can't hurt to consult the rules that Orwell penned more than 60 years ago. He was addressing the broad problem of unclear and even misleading communication. See his basic prescription below (but you should read his whole essay):

1. Never use a metaphor, simile, or other figure of speech which you are used to seeing in print.
2. Never use a long word where a short one will do.
3. If it is possible to cut a word out, always cut it out.
4. Never use the passive where you can use the active.
5. Never use a foreign phrase, a scientific word or a jargon word if you can think of an everyday English equivalent.
6. Break any of these rules sooner than say anything outright barbarous.

Analyze

1. Griswold begins her essay by claiming that proper grammar is declining "even in the office." What distinction is she drawing between the workplace and other spaces where language is used?
2. How does Alice Harris's point about language changes occurring from the bottom up help us understand the complexities of word usage?
3. As the English language evolves, should its users always strive to use correct grammar? Why or why not?

Explore

1. What are some of the most common grammar mistakes that you have heard or seen? Make a list of these errors and explain the correct usage.
2. Write a short essay in which you examine some contemporary verbs that started out as nouns and discuss the reasons that might have led to the change.
3. Griswold emphatically states that "the natural evolution of language cannot and should not be used to dismiss all grammar mistakes." Construct an argument in which you explore the validity of this position. Develop your own response by consulting scholarly resources that present different points of view.

Kate Dailey
Are Language Cops Losing War Against "Wrongly" Used Words?

Prior to joining the staff of the *BBC News Magazine* as a writer, Kate Dailey wrote about health, life, and culture at the magazines *Newsweek* and *Women's Health*. The following article appeared on April 12, 2012 on *BBC News Magazine* online, a department of the British Broadcasting Corporation. While sympathizing with language purists who lament the current misuse of the English language, Dailey recognizes that it is often through an apparent misuse that the English language evolves. For example, should we shake a finger at the technically incorrect expression "I feel nauseous" and correct it to "I feel nauseated," if the former is the more common expression?

While some scholars suggest that we must accept the evolution of word usage, to what extent should we accept the evolution of word meaning?

The editors of the *Associated Press (AP) Stylebook* announced that after careful consideration, they had changed the usage rules for the word "hopefully".

The *AP Stylebook* is one of the premier guides for American writers and copy-editors, and its rules dictate how the vast majority of newspapers and magazines use words, phrases, grammar and punctuation.

Before the change, "hopefully" could only be used to mean "in a hopeful manner". ("Is dinner ready?" she asked hopefully.) Now, it can also take the more modern meaning, "it is hoped". (Hopefully, dinner will be ready soon).

Though the *AP Stylebook* is primarily used in the US, the question of what words can be used in which ways is a universal one. The debate about proper ways to use the English language occurs wherever English is read, written or spoken.

5   The use of "hopefully" is no longer as controversial as it once was, there exists no shortage of words that trigger arguments amongst language formalists.

But how long before these constructions that make prescriptivists cringe are considered proper usage?

Begs the question This phrase is guaranteed to raise the ire of language purists. It describes a logical fallacy where one tries to prove a point by assuming the point is already valid: "Eating meat is immoral because meat is murder." But "to beg the question" is often used to mean "to raise the question", and that usage increasingly dominates, says Mignon Fogarty, author of the book *Grammar Girl's Quick and Dirty Tips for Better Writing*.

Fogarty set out to defend the traditional usage in her upcoming book, *101 Troublesome Words*. "After scouring articles and blog posts and being unable to find it used in the traditional way I became convinced it was a lost cause," she says.

Bemused Bemused means puzzled or confused, but is often used to mean slightly amused or entertained. It's one of a class of words that the linguist Bryan Garner calls "skunked". Those who know the word's proper meaning are upset when they see it misused, those who don't know the proper meaning are confused when it's used correctly.

"A lot of editors will avoid it altogether," says Colleen Barry, a copyeditor for IDG Enterprise and creator of the @CopyCurmudgeon Twitter handle. Instead, editors and journalists will often find a way to edit out skunked words, which disappear from traditional publications. However, they can still live on in Tweets, blog posts and other unedited web content, where the meaning is less likely to adhere to traditional rules of style—and as a result, the "inaccurate" definition becomes more accepted.

Disinterested In the same way that interested once meant having a stake—interested parties, for example—disinterested meant having no bias or gain. If she's disinterested in the Olympics, she won't benefit financially from the games, or have a family member participate. "Interested" is rarely used in that form, which puts disinterested at risk.

"When the positive goes, you can't expect to keep the negative around," says Nunberg.

Now, disinterested is often used synonymously with "not interested".

"That's too bad, because there is an uninterested already which means the same thing," says Ben Yagoda, professor of English and journalism at the University of Delaware, and author of *When You Catch an Adjective,*

10

Kill It. "Disinterested is kind of a cool word, there's no other word that means just that."

15 **Nauseous** Nauseous is the descriptor given to something that makes you feel sick, eg a nauseous odour. But people who are feeling unwell often say "I feel nauseous". Purists argue that they should say "nauseated". Many dictionaries and usage guides now list both definitions—and do so in response to the way people have continuously misspoke. "Dictionaries are about words as they're used, not as they think they should be used," says Barry.

Who/Whom Whom is on the way to becoming as archaic as "thou" or "thee", says John McIntyre, the night editor at the *Baltimore Sun* newspaper. It was his letter to the AP that prompted the change to "hopefully". "It's pretty much gone in spoken English and is increasingly abandoned in written English. You can see how precarious it is because when people use it, they often misuse," he says. "Increasingly it makes sense not to bother."

Analyze

1. How, according to the *AP Stylebook*, has the meaning of the word "hopefully" changed recently? Explain the difference you notice between the two forms of usage.
2. Why did the original meaning of the phrase "begs the question" fall into disuse? Consider some factors that might have led to the change in meaning.
3. Do you agree that words (e.g., "whom") should become obsolete simply because some people do not use them in speech or writing? How would such a trend affect the English language?

Explore

1. What are your views on the proper ways to use the English language? How concerned are you about the misuse of particular words?
2. Dailey mentions that "skunked" words have started to disappear from traditional publications. Write a paper where you discuss some of the "skunked" words in English as you trace their original meaning and examine how and why the words changed.

3. Conduct research on words and phrases that are in danger of disappearing from the English language. What are some of the reasons for the decline in usage? Are these words acquiring new meaning, and if so, what do they reflect about the way language functions?

Linton Weeks
R Grammar Gaffes Ruining the Language? Maybe Not

Linton Weeks, a former writer and editor for the *Washington Post,* joined National Public Radio as a correspondent in 2008. In the following article, which appeared on August 2, 2012 on NPR's website, Weeks joins the conversation sparked by Sue Shellenbarger and Kyle Wiens (in this chapter), positing that the diminution of English language grammar skills is not, in fact, destroying the language, but rather bringing it a renewed vibrancy and relevance. Weeks cites a professor's observation that, although students were writing correctly 30 years ago, they were not necessarily writing coherently. Thus, today's student writers might not always use correct grammar, but their writing is in many ways "better" at communicating.

Is correctness or clarity of language more important to you as a writer? Is it possible to have one without the other?

Good grammar may have came and went.

Maybe you've winced at the decline of the past participle. Or folks writing and saying "he had sank" and "she would have went." Perhaps it was the singer Gotye going on about "Somebody That I Used to Know" instead of "Somebody Whom I Used to Know." Or any of a number of other tramplings of traditional grammar—rules that have been force-fed to American schoolchildren for decades—in popular parlance and prose.

You can find countless examples of poor construction in the news, like this report from a radio station's website about a thief who "had ran out of gas" or this Fox News item about a dog owner who said "her dog had ran away" or this gossipy blog post about actress Demi Moore and her daughter, Rumer, "when her and Rumer attended the Friends Cinema for Peace event in Los Angeles and posed for photos on the red carpet!"

Such cacology drives some people to distraction. "I won't hire people who use poor grammar," Kyle Wiens, CEO of the iFixit online community and founder of Dozuki software, writes in a recent *Harvard Business Review* blog post.

5   In *The Wall Street Journal*, Sue Shellenbarger observes: "Managers are fighting an epidemic of grammar gaffes in the workplace. Many of them attribute slipping skills to the informality of email, texting and Twitter, where slang and shortcuts are common. Such looseness with language can create bad impressions with clients, ruin marketing materials and cause communications errors, many managers say."

Sure enough. Reading and listening to contemporary English, you just might think that the language is going to hell, and there is plenty of evidence to help make your argument. "Every year fewer and fewer students enter college knowing the difference between 'lie' and 'lay,'" says Connie C. Eble, an English professor at the University of North Carolina.

But Eble and some others who study the contemporary tongue do not think that bad grammar is necessarily destroying the English language. Instead, some posit, it may be making the way we talk and write more vibrant and relevant.

Oh sure, Eble says, students may confuse certain words or be ignorant of the correct pronoun case when two noun phrases are joined by "and." For instance, someone might say "Michael and me rented a car" or "between you and I."

But, she says, "today's students are actually much better writers than they were 30 years ago." Back then young people often used proper grammar to write incoherent essays.

10   Students are no longer being drilled endlessly in grammar, Eble says, "but they are being taught about topic sentences and paragraph coherence and overall organization."

If clarity of communication is the aim, most prescriptive rules of usage do not really cause misunderstanding, she says. "Between you and I" gets the point across as well as "between you and me."

Other scholars agree. Matthew Gordon, a linguist at the University of Missouri, says that with the advent of the Internet "a new wrinkle has been added to the complaint tradition."

In the pre-digital era, he says, "most texts we read came from published works—books, newspapers, journals, et cetera. This means they represented the variety of English associated with such media—generally formal, edited prose using the grammatical and orthographic conventions of 'standard English.'"

Such texts are still part of our world today, Gordon says, "but we also encounter very different kinds of writing online and sometimes elsewhere." He cites the use of "U" to represent "you," confused homophones such as "you're" and "your" or "it's" and "its," and the use of newish terms like "LOL" for "laughing out loud" and "totes" for "totally."

But it would be wrong to take such contemporary usages as indicative of   15
the deterioration of the language or even a relaxing of the rules of grammar, Gordon says. "They are trivial matters in terms of the overall structure of English."

Such liberties are not new. "People have always had trouble with homophones," he says, "and they have always used language creatively, coining new words or respelling established words. ... What's different today is that we can see these 'mistakes' more commonly because we're encountering a broader swath of writing on the Internet."

Carter Revard, a professor emeritus at Washington University who taught the history of the English language for more than 35 years, says that in almost all cases, the new developments in language—new constructions, new words, new meanings—spring from the past.

"They grow from roots that may be out of sight," Revard says, "or take root from seeds or spores spread by word of mouth or Tweety Bird droppings. They may suddenly be noticed but usually have been in use for quite some time before people notice them as 'new and different.'"

Wiens, the high-tech CEO, isn't buying the academic defense of dynamic language. Yes, language is constantly changing, he writes in his essay, "but that doesn't make grammar unimportant."

Those who pay attention to the rules of good grammar, Wiens says, will   20
probably pay attention to other details as well.

As he puts it, "Good grammar is credibility, especially on the Internet. In blog posts, on Facebook statuses, in e-mails, and on company websites, your words are all you have. They are a projection of you in your physical absence. And, for better or worse, people judge you if you can't tell the difference between their, there, and they're."

In other words, Wiens is saying to those who argue that bad grammar is not all bad, there may be a real-world reality in their argument they're not reckoning with.

Analyze

1. Why does Weeks start his essay with several examples of grammatically incorrect phrases? Identify and correct as many incorrect phrases as you can find, and compare your findings with a classmate.
2. What distinctions does the article make between pre-digital-era writing and online writing? What additional differences do you notice?
3. Examine some of the arguments presented in the article that explain why bad grammar, although increasingly common, is not necessarily destroying the English language. How convinced are you by these arguments?

Explore

1. Consider Eble's point that although students in the past wrote "incoherent essays," their grammar was perfect. In your experience, what does it mean to write a "coherent" essay? Does grammar have anything to do with coherence? Why or why not?
2. Examine how language is used in your community. How often do speakers invent new words or change currently used words? What impact does this have on your community? Interview a friend, relative, or family member and include his or her perspective as evidence for your argument.
3. The article presents the argument that contemporary usage (e.g., OMG or LOL) does not necessarily reflect the decline of English. Write a research paper in which you examine how such usage has affected the English language. What do language experts think about this change in attitude?

Robert Lane Greene
OMG, ETC.

Robert Lane Greene, a Brooklyn-based journalist and business correspondent for the British magazine *The Economist*, is fluent in five languages (German, Spanish, French, Portuguese, and Danish) and conversant in three more (Russian, Arabic, and Italian). "OMG, ETC.," appeared in the fall 2010 edition of *Intelligent Life*, the bimonthly lifestyle and culture magazine from

The Economist. In his article, Greene asserts that younger people are not the only ones using acronyms in language in their electronic communiqués; many professionals, he observes, are just as likely to use acronyms in the workplace, especially when referring to roles, initiatives, and processes. Greene recognizes that acronyms are linguistic tools, and in and of themselves are not particularly offensive; they are, he claims, "no better or worse than the people who enliven or burden our lives with them."

In what contexts are you most likely to use acronyms? Are there any writing situations in which you wouldn't dare use the same acronyms?

Perhaps the perfect modern movie is the cult classic *Office Space.* The anti-hero, Peter, begins his working day with a dressing-down from a droning boss about forgetting to put the cover-sheets on his TPS reports. We never find out what a TPS report is. Nor do we have to; the name alone tells us all we need to know about the life seeping out of Peter's days, three capital letters at a time.

Acronyms have become so prevalent that they suffer what anything does when coined without end: devaluation. "Oh, my God" still packs quite a punch in the right circumstances. "OMG", by contrast, is barely effective as a plaything any more. ("OMG he's cute." "OMG is it ten already?") LOL began life as "laughing out loud", a way for internet chatterers to explain a long pause in typing. Now, LOL means "you just said something so amusing my lip curled for a moment there." And how many BFFs will truly be best friends forever? Teens, with their habit of bleaching once-mighty words (from "awesome" to "fantastic"), can quickly render a coinage banal.

The kids are not ruining the language, though. Grown-ups play the same inflationary game. Walk into any business and a cloud of three-lettered titles surrounds you. The one who used to be just the boss, or the managing director, now styles himself the CEO, for chief executive officer. This alone would be one thing, but it turned into a viral infection: CIO, CTO, CFO, COO, CLO, and so on, for what used to be the heads of technology, finance and operations, and the company lawyer. The so-called C-suite is an allegedly prestigious club, but whither prestige as its ranks swell? Throw in the VPs and SVPs who swarm all over American offices—not just vice-presidents, but senior ones—and everyone is a manager. A study of Linked-In, the networking site, found the number of C- and VP-level members growing three to four times faster than the membership overall. Who, then, is managed any more?

All this seems natural in a technological age, when almost anything we do depends on computers. The first modern computers had acronymic names (ENIAC and UNIVAC), and they set the tone for the subsequent half-century; in fact ever since IBM gave us the cheap PC, homes have been flooded with CPUs (central processing units) that grow in power at an alarming rate, progressing from reading CD-ROMS to downloading MP3s (formerly known as songs) to controlling your HDTV. No one knows what the future of technology holds, but we can be confident it will arrive in a swirl of capital letters.

5   Acronyms have become so ubiquitous that we look for them even where they don't exist. They are a major source of the folk etymologies that ping around the internet, etymologies for words that aren't actually acronyms. "Fuck" isn't short for "for unlawful carnal knowledge", "posh" has nothing to do with "port out, starboard home", and a "tip", while it might be to insure promptness, certainly doesn't derive its name from that phrase. All these words are much older than the profusion of acronyms in English. When, in fact, did we start talking in acronyms, and why?

The armed forces have much to do with it. And the American army seems to have contributed more than its share. But acronyms don't have a particularly long pedigree. You won't find them in the papers of GEN George Washington or LTG Ulysses Grant. (Grant was occasionally referred to as USG, but this was long before the "United States Government" he fought for was universally known by those same letters in bureaucratese, as it is today.) David Wilton, a linguist, says that a 19th-century "smattering" turned into a flood with the first world war, when one of the most famous among them, AWOL ("absent without leave"), is definitively attested for the first time.

The smattering became a smorgasbord with the coming of FDR—the first president (1933–45) to be known so frequently by his initials alone. Roosevelt brought the New Deal economic programme, and many a ointy-headed planner, to Washington, DC. In the midst of the Great Depression, these idealists thought they could remake society with a host of new government programmes. The long names begged for a shorthand: when the Tennessee Valley Authority and the Works Progress Administration were being rushed out of the door, it was natural to dub them the TVA and the WPA.

There may have been another temptation as well. The use of letters as symbols began with the physical sciences: Jons Jacob Berzelius had invented the one- and two-letter system for the chemical elements in 1813, and physicists had unlocked the secrets of the universe with insights from $F=MA$ to $E=MC$. By analogy, perhaps, something that had an acronym felt scientific and controllable, tempting to government planners in the chaotic world of the mid-20th century. Enter the FBI to police the country, the CIA to spy on others, and the SEC to wrestle with financial markets.

If acronyms meant trying to define something so it could be controlled, this was especially tempting in medicine. Diseases, physical and mental, used to get curt, Germanic names: mumps, measles, madness. (When my paediatrician told me my son had croup, I felt transported to a mud-and-thatch hut in medieval Europe.) But as science progressed, the ailments began to get more Latin- and Greek-derived names: typhoid, cholera, mania, melancholy. Then the late-20th-century version of this trend came along: stringing together a long series of polysyllables to describe an illness—acquired immunodeficiency syndrome, chronic obstructive pulmonary disease and so on. It's only natural that these would become AIDS and COPD. If croup were discovered today, its lovable monosyllable would have no chance: it would be called acute laryngeal irritation disorder or ALID.

At the same time, clever marketing people seized the chance to get into 10 the medical, or quasi-medical acronym game. Having a hard time getting men to talk to their doctor about certain boudoir-related issues? A clever two-step solves the problem: dub it "erectile dysfunction", and then since nobody wants to say that either, "ED". Before you know it, celebrities are advertising your medication.

The principle of inflation applies here too, though. When I first saw an advertisement promising treatment for "restless leg syndrome, or RLS", I thought "now they're just making it up," trying to sell drugs. It turns out that RLS is a real thing, also known as Wittmaack-Ekbom's syndrome (as usual, after two of its discoverers). The names of a German and a Swedish scientist seem to me to give a lot more solidity to the syndrome than that triad of capital letters.

Psychology is another realm where many are not convinced that acronymic new "syndromes" and "disorders" are real. No one is insane any more, or even eccentric, or highly strung; they have BPD or OCD (borderline personality disorder or obsessive-compulsive disorder). And it's tempting to think that we might be over-medicalising kids when we talk about their ODD (oppositional-defiant disorder) and ADHD (attention-deficit hyperactivity disorder). In the old days, conservatives grumble, we had a different label for these kids—"badly behaved"—and we treated their condition with a good hard swat. The grumpy reaction against acronymic inflation may be making us ignore real advances in psychology, throwing the scientific baby out with the alphabet-filled bathwater.

The conservative anti-acronym crusader may grind to a halt when considering the business world, which is a long-standing source of acronymy. In 1901 the National Biscuit Company sought a trademark for a new short form of its name—Nabisco. The "co" trend took off, especially with oil companies (Texaco, Conoco, Sunoco), using a different kind of acronym, one that pulls together first syllables, not just letters. But the rise of the initialism and acronym proper were not far off; the stock-ticker and other space-compressed media did not cause, but helped accelerate, the trend towards shorter names. The century-long process that gave birth to IBM, GE and AT&T has culminated with many companies preferring not to be known by their original names. IBM may still do international business but it no longer makes most of its money selling machines. GE does so much more than electronics that it rarely refers to itself as General Electric. AT&T would prefer you forget the "telegraph" in its name, though American iPhone users might prefer a telegraph to the much-derided voice service bundled with their handset by AT&T. The desire to shed an old association goes doubly for the second word in Kentucky Fried Chicken, now served up by a company called KFC. God bless Radio Shack for resisting the trend. But how long before they become RS.com?

There's a whiff of the American about many acronyms. This may be the reason that a Chinese ministry, which went unnamed in press reports, quietly told media outlets to stop using roman-letter acronyms; F1 (Formula One motor racing) and the NBA (America's National Basketball Association) were no longer to be so called in the columns of Chinese newspapers. But even the mighty Chinese government can only do so much; CCTV, the state-controlled Chinese Central Television, still has a large Roman "CCTV" in its logo, perhaps because its web address consists of those letters, not the Chinese characters, which cannot be used in web addresses.

There is nothing inherently American, or even Anglo-phone, about 15 acronyms. Chinese itself has them, despite its remarkable character-based writing system. Many words consist of more than one character, and Chinese acronyms will use one character from each word (often, but not always, the first one). But of course acronyms are more suited to alphabets. The fish became a Christian symbol largely because the Greek word for it, *ichthos*, is an acronym for *iesous christos theou ouios soter*, "Jesus Christ, Son of God, Saviour". The Jews enjoyed making acronyms too, and even the name of the Bible is the *tanakh*, an acronym for *torah nevi'im ketuvim*, "Torah, prophets, writings", the three main sections of the Hebrew Bible.

The proliferation of acronyms through texting seems particularly Anglophone. The standard term for a text in America is itself a set of capitals (SMS, short message service). Now other languages are following suit. In German, the initialism SMS has become an acronym proper, pronounced "zims". It has also been made into a verb, *smsen*, so that it's perfectly natural to say *Ich habe ihr gesmst*, "I texted her."

The French too are playing with text-speak. Though many will happily import LOL from English tout court, they may also write MDR, *mort de rire*, "dead from laughing". And just as English texters can play with the rebus principle to write things like CUL8R ("see you later"), so the French have @+ (*à plus*, short for "see you later") and OQP, *occupé*, "busy".

This trend points to good news as we drown in ever more acronyms. They are a mere microcosm of language, sharing most of the properties of language generally. So just as the bureaucrats coin jargon, waffle and acronyms, the grunts and drones will continue to fight back against the plodding predictability of acronymic churn. And kids will continue to speed up the process by replacing anything that catches on too broadly—to the next generation, "LOL" could be about as groovy as "groovy" is today.

Slang initialisms and nonce-acronyms survive in the crowded marketplace of language because they fill a useful function. A SNAFU (situation normal: all fucked up) filled a void; it's not just any screw-up, it's the screw-up caused by some title-inflated CTO or SVP trying to impose TQM (total quality management) on his remaining subordinates. Soldiers, who have to face the reality of life and death on the battlefield along with the fact that they work for a giant bureaucracy, are a prolific source of subversive acronyms. The American military mindset that gave us CENTCOM

(Central Command), NORAD (North American Aerospace Defence Command) and NETWARCOM (Naval Network Warfare Command) has also come up with SNAFU and FUBAR (fucked up beyond all recognition). In the famous profile in *Rolling Stone* that led to Stanley McChrystal's resignation as America's commander in Afghanistan, some troops were quoted as mocking the non-Americans serving with them in the International Stabilisation Force for Afghanistan: ISAF, they said, really stood for "I suck at fighting". Soldiers will subvert acronyms as long as superiors think they can drive off the fog of war with the seductive quasi-certainty of the caps-lock key.

20   Ultimately, there's nothing wrong with acronyms. They may be a quintessentially modern annoyance, fooling us into thinking we have a greater grip on life's complexities than we really do. But that goes hand in hand with the wonders of the modern world: I'll take COPD and modern drugs over tuberculosis in 1910 any day. Acronyms are tools, no better or worse than the people who enliven or burden our lives with them.

Analyze

1. Greene provides many examples of acronyms from various fields such as business, technology, and medicine. In your opinion, which of these fields are most justified in using shortened forms of words? Why?

2. Examine Greene's discussion of the use of acronyms in psychology. How have the invention of these acronyms contributed to "real advances in psychology"?

3. Given the examples of acronyms that Greene cites, do you agree that acronyms are not inherently problematic but merely linguistic tools? Refer to some of the acronyms referred to in the article in your response.

Explore

1. To what extent has the increase in digital communication (such as email, texting, tweets, and social media updates) had an effect on the creation and use of acronyms? Reflect on your personal experience with these modes of communication and list some popular acronyms that are currently in use.

2. Greene states that acronyms and abbreviated words often serve a useful function in a particular context. Do you agree with this premise?

Write a brief essay in which you examine the complex nature of language use as you develop an argument about how acronyms function in a particular field.

3. Because they are shortcuts, acronyms often tend to become words in themselves, making the full version useless. Is it possible that this could pose a threat to the preservation of language? Or do acronyms reflect linguistic advancement and add to our understanding of how language works? Find two scholarly articles through your library database that address the value of acronyms, and examine the views held by language experts on the subject.

Forging Connections

1. The readings in this section, which often respond to and build on one another, reflect the current debate raging over language correctness. Given various viewpoints presented by the authors, do you think that grammar rules should be followed with utmost care? Or should rules be flexible enough so that language can be adapted to our needs? Refer to at least two readings from this chapter as you develop your argument.

2. We are constantly exposed to writing by friends, family, co-workers, and other acquaintances in the form of text messages, emails, tweets, blog entries, and Facebook updates. Choose five postings or responses from any of these sources and examine them to see how closely the writers adhere to the rules of grammar and usage. What type of errors do you notice, if any, and what do these errors tell you about the value of grammar and correctness?

Looking Further

1. Although dialects, slang, and other informal linguistic forms often do not follow the rules that govern standardized languages, would you agree that these are legitimate means of communication? In an essay that examines the place of nonstandard forms of languages in our culture, consider why we place so much emphasis on proper use of language and what we sacrifice when we insist on grammatical correctness. Refer to at least one of the selections in Chapter 6, "Language and Race," to support your argument.

2. Each of authors in this chapter is concerned about the importance of using language correctly and communicating well. Many of the selections in Chapter 3, "Language and Writing," are also concerned with the importance of audience awareness to a writer's work. Look through your favorite magazine, newspaper, website, or blog and analyze a piece of writing of your choice. How are the ideas expressed? How aware is the author of grammar and correctness? Does this awareness (or lack thereof) make any difference to the quality of writing? How would Linda Flower ("Writing for an Audience," Chapter 3), or Ellen Collett ("The Art of the Police Report," Chapter 3) evaluate the writer's audience awareness compared to his or her overall "correctness"?

5 Language & Gender

Language has the power to define, redefine, or challenge who we are. As the social roles we play in our families, communities, and workplace grow increasingly complex, our gender identity—however we choose to define it, as well as whatever identity is imposed on us by others—has the potential either to label or liberate. The selections in this chapter all focus on the power of language to define identity, and encourage readers to dwell on the interconnectedness of language and perceptions of gender. If gender barriers can be created and reinforced through our use of language, is it also possible for language to challenge stereotypes and break barriers? Can small shifts in meaning and usage result in larger shifts in gender equality? Even as they touch on topics as diverse as sports and workplace attitudes, these readings point to the close relationship between language and identity as they help us reconsider common interpretations of gendered language and challenge our assumptions about how gender operates.

In "The Soccer Mom," blogger and columnist Jason Davis explains that, despite the original intent behind the creation of the term "soccer mom," the concept has had an unexpected influence on our perception of both of suburban women and soccer. In "Hey Dude," Robert Lane Greene takes pleasure in discussing how the word "dude" has evolved from denoting urban hipness to reflecting parent–child bonding. For her own part, in "Let's Talk About Gender, Baby" political writer Wendy Kaminer ponders the confusion that arises when the terms "sex" and "gender" are used interchangeably. Amy Reiter, a freelance writer, analyzes the effect of a gendered power structure on the workplace in her essay "Why Being a Jerk at Work Pays." Across the Atlantic, Nathalie Rothschild, a Swedish journalist, reports in "Sweden's New Gender-Neutral Pronoun: *Hen*" that for better or worse, Sweden's movement toward gender neutrality has started a linguistic revolution. Finally, British sociologist Mark McCormack strikes a hopeful note in "Don't Call Me Homophobic: The Complexity of 'That's So Gay'" when he draws on his research to make the case that language is supple enough to resist entrenched connotations and adapt new, more positive meanings.

Jason Davis
The Soccer Mom

Jason Davis is a Virginia-based writer, podcaster, and columnist. He is the founder and lead writer for *Match Fit USA*, a soccer blog that attempts to "deconstruct" the sport. His blog post "The Soccer Mom" appeared in March 2012 on *Run of Play*, another soccer blog. Republicans coined the phrase "soccer mom" during the 1996 presidential election, bringing national attention to a newly important demographic of swing voters: middle- and upper-middle-class suburban mothers. However, because of the resulting association between soccer and a particular political viewpoint, Davis claims that such attention had a negative impact on the American public's perception of soccer.

What does the phrase "soccer mom" mean to you? What other phrases can you think of that might result in the same knee-jerk reactions in people that Davis describes?

Sometime during the run-up to the 1996 Presidential election, a Republican political advisor named Alex Castellanos told a reporter from the *Washington Post* that incumbent Bill Clinton was going after a newly identified demographic of American voters called "soccer moms." Middle-class, suburban, and constantly on the go in her loaded Dodge Caravan, the Soccer Mom represented a burgeoning group of swing voters key to the outcome of the election. Soccer Moms were family-first, possibly affluent, generally moderate, not necessarily assured of voting lockstep with their husbands, and therefore totally up for grabs.

In other words, Soccer Moms were America's political future.

The '96 election set in motion a series of events that culminates with this writing. After more than 15 years and the loss of countless hairs while watching the good name of soccer being dragged through the mud as part of a phrase that sums up everything soccer *isn't* supposed to be, I've been compelled to lash out against this ruinous phrase.

I detest the Soccer Mom.

No, that's not right. I detest the *phrase* "Soccer Mom." I hate what the phrase   5 "Soccer Mom" has come to imply. I hate the careless willy-nilly usage of it. I hate the laziness inherent in its application. I hate the idea that in the United States of America, the phrase "soccer mom" has been appropriated to mean (almost exclusively) white, middle-to-upper class, suburban women with children who may or not play soccer. I hate that the phrase paints with broad strokes an entire group while simultaneously leaving out multiple millions of mothers with soccer-playing children who don't meet the very narrow definition concocted by a few political strategists. Why should that subset of a subset be the only women graced with the title "Soccer Mom"?

More than anything, I rue that the aspect of suburban life used to identify the demographic is soccer. Not because I don't like that there's a group of women marked by their connection to the sport, even though not all of the women so haphazardly labelled "Soccer Mom" are actually, in fact, soccer moms, but because the phrase, by virtue of who it has come to mean, embodies so much of what's wrong with soccer's place in American culture. The Soccer Mom, as she is portrayed, is a mythical creature concocted by political operatives and subsequently co-opted by pop culture. Soccer moms, without the political or demographic overtones, are not universally anything save for moms who have kids who play soccer. Actual soccer moms don't even have to drive their kids to practice to qualify as soccer moms. They certainly don't have to be white, affluent, live in the suburbs, or represent a specific type of American woman.

Back in 1996, no one was really sure what a Soccer Mom *was*, at least in the context meant by Castellanos. Stripped of all socioeconomic trappings, the phrase is self-explanatory. But in the arena of American politics, there was significant disagreement over just what constituted the fabled Soccer Mom demographic. Were Soccer Moms affluent housewives with time to spare and a laser focus on kids and family? Were they working moms shuttling kids to and from soccer practice while juggling a job and stretching every family dollar? Or were they something in between, both professional and domestic?

Jacob Weisberg addressed the problem of the Soccer Mom label for *Slate* in October of '96, just before the election and when Soccer Mom fever was at its height. First, the issues with pinning down just what a Soccer Mom was all about.

> Who exactly, we must ask, are these soccer moms who hold the nation's fate in their hands? "They can be found," a CNN correspondent informs us, "shuttling the kids to practice in minivans, nervously pacing the sidelines, juggling the demands of family and career." Well naturally, but what sort of women take their kids to soccer practice? According to one South Carolina paper, soccer mom is "a well-heeled super-parent whose primary mission in life is to do too much for her children. She got on a waiting list early for the right day-care center, sent junior to Montessori, started violin lessons at 5, private school the same year and, the next year— soccer." According to the *Rocky Mountain News*, however, soccer mom is "financially stressed." Opinion is similarly divided on her employment status. In the view of the *Cleveland Plain Dealer*,

soccer mom is a career woman who has "temporarily taken up child rearing." According to the *Buffalo News*, however, she is "balancing the demands of work and family." The consensus seems to be that soccer moms are some subset of middle-class, white suburban women. They "care about their kids" (as opposed, presumably, to urban "rap moms" who do not), and they are incredibly busy. If you can't find a soccer mom for your story, don't worry. Part of the shtick is that she hasn't got time to talk to reporters.

Weisberg was writing from a political perspective on the application of the label, but the size of the supposed key demographic presages the problems with the later creep of the phrase into popular culture. Now that—15 years later—"Soccer Mom" has fully transitioned from a name for a specific voting bloc to mainstream label for any white, un-hip, suburban mother, the disproportionate impact it has had on the image of soccer is a gut-shot to those of us who know the sport is much more than carpools and orange slices (and wishes more of America would wake up to that fact).

Narrowly defined as married, college-educated, suburban women with school-age children, soccer moms constitute only 4 percent or 5 percent of the electorate. Broadly defined as suburban white women with school-age kids, they add up to 11 percent or 12 percent. But then, as Hickman points out, that 12 percent covers both working-class women who live in two-bedroom ramblers and professionals in Westchester County with inherited wealth. As voters, these women have little in common from election to election. It was a cruel stroke of fate that the rise of Soccer Moms, as small a group as they proved to be, came just as professional soccer in the United States was getting a fresh start with the launch of MLS. It can't be a coincidence that Major League Soccer wasted so many years marketing almost exclusively to families, and specifically to Soccer Moms (the presumed gatekeeper of the entertainment dollar), just as the nation became enraptured with the possibility that these women would determine the outcome of a presidential election. Pro soccer was already behind the eight ball thanks to the lily-white image of the game (an image earned honestly over two decades of soccer's failure to catch on anywhere but suburbia). Falling into the trap of selling the sport counter to its intrinsic nature as a game of passion and commitment set the American league back by as much as a generation.

Without the Soccer Mom craze of '96, MLS might have corrected its course much sooner. If it weren't for Soccer Moms, or more accurately the attachment of soccer to their image, who knows where MLS might be. Bigger than NASCAR, I bet. Definitely bigger than NASCAR.

In 2012, "soccer mom" gets attached to stories about 40-something suburbanite women running brothels in New York, and counts as an archetype into which the knocked-up member of the Jersey Shore cast should fit perfectly. The phrase is a catch-all that only involves soccer tangentially; mostly it's about the placid, affluent, prosaic existence white women in the suburbs—if we believe what media tell us—can't help but live. The madam running the brothel is labelled a "Soccer Mom" in headlines because the phrase is code for "boring, family-focused, and middle-class." It makes the story that much more shocking. Taking her kids to soccer practice *and* running a brothel? Gasp! Even the English transfer the phrase without the usual translation of the word "soccer" into "football" because "soccer mom" is idiomatic. A Soccer Mom might be a soccer mom, technically just a mother with soccer-playing kids, but she's also a certain type of American woman. The phrase conveys that message even to a non-American readership.

> "Soccer Mom therefore isn't a descriptor, it's a borderline insult."

Like so many other women throughout history, Soccer Moms are relieved of their individuality en masse and without consultation. The media defines them by their kids and by their kids' activities, around which their lives supposedly orbit. Soccer Mom therefore isn't a descriptor, it's a borderline insult. It's marginalization through labeling. It implies groupthink.

15   From a soccer perspective, there's not much that sums up the sport's image problem in America better than the phrase "Soccer Mom." It's is loaded with connotations that run directly counter to soccer's natural populist character. It fully expresses—because the perceived affluence of a Soccer Mom has apparently settled in the upper-middle-class range, judging by contemporary media usage—just how upside-down access to the sport in the United States has been over the last four decades. Now that Soccer Moms are viewed as women of privilege (which makes their kids children of privilege), the phrase further exacerbates soccer's image as a sport for rich white suburbanites. I don't begrudge anyone the right to be successful. But that's not what soccer is, and it's certainly not how I want to the country at large to view it. Soccer is the people's game. Soccer Moms are not the people.

I'd like to talk to Alex Castellanos. I'd like to ask him why he and his fellow Republican strategists had to go and tarnish soccer's good name like that back in '96. Yes, the suburban soccer boom was in full swing in the mid-90s, but there were so many other ways to go. What about "minivan mom" (alliteration!) or a singular personification like "Susie Suburbia" (in the great tradition of Joe Sixpack)? If it's necessary to boil millions of individual American women down into one catchy phrase, both would provide the same sort of easy identification.

Soccer is an innocent bystander in all of this. The phrase "Soccer Mom" likely explains the militant nature of so many of the "football not soccer" zealots pinging around the internet. For them, "soccer" is irrevocably linked with the Soccer Mom and her insipid existence of suburban banality. Can we blame them for wanting to separate the sport they love from the painfully square image of the oblivious mom and her recreational soccer-playing kids?

Meanwhile, mainstream American sports fans look down their noses at a game they see as juvenile. To the aforementioned Joe Sixpack, soccer is exercise masquerading as sport, with shrieking, over-bearing, self-involved, oblivious women pacing the sideline exhorting little Johnny to "kick it in the goal!" while wearing t-shirts with their son's or daughter's picture on them. Thanks, Soccer Mom.

It turns out Soccer Moms were hardly America's political future. They still pop up as a voting demographic occasionally, but they are now much more influential in the world of marketing. Sometime shortly after the '96 election, the Soccer Mom stopped being a sought-after voter and became a coveted consumer. Everything from automobiles to cereal was advertised to appeal to the mythical "Soccer Mom". Despite many companies (particular the car companies) abandoning Soccer Mom-focused campaigns in an effort to become more hip in the middle part of the last decade, the Soccer Mom, with all of her presumed attributes, remains the target for many American advertisers.

In fact, Major League Soccer still makes it a point to market to Soccer 20 Moms, although on a much lower level than they did back in the early days of the league. As much as that pains me, I see the wisdom in it. Soccer Moms exist, as least in the strictest definition of the word, and it seems natural for a local professional soccer club to try and connect with them and convince them to spend a family night out at the soccer park. As long as there are supporters singing behind the goal and MLS doesn't revert to its family-friendly past, I can handle giving the Soccer Mom a smidgen of attention.

Of course, the phrase is so loaded with coded meanings now that no woman should want to self-identify as a Soccer Mom. Clubs should be careful about invoking it. The phrase conjures up images that don't do the sport in America any favors, and it presents suburban motherhood as an exercise in waiting hand-and-foot on one's children. It presumes a supreme lack of individuality. It colors soccer as the sport of privilege, indirectly alienating the bulk of the American population who should be most inclined play and watch.

In 1996, political commentators had trouble locking in on the exact definition of the phrase. In 2012, we know exactly what it means because society at large has collectively chosen to give the Soccer Mom a stereotypical identity.

And I hate it. Begone, Soccer Mom.

Analyze

1. What, according to Davis, are some of the problems associated with the term "Soccer Mom" that make him detest it so much?
2. Davis contends that "Soccer Mom" is not so much a descriptive term but a "borderline insult." How does this particular description of a broad group of women affect the way they are perceived?
3. What argument does Davis make about the place of soccer in American society?

Explore

1. Given your own experiences, how would you define a "Soccer Mom"? Do you agree with Davis's definition of the term?
2. Examine whether a gendered term such as "Soccer Mom" has a greater impact on the role of women in society than on the reputation of a particular sport. Refer back to the article and other published sources as you develop your argument.
3. Would you agree that soccer's "image problem" in the United States is further hampered by the phrase "Soccer Mom"? Write an essay in which you use researched sources to examine the history of soccer in this country and how, if at all, "Soccer Moms" affect the popularity of the sport.

Robert Lane Greene
Hey Dude

Robert Lane Greene, a Brooklyn-based journalist and business correspondent for the British magazine *The Economist*, is fluent in five languages (German, Spanish, French, Portuguese, and Danish) and conversant in three more (Russian, Arabic, and Italian). Greene is best known for his book on the politics of language, *You Are What You Speak* (Random House, 2011). His article, "Hey Dude," appeared in *Intelligent Life*, a bimonthly lifestyle and culture magazine published by *The Economist*. Greene describes the staying power of the slang term, "Dude," which first appeared in print in 1883 in an American magazine. Since then, the meaning of the term has evolved and its usage has crossed gender lines.

Think of a slang term that you use often in your daily vernacular—does its meaning change depending on the context in which you use it?

S lang rarely has staying power. That is part of its charm; the young create it, and discard it as soon as it becomes too common. Slang is a subset of in-group language, and once that gets taken up by the out-group, it's time for the in-crowd to come up with something new. So the long life of one piece of American slang, albeit in many different guises, is striking. Or as the kids would say, "Dude!"

Though the term seems distinctly American, it had an interesting birth: one of its first written appearances came in 1883, in the American magazine, which referred to "the social 'dude' who affects English dress and the English drawl". The teenage American republic was already a growing power, with the economy booming and the conquest of the West well under way. But Americans in cities often aped the dress and ways of Europe, especially Britain. Hence dude as a dismissive term: a dandy, someone so insecure in his Americanness that he felt the need to act British. It's not clear where the word's origins lay. Perhaps its mouth-feel was enough to make it sound dismissive.

From the specific sense of dandy, dude spread out to mean an easterner, a city slicker, especially one visiting the West. Many westerners resented the dude, but some catered to him. Entrepreneurial ranchers set up ranches for tourists to visit and stay and pretend to be cowboys themselves, giving rise to the "dude ranch".

By the 1950s or 1960s, dude had been bleached of specific meaning. In black culture, it meant almost any male; one sociologist wrote in 1967 of a group of urban blacks he was studying that "these were the local 'dudes', their term meaning not the fancy city slickers but simply 'the boys', 'fellas', the 'cool people'."

5   From the black world it moved to hip whites, and so on to its enduring associations today—California, youth, cool. In *Easy Rider* (1969) Peter Fonda explains it to the square Jack Nicholson: "Dude means nice guy. Dude means a regular sort of person." And from this new, broader, gentler meaning, dude went vocative. Young men the world over seem to need some appellation to send across the net at each other that recognises their common masculinity while stopping short of the intimacy of a name. It starts in one country or subculture, and travels outwards. Just as the hippies gave us "man", and British men are "mate" to one another, so, by the late 1970s or early 1980s, "dude" was filling that role. And all three words are as likely to go at the start of the sentence as the end.

Sean Penn's surfer-stoner in *Fast Times at Ridgemont High* (1982) says "Make up your mind, dude." By 2000, the vocative use and whiff of stoner culture was firm. The title line of *Dude, Where's My Car?* is spoken by a character waking up from a big night out. In *BASEketball* (1998), the creators of *South Park*, Trey Parker and Matt Stone, play Coop and Remer, two friends having an argument:

Coop: Dude, I'm not gonna cave in! End of story, Dude!
Remer: Dude?
Coop: Dude!
Remer: Dude!
Coop: Dude.
Remer: Dude!
Coop: DUDE!
Remer: Dude! . . . (Coop opens his mouth but says nothing. Remer continues, firmly) Dude.
Coop: I guess you got a point there.

Also in 1998, *The Big Lebowski* gave us the most lovable dude yet: Jeff Lebowski, the role that relaunched Jeff Bridges' career. "The Dude", as everyone calls the stoner Lebowski, is being lectured by a rich old man of the same name. The Dude finally snaps:

> I am not "Mr Lebowski". You're Mr Lebowski. I'm the Dude. So that's what you call me. You know, that or, uh, His Dudeness, or uh, Duder, or El Duderino if you're not into the whole brevity thing.

With his bathrobe and his milk-soaked moustache, the Dude had come a long way from the east-coast dandy of the 1880s.

Now the vocative "Dude!" is mainstream—and no longer just for dudes. Young "dudettes", as women could once be called, routinely call each other "dude". And even married couples do it. The first time I heard it leap the gender divide, it was startling; now I find it sweet, somehow even more intimate than "baby", showing the couple as friends, not just lovers. My wife and I never made a decision to be "dude" to each other, it just fills in the cracks in domestic life: "Dude, you have got to stop leaving the closet light on . . . "

I knew its journey was complete when my 11-year-old son was trying to grab my attention the other day. "Dude!" he said, as I flailed away at one of his video games, "you're doing it wrong."

At first I wanted to say, "I'm not a dude. I'm your dad." But something stopped me. Dude is now all about solidarity. My son just called me "dude!" It was about the nicest thing he could have said.

Analyze

1. How does the author's detailed reference to the origin of the term "dude" help you to understand its current usage?
2. What point is Greene trying to convey by presenting the short exchange between two characters from the movie *BASEketball*?
3. Greene explains how the meaning and scope of the term "dude" has expanded over time. What do you think contributed this expansion?

Explore

1. A "vocative" is a personal name used to address a listener directly. Think of some of the vocatives you use to refer to friends, family, and acquaintances and explore the meaning that these words carry.

2. While the word "dude" evolved to refer to women as well, other vocatives such as "man" or "mate" have a "common masculinity" or distinctively male feel. Explore the use of vocatives among your friends by conducting an interview with at least two individuals. Who do they address when they use these terms? Are these terms gender neutral? Why?

3. Words, however innocent they might seem, often carry entrenched meanings that are hard to shake off. In a short research essay investigate how a particular vocative has been used to mark a certain gender. Has this usage changed over time? How?

Wendy Kaminer
Let's Talk About Gender, Baby

Before embarking on her writing career, Wendy Kaminer served as staff attorney at the New York Legal Aid Fund. She is now a contributing editor at *The Atlantic Monthly* and a former correspondent for *The American Prospect,* in which the following article appeared on December 19, 2001. Founded in 1990, The *American Prospect* is a liberal, bimonthly print and online political magazine based in Washington, DC. Although Kaminer applauds her fellow feminists for trying to remove all "gender language" from their vocabularies, she also observes how these same feminists fail to recognize other more blatant misuses: "Why do they tolerate, and even promote, use of the word *woman* (or the plural *women*) as an adjective? . . . We have 'women doctors' . . . but no 'men doctors'. . . . We do, however, have 'manservants.' It's not hard to figure out why. Servants are presumptively female, just as senators are presumptively male."

Do you believe that people's conscientious integration (or lack thereof) of nongendered language has an impact on male–female equality in the United States?

F eminists have long been ridiculed for their efforts to purge sexism from language by using words like *chairperson* and avoiding the use of male pronouns as universal signifiers of both sexes. The results have not always been pretty: "He knows what's good for him" is a far more felicitous phrase than "He/she knows what's good for him/her." And we can probably achieve equality without ever using the word *herstory*. Still, I'm grateful that common usage no longer completely ignores the existence of women with words like *mankind*.

Besides, I grew up in a predigital age, when concern about grammar and usage was not dismissed as pedantry. So in my view, while feminist language police are sometimes hypervigilant, sometimes they're not vigilant enough. Why do they tolerate, and even promote, use of the word *woman* (or the plural *women*) as an adjective? It's a noun. We have "women doctors" and "women senators" but no "men doctors" or "men senators." We do, however, have "manservants." It's not hard to figure out why. Servants are presumptively female, just as senators are presumptively male. When we incorrectly describe a female politician as a "woman politician," we confirm that, like a "manchild," she's an oddity, an oxymoron.

Equally irritating is our conflation of *sex* and *gender*. In a society that vacillates between Puritanism and permissiveness, there are obvious reasons to avoid using the word *sex*. People fear that it arouses prurient interest by recalling what teenagers do in the backseats of cars or what hookers do in the front. But in addition to various acts, *sex* refers to the biological categories male and female; *gender* refers (or used to refer) to cultural norms of masculinity and femininity. To say that you're a member of the female sex is simply to say that you're a woman. To say that you're a member of the female gender is to say that you behave the way a woman is supposed to behave. Sexual differences can only be accommodated; gender differences can and do change. Men can't get pregnant, but they can learn to type, as the computer age has shown.

So I don't think my complaint is mere pedantry. When we use these terms interchangeably, we lose important distinctions between biology and culture and risk confusing our standards of law. We shouldn't use the term *gender discrimination* to describe discrimination against a person because she's a female. Instead, it means (or should mean) discrimination against a woman who dresses like a man, for example, or has adopted a masculine style. A sign that says "No men need apply" constitutes sex discrimination. Gender discrimination is a sign that says "No men in skirts need apply."

Fortunately, the U.S. Supreme Court has managed, barely, to outlaw 5 discrimination based on gender, without ever recognizing how it differs from discrimination based on sex. In the 1989 case *Price Waterhouse v. Hopkins,* a plurality of the Court ruled in favor of a woman who had been passed over for partnership at the accounting firm of Price Waterhouse because she was deemed insufficiently ladylike. One partner advised her to "walk more femininely, talk more femininely, dress more femininely, wear make-up, have her hair styled, and wear jewelry."

Or consider the 1998 case of Joseph Oncale, a former oil rig worker who claimed to have been subjected to highly sexualized, physical assaults and threatened with rape by his male colleagues. In *Oncale v. Sundowner Offshore Services,* the Supreme Court allowed Oncale to pursue his "same-sex" harassment case under federal equal-employment law. The Court stressed that federal law prohibits sex discrimination, even when practiced by members of the same sex against one another. The trouble is that Oncale suffered gender discrimination, not sex discrimination. He was reportedly singled out for abuse not because he is a man but because he is a relatively slight man whose masculinity was questioned. There was no general hostility toward men in Oncale's all-male workplace; there was, it seems, hostility toward men deemed to possess insufficient machismo.

Misuse of *sex* and *gender* is steadily worsening: As if "single-sex schools" weren't bad enough, we now have "single-gender schools," which I imagine as places in which men learn to walk like women and women learn to whistle. Instead of "transsexuals," we have "transgendered people"—a term that might apply to any woman who exercises authority in what is labeled a masculine style or to any man who carries a purse. We even have surveys asking us to specify our "sex or gender." "Male gender," I replied once, when I was wearing a mannish suit; "female sex."

How did we get so confused? Supreme Court Justice Ruth Bader Ginsburg is sometimes blamed or credited for introducing the term *gender discrimination* in the early 1970s, when she was arguing landmark sexual-equality cases before the Supreme Court. According to my favorite rumor, she did not want to use the word *sex* before the Court and so offered up the word *gender.* I've always been quite grateful to Justice Ginsburg for the rights she helped secure, and I understand that every revolution has its casualties. But why must language always be among them?

Analyze

1. When used as adjectives, what effect do gender descriptors such as "man" and "woman" have in describing social roles?
2. Who exactly are the "feminist language police"? What kinds of linguistic practices do you think they would like to control?

3. Why should the terms "sex" and "gender" not be used interchangeably? Explain the distinction that Kaminer draws between these two concepts, and look for other examples of misuses of both terms in the media.

Explore

1. To what extent is sexist language a serious threat to equality among men and women? Consider some of the gender-specific words that are commonly used around you and discuss what they reflect about the target population.
2. Make a list of some of the gender-neutral words that exist in the English language. How effective are these words in conveying a sense of equality among the sexes?
3. Our sense of what is masculine and what is feminine is deeply influenced by what we hear, read, and see. Write a research essay in which you explore how language used in popular media such as television movies, videos, Facebook, and so on, shapes our understanding of gender.

Amy Reiter
Why Being a Jerk at Work Pays

Formerly a staff writer and editor for *Salon*, the online news and information site, Amy Reiter is now a freelance writer. Her work has appeared in numerous print and online publications, including the *New York Times*, the *Washington Post*, *Glamour*, and *Huffington Post*. "Why Being a Jerk at Work Pays" appeared on October 20, 2011 at *The Daily Beast*, an online publication dedicated to breaking news and sharp commentary. Reiter observes how those individuals who wield the most power and authority in the workplace are frequently rude, impolite, and disagreeable; however, public perceptions of men who behave this way are quite different from perceptions of women who behave in this fashion.

Consider your own workplace, classroom, and social interactions. Do Reiter's observations about polite versus impolite communication styles ring true for you?

For years, I tried to be a very nice person at work—a dream colleague, a team player, the sort of woman who gave women a good name in the workplace. I thanked people. I apologized. I expressed concern. I took responsibility for making things right, even when I wasn't the one who had made them go wrong.

Then one day I looked up from my under-challenging, midlevel job and noticed that my boss, who was generally regarded as kind of a jerk, but a smart and talented one, never, ever thanked people. He never apologized. And he didn't appear to give a rip about what was going on in the lives of anyone around him. He never took responsibility when things went wrong, preferring instead to label someone else the culprit and chew them out.

It suddenly occurred to me: he had gained responsibility, power and a big, cushy salary not despite the fact that he was a jerk, but because of it. Maybe no one liked him, but everyone respected him. Whereas I, arguably no less competent, but assuredly a whole lot more pleasant and agreeable, was drifting along in a rudderless career—pal to all, boss to none.

I'm not alone in my thinking: A recent study examining the relationship between agreeableness, income and gender, published in *Journal of Personality and Social Psychology*, found that the workplace does tend to reward disagreeable behavior. Disagreeable men tend to earn more than agreeable men, and disagreeable women, though they earn less than both nice and not-nice guys, earn more than agreeable women, researchers found.

5   The study, entitled "Do Nice Guys—and Gals—Really Finish Last?" (conducted by Timothy A. Judge of the University of Notre Dame's Mendoza College of Business, Beth A. Livingston of Cornell University's School of Industrial and Labor Relations, and Charlice Hurst of University of Western Ontario's Richard Ivey School of Business) provided an analysis of the data from three separate surveys conducted over the past two decades including responses from thousands of workers of various ages, salary levels, and professions. The authors also conducted a survey of their own, asking 460 business students to weigh in on hypothetical personnel decisions.

"'Niceness"—in the form of the trait of agreeableness—does not appear to pay, the authors concluded.

Although I could never pull off my boss's level of rudeness (nor would I have wanted to), I nevertheless decided to shed just a bit of my workaday warmth by making two seemingly small changes: to stop saying "thank you" or "I'm sorry." Straightaway. Cold turkey. Just to see what would happen.

I started with email, where I had often signed off with a chipper "thanks!" or apologized for inconveniencing someone with a request or for taking a while to reply. I was no longer sorry it took so long to get back to anyone. Neither did I feel either regretful about asking them to do something or grateful to them in advance for doing it.

I painstakingly reread every message to make sure neither polite phrase had sneaked through. And after I'd carefully excised each self-effacing slip, I hit send with a new set to my jaw, a hard glimmer in my eyes.

The effect was immediate: Colleagues began to treat me with more respect. Celebrity publicists—a notably power-aware lot whom I often contacted in my job—were more responsive. Even interns (those pecking-order experts) seemed to regard me with a new sort of awe.   10

Emboldened, I sought to eliminate "sorry" and "thank you" from my spoken workplace interactions as well, sometimes literally covering my mouth (passing it off as a "thoughtful" pose) during meetings to keep from uttering them. I found myself smiling less and bargaining harder.

My new confidence gave me the inner wherewithal to launch a freelance business (I'm now my own boss). My career—and my income—lurched upward.

At first, my new sense of power and its rewards felt thrilling. I learned to bargain firmly and unapologetically and was paid fairly—and it seemed to me that, when people paid more for my work, they tended to value it (and me) more highly, further increasing my own sense of worth. But there were also times I pushed too hard and lost assignments. And I began to worry about my reputation. Had my new self-assurance made me overly demanding? Were people starting to think of me as a diva?

My concerns may have been valid. The recent study also found that the rewards of disagreeableness for women are limited—far more so than for men. What's more, if women push their disagreeable behavior in the workplace too far, they risk a major backlash.

"People attribute disagreeable—i.e. self-interested, tough, argumentative—   15
behavior in men and women differently," study coauthor Judge told me. "If a man is disagreeable, he is thought to be tough and leader-like. If a woman is disagreeable, the 'b-word' is applied to her."

I had found myself bumping against these very boundaries: placing a higher value on respect and remuneration than likability, I had advanced, but I feared I was becoming unlikable. Had I become, as Judge politely put it, a "b-word"?

This past summer, I had a breakthrough. It happened when I wrote an essay that was included in a collection of works by "mommy bloggers." An email group was formed so that those of us who were involved could introduce ourselves to each other. Every single person, in their initial emails, included a sort of apology ("I've never been included in something like this before!") and an expression of thanks ("I'm so honored").

Reading through the email chain, I saw these expressions not as displays of powerlessness, but of kindness, openheartedness and candor, a desire for connection and support. We were thankful. We were sorry. We were also in it together. I added my own expressions of modesty and gratitude to the highly agreeable chain, and felt the camaraderie surround me like a warm blanket.

In the intervening months, I've sought to find a middle ground. I will now allow the occasional "thank you" to pass, and I will apologize if I feel it is justified, though I still try not to do either reflexively.

20   That's the sort of balanced approach Judge, the study coauthor, recommends. "I tell women there is a difference between disagreeing and being disagreeable," he says. "Be firm, logical, assertive, and persistent—but do not ever show hostility, anger, or other negative emotions."

We women are held to different standards of agreeability than men, Judge cautions, adding, "This of course is not fair—but fair does not always describe the world in which we live."

Sorry to break the news. And thanks!

Analyze

1. Reiter describes her boss as a "kind of jerk" because of his attitude and ways of communication. Is the word "jerk" gender-specific? Do you think Reiter would have used the word just as easily to describe a woman?

2. How, according to the research cited in the essay, does the workplace reward disagreeable behavior? Do you think it is fair to reward such behavior?

3. What lesson does the author learn about gender roles in the workplace by adopting a more aggressive attitude?

Explore

1. Write about a time when you experienced some form of discrimination because of your sex or gender. What gender stereotypes, do you think, led to this discriminatory attitude?

2. Reiter's essay seems to point to a double standard in the workplace when it comes to gender and authority. Consider how employees are treated in a workplace with which you are familiar. What differences do you notice?

3. Traditionally, power and authority have been viewed as male domains and women have been relegated to the realm of domesticity. Look into scholarly sources to find out what feminist scholars have to say about how these gendered roles have affected the language that is used to define the two groups.

Nathalie Rothschild
Sweden's New Gender-Neutral Pronoun: *Hen*

Born in Stockholm, Sweden, freelance journalist Nathalie Rothschild has covered a range of topics—from Rastafarians in Israel to Orthodox Jewish fashion bloggers in the United States. She is a regular correspondent for the U.S. *Christian Science Monitor,* the UK *Jewish Chronicle,* and the Swedish *Judisk Krönika* (*Swedish Jewish Chronicle*). The following article was posted on April 11, 2012 in *Slate,* a web-based daily magazine founded in 1996 that offers reporting, analysis, and commentary about politics, news, business, technology, and culture. In her article, Rothschild discusses Sweden's push toward not only gender *equality,* but gender *neutrality.* So intent is the aim to obliterate the distinctions between male and female that the Swedes have proposed adding a new pronoun to their current vocabulary: *hen* (gender-neutral) to replace *han* (he) and *hon* (she).

Rothschild suggests that Sweden's attempt to erase all gender distinctions might be particularly difficult for young children who are already born with a sense of gender and their gender roles. What are your thoughts?

B y most people's standards, Sweden is a paradise for liberated women. It has the highest proportion of working women in the world, and women earn about two-thirds of all degrees. Standard parental leave runs at 480 days, and 60 of those days are reserved exclusively for dads, causing some to credit the country with forging the way for a new kind of nurturing masculinity. In 2010, the World Economic Forum designated Sweden as the most gender-equal country in the world.

But for many Swedes, gender equality is not enough. Many are pushing for the Nordic nation to be not simply gender-*equal* but gender-*neutral*. The idea is that the government and society should tolerate no distinctions at all between the sexes. This means on the narrow level that society should show sensitivity to people who don't identify themselves as either male or female, including allowing any type of couple to marry. But that's the least radical part of the project. What many gender-neutral activists are after is a society that entirely erases traditional gender roles and stereotypes at even the most mundane levels.

Activists are lobbying for parents to be able to choose any name for their children (there are currently just 170 legally recognized unisex names in Sweden). The idea is that names should not be at all tied to gender, so it would be acceptable for parents to, say, name a girl Jack or a boy Lisa. A Swedish children's clothes company has removed the "boys" and "girls" sections in its stores, and the idea of dressing children in a gender-neutral manner has been widely discussed on parenting blogs. This Swedish toy catalog recently decided to switch things around, showing a boy in a Spider-Man costume pushing a pink pram, while a girl in denim rides a yellow tractor.

The Swedish Bowling Association has announced plans to merge male and female bowling tournaments in order to make the sport gender-neutral. Social Democrat politicians have proposed installing gender-neutral restrooms so that members of the public will not be compelled to categorize themselves as either ladies or gents. Several preschools have banished references to pupils' genders, instead referring to children by their first names or as "buddies." So, a teacher would say "good morning, buddies" or "good morning, Lisa, Tom, and Jack" rather than, "good morning, boys and girls." They believe this fulfills the national curriculum's guideline that preschools should "counteract traditional gender patterns and gender roles" and give girls and boys "the same opportunities to test and develop abilities and interests without being limited by stereotypical gender roles."

5   Earlier this month, the movement for gender neutrality reached a milestone: Just days after International Women's Day a new pronoun, *hen*

(pronounced like the bird in English), was added to the online version of the country's *National Encyclopedia*. The entry defines *hen* as a "proposed gender-neutral personal pronoun instead of he [*han* in Swedish] and she [*hon*]." The *National Encyclopedia* announcement came amid a heated debate about gender neutrality that has been raging in Swedish newspaper columns and TV studios and on parenting blogs and feminist websites. It was sparked by the publication of Sweden's first ever gender-neutral children's book, *Kivi och Monsterhund* (Kivi and Monsterdog). It tells the story of Kivi, who wants a dog for "hen's" birthday. The male author, Jesper Lundqvist, introduces several gender-neutral words in the book. For instance the words *mammor* and *pappor* (moms and dads) are replaced with *mappor* and *pammor*.

The free lifestyle magazine, *Nöjesguiden*, which is distributed in major Swedish cities and is similar to the *Village Voice*, recently released an issue using *hen* throughout. In his column, writer Kawa Zolfagari says, "It can be hard to handle the male ego sometimes. I myself tend to get a stinging feeling when a female friend has had it with sexism or has got hurt because of some guy and desperately blurts out some generalisation about men. Sometimes I think 'Hen knows me, hen knows I am not an idiot, why does hen speak that way of all men?' *Nöjesguiden*'s editor, Margret Atladottir, said *hen* ought to be included in the dictionary of the Swedish Academy, the body that awards the Nobel Prize in literature.

Hen was first mentioned by Swedish linguists in the mid-1960s, and then in 1994 the late linguist Hans Karlgren suggested adding *hen* as a new personal pronoun, mostly for practical reasons. Karlgren was trying to avoid the awkward he/she that gums up writing, and invent a single word "that enables us to speak of a person without specifying their gender. He argued that it could improve the Swedish language and make it more nuanced.

Today's *hen* champions, however, have a distinctly political agenda. For instance, Lundqvist's book is published by a house named Olika, which means "different or diverse." Olika only publishes books that "challenge stereotypes and obsolete norms and traditions in the world of literature." Its titles include *100 möjligheter Istället för 2!* ("100 possibilities instead of 2!"), a book for adults who "want to give children more opportunities in gender-stereotyped everyday life"; and *Det var en gång . . . en ritbok!* ("Once upon a time there was . . . a drawing book!"), the first "gender-scrutinizing" drawing book for children that "challenges traditional and diminishing conceptions of girls and boys, men and women."

But not everyone is keen on this political meddling with the Swedish language. In a recent interview for *Vice* magazine, Jan Guillou, one of Sweden's most well-known authors, referred to proponents of *hen* as "feminist activists who want to destroy our language." Other critics believe it can be psychologically and socially damaging, especially for children. Elise Claeson, a columnist and a former equality expert at the Swedish Confederation of Professions, has said that young children can become confused by the suggestion that there is a third, "in-between" gender at a time when their brains and bodies are developing. Adults should not interrupt children's discovery of their gender and sexuality, argues Claeson. She told the Swedish daily, *Dagens Nyheter,* that "gender ideologues" have managed to change the curriculum to establish that schools should actively counter gender roles.

10   Claeson might have a point. The Swedish school system has wholeheartedly, and probably too quickly and eagerly, embraced this new agenda. Last fall, 200 teachers attended a major government-sponsored conference discussing how to avoid "traditional gender patterns" in schools. At Egalia, one model Stockholm preschool, everything from the decoration to the books and toys are carefully selected to promote a gender-equal perspective and to avoid traditional presentations of gender and parenting roles. The teachers try to expose the pupils to as few "gendered expressions" as possible. At Christmastime, the Egalia staff rewrote a traditional song as "*hen* bakes cakes all day long." When pupils play house, they are encouraged to include "mommy, daddy, child" in their imaginary families, as well as "daddy, daddy, child"; "mommy, mommy, child"; "daddy, daddy, sister, aunty, child"; or any other modern combination.

To those who feel gender equality or gender neutrality ought to be intrinsic to a modern society, it probably makes sense to argue for instilling such values at an early age. The Green Party has even suggested placing "gender pedagogues" in every preschool in Stockholm, the Swedish capital, who can act as watchdogs. But of course toddlers cannot weigh arguments for and against linguistic interventions and they do not conceive of or analyze gender roles in the way that adults do.

Ironically, in the effort to free Swedish children from so-called normative behavior, gender-neutral proponents are also subjecting them to a whole set of *new* rules and *new* norms as certain forms of play become taboo, language becomes regulated, and children's interactions and attitudes are closely observed by teachers. One Swedish school got rid of its toy cars because boys "gender-coded" them and ascribed the cars higher status than other toys. Another preschool removed "free playtime" from its schedule because, as a pedagogue at the school put it, when children play freely "stereotypical gender patterns are born and cemented. In free play there is hierarchy, exclusion, and the seed to bullying." And so every detail of children's interactions gets micromanaged by concerned adults, who end up problematizing minute aspects of children's lives, from how they form friendships to what games they play and what songs they sing.

Analyze

1. Discuss the changes Sweden has adopted as it moves toward gender neutrality. How is gender neutrality different from gender equality?
2. What might be some of the benefits of developing the kind of gender-neutral language that Swedish society has created? What are the drawbacks?
3. Are you convinced by the argument that free play leads to "hierarchy, exclusion, and . . . bullying"? What does gender have to do with these issues?

Explore

1. Do you think gender-specific language, particularly names and pronouns, has an impact on the way people are treated? Weigh the advantages and disadvantages of gendered language in a brief essay using personal or anecdotal experience as supporting evidence.
2. The toy industry in the United States is known for marketing gender-specific children's products. Pick a toy company and describe some of their most popular toys. What message about gender roles do these best-sellers convey and how do they influence the development of children's sense of themselves?
3. Is it possible for children to have a natural, engrained sense of gender roles and identity? Or is gender socially constructed? Explore this issue in a research essay by referring to scholarly articles that examine the origins of gender development.

Mark McCormack
Don't Call Me Homophobic:
The Complexity of "That's So Gay"

Mark McCormack is a sociologist of masculinities and sexualities at Durham University, England. His research on the relationship between the impact of declining homophobia on gender expectations and sexual identities in Britain and the United States has garnered considerable media attention. McCormack's work has appeared in several academic journals, as well as online at the *Huffington Post* and *Open Democracy*. *Open Democracy*, where this article was posted on April 30, 2012, encourages a global perspective on principles and the arguments and debates about those principles. In the following article, McCormack challenges the notion that the phrase "That's so gay" always carries negative undertones. He suggests that the immediate impulse to classify it as "homophobic" fails to consider its alternate meanings, as well as the cultural and social contexts in which the phrase is used: "calling people homophobic for saying it is both wrong and counterproductive."

Is it ever acceptable to use language that some might perceive as offensive or discriminatory if the speaker meant no offense?

You wouldn't say "that's so jew" or "that's so black"—that would be so racist—so you should also refrain from saying "that's so gay". This is the end of the argument for many parents, teachers and equality activists. Yet educators find that when they reprimand young people for using this term, they often face an angry rebuttal from kids, who say, "I'm not homophobic, I've got gay friends".

So what are we to make of this defense? The easy answer is to say that the denial of homophobia is a tokenistic rejection of what has become a socially unacceptable attitude. It is certainly the answer given by gay rights group, Stonewall, when they argue that such expressions are evidence of continued homophobia. Yet to automatically assume homophobia in youth, without listening to their perspectives, is to pre-judge them. In my new book, *The Declining Significance of Homophobia*, where I spent a year researching what it means to be a guy in school today, I found that the default position for straight male youth is to be *supportive* of gay rights, *inclusive* of gay peers and *critical* of homophobia.

I have written for *Open Democracy* before about the erosion of homophobia and the softening of masculinity in the sixth forms where I collected data. Then, I argued that the success of the gay rights movement, increased visibility of LGBT people in the media, and the democratizing power of the Internet has resulted in a profound change in heterosexual young people's attitudes toward homosexuality. I argued that this led to a softening of masculinity, with a marked expansion of acceptable gendered behaviours. And as the attitudes of these young men changed, so did the way they talked about homosexuality.

Many of my participants did not use the phrase 'that's so gay', but those who did insisted that it was not homophobic. Their argument rested on two key points. First, they pointed out that there were two meanings for the word gay: one meaning 'rubbish' and the other referring to sexual identity. For example, Alex said, "It isn't meant homophobically. When I say 'that's so gay', I don't mean homosexual". Angered by the suggestion that some might perceive it as homophobic, Lewis was more forceful in response. "What?" he said, "So saying 'it's so gay that I got homework' means that I think my homework is a guy and is attracted to other guys? That doesn't make sense". Zak said, "I say it all the time. But I don't mean anything by it. I've got gay friends".

Many adults who grew up in cultures of intense homophobia will find 5 both parts of this argument to be lacking credibility. After all, when I was at school, "that's so gay" was said by students who also used homophobic pejoratives and bullied students who were camp or feminine. And these young men certainly would not have had gay friends. Yet in today's gay-friendly environment, students use language in new ways, with different meanings. The key issue is that words can have multiple meanings, and we distinguish between them based on the context of their use and the way in which they are spoken.

Consider the following scenario: You are walking along the street, when a friend urgently shouts "DUCK!" What do you do? I suggest that your first reaction is not to look for a bird waddling along the road going 'quack quack'. No, rather, you will lower your head, pretty quickly. 'Duck' has two distinct meanings, and we accept we are able to interpret the meaning by the manner in which it is said. Why is 'gay' so different?

One argument is that the difference lies in the psychological associations 'gay' has with a sexual identity and its history of homophobic oppression. This is a valid point, but the young people in my research did not see it this way. For them, 'gay' has two distinct meanings just like 'duck'. Thus, I argue the difference in interpretation occurs because older generations may not be able to cognitively separate the two. Older generations have not learned to understand the use of the word in the same way and they are judging young people from an adult perspective, without considering their viewpoint. By listening to the voices of the young people in my study, I found they had a sophisticated understanding and use of language. It's just that it's different to our own perspective.

When it comes to understanding the meanings and effects of language, context is all-important. "That's so gay" *can* be homophobic, if it is said with negative intent or within a homophobic environment. But when it is said in settings where sexual minorities are open, out and proud, and heterosexual men are friends with their openly gay peers, it takes on different meanings. In such a context, it is not homophobic. As openly gay student Eddie commented, "I don't mind straight people saying 'that's so gay'. I say it, so it would be hypocritical if I had an issue with it".

Further supporting this dual meaning, I found that heterosexual and gay students bonded through use of the word 'gay'. For example, Max, an openly gay student, was working alongside Cooper and James in an English lesson. While Cooper was doodling in his book, he looked up and asked Max, "Is this really gay what I'm doing?" Max started laughing and said, "Yeah, it's pretty gay". Another time, openly gay student Greg was playing catch with Lewis and some other heterosexual friends. As Lewis threw the ball, it slipped out of his hand, travelling only a few metres. Greg shouted, "Lewis, you're gayer than me!" Such forms of banter strengthened the students' friendship, and also appeared to expunge the negativity from use of the word—consolidating the dual meaning of the word "gay".

10   To be clear, I am not advocating for the use of the phrase "that's so gay". One of the problems with it is that older generations will hear homophobia even where none is intended. Indeed, some of the LGBT students I spoke to felt uncomfortable with the phrase at the same time as they argued it did not connote homophobia. In *The Declining Significance of Homophobia*, I develop a new model for understanding this changing use of language, which highlights how the intent, effect, and environment within which words are used are vitally important in determining whether homophobia is present or not.

My point here is not to defend usage of the phrase. Rather, it is to argue that calling people homophobic for saying it is both wrong and counterproductive. Instead, it is crucial we listen to young people's perspectives. When someone says "that's so gay", we should also consider discussing with them why some people might find it offensive, the history of gay oppression and the value of empathy. By engaging with young people about this issue, we might even find that we learn something about their increasingly positive attitudes toward homosexuality.

Analyze

1. Are there good reasons for gay rights groups to continue to hold the position that the phrase "that's so gay" does reflect homophobic attitudes? What might these reasons be?
2. According to the subjects interviewed by the author, the word "gay" had taken on a new meaning—"rubbish." What does this tell you about the evolution of the word and its associations?
3. What do you think McCormack means by "softening of masculinity" and "expansion of acceptable gendered behaviors?" Consider some specific examples as you respond to this question.

Explore

1. McCormack's research findings reveal a decline in homophobic attitudes among straight male youth. Do your own experiences support this view? Write a brief personal essay that addresses the attitude of your friends, family, or community members toward issues of gender identity and lifestyle choices.
2. Given that gay rights issues are still hotly debated in the United States, can a more nuanced and sophisticated use of language broaden people's perspectives? In a brief essay, explain how language can shape thinking as new and positive meanings can be attached to historically negative words.
3. Examine the impact that the "increased visibility of LGBT people in the media" has had on society. Conduct research on a particular celebrity, popular musician, or a character from a television show or movie and analyze how he or she has contributed to a greater awareness and acceptance of LGBTs.

Forging Connections

1. Does language contribute to gender discrimination, or does the gender gap help create language that perpetuates such discrimination? Examine the ideas, arguments, and examples of some of the authors in this chapter as you develop a response.

2. Writers such as McCormack and Rothschild demonstrate how linguistic changes can occur both formally and informally. Consider how the government, educational institutions, media, and social networks can influence and possibly reverse gender bias.

Looking Further

1. Although women have made significant strides in American politics, the number of elected officials who are female is still not representative of the American population as a whole. What kinds of obstacles do women politicians face as they work to overcome the perception, still held in many quarters, that politics is a man's job? In what ways do women politicians use language to assert their leadership as well as convey their own perspectives and priorities? Conduct research on a female politician and describe the specific language and rhetorical choices she made (or continues to make) that contribute to her success. Refer back to Amy Reiter's argument ("Why Being a Jerk at Work Pays") or Julie Sedivy's "Are You a Mac or a Mac User? How the Language of Identity Persuades" (Chapter 7) to support your observations.

2. In "The Soccer Mom," Jason Davis deplores the cynicism with which politicians deploy figurative language to target (or dismiss) entire demographics, or groups of people. The side effect of the particular image of the "soccer mom," Davis argues, was to create a misleading stereotype of people who actually play and enjoy soccer. How would you define your own particular demographic? In what ways do politicians or advertisers tailor their messages to appeal to your demographic to persuade you to buy something, or to vote a certain way? Refer to Davis's essay as well as Julie Sedivy's "Are You a Mac or a Mac User? How the Language of Identity Persuades" and at least one additional selection in Chapter 7, "Politics and Language," to support your argument.

6 Language & Race

As the Chicana writer Gloria Anzaldua eloquently observed: "Ethnic identity is twin skin to linguistic identity." With these words she captured what we all understand to be an indisputable fact—we literally are what we speak. Yet we know that the reverse holds true as well; our lives, our experiences, and our identities deeply influence the languages we speak. Thus we create language even as we are created by it. The constant interplay between our intuitive sense of self and its expression in spoken and written words helps shape our identities, enables us to understand our place in the world, and reminds us of the formative power of language. All the authors in this chapter are profoundly aware of how their racial and ethnic selves are shaped by the complex nature of the language they use or that is used against them.

They point out that although language can be used to conquer, repress, and forget, it can also be used to survive, adapt, and create. The ideas and experiences they discuss in the chapter illustrate that the expansive capacity of spoken tongues helps people adjust to new lands, new realities, and new experiences regardless of their national, racial, or ethnic identity.

James Baldwin, a preeminent American novelist, essayist, and playwright, and author of *Go Tell It on the Mountain*, places Black English in its historical context and makes a case for its legitimacy in his provocatively titled essay "If Black English Isn't a Language, Then Tell Me, What Is?" In "Speaking Swahili for Kwanzaa?" John McWhorter, an American linguist, wonders whether there is one "ancestral" African language that has the power to unite Americans of diverse African backgrounds. Nigerian-born poet and writer Bassey Ikpi writes defiantly about how the proliferation of myths and misconceptions about Africa has tarnished the continent's image in "Why the Whole 'Poor Africa' Thing Isn't Cool." Tracing the rise of Spanglish as an authentic language in "Spanglish Moves Into Mainstream," Daniel Hernandez, a news assistant for the *Los Angeles Times* its in Mexico City bureau, gives us a glimpse into how the language is actually created. On the other hand, in her essay "Saying 'Adios' to Spanglish" *Newsweek* contributor Leticia Salais takes great pride in transitioning from Spanglish into "proper" Spanish and becoming, from her perspective, truly bilingual. In "Regarding Spanglish," Felipe de Ortego y Gasca, a scholar in residence at Western New Mexico University, critiques Salais's rejection of Spanglish and develops a compelling argument in favor of linguistic diversity. Finally, in "Writing Like a White Guy," Chicago-born poet Jaswinder Bolina ponders a uniquely American problem as his racial and writerly identities collide.

James Baldwin
If Black English Isn't a Language, Then Tell Me, What Is?

Born and raised in Harlem, New York City, James Baldwin (1924–1987) spent most of his adult life abroad, which afforded him the distance he needed to write about his experience in America. In his many celebrated books, including *Go Tell It on the Mountain* (1953) and *Notes of a Native Son* (1955), he examined issues of deeply social relevance: interracial marriages, homosexuality, Black identity, and racial struggles in America. The following article originally appeared in the *The New York Times* in 1979. In it Baldwin asserts that Black English is as legitimate a language as any other because it was formed out of necessity and articulates the experiences of those who speak it.

Are Baldwin's observations about Black English, and language in general, still relevant today? What changes in contemporary American culture support his argument?

The argument concerning the use, or the status, or the reality, of black English is rooted in American history and has absolutely nothing to do with the question the argument supposes itself to be posing. The argument has nothing to do with language itself but with the *role* of language. Language, incontestably, reveals the speaker. Language, also, far more dubiously, is meant to define the other—and, in this case, the other is refusing to be defined by a language that has never been able to recognize him.

People evolve a language in order to describe and thus control their circumstances, or in order not to be submerged by a reality that they cannot articulate. (And, if they cannot articulate it, they *are* submerged.) A Frenchman living in Paris speaks a subtly and crucially different language from that of the man living in Marseilles; neither sounds very much like a man living in Quebec; and they would all have great difficulty in apprehending what the man from Guadeloupe, or Martinique, is saying, to say nothing of the man from Senegal—although the "common" language of all these areas is French. But each has paid, and is paying, a different price for this "common" language, in which, as it turns out, they are not saying, and cannot be saying, the same things: They each have very different realities to articulate, or control.

What joins all languages, and all men, is the necessity to confront life, in order, not inconceivably, to outwit death: The price for this is the acceptance, and achievement, of one's temporal identity. So that, for example, though it is not taught in the schools (and this has the potential of becoming a political issue) the south of France still clings to its ancient and musical Provençal, which resists being described as a "dialect." And much of the tension in the

Basque countries, and in Wales, is due to the Basque and Welsh determination not to allow their languages to be destroyed. This determination also feeds the flames in Ireland for many indignities the Irish have been forced to undergo at English hands is the English contempt for their language.

It goes without saying, then, that language is also a political instrument, means, and proof of power. It is the most vivid and crucial key to identify: It reveals the private identity, and connects one with, or divorces one from, the larger, public, or communal identity. There have been, and are, times, and places, when to speak a certain language could be dangerous, even fatal.

Or, one may speak the same language, but in such a way that one's antecedents are revealed, or (one hopes) hidden. This is true in France, and is absolutely true in England: The range (and reign) of accents on that damp little island make England coherent for the English and totally incomprehensible for everyone else. To open your mouth in England is (if I may use black English) to "put your business in the street": You have confessed your parents, your youth, your school, your salary, your self-esteem, and, alas, your future.

> "Language is . . . a political instrument, means, and proof of power."

5   Now, I do not know what white Americans would sound like if there had never been any black people in the United States, but they would not sound the way they sound. *Jazz*, for example, is a very specific sexual term, as in *jazz me, baby*, but white people purified it into the Jazz Age. *Sock it to me,* which means, roughly, the same thing, has been adopted by Nathaniel Hawthorne's descendants with no qualms or hesitations at all, along with *let it all hang out* and *right on! Beat to his socks* which was once the black's most total and despairing image of poverty, was transformed into a thing called the Beat Generation, which phenomenon was, largely, composed of *uptight*, middle-class white people, imitating poverty, trying to *get down*, to get *with it*, doing their *thing*, doing their despairing best to be *funky*, which we, the blacks, never dreamed of doing—we *were* funky, baby, like *funk* was going out of style.

Now, no one can eat his cake, and have it, too, and it is late in the day to attempt to penalize black people for having created a language that permits the nation its only glimpse of reality, a language without which the nation would be even more *whipped* than it is.

I say that the present skirmish is rooted in American history, and it is. Black English is the creation of the black diaspora. Blacks came to the

United States chained to each other, but from different tribes: Neither could speak the other's language. If two black people, at that bitter hour of the world's history, had been able to speak to each other, the institution of chattel slavery could never have lasted as long as it did. Subsequently, the slave was given, under the eye, and the gun, of his master, Congo Square, and the Bible—or in other words, and under these conditions, the slave began the formation of the black church, and it is within this unprecedented tabernacle that black English began to be formed. This was not, merely, as in the European example, the adoption of a foreign tongue, but an alchemy that transformed ancient elements into a new language: *A language comes into existence by means of brutal necessity, and the rules of the language are dictated by what the language must convey.*

There was a moment, in time, and in this place, when my brother, or my mother, or my father, or my sister, had to convey to me, for example, the danger in which I was standing from the white man standing just behind me, and to convey this with a speed, and in a language, that the white man could not possibly understand, and that, indeed, he cannot understand, until today. He cannot afford to understand it. This understanding would reveal to him too much about himself, and smash that mirror before which he has been frozen for so long.

Now, if this passion, this skill, this (to quote Toni Morrison) "sheer intelligence," this incredible music, the mighty achievement of having brought a people utterly unknown to, or despised by "history"—to have brought this people to their present, troubled, troubling, and unassailable and unanswerable place—if this absolutely unprecedented journey does not indicate that black English is a language, I am curious to know what definition of language is to be trusted.

A people at the center of the Western world, and in the midst of so hostile a population, has not endured and transcended by means of what is patronizingly called a "dialect." We, the blacks, are in trouble, certainly, but we are not doomed, and we are not inarticulate because we are not compelled to defend a morality that we know to be a lie.

The brutal truth is that the bulk of white people in America never had any interest in educating black people, except as this could serve white purposes. It is not the black child's language that is in question, it is not his language that is despised: It is his experience. A child cannot be taught by anyone who despises him, and a child cannot afford to be fooled. A child cannot be taught by anyone whose demand, essentially, is that the child repudiate his experience, and all that gives him sustenance, and enter a limbo in which he will no longer be black, and in which he knows that he can never become white. Black people have lost too many black children that way.

And, after all, finally, in a country with standards so untrustworthy, a country that makes heroes of so many criminal mediocrities, a country unable to face why so many of the nonwhite are in prison, or on the needle, or standing, futureless, in the streets—it may very well be that both the child, and his elder, have concluded that they have nothing whatever to learn from the people of a country that has managed to learn so little.

Analyze

1. What tone of voice does Baldwin adopt in the first paragraph of his essay? Is it effective?
2. According to Baldwin, how did Black English develop in the United States? Analyze the historical references in the essay as you respond.
3. What point is Baldwin trying to make when he draws a connection between language and education?

Explore

1. According to Baldwin, languages arise out of need to survive, to "confront life." Write about a time when you had to be creative about the words you used to adjust to or deal with a particular life situation. How did you go about creating these words? What effect did the words have on the situation?
2. Linguists have debated over whether Black English is a dialect or a language. In a researched essay, examine some of the claims made about Black English and develop your own position as you analyze these claims. Be sure that you understand the difference between a dialect and a language, according to linguistic scholarship.
3. How closely is language tied to racial identity? Interview a friend or acquaintance who speaks a language in addition to English to find out how his or her identity is shaped by that language. How do the words themselves influence your interview subject's sense of self?

John McWhorter
Speaking Swahili for Kwanzaa?

John McWhorter, an American linguist who specializes in language change and language context, is the William T. Simon Fellow at Columbia University. He writes and comments on ethnicity and cultural issues for the Manhattan Institute, a conservative public policy think tank, and is a contributing editor to the Institute's urban policy magazine, *City Journal*. He is also a regular contributor to *The Root*, a leading online source of news and commentary from an African American perspective, founded by Henry Louis Gates, Jr. (a professor of African American studies at Harvard University) in 2008. "Speaking Swahili for Kwanzaa?" was posted on *The Root* in December 2010.

How far back in your lineage do you have to go to find a speaker of what you consider your "ancestral" language? If you speak or understand that language now, how does it connect you to your heritage? If you do not speak or understand it, do you feel a sense of loss?

"**J**ambo" may mean hello in Swahili, but a slave brought to the United States would not have recognized that greeting. There may not have been a single Swahili-speaking African brought to these shores amid the slave trade. If there were any, it was very few.

I get to thinking about this during the holidays as we start hearing about Kwanzaa, which starts the day after Christmas and runs until New Year's Day. Kwanzaa is fine, but it was rooted in a '60s fashion for treating Swahili as black America's "ancestral" language. The choice of Swahili out of the thousands of languages spoken in Africa was innocent, and made a certain sense in that it is a lingua franca across several African nations where hundreds of other languages are spoken.

But the nations where it's spoken are in East Africa. Black Americans' ancestors came mostly from West Africa. And as we all know, Africa is enormous.

The thing is this: To treat Swahili as meaningfully ancestral to black Americans because it's "African" is to lump diverse peoples together in a way that might seem less appropriate if done by whites. Or, imagine someone with roots in Wales cooking borscht and toasting with vodka in salute to their "Europeanness."

5   If black Americans are to seek an ancestral language, shouldn't it be one that our ancestors actually spoke?

Picking just one is tough, though. No one African language is used as common coin from Senegal all the way down to Angola, and slaves brought to the United States came from places throughout this stretch. In the past, I have suggested Mende of Sierra Leone, the language of the songs that some Gullah speakers in South Carolina still remember in fossilized form. But there aren't that many Mende speakers in the U.S., and there are virtually no books in print for learning it (and not many even out of print in libraries). Nigeria's Yoruba is a tempting alternative, presenting neither of those problems. But its speakers were never a significant proportion of slaves brought to the United States.

If there is one West African language that a great many slaves in America spoke and is also realistically available to us, it is Twi. It's spoken in Ghana and is the lingua franca there for speakers of dozens of smaller local languages. Many slaves brought to the New World by the English, or sold to them, were from Ghana, then known famously as the Gold Coast, where Twi was a dominant local language. Just as important, a great many Ghanaians have relocated to the United States in the past 40 years, and therefore, someone trying to pick up some Twi could have native speakers to practice with.

Twi, unlike Swahili, will not throw you with piles of prefixes and nouns divided into seven different classes (which means that Swahili has seven "genders" instead of the two that are hard enough to deal with in French and Spanish). Twi is a language in which, while words are on the short side, the same one means different things, depending on what tone you say it with. This trait is why many African groups can communicate with drums set to different tones.

Say "fa" with a high tone and it means "festival." Say it in a low tone and it means "take." It gets interesting: Say the word for "my" when it's referring to part of your body, and you say it with a low tone. But if you are saying "my (something else)," like an umbrella or a table, then you say it with a high tone.

10   Yet the fact is that Rosetta Stone, Living Language, Berlitz and the other grand language-teaching outfits haven't gotten to Twi the way they have to Swahili. One way we could get their attention is to start buying up what education sources there are. If you just want to get your feet wet, Pimsleur has a neat little intro kit. If you really want to get into it, then get

this offering and remember to get the audio materials, too, since they're the only way to get the knack of the tones.

Imagine black America reuniting with a language that its ancestors actually used.

For the record, the name "Kwame" and the Anancy spider of folklore are Twi. Let's fill things in from there—especially because of one other fact: Twi is actually quite similar grammatically to none other than Chinese. Anyone who has even played with Twi a bit will be in a good position to pick up Mandarin, which will be a handier business decision by the year for *all* Americans.

So, "jambo" means "hello"? Well, in Twi, *biakong, abieng, abiesang* is "one, two, three." Try that on a Ghanaian you know, and watch someone delighted to see you making the acquaintance of a language that at least one of your ancestors probably spoke.

Analyze

1. Why might it be important for Americans of African descent to familiarize themselves with a language closest to their ancestors? What effect might such language-learning have on their identity?
2. McWhorter notes that language teaching programs tend to popularize Swahili rather than Twi. What could be some of the reasons for this?
3. Who is the audience for McWhorter's essay? What message does the essay convey to this audience?

Explore

1. What, from your point of view, is the significance of "ancestral language"? Refer to your own experience as you develop a personal essay that examines the importance of the role of one's native language or mother tongue in a time when we are surrounded by multiple, competing languages.
2. In a brief analytical essay discuss the historical significance and uniqueness of Swahili as an African language. How did it develop? Who was expected to use it? Why?
3. What are some of the features of Black English? How is it different from mainstream or standard written English? Refer to scholarly as well as popular sources as you both describe Black English and address the controversy that surrounds it.

Bassey Ikpi
Why the Whole "Poor Africa" Thing Isn't Cool

Bassey Ikpi is a Nigerian-born poet and performer who grew up in Oklahoma and now lives in Brooklyn, New York. She is the founder of the Siwe Project, a global nonprofit dedicated to promoting mental health awareness throughout the global Black community. The following post appeared on *xoJane. com* in March 2012. Created by former writers and editors of the print magazines *Sassy* and *Jane*, *xoJane* features strong female voices on the topical and cultural issues affecting the lives of young women today. In her essay, Ikpi explores the attitude of pity many people assume toward Africa. For Ikpi, this attitude only serves to perpetuate a sense of helplessness about Africa—a helplessness that does not consider or account for the astonishingly diverse ways in which contemporary Africans live.

What are the most recent news reports you have heard about Africa? How do those reports compare to the kinds of stories you hear reported about other regions of the world?

W hen I was in college, my father admitted that the reason my parents never taught me our native language was because they wanted me to have an "unaccented existence." I don't know if that's even possible.

See, I was born in Ikom, Cross River State in Nigeria. I moved to Stillwater, Oklahoma when I turned 4 in 1980 and lived there until 8th grade. I got a green card when I was 9 years old, but I never felt like going the extra step to become an official American was necessary.

My English as a Second Language class consisted of me repeating dialogue from "Three's Company." My parents were both in grad school when I was younger and they didn't have the time to teach me our original language. Because we weren't Hausa, Igbo or Yoruba (the big three of Nigerian languages) there weren't other Nigerian families that I could learn from. So English was my only option.

Stillwater was a carefully and cautiously racist college town. My father saw how his thick accent kept him from opportunities. He had several degrees but worked as a janitor in the town's movie theaters. He was told time and time again that he was unsuitable for any type of employment that involved him supervising employees.

"They're just not going to understand you."   5

He wanted to make sure his American-raised daughter faced no such barriers.

But despite all that, I owe my "Naija pride" to my father. He taught me and my siblings that above all, we were Nigerian. We waved our green-white-and-green flag high. I made it a point to tell anyone I suspected of being African that I too was Nigerian. Because of my unaccented English, straight hair and general regular American kid demeanor, I was often challenged.

Most first-generation immigrants raised in this country are often reminded to the point of exhaustion about how much sacrifice and responsibility came with privilege of being in America. For better or worse, many of us became high achievers in order to repay our parents for this gift. But, while we were coached to be proud to be in America, we were rarely encouraged to actually be American. For every, "You're so lucky to be here" speech we heard, there was the "but you are a Nigerian. Full stop" disclaimer. My father would say over and over that our duty was to make "the country" proud and he wasn't talking about America. We were to make Nigeria proud.

But not everyone was as proud of our homeland as we were taught to be. Elementary school was the height of the "We Are the World"–Live Aid movement. Images of the poverty-stricken Ethiopian child with the swollen belly and flies crawling across their painfully emaciated faces were the norm. In my majority white community, I was asked about whether or not I felt lucky to have escaped that.

During one rare opportunity to spend the night at a friend's house, her   10
father said something that stuck with me for years.

"You need to eat all your dinner. There are people in Bassey's family who don't get anything to eat. Isn't that right, Bassey?"

I was stunned. The answer was probably yes, but also no. I was too polite to correct an adult, so I nodded shamefully, forcing the dry macaroni and cheese down my throat. And those were the well-meaning comments. I had my share of the nonsensical yet hurtful "African Booty Scratcher" jokes hurled at me.

The recent Stop Kony movement felt no different. I could only stomach about five minutes of the video. It made my face burn. All I could think was, *Where's the rest of the story?* What of the Ugandan people who have been working tirelessly to save child soldiers for a generation? What about the fact that Joseph Kony, at this time, is the least of their worries?

As an African in America, it's difficult for me to dismiss this type of activism as "well-meaning." Critics and supporters of the "movement" are debating whether or not it even matters if the people behind Stop Kony were 100 percent truthful when it came to factual information about the country they're trying to save. Of course it matters. It serves no one, least of all Ugandan people, to muddy the facts of such a complex situation just to manipulate people with charity propaganda.

15   All this reminds me of a story my father once told about an incident in our village of Ugep. When he was a little boy, a group of men from England had come bearing cameras. They were eager to capture the everyday comings and goings of our small village.

In late August, we celebrate an event known as The New Yam Festival. It's like a carnival in other parts of the world. Everyone in the village assumed that the English men were there to take photographs of this rich and beautiful aspect of our culture. But they weren't there for that at all. They were there to push their own agenda.

When they saw anyone who fit their idea of what Africa was, that's when their cameras switched on. They ignored the pageantry of the festival and zoomed in on a few young kids who were naked or dirty. These are the same images that go on to be used to represent all of Africa. Each village, each language, each country, each region gets clumped into this congealed pot of "poor Africa."

That's what Stop Kony is doing—perpetuating the notion that Africa is a place soft enough to land after a guilt trip. Furthering the myth that Africans are constantly in need of saving only serves to dehumanize its people. Nearly three decades after "We Are the World," I'm still fighting misconceptions about the continent.

For those of us who call a country in Africa home, constantly having to battle these misconceptions causes cultural fatigue. It's easier to change your accent and adopt an anglicized name than it is to constantly have your people and their lives invalidated. As happy as I am to live in America, I'm not here because the Nigeria of my birth was some horrid place. And that's true of most immigrants. We shouldn't have to choose between loving where we are and honoring where we came from.

Analyze

1. What idea about the intersection of language and identity does the term "unaccented existence" force you to consider?
2. Ikpi writes about her experiences as a Nigerian growing up in America. What effect did these experiences have on her?
3. What impression of Africa does Ikpi's essay leave on you? Why?

Explore

1. Often the images that the media presents of underdeveloped, non-Western nations are those of poverty and inhumanity. Why do you think this is so? Select a photograph that reflects such a nation and write about what you see in the image. What assumptions do you make about that nation? Why?
2. Africa is a vibrant and culturally diverse continent but, as Ikpi points out, Africans have to "battle misconceptions" about their land. In an essay, critically examine some of your beliefs about an African country by first describing those beliefs, explaining how you developed these beliefs, and finally consulting other sources (both journalistic and academic) to test the validity of those beliefs.
3. View the "KONY 2012" video and write an essay that describes and analyzes the message behind the film. Refer to external sources that shed light on the purpose of the video and its effect on the global community.

Daniel Hernandez
Spanglish Moves Into Mainstream

Daniel Hernandez is a news assistant in the Mexico City bureau of the *Los Angeles Times*, where he contributes to the *World Now* news blog and also to the print edition for news and arts. His interests lie in the fusion and mixing of all cultures, nations, and borders, as evident in much of his writing, including the following article, which originally appeared on *Boston.com* in January 2004. *Boston.com*, which is affiliated with the newspaper the *Boston*

Globe, was launched in October 1995 as a regional news and information site. In this article, Hernandez observes how Spanglish has entered the mainstream, arguing that there is more to the language beyond the mere corruption of English or Spanish words; it also involves complex code-switching. More important, it serves as a vehicle through which young, U.S.-born urban Hispanics are able to bridge two cultures: that of the largely Spanish-speaking world of their parents and the English-speaking world of their peers.

Consider the language you use with your parents or among your family, and the language you use among your friends and peers—in what ways do they differ?

On a muggy Sunday afternoon at the Duenas, mariachi music jumped from a boombox on the concrete in the driveway. The roasted smells of "carne asada" lingered over a folding picnic table, like the easy banter between cousins.

"Le robaron la troca con everything. Los tires, los rines," a visiting cousin said.

Translation: "They robbed the truck with everything. The tires, the rims."

"Quieres watermelon?" offered Francisco Duenas, a 26-year-old housing counselor, holding a jug filled with sweet water and watermelon bits.

5   "Tal vez tiene some of the little tierrita at the bottom."

Translation: "Want watermelon? It might have some of the little dirt at the bottom."

When the Duenas family gathers for weekend barbecues, there are no pauses between jokes and gossip, spoken in English and Spanish. They've been mixing the languages effortlessly, sometimes clumsily, for years, so much so that the back-and-forth is not even noticed.

Spanglish, the fluid vernacular that crosses between English and Spanish, has been a staple in Hispanic life in California since English-speaking settlers arrived in the 19th century. For much of that time, it has been dismissed and derided by language purists—"neither good, nor bad, but abominable," as Mexican writer Octavio Paz famously put it.

The criticism has done little to reduce the prevalence of Spanglish, which today is a bigger part of bilingual life than ever.

10   Now, it's rapidly moving from Hispanic neighborhoods into the mainstream. Spanglish is showing up in television and films, as writers use it to

bring authenticity to their scripts and get racy language past network executives.

Marketers use it to sell everything from bank accounts to soft drinks. Hallmark now sells Spanglish greeting cards. McDonald's is rolling out Spanglish TV spots that will air on both Spanish- and English-language networks.

In academia, once a bastion of anti-Spanglish sentiment, the vernacular is studied in courses with names like "Spanish Phonetics" and "Crossing Borders." Amherst College professor Ilan Stavans published a Spanglish dictionary with hundreds of entries—from "gaseteria" (which means "gas station") to "chaqueta" (for "jacket," instead of the Spanish word "saco"). Stavans said new Spanglish words are created all the time, altering traditional notions of language purity that remained strong a generation ago.

Growing up, "I was told in school that you shouldn't mix the languages," said Stavans, whose college plans to hold the first Conference of Spanglish in April. "There used to be this approach that if you use a broken tongue, you have a broken tongue. It's not about broken tongues; it's about different tongues, and they are legitimate. I think you're going to see a lot more of that."

The rise of Spanglish says a lot about the demographic shifts in California and other states with large Hispanic populations.

Migration movements are traditionally accompanied by the mixing of the native language with the newly acquired one. Within a generation or two, the old-country tongue—whether Polish, Chinese, or Italian—usually recedes.

But unlike immigrants from Europe and Asia, Hispanics are separated from their cultural homeland, not by vast oceans, but by the border with Mexico and the 90 miles between Cuba and the Florida Keys.

The Hispanic immigrant population is constantly replenishing itself. Meanwhile, Spanish-language media, such as industry giants Telemundo and Univision, continue to grow, meaning the immigrants' original language remains a force in the community.

Today, Spanglish is especially popular among young urban Hispanics who are US-born—people like Francisco Duenas, who was raised in South Gate, Calif., lives near downtown Los Angeles, and works in an office in South Los Angeles. Spanglish, he said, allows him to bridge two cultures: the largely Spanish-speaking world of his parents and the English-language world of work and friends.

"I think this Spanglish, it's a way of saying, 'Look, I can do both,'" Duenas said. "And I think here in Los Angeles particularmente, it's not necessary to speak just Spanish or English. No puedes describir la vida aqui (you can't describe life here) without speaking both."

20   As Spanglish spreads, academics and marketers are finding that it's much more complicated than simply forming sentences with both Spanish and English words.

The most basic part of Spanglish is "code-switching," in which someone inserts or substitutes words from one language into another. For instance, Spanglish might sound like "Vamos a la store para comprar milk." ("Let's go to the store to buy milk.")

A more complicated form of Spanglish involves making up words, essentially switching languages within a word itself. It can happen when a word or phrase is translated literally, like "perro caliente" for "hot dog." In other instances, Spanglish is created when an English word is Hispanicized, such as "troca" or "troque" for "truck."

Just where the sudden popularity of code-switching will end is a matter of debate. Jim Boulet Jr., executive director of English First, a lobbying group opposed to bilingual education and which has railed against Spanglish, thinks the boom is a fleeting trend. He and other critics see Spanglish as a form of slang, not a new language.

"There's always been some form of that," he said. "At one point it was Yiddish, then the black urban slang, and now Spanglish is the new 'in' thing."

25   But while academics try to break down Spanglish to understand how it is used, others say it's a code so spontaneous that it's impossible to fully unravel.

It's "a state of mind," said San Diego cartoonist Lalo Alcaraz, whose nationally syndicated strip "La Cucaracha" includes code-switching. "It's the schizophrenia of trying to deal with two worlds in one."

First-generation Hispanics roughly between the ages of 14 and 28 represent the fastest-growing youth demographic, according to the US Census Bureau.

Analyze

1. How does Hernandez's introduction use description, dialogue, and narration to illustrate how Spanglish works? Is this an effective rhetorical strategy?

2. What does the phrase "broken tongue" mean to you? What are the implications of using the word "broken" when it comes to language use?

3. Do you think that Spanglish is a form of slang, or is it instead "a state of mind"? Support your ideas by looking at some of the examples from the essay.

Explore

1. Is Spanglish unique in the way it combines two languages, or are such linguistic innovations common among other immigrant groups as well? What examples can you think of?

2. Examine the role of Spanglish in the Hispanic community. What effects does it have on the individuals who use the language?

3. Code-switching is the subject of much recent research in linguistics. In a researched essay, define "code-switching" within a specific community and draw from at least three academic sources to explain how this community developed its own type of "code-switching."

Leticia Salais
Saying "Adios" to Spanglish

Leticia Salais, a contributor to *Newsweek* magazine, grew up in El Paso, Texas. Eventually she married and moved to Tuscon, where she felt a sense of comfort and freedom among her community of non–Spanish-speaking, non-Hispanic neighbors. In the following article, which first appeared in *Newsweek* in December 2007, Salais describes how she overcame a sense of denial of her heritage and language. Although she taught her first son to speak only English, she switched gears with her second son, speaking only Spanish with him while her husband spoke only English. In so doing, she instilled in her son the value of bilingualism.

Do you believe that by not learning your ancestral tongue you are denying your ancestral heritage?

*N*iños, vengan a comer. My 18-month-old son pops out from behind the couch and runs to his high chair. My 7-year-old has no idea what I just said. He yells out from the same hiding spot: "What did you say?" My older son does not suffer from hearing loss. He is simply not bilingual like his brother, and did not understand that I was telling him to come eat.

Growing up in the poorest neighborhoods of El Paso, Texas, I did everything I could to escape the poverty and the color of my skin. I ran around with kids from the west side of town who came from more-affluent families and usually didn't speak a word of Spanish. I spoke Spanish well enough, but I pretended not to understand it and would not speak a word of it. In school, I refused to speak Spanish even with my Hispanic friends. I wanted nothing to do with it. While they joined Chicano clubs, all I wanted to do was be in the English literacy club. Even at home, the only person to whom I spoke Spanish was my mom, and that's only because she wouldn't have understood me otherwise.

After I got married and moved to Tucson, Ariz., I thought I was in heaven. Though I was actually in the minority, I felt right at home with my Anglo neighbors. When I got pregnant with my first son, I decided that English would be his first language and, if I could help it, his only language. I never spoke a word of Spanish around him, and when his grandparents asked why he did not understand what they were saying, I made excuses. He understands but he's very shy. He understands the language but he refuses to speak it. In reality, I didn't want him to speak it at all.

In a land of opportunity, I soon realized I had made a big mistake. I was denying my son one of the greatest gifts I had to offer: the ability to be bilingual. I saw the need for interpreters on a daily basis in the health field where I worked. Even trips to the grocery store often turned into an opportunity to help someone who could not understand English or vice versa.

5   In the nursing home where I worked, I met a wonderful group of Spanish-speaking individuals, whom I bonded with right away. I longed to speak like they did, enunciating the words correctly as they rolled off their tongues. It sounded like music to me. I started watching Spanish telenovelas and listening to Spanish morning shows on the radio just to improve my vocabulary. I heard words that had never been uttered around me growing up in a border town where people spoke a mixture of Spanish and English. A co-worker from Peru had the most eloquent way of speaking in a language that I recognized as Spanish yet could not fully comprehend. Did I also cheat myself of being bilingual?

Today I can take any English word and, like magic, easily find its Spanish equivalent. I now live a life that is fully bilingual. I hunger for foreign movies from Spain and the interior of Mexico just to challenge myself by trying to guess what all the words mean. I even surprise my mom when she doesn't understand what I'm saying. I know she is proud that I no longer speak Spanglish, and I am no longer embarrassed to speak Spanish in public. I see it as a secret language my husband and I share when we don't want those around us to understand what we are saying. I quickly offer the use of my gift when I see someone struggling to speak English or to understand Spanish, and I quietly say a prayer of thanks that I am not in his or her shoes. I feel empowered and blessed that I can understand a conversation in another language and quickly translate it in my head.

My second son has benefited from my bilingual tongue. I speak only Spanish to him while my husband speaks only English; I am proud to say that his first language was Spanish. My 7-year-old, on the other hand, still has a way to go. I'm embarrassed that I foolishly kept my beautiful native language from him. I hope I have not done irreversible damage. A couple of years ago, I began speaking to him only in Spanish, but I had not yet heard him utter a complete sentence back.

Then, as if my prayers were answered, from behind the couch, I heard a tiny voice exclaim, *Ven, mira esto.* It was my older son instructing his little brother to come look at what he was doing. Maybe I won't be his first bilingual teacher, but it looks like he's already learning from another expert— his bilingual brother. Maybe it's not too late after all.

Analyze

1. Salais considers the ability to speak two or more languages "the greatest gift." Do you agree? Why or why not?
2. Examine the author's experiences as she becomes a truly bilingual person. What other steps can one take to fully immerse oneself in another language?
3. What *might* be some of the personal and social benefits of being bilingual or multilingual?

Explore

1. If you are monolingual (i.e., you speak only one language), write about a time when you had to communicate in a new language. Describe how

you went about learning this language and how you felt about being bilingual.

2. Examine the argument that linguists make in favor of or against bilingualism by analyzing at least two scholarly articles from your library database. How convinced are you by the positions taken by the authors? Why?

3. Consider how educational policies related to bilingualism serve the individual student. What effect does it have on the learner? Refer to legitimate scholarly sources as you respond.

Felipe de Ortego y Gasca
Regarding Spanglish

Felipe de Ortego y Gasca, a professor at Western New Mexico University, is considered to be a principal scholar of the Chicano Renaissance. He teaches courses on the history and philosophy of education, Chicano literature, critical theory, and second-language acquisition. In the following essay, which appeared in April 2008 on *Newspaper Tree*, an online news and culture publication based in El Paso, Texas, Ortego responds to Letitia Salais's article "Saying 'Adios' to Spanglish." To Ortego, Spanglish is the product of "languages [that come] in contact with each other, enriching the discourse of expression."

As America becomes increasingly diverse, who benefits from upholding the notion of a "proper" language? Who benefits from challenging what's "proper"?

I was amused by Leticia Salais' piece on "Saying 'Adiós' to Spanglish" in *Newsweek* (December 17, 2007), in part because it reflects how little so many people know about language and its centrality in human intercourse and development. I was also saddened by the article because it tells us much about dysphoria (alienation) and its effects on self identity.

Leticia Salais caterwauls about the loss of the Spanish language her children have suffered. It turns out, however, that it's not their loss of the Spanish language she bemoans but her own loss of a Spanish she never learned because the *koine* of the Southwest (especially El Paso where she grew up) was Spanglish, that mixture of Spanish and English so prevalent in the borderlands between Mexico and the United States. She explains how she did everything she could to escape the poverty and the color of her skin, having grown up in the poorest neighborhoods of El Paso, Texas.

Poverty is everywhere, and economic circumstances can change that. But the color of one's skin is another story. Dysphorically, however, her escape was from her identity as a "Mexican." In the U.S.– Mexico borderlands, it doesn't matter which side of the border you're from. If you're a Mexican, you're a Mexican. Never mind that Mexican Americans are mexicans with a lower case "m" and Americans with a capital "A." This situation has prevailed for more than 160 years.

Hegemonically subject to the apodictic values of American society since 1848, far too many Mexican Americans have sought escape from the prison of the skin. Being mexican in the Southwest has been like being african (lower case "a") in the South. Salais' escape was to "run around with kids from the west side of town who came from more-affluent families."

Though she spoke Spanish "well enough" she "pretended not to under- 5 stand Spanish and would not speak a word of it." In school she refused to speak Spanish even with her Chicano friends. While they joined Chicano clubs, all she wanted was to be in the English literacy club. At home, the only person she would speak Spanish with was her mother who knew no English.

She married and moved to Tucson, Ariz. where she was in heaven with her Anglo neighbors. When she got pregnant with her first son, she decided that English would be his first language and, if she could help it, his only language. But she saw the error of her decision—she realized the profitability of being bilingual "in a land of opportunity" that needed interpreters in so many of the professions and occupations. But her epiphany went beyond the realization of profitability. It took a turn towards the Spanish of propriety— good Spanish, the enunciation of words rolling correctly off one's tongue. None of that Spanglish.

Spanglish is actually code-switching from English to Spanish or vice-versa in utterances or sentences that may be syntactically English or Spanish, what linguists call "intra-sentential alternation." For example: "Bueno bye" when saying "goodbye" or "Hasta later" for "Until later." Hyperbolically, the permutations are infinite. Spanglish works both ways—bi-directionally; and has a code for its intra-sententialism. In other words, code-switching occurs logically in its sentences. This means that Spanglish has developed a grammar of its own.

Along any boundary between two nations speaking different languages more code-switching occurs than one is aware of, not to mention the phenomenon of borrowed words. Most languages are studded with scads of borrowed words. Early on, English speakers in the Hispanic Southwest made English words out of such Spanish words as "calabozo" turning it into "calaboose." Or "juzgado" into "hoosegow." Or "mesteño" into "mustang" Or "la riata" into "lariat" incorporating the Spanish article "la" into the noun and prefacing it with the English article "the" so that, in effect, the utterance is "the the rope."

Along the contiguous border between Mexico and the United States, English and Spanish fertilize each other. Languages in contact zones are like consenting adults creating words full of pregnant meaning enriched like DNA by the power of their constituents. Both American and Mexican elitists decry the presence and use of Spanglish along the U.S.–Mexico borderlands, calling it bad English and bad Spanish—substandard and ungrammatical.

10   But Spanglish does not emerge just from the U.S.–Mexico borderlands. It emerges where there are communities of Spanish-speaking Hispanics in the United States from any Spanish-speaking country. Cubans in Miami speak Spanglish. Puerto Ricans in New York and Chicago speak Spanglish. Dominicans in DC speak Spanglish. Latinos everywhere in the United States speak Spanglish to varying degrees.

The linguistic phenomenon of Spanglish is part of the *efficient continuity* of language, that is, in their evolution, all languages tend toward more efficient articulations and expressions. This is what accounts for abbreviations in English like "What'll you have?" for "What will you have?" "I'll" for "I will." Or the abbreviations in text-messaging. In part, this *efficient continuity* explains how languages change. How Latin became French and Spanish and Italian and Portuguese and Romanian. Unfortunately, some English language purists pooh-pooh these notions, labeling instead the Spanglish phenomena as bad English and bad Spanish mixed together.

As a native speaker of Spanish and a professor of English for more than five decades, I speak Spanglish—and that's not a sign of bad English and bad Spanish mixed together. It's what happens with languages in contact with each other, enriching the discourse of expression. That mixture does not impoverish either language. Linguistically we must come to terms with the phenomenon that is Spanglish before it becomes a *cause célèbre*.

In Spanglish I can say "*voy al show*" which means "I'm going to the movies." Using the word "show" doesn't mean I don't know the Spanish word "*cine*" or "*vistas*"—it means I have linguistic options of using either the English word "show" or the Spanish words "*cine*" or "*vistas*." This is the same process as using a French word, say, in an English expression, such as "*cause célèbre*." This is binary phenomena. A good example of binary phenomena is Ezra Pound who sprinkled his poetry with foreign words and expressions without bothering to explain them to the reader. Language is an amalgamation.

Even today, as when I was a child in San Antonio, Texas, one hears the judgment of the *populi* about Chicanos and their language. That *vox populi* contends that Chicanos don't speak English and they don't speak Spanish. The populi explain that what they speak instead is a bastardization of English and Spanish. Some commentators of that phenomenon have gone so far as to suggest that Chicanos are "alingual"—that is, they are without language.

The distinction between Spanglish and Tex-Mex (a corollary manifestation of languages in contact) is that the latter is a process of taking an English word and transforming it ostensibly into a Spanish word. The English word "truck," for example, is transformed into "troca" just as the English word "muffler" is transformed into the word "mofle." Both "troca" and "mofle" are not Spanish words per se, but part of the growing Spanglish lexicon which is well understood by "bilingual" residents along the U.S.–Mexico border. Interestingly, words like "troca" and "mofle" have migrated into Mexico and beyond and have become part of the extended lexicon of the borderlands such that in Mexico both words are used with aplomb.

Many if not all Chicanos use Hispanicized English words in their speech, not because they don't have a lexicon of standard English but because it's easier to use Hispanicized English words in their utterances. For example, in Spanish "to type" is "escribir a maquina." With a little bit of "linguistic tweaking" the English language word "type" becomes "taipear," the Hispanicized version, considerably shorter and more efficient than "escribir a maquina"—to write with a machine.

The same is true of the word "parquear"—for "to park" instead of the Spanish word "estacionar." Here it's not the length of the Spanish word that engenders preference for the creolized word "parquear" but popularity of the word "park." Preference for "parquear" is not because Chicanos don't know the Spanish word "estacionar." What is operational in that preference is the density of usage for the word "parquear." It has become "la moda"—the mode of parlance among Chicanos.

Creation of a "language" springing from two languages in contact is not uniquely a Chicano phenomenon. Creation of "blended nouns and verbs" occur everywhere languages "live" side by side or in proximity to each other. Because of the historical presence of American troops in Korea, Koreans have added the word "hom-reon" for "homerun" to their lexicon in the same way that Mexicans added the word "hon-ron" for "homerun" to their lexicon. For "hotcakes," Koreans say "hat-kei-i-keu" just as speakers of Spanglish use "keke" for "cake."

To their lexicon, Chicanos have added words like "wachate" for "watch yourself." Many Chicanos use the word "dematriation" as the English version of "desmadre" (riot) as Ricardo Sanchez, the Chicano poet, used the word. In Korea these kinds of hybrid words are called "Konglish" which also reflects words from Japanese.

20   In English we interject many Spanish words into our speech, words like enchilada, tacos, tamales, and tortillas as well as plaza, patio, and barbeque (from barbacoa). This is not bad English, just the way of the word. Our speech becomes more colorful and indicates just how languages syncretize. As a consequence of the American presence in Japan, the Japanese word for "rifle" has become "rifu." This is not bad Japanese, just an indication of how English has influenced Japanese.

In my Chaucer classes, I point out that Chaucer spoke more French than English, and we discuss how much French there is in the Canterbury Tales, especially in "The Wife of Bath's Tale." When we speak of Chaucer's language, we do not call it "Frenglish." Nor do we call Chaucer's use of "axe" for "ask" or "na moe" for "no more" bad English. English did not become English until after it was fertilized by 400 years of French. And Spanish did not become Spanish until after it was fertilized by 700 years of Arabic. In like fashion, Latin became French after consorting with the Gallic languages of Gaul; and in Iberia, Latin transmogrified into Spanish after consorting with the Iberian language of Hispania (Roman designation for Spain).

Spanglish is a battle over symbols. The symbolic values of English are changing and will continue to change in the cauldron of linguistic diversity. The English language of today is not the English language of 200 years ago. The speakers of English in 1807 would be hard pressed to understand today's English just as the speakers of English in the year 2207 will be hard pressed to understand today's English. [The language of the United States is nominally English, but it has evolved sufficiently different from the English of England that it merits calling it "the American language" as H.L. Mencken did.]

There is no accurate count of the number of Americans of Mexican descent in the United States, but the most consistent figures presently suggest a population of approximately 30 million, two-thirds of the 45 million American Hispanics, most of whom in their bilingual identity speak Spanglish as well as English and Spanish with varying degrees of fluency. Speakers of Spanglish represent a linguistic community.

It's important to bear in mind that characterizing the speech of that linguistic community as "Spanglish" is a pejoration reflecting attitudes of linguistic imperialism couched in terms of "good English" and "good Spanish." It's this linguistic imperialism that internalizes in Mexican Americans the notion that Spanglish is an inferior language. This internalization promotes dysphoria.

On a recent morning talk-show in El Paso, Texas, where the topic was corruption in the El Paso County government, a Mexican American called in to the show, commenting that the corruption was because the county government had so many Mexicans. Adding that "as everybody knows all Mexicans are corrupt," to which the host objected strenuously. The point here is how dysphoria alienates Mexican Americans from themselves.

This is the dysphoria that drove Leticia Salais to reject Spanglish and the culture that spawned it believing that no good could come of being identified as part of that culture, and certainly no good in speaking its language since it is not "proper English" nor "proper Spanish." Thus, fleeing from one dysphoric situation, Salais has embraced an equally dysphoric solution, going from the frying pan into the fire, so to speak.

What is happening in Spanglish is what happened to Spanish as it emerged from Latin and as other languages emerged from Latin also. This phenomenon is not limited to romance languages. Though considered a

Germanic language, English is also a product of its Latin roots both as a province of Rome for 500 years and as a captive nation of the French speaking Normans for 400 years. Chaucer was part of the latter milieu, working at literature in the forge of an emerging language, much the way many Chicano writers have been working at the forge of the emerging languages of Chicano English and Chicano Spanish.

Current views about language, culture, and behavior are still influenced by historical and traditional concepts. In most instances, these concepts insufficiently explain the intricate relationship between language, culture, and behavior. Ergo the public opprobrium towards Spanglish. And also the current public opprobrium in the United States towards Spanish in general and at large, producing the backlash of English Only attitudes. Unfortunately these attitudes tend to reinforce existing stereotypes about Spanish-speaking American Hispanics and to perpetuate a variety of psycho-social propositions about Mexican Americans in particular. Historically, until 1970 one such proposition identified Spanish-speaking Mexican American children in the public schools of the Hispanic Southwest as retarded.

This was the state of Mexican American children in the American educational system as I pointed out in my cover story on "Montezuma's Children" (*The Center Magazine*, November/December, 1970). Forty years ago Mexican American children were considered retarded because they could not speak English. Though research since then has established that that psycho-social sentiment was engendered because they were "Mexicans."

30   There is no "proper Spanish" just as there is no "proper English." There is the Spanish and English of usage and convention. We tend to identify one brand of English as "standard English" and one brand of Spanish as "standard Spanish" in hopes of creating some kind of national cohesion via language. Unfortunately, however, language is not the glue of national unity. Across the globe there is internecine conflict between peoples who speak the same language. Respect for the individual regardless of the language he or she may speak and the way it's produced (accent) is the key to national unity. African Americans, for example, speak English (American English) yet have remained only marginally part of the national polity.

Leticia Salais has not achieved an epiphany. She is now ensconced in a linguistic ivory tower passing judgment on those who speak Spanglish. She prefers the mellifluous sounds of Peruvian Spanish, as she indicates in her

Newsweek piece, rather than the cacophonous sounds of Spanglish, failing to realize that in Peru the Spanish language has undergone a comparable evolution to the Spanish language in Mexico where the indigenous languages in contact with Spanish have influenced each other and produced a Spanish unique to Peru. A Spanish that is not Peninsular Spanish.

While I was an undergraduate at Pitt in Comparative Studies (languages and literatures), many students from Latin America would exclaim that their country had preserved *el mero castellano*—the pure or true Spanish. The most notorious in this regard were Argentines and Colombians, neither aware of how phonologically different their Spanish was from Peninsular Spanish. In Spain I heard many varieties of Spanish.

At the beginning of my linguistic studies at Pitt I imagined code-switching as a dual track in the brain where at appropriate places a synaptic spark enabled the switch from, say, Spanish to English or English to Spanish, much like switching trains on tracks. This was also when I accepted the proposition that one thought in specific languages. We now consider that "thinking in a language" involves coded electro-chemical impulses that are translated into aural signals at a voicing point. We don't think in languages but in electro-chemical codes. Consider that when we press the letter key for "R" on a computer keyboard, the letter "R" is not traveling from the keyboard to the computer screen but a coded form of the letter and transformed into print at an appropriate place in the transmission process: the monitor or the page.

I'm reminded here of how many times I've heard non-Spanish speakers in the U.S.–Mexico borderlands express a desire to learn Spanish, adding the caveat: not "kitchen Spanish," explaining that "kitchen Spanish" is the Spanish the maids use. They want to learn Castillian Spanish. Shades of the Mexican-Dixon Line! In the U.S.–Mexico borderlands the maids are almost always Mexican as are the gardeners and those who work at the jobs of last resort.

Linguistic truths give way to invidious fallacies and, before long, Mexican   35
Americans are considered once more as lazy, unambitious, stupid and retarded because they fail to meet the linguistic standards of the English language.

Analyze

1. Why does Ortego feel compelled to respond to Leticia Salais's essay? Does he fully explain why he is both "amused" and "saddened" by her essay?

2. What is "efficient continuity"? Explain the meaning of the term by referring to some of Ortego's examples.
3. Ortego claims that "the English language of today is not the English language of 200 years ago." What kind of evidence is used to support this claim? Do you find the evidence convincing? Why?

Explore

1. Throughout his essay Ortego uses words ("hegemony" and "apodictic," among others) that might be unfamiliar to you. Write a response that reflects the effect of Ortego's diction on your understanding of his essay. Is he writing for the same audience as Leticia Salais?
2. What are the implications of privileging "proper Spanish" over Spanglish? What does this have to do with "linguistic imperialism?" Consider some of your preconceptions about how language *should* be used and how it is *actually* used. Refer to examples of patterns of word usage you've noticed in your community, on television, or on social networks.
3. Respond to Ortego's claim that "language is not the glue of national unity." Test this claim by considering the term "national unity." What does it mean and what does it have to do with what and how one speaks? Refer to published sources as you explore how different languages and dialects might affect those who use them.

Jaswinder Bolina
Writing Like a White Guy

Chicago-born poet Jaswinder Bolina teaches creative writing at Lesley University. He is the author of two collections of poetry: *Phantom Camera* (2013), which won the 2012 Green Rose Prize; and *Carrier Wave* (2007), which won the 2006 Colorado Prize for Poetry. "Writing Like a White Guy" appeared in November 2011 on the website of the Poetry Foundation, an independent literary foundation established in 1941 that publishes *Poetry* magazine and seeks to enhance the standing of poetry within American culture. In an interview with *Mandala Journal* (2011–2012) about "Writing Like a White Guy," Bolina noted that, "When I do manage to write anything about my background, it isn't because I mean to at first. It's because in the effort to write something new, the phrases and descriptions I'm working on start to take up orbit around the subject of race. It isn't intentional."

In what ways is it powerful to draw on your own identity and personal experience when writing about social or political issues?

My father says I should use a pseudonym. "They won't publish you if they see your name. They'll know you're not one of them. They'll know you're one of us." This has never occurred to me, at least not in a serious way. "No publisher in America's going to reject my poems because I have a foreign name," I reply. "Not in 2002." I argue, "These are educated people. My name won't be any impediment." Yet in spite of my faith in the egalitarian attitude of editors and the anonymity of book contests, I understand my father's angle on the issue.

With his beard shaved and his hair shorn, his turban undone and left behind in Bolina Doaba, Punjab—the town whose name we take as our own—he lands at Heathrow in 1965, a brown boy of 18 become a Londoner. His circumstance then must seem at once exhilarating and also like drifting in a lifeboat: necessary, interminable. I imagine the English of the era sporting an especially muted and disdainful brand of racism toward my alien father, his brother and sister-in-law, toward his brother-in-law and sister, his nieces and nephews, and the other Indians they befriend on Nadine Street, Charlton, just east of Greenwich. The sense of exclusion arrives over every channel, dull and constant.

At least one realtor, a couple of bankers, and a few foremen must have a different attitude. One white supervisor at the industrial bakery my father labors in invites him home for dinner. The Brit wants to offer an introduction to his single daughters. He knows my father's a hard worker, a trait so commonly attributed to the immigrant it seems sometimes a nationality unto itself, and maybe the quietude of the nonnative speaker appeals to the man's sense of civility. As a result he finds my father humble, upstanding, his complexion a light beach sand indicative of a vigor exceeding that of the pale English suitors who come calling. In my imagination, my father's embarrassed and placid demeanor, his awkward formality in that setting, is charming to the bashful, giggly daughters, and this impresses the supervisor even further. But nothing much comes of that evening. My father never visits again. He marries my mother, another Sikh Punjabi also, a few years later, but that event is evidence that one Englishman considered my father the man, not my father the "paki."

When he moves to hodgepodge Chicago nine years after arriving in England, he becomes another denizen of the immigrant nation, the huddled masses. He might be forgiven for thinking he will not be excluded here, but he isn't so naïve. America in 1974 is its own version of the UK's insular empire, though the nature of its exclusion is different, is what we call institutional. He knows that in America nobody should be rejected, not unabashedly and without some counterfeit of a reason, but all my father's nearly three decades as a machinist at the hydraulics plant near the airport teach him is that economies boom and economies bust, and if your name isn't "Bill" or "Earl" or "Frank Malone," you don't get promoted. You mind the machines. "Bills" and "Earls" supervise. "Frank" is the name the bosses go by, all of them hired after my dad but raised higher. So when my father suggests I use a pseudonym, he's only steadying my two-wheeler, only buying me a popsicle from the cart at Foster Avenue Beach. This is only an extension of covering my tuition, of paying my room and board.

5   At the time, I'm only a year or so into an MFA. I stop by the office of a friend, an older white poet in my department. Publication to me feels impossible then, and the friend means to be encouraging when he says, "With a name like Jaswinder Bolina, you could publish plenty of poems right now if you wrote about the first-generation, minority stuff. What I admire is that you don't write that kind of poetry." He's right. I don't write "that kind" of poetry. To him, this is upstanding, correct, what a poet ought to do. It's indicative of a vigor exceeding that of other minority poets come calling. It turns out I'm a hard worker too. I should be offended—if not for myself, then on behalf of writers who do take on the difficult subject of minority experience in their poetry—but I understand that my friend means no ill by it. To his mind, embracing my difference would open editorial inboxes, but knowing that I tend to eschew/exclude/deny "that kind" of subject in my poetry, he adds, "This'll make it harder for you." When, only a few months later, my father—who's never read my poems, whose fine but mostly functional knowledge of English makes the diction and syntax of my work difficult to follow, who doesn't know anything of the themes or subjects of my

poetry—tells me to use another name, he's encouraging also. He means: Let them think you're a white guy. This will make it easier for you.

The one thing I least believe about race in America is that we can disregard it. I'm nowhere close to alone in this, but the person I encounter far more often than the racist—closeted or proud—is the one who believes race isn't an active factor in her thinking, isn't an influence on his interaction with the racial Other. Such blindness to race seems unlikely, but I suspect few of us entirely understand why it's so improbable. I'm not certain either, but I've been given some idea. At a panel discussion in 2004, a professor of political philosophy, Caribbean-born with a doctorate from the University of Toronto, explains that he never understood why the question in America is so often a question of race. A scholar of Marxist thinking, he says in nearly every other industrialized nation on Earth, the first question is a question of class, and accordingly class is the first conflict. He says it wasn't until he moved to the United States in the early '70s—about the same time my father arrived—that he intellectually and viscerally understood that America is a place where class historically coincides with race. This, he says, is the heaviest legacy of slavery and segregation.

To many immigrants, the professor and my father included, this conflation between success and skin color is a foreign one. In their native lands, where there exists a relative homogeneity in the racial makeup of the population or a pervasive mingling of races, the "minorities" of America are classed based on socioeconomic status derived from any number of factors, and race is rarely, if ever, principal in these. You can look down on anybody even though they share your skin color if you have land enough, wealth enough, caste and education enough. It's only arriving in England that the Indian—who might not even recognize the descriptor "Indian," preferring instead a regional or religious identity to a national one—realizes anyone resembling him is subject to the derision "coolie." It's only in America that such an immigrant discovers any brown-skinned body can have a "camel fucker" or a "sand nigger" hurled at him from a passing car—a bit of cognitive dissonance that's been directed at me on more than one occasion. The racially African but ethnically Other philosophy professor understands the oddness of this as well as anyone. He explains that in the United States, as anywhere, the first question remains a question of class, but the coincidence between class and color makes the first American social conflict a conflict of race. As such, for the racial immigrant and his offspring, racial difference need be mitigated whenever possible, if only to lubricate the cogs of class mobility: nearer to whiteness, nearer to wealth.

If the racial Other aspires to equal footing on the socioeconomic playing field, he is tasked with forcing his way out of the categorical cul-de-sac that his name and appearance otherwise squeeze him into. We call the process by which he does this "assimilation." Though the Latin root here—shared with the other word "similar"—implies that the process is one of becoming absorbed or incorporated, it is a process that relies first on the negation of one identity in order to adopt another. In this sense, assimilation is a destructive rather than constructive process. It isn't a come-as-you-are proposition, a simple matter of being integrated into the American milieu because there exists a standing invitation to do so. Rather, assimilation first requires refuting assumptions the culture makes about the immigrant based on race, and in this sense assimilation requires the erasure of one's preexisting cultural identity even though that identity wasn't contingent upon race in the first place.

The first and perhaps essential step in assimilating into any culture is the successful adoption of the host country's language. What's unusual in America is that this is no different for the immigrant than for the native-born nonwhite. This is most obvious when I consider African Americans, whose language is variously described as "urban" (as in "of the slums of the inner city"), "street" (as in "of the gutter"), and "Ebonic" (as in "of ebony, of blackness"). These descriptors imply that whatever it is, black vernacular isn't English. Rather, it's "broken English," which is of course what we also call the English of the nonnative speaker. I'm tempted to categorize so-called "countrified" or "redneck" dialects similarly, except I remember that any number of recent U.S. presidents and presidential candidates capable in that vernacular are regarded as more down-to-earth and likable rather than less well-spoken or intelligent. It seems that such white dialect serves as evidence of charisma, charm, and folksiness rather than of ignorance.

10   In 2007, the eventual vice president campaigning in the primary election against the eventual president says, "I mean, you got the first mainstream African American who is *articulate* and bright and *clean* and a nice-looking guy. I mean, that's a storybook, man." The ensuing kerfuffle is almost entirely unsurprising. Though the white candidate believes he's merely describing the candidate of color and doing so with ample objectivity and perhaps even with generosity, the description implies that the black man's

appearance and eloquence constitute an exception to his blackness, which is a function of genetics, which only further suggests that the black candidate is an exception to his basic nature. The implication is that he is being praised for his approximate whiteness. Not shockingly, this very conflation of his eloquence with white racial identity leads pundits in another context to ask the obnoxious question, "But is he black enough?" The conundrum the candidate faces is that he need be an exceptional speaker and writer, but part of the "exceptional" here is the idea that he's an "exception" to his race. He has co-opted the language of whiteness. If he then neglects to take on the subject of race with that language, with the fierce urgency of now, he might further be accused of rejecting his own racial identity. Is he a candidate or a black candidate? If it's the former, he might not be "black enough." If it's the latter, he can't win.

In a country where class and race structurally overlap, what we call "standard" English reflexively becomes the English of whiteness rather than simply the English of the educated or privileged classes. When I adopt the language I'm taught in prep school, in university, and in graduate school, I'm adopting the English language, but in the States, that language is intrinsically associated with one race over any another. By contrast, in the England of history, the one prior to the more recent influx of immigrants from its imperial colonies, Oxford English is spoken by subjects as white as those who bandy about in Cockney. Adeptness of language usage isn't a function then of melanin but of socioeconomic location. Color isn't the question; class is. Unlike the Cockney of England or the dialects of India, none of which are contingent upon racial difference, alternate dialects in American English are inherently racialized. Assimilation in America then comes to mean the appropriation of a specific racial identity by way of language. The conundrum for the poet of color becomes no different than the one that faces the candidate of color: Am I a writer or a minority writer?

The day I'm born, my father engages in the American custom of handing out cigars to the "Bills" and "Earls" and "Franks" of the factory floor, even though he has never smoked in his life. Smoking is anathema to his Sikh Punjabi identity. Drinking, on the other hand, is most certainly not, and he gets gleefully and mercilessly drunk with his brothers at home. He boasts everywhere, "My son will be president." He believes it. Twenty-four years later, in 2002, when he counsels me to use a pseudonym, he knows I'm already adept in the language. I've been educated in it, and in spite of all his diligence and intelligence, this is a key he's never been given. I talk like them. I write like them. I'm an agile agent in the empire so long as nobody grows wise. He no longer expects a presidency, but he sees no limit to potential success in my chosen field, except for the limits placed on me by my racial difference from the dominant culture. He doesn't consider the possibility that I write about race in my work, that I might want to embrace the subject, because he knows, like the candidate of black Kenyan and white Kansan bloodlines, I've been conditioned to resist making race the essential issue.

And it's true. The manner with which I avoid the subject of race in my first book is nearly dogmatic. Race is a subject I don't offer any attention to. To do so would seem only to underscore my Otherness, which would only result in the same sorts of requisite exclusions I experienced growing up in mostly white schools and neighborhoods. Assimilation in those circumstances isn't a choice so much political as it is necessary. Some remnant of a survival instinct kicks in, and one's best efforts are directed at joining rather than resisting the herd. To be racialized is to be marginalized. When another Asian kid joins the playground, we unwittingly vie to out-white each other. This tactic I learned from practice but also from my immigrant family. When your numbers are few, assimilation is the pragmatic gambit.

It's not something that we engage in without a queasy feeling. When my father suggests I Wite-Out my name, he's entirely aware that he's suggesting I relinquish the name he and my mother gave me. This isn't an easy thing, but growing up, I've never been kept from doing what the "American" kids do—though I'm born here and though my parents have long been citizens, "American" remains a descriptor my family uses to signify whiteness. Like the white kids, I join the Cub Scouts and play football at recess, I attend birthday parties at my American classmates' houses and go to junior high socials. In high school, after years of elementary school mockery, I attempt—not unlike the young Barry Obama—to anglicize my name, going by "Jason" instead, a stratagem that those who become my friends quickly reject after only a few weeks. I go to the homecoming dance. I go to the prom. I stay out past curfew and grow my hair long. I insist that my mother close all the bedroom doors when she cooks so my clothes don't reek of cumin and turmeric. I resist any suggestion that I study the sciences in order to prepare for a career in medicine or engineering. I never meet an Indian girl; there aren't any in the philosophy and English departments I'm a member of anyway. My parents know I'm bereft of their culture. They must at times feel a lucid resentment, a sense of rejection and exclusion. Their son has become one of the English-speakers, as "Frank" or "Bill" to them as any American. But this, they know, is necessary. If the first generation is to succeed here, it's by resisting the ingrained cultural identity and mores of its immigrant forebears. If their son is to become president, my parents know it won't happen while he's wearing a turban. This is why they never keep me from engaging American culture, though it quickly comes to supplant their own. Assimilation is pragmatic, but pragmatism calls for concessions that compound and come to feel like a chronic ache.

It's because of the historical convergence of race and class in America 15 that we conflate the language of the educated, ruling classes with the language of a particular racial identity. If I decouple the two, as I might be able to do in another nation, I realize that what's being described isn't the language of whiteness so much as the language of privilege. When I say "privilege" here, I mean the condition of not needing to consider what others are forced to consider. The privilege of whiteness in America—particularly male, heteronormative whiteness—is the privilege to speak from a blank slate, to not need to address questions of race, gender, sexuality, or class except by choice, to not need to acknowledge wherefrom one speaks. It's the position of no position, the voice from nowhere or from everywhere. In this, it is Godlike, and if nothing else, that's saying something.

To the poet, though, the first question isn't one of class or color. The first question is a question of language. Poetry—as Stéphane Mallarmé famously tells the painter and hapless would-be poet Edgar Degas—is made of words, not ideas. However, to the poet of color or the female poet, to the gay or transgendered writer in America, and even to the white male writer born outside of socioeconomic privilege, a difficult question arises: "Whose language is it?" Where the history of academic and cultural institutions is so dominated by white men of means, "high" language necessarily comes to mean the language of whiteness and a largely wealthy, heteronormative maleness at that. The minority poet seeking entry into the academy and its canon finds that her language is deracialized/sexualized/gendered/classed at the outset. In trafficking in "high" English, writers other than educated, straight, white, male ones of privilege choose to become versed in a language that doesn't intrinsically or historically coincide with perceptions of their identities. It's true that minority poets are permitted to bring alternative vernaculars into our work. Poets from William Wordsworth in the preface to *Lyrical Ballads* to Frank O'Hara in his "Personism: a manifesto" demand as much by insisting that poetry incorporate language nearer to conversational speech than anything overly elevated. Such calls for expansions of literary language in conjunction with continuing experiments by recent generations of American poets are transforming the canon for sure, but this leaves me and perhaps others like me in a slightly awkward position. I don't possess a vernacular English that's significantly different from that of plain old Midwestern English. As such, it seems I'm able to write from a perspective that doesn't address certain realities about myself, and this makes me queasy as anything. The voice in my head is annoyed with the voice in my writing. The voice in my head says I'm disregarding difference, and this feels like a denial of self, of reality, of a basic truth.

It isn't exactly intentional. It's a product of being privileged. In the 46 years since my father left Punjab, the 40 or so years since my mother left also, my parents clambered the socioeconomic ladder with a fair amount of middle-class success. We're not exactly wealthy, but I do wind up in prep school instead of the public high school, which only isolates me further from those with a shared racial identity. Later I attend university, where I'm permitted by my parents' successes to study the subjects I want to study rather than those that might guarantee future wealth. I don't need to become a doctor or a lawyer to support the clan. I get to major in philosophy and later attend graduate school in creative writing. Through all of this, though I experience occasional instances of bigotry while walking down streets or in bars, and though I study in programs where I'm often one of only two or three students of color, my racial identity is generally overlooked or disregarded by those around me. I've become so adept in the language and culture of the academy that on more than one occasion when I bring up the fact of my race, colleagues reply with some variation of "I don't think of you as a minority." Or, as a cousin who's known me since infancy jokes, "You're not a minority. You're just a white guy with a tan." What she means is that my assimilation is complete. But she can't be correct. Race is simply too essential to the American experience to ever be entirely overlooked. As such, I can't actually write like a white guy any more than I can revise my skin color. This, however, doesn't change the fact that if a reader were to encounter much of my work not knowing my name or having seen a photograph of me, she might not be faulted for incorrectly assigning the poems a white racial identity. This is a product of my language, which is a product of my education, which is a product of the socioeconomic privilege afforded by my parents' successes. The product of all those factors together is that the writing—this essay included—can't seem to help sounding *white*.

Recently, I was invited to give a few poetry readings as part of a literary festival taking place in a rural part of the country. I borrow my father's compact SUV and let its GPS guide me for a few days on the road. I spend afternoons and evenings reading poems with local and visiting writers in front of small audiences at community centers and public libraries. The audiences are largely made up of kind, white-haired, white-skinned locals enthusiastic to hear us read from and speak about our work, even when they've never heard of most of us. They at least appreciate poetry, a rarity I'm grateful for. During the introductions that preface each event, even the organizers who've invited me have difficulty getting my name right, and in one school library, I enunciate it over and over again. I say, "*Jas* as in the first part of *justice*; *win* as in the opposite of defeat; *der*, which rhymes with *err*, meaning to be mistaken." I say, "JasWINder," lilting the second syllable, and smile as about a dozen audience members mouth each syllable along with me until they feel they have it right. When they do, they grin broadly. After each event, I chat with them one or two at a time, and I do my best to reflect their warmth. They're complimentary about the work, and though I don't expect they're a demographic that'll especially like my poems—even when you write poems like a white guy, you might not be writing poems everyone will like—the compliments are earnest.

Still, in all this pleasantness, the awkward moment occurs more than once. It's some variation on a recurring question I get in town after town. The question usually comes up as a matter of small talk while I'm signing a book or shaking someone's hand. No one delivers it better, with so much beaming warmth and unwitting irony, than the woman who says she enjoyed my poems very much and follows this quickly with an admiring "You're so Americanized, what nationality are you?" She doesn't pick up on the oxymoron in her question. She doesn't hear the hint of tiredness in my reply. "I was born and raised in Chicago, but my parents are from northern India." Once more, I ought to be offended, but I'm not really. Hers is an expression of curiosity that's born of genuine interest rather than of side-show spectacle. I'm the only nonwhite writer at the events I participate in. I'm the only one who gets this question. It makes me bristle, but I understand where it comes from.

20   After my brief tour is over, I make the 500-mile trip to suburban Chicago
to return the Toyota to my parents. I eat dinner at home, and after, my
father drops me back in the city. Invariably, the trip down the Kennedy
Expressway toward the skyline makes him nostalgic for his early, underpaid
days in small apartments on the North Side, his city long before it became
my city. He tells a story or two, and we talk as usual about the news, politics, the latest way my uncle annoys him. He goes on a while before his attention returns to the moment, and he asks how my trip went. I tell him it
went well. I say the audiences were kind and the drives were long. I say, out
there, the country looks like a painting of itself. I don't mention what
the woman asked, the recurring question echoed by others. "You're so
Americanized, what nationality are you?" It won't matter that she asked it
while eagerly shaking my hand. It won't matter that she asked while asking
me also to sign a copy of my book for her. It won't matter that she offered
her gratitude that I'd come all that way to read in her hamlet on the out-
skirts of America. Though she might have meant the opposite, he'll hear
the question as the old door closing again. The doorway, then, is both welcome and departure, is border guard and border crossing, and though I'm
not on the woman's side of it, I'm not entirely on my father's side either.

Perhaps for this reason, there's the continuing sense that I *ought* to write
about race even as I resent that I need be troubled by the subject in the first
place. After all, I should permit myself to be a poet first and a minority
second, same as any male, white writer. But even as I attempt to ignore the
issue altogether, I find myself thinking about it, and I realize now that this
fact more than any other makes it so that I can't write like a white poet.
Writing is as much the process of arriving at the point of composition as it
is the act of composition itself. That my awareness of racial identity so often
plays a part in my thinking about my writing makes it so that I can't engage
in that writing without race being a live wire. Even one's evasions are born
of one's fixations. More to the point, what appears to be an evasion might
not be exactly that at all. John Ashbery doesn't make a subject matter of his
sexuality, but this doesn't mean he's unable to inhabit the identity of a gay
writer. Similarly, even though Mary Ruefle might not take on gender identity overtly in a given poem, it doesn't make that poem an adversary to the
cause of feminism. I don't bring all this up to absolve myself exactly, though
it's true I'm trying to figure out a way to alleviate a guilt I'm annoyed to feel
in the first place. I imagine male, white poets will recognize this feeling.
I bet any poet of conscience who doesn't actively write about sociopolitical

subjects knows this feeling, but the poet is trying to write the original thing, and that originality might not take up orbit around a more obvious facet of a poet's identity. When any of us doesn't take on such a subject in our writing, it might not be because we neglected to do so. Rather, it might be that the subject informed every bit of our deciding to write about something else.

More importantly, when it comes to writing about difficult issues of identity, especially those with far-reaching political and cultural implications, maybe the choice needn't be a dichotomous one. Maybe I don't need to choose between being the brown guy writing like a white guy or the brown guy writing about being Othered. Instead, maybe I need only be a brown guy writing out his study of language and the self—the same as the Paterson doctor, the Hartford insurance executive, the lesbian expat in Paris, the gay Jew from New Jersey, the male white poet teaching at the University of Houston, or the straight black female professor reading her poem at the American president's inauguration. Though "high" English might be born of a culture once dominated by straight white men of privilege, each of us wields our English in ways those men might not have imagined. This is okay. Language, like a hammer, belongs to whoever picks it up to build or demolish. Whether we take language in hand to deconstruct itself, to confess a real experience or an imagined one, or to meditate upon the relationship between the individual and the political, social, historical, or cosmological, ownership of our language need not be bound up with the history of that language. Whether I choose to pound on the crooked nail of race or gender, self or Other, whether I decide on some obscure subject while forgoing the other obvious one, when I write, the hammer belongs to me.

Analyze

1. Bolina's friend encourages him to write under his real name but his father recommends a pseudonym. What are some of the reasons for this?

2. What does the author mean when he says that "the coincidence of class and color" makes the "conflict of race" the biggest social conflict in the United States?

3. Explain why Bolina believes that in America, "standard" English is also considered to be the "English of whiteness." What does he mean?

Explore

1. Do you agree that assimilation naturally implies "the negation of one identity in order to adopt another"? Draw on personal or anecdotal experience as you write about what assimilation means to you and how it might or might not be different from the author's experience.

2. What exactly is a "language of privilege"? Who do you think uses such language and in what types of situations? Analyze an example from a song, dialogue from a movie, a television show, a political speech, or another popular source to show what particular features qualify it as "language of privilege."

3. Select a minority writer—a poet, a novelist, an essayist, a blogger—and do some research on the way he or she uses language. Is the writer's racial identity obvious in the writing itself? How so?

Forging Connections

1. Is it possible for language to erase stereotypical perceptions of racial and ethnic minorities? What sorts of linguistic changes would have to take place to ensure true equality for all? Be sure to draw from at least two selections in this chapter to support your argument.

2. As the numbers of language minorities continue to grow in our society, they are bound to create hybrid languages that do not follow the traditional rules of any one language. What new linguistic forms are currently developing in your community? What do they sound like and what effect do they have on its users? Refer to the concept of "code-switching" as defined by Daniel Hernandez and Felipe de Ortego y Gasca as you describe these new, hybrid forms of language.

Looking Further

1. The authors represented in Chapter 6 remind us of the need to respect—and even celebrate—linguistic diversity as an integral part of racial and cultural diversity. What are some of the steps that you can take to learn more about those in your community who speak Spanglish, Chinglish, or another hybrid language? Visit a campus or community cultural center and arrange an interview with someone who speaks a hybrid language, or practices "code-switching" as defined by Daniel Hernandez ("Spanglish Moves Into Mainstream") or Jin Zhao ("Oh My Lady

Gaga! This Is So Gelievable!"': Chinglish Entering Globish?," Chapter 9). Based on your research, is there more that your campus or community could do to celebrate its linguistic diversity?

2. As the selections in Chapter 10, "Endangered Languages," make clear, many of the world's smaller languages are languishing or disappearing altogether. Should speakers of these endangered languages adapt to more widespread languages (like English) and consider hybrid languages such as Chinglish and Spanglish as models? Or should they maintain the purity of these languages, even if the language risks extinction? Why or why not? Refer to the arguments set forth by some of the authors of this chapter as well as Chapter 10 as you write your essay.

7 Language & Politics

Rhetoric is generally understood to be the art of persuasion. Today, we are confronted with (and surrounded by) rhetoric that aims to coax, manipulate, assure, and convince us. But as often as we are persuaded by such language, there are times when we are suspicious of what we hear. Can we trust a politician to follow through with the passionate promises offered in a campaign speech? Can a product actually live up to the ambitious claims of its advertisers? Indeed, the line between politics and advertising has been blurred: political candidates become marketable commodities, carefully constructed to appeal to the public, and consumer products take on the stature and loyal following that was, in the past, reserved for political leaders.

The selections in this chapter deal with this politicization of language. Together, they remind us that the language of commerce and the language of politics have become eerily similar, urging us to ask what this does for— and in some ways, does to— us, the average citizen.

Finding nothing redeeming about "language which pretends to communicate but doesn't," in "Doubts About Doublespeak" William Lutz, former editor of the *Quarterly Review of Doublespeak* and English professor, describes how the four main types of doublespeak—euphemism, jargon, bureaucratese, and inflated language—challenge our perception of reality. George Orwell's classic essay "Politics and the English Language" is both a scathing criticism of pretentious political prose and an illustration of the value of simple, direct language. Orwell's chilling insights on the use of metaphor as a symptom of careless thinking seems to have predicted Alexis Madrigal's reporting in "Why Are Spy Researchers Building a 'Metaphor Program'?" Madrigal discusses how cultural insights can be gained from developing a software program that interprets and stores metaphors related to specific languages—and how those insights can be used as a powerful weapon to manipulate political opinion. In "'Kinetic' Connections," Neal Whitman, a writer and blogger, further explores Orwellian uses of language, explaining that if the word "kinetic" sounds familiar it is because its persistent and euphemistic use by the American government has made it ever so popular. Finally, the cognitive scientist Julie Sedivy's "Are You a Mac or a Mac User? How the Language of Identity Persuades" is a sobering reminder of how our sense of self is shaped by the language of commerce—and how that sense of self can be skillfully manipulated by advertisers as well as politicians.

William Lutz
Doubts About Doublespeak

William Lutz received the 1996 George Orwell Award for Distinguished Contribution to Honesty and Clarity in Public Language from the National Council of Teachers of English. Lutz, an English professor and a lawyer, served as the editor of the *Quarterly Review of Doublespeak* for many years. His books include *The New Doublespeak: Why No One Knows What Anyone's Saying*

Anymore (HarperCollins, 1996) and *Doublespeak Defined: Cut Through the Bull**** and Get the Point* (HarperCollins, 1999). The following essay originally appeared in *State Government News* in July 1993.

Is it more important to say what you mean or to mean what you say?

During the past year, we learned that we can shop at a "unique retail biosphere" instead of a farmers' market, where we can buy items made of "synthetic glass" instead of plastic, or purchase a "high velocity, multipurpose air circulator," or electric fan. A "waste-water conveyance facility" may "exceed the odor threshold" from time to time due to the presence of "regulated human nutrients," but that is not to be confused with a sewage plant that stinks up the neighborhood with sewage sludge. Nor should we confuse a "resource development park" with a dump. Thus does doublespeak continue to spread.

Doublespeak is language which pretends to communicate but doesn't. It is language which makes the bad seem good, the negative seem positive, the unpleasant seem attractive, or at least tolerable. It is language which avoids, shifts, or denies responsibility; language which is at variance with its real or purported meaning. It is language which conceals or prevents thought.

> "Doublespeak is language which pretends to communicate but doesn't."

Doublespeak is all around us. We are asked to check our packages at the desk "for our convenience" when it's not for our convenience at all but for someone else's convenience. We see advertisements for "preowned," "experienced," or "previously distinguished" cars, not used cars and for "genuine imitation leather," "virgin vinyl," or "real counterfeit diamonds." Television offers not reruns but "encore telecasts." There are no slums or ghettos, just the "inner city" or "substandard housing" where the "disadvantaged" or "economically nonaffluent" live and where there might be a problem with "substance abuse." Nonprofit organizations don't make a profit, they have "negative deficits" or experience "revenue excesses." With doublespeak it's not dying but "terminal living" or "negative patient care outcome."

There are four kinds of doublespeak. The first kind is the euphemism, a word or phrase designed to avoid a harsh or distasteful reality. Used to mislead or deceive, the euphemism becomes doublespeak. In 1984 the U.S.

State Department's annual reports on the status of human rights around the world ceased using the word "killing." Instead the State Department used the phrase "unlawful or arbitrary deprivation of life," thus avoiding the embarrassing situation of government-sanctioned killing in countries supported by the United States.

5   A second kind of doublespeak is jargon, the specialized language of a trade, profession, or similar group, such as doctors, lawyers, plumbers, or car mechanics. Legitimately used, jargon allows members of a group to communicate with each other clearly, efficiently, and quickly. Lawyers and tax accountants speak to each other of an "involuntary conversion" of property, a legal term that means the loss or destruction of property through theft, accident, or condemnation. But when lawyers or tax accountants use unfamiliar terms to speak to others, then the jargon becomes doublespeak.

In 1978 a commercial 727 crashed on takeoff, killing three passengers, injuring 21 others and destroying the airplane. The insured value of the airplane was greater than its book value, so the airline made a profit of $1.7 million, creating two problems: the airline didn't want to talk about one of its airplanes crashing, yet it had to account for that $1.7 million profit in its annual report to its stock-holders. The airline solved both problems by inserting a footnote in its annual report which explained that the $1.7 million was due to "the involuntary conversion of a 727."

A third kind of doublespeak is gobbledygook or bureaucratese. Such doublespeak is simply a matter of overwhelming the audience with words—the more the better. Alan Greenspan, a polished practitioner of bureaucratese, once testified before a Senate committee that "it is a tricky problem to find the particular calibration in timing that would be appropriate to stem the acceleration in risk premiums created by falling incomes without prematurely aborting the decline in the inflation-generated risk premiums."

The fourth kind of doublespeak is inflated language, which is designed to make the ordinary seem extraordinary, to make everyday things seem impressive, to give an air of importance to people or situations, to make the simple seem complex. Thus do car mechanics become "automotive internists," elevator operators become "members of the vertical transportation corps," grocery store checkout clerks become "career associate scanning professionals," and smelling something becomes "organoleptic analysis."

Doublespeak is not the product of careless language or sloppy thinking. Quite the opposite. Doublespeak is language carefully designed and constructed to appear to communicate when in fact it doesn't. It is language designed not to lead but mislead. Thus, it's not a tax increase but "revenue enhancement" or "tax-base broadening." So how can you complain about higher taxes? Those aren't useless, billion dollar pork barrel projects; they're really "congressional projects of national significance," so don't complain about wasteful government spending. That isn't the Mafia in Atlantic City; those are just "members of a career-offender cartel," so don't worry about the influence of organized crime in the city.

New doublespeak is created every day. The Environmental Protection   10
Agency once called acid rain "poorly-buffered precipitation" then dropped that term in favor of "atmospheric deposition of anthropogenically-derived acidic substances," but recently decided that acid rain should be called "wet deposition." The Pentagon, which has in the past given us such classic doublespeak as "hexiform rotatable surface compression unit" for steel nut, just published a pamphlet warning soldiers that exposure to nerve gas will lead to "immediate permanent incapacitation." That's almost as good as the Pentagon's official term "servicing the target," meaning to kill the enemy. Meanwhile, the Department of Energy wants to establish a "monitored retrievable storage site," a place once known as a dump for spent nuclear fuel.

Bad economic times give rise to lots of new doublespeak designed to avoid some very unpleasant economic realities. As the "contained depression" continues so does the corporate policy of making up even more new terms to avoid the simple, and easily understandable, term "layoff." So it is that corporations "reposition," "restructure," "reshape," or "realign" the company and "reduce duplication" through "release of resources" that involves a "permanent downsizing" or a "payroll adjustment" that results in a number of employees being "involuntarily terminated."

Other countries regularly contribute to doublespeak. In Japan, where baldness is called "hair disadvantaged," the economy is undergoing a "severe adjustment process," while in Canada there is an "involuntary downward development" of the work force. For some government agencies in Canada, wastepaper baskets have become "user friendly, space effective, flexible, deskside sortation units." Politicians in Canada may engage in "reality augmentation," but they never lie. As part of their new freedom, the people of Moscow can visit "intimacy salons," or sex shops as they're known in other countries. When dealing with the bureaucracy in Russia, people know that they should show officials "normal gratitude," or give them a bribe.

The worst doublespeak is the doublespeak of death. It is the language, wrote George Orwell in 1946, that is "largely the defense of the indefensible . . . designed to make lies sound truthful and murder respectable, and to give an appearance of solidity to pure wind." In the doublespeak of death, Orwell continued, "defenseless villages are bombarded from the air, the inhabitants driven out into the country-side, the cattle machine-gunned, the huts set on fire with incendiary bullets. This is called pacification. Millions of peasants are robbed of their farms and sent trudging along the roads with no more than they can carry. This is called transfer of population or rectification of frontiers." Today, in a country once called Yugoslavia, this is called "ethnic cleansing."

It's easy to laugh off doublespeak. After all, we all know what's going on, so what's the harm? But we don't always know what's going on, and when that happens, doublespeak accomplishes its ends. It alters our perception of reality. It deprives us of the tools we need to develop, advance, and preserve our society, our culture, our civilization. It breeds suspicion, cynicism, distrust, and, ultimately, hostility. It delivers us into the hands of those who do not have our interests at heart. As Samuel Johnson noted in 18th century England, even the devils in hell do not lie to one another, since the society of hell could not subsist without the truth, any more than any other society.

Analyze

1. In defining "doublespeak," Lutz reveals a particular way language is used to communicate. Analyze his definition and discuss how doublespeak functions in society.

2. Lutz identifies four types of doublespeak. With which ones of these are you most familiar? Provides some clear examples and explain their purpose.

3. What is Lutz's position with regard to doublespeak? Do you agree with this position? Why or why not? Examine and quote from specific parts of the text as you respond.

Explore

1. Although Lutz states that doublespeak is "language carefully designed . . . not to lead but to mislead," do you think that it can ever be a useful means of communication? Think of a time when you had to use some form of doublespeak. What was the situation and what was the effect of the particular choices of words?

2. Consider the effect of "jargon" or "bureaucratese" on your day-to-day life. Where do you encounter these the most? Write a narrative essay in which you provide examples of these types of doublespeak, how you interpret them, and what it tells you about the society you live in.

3. Analyze a speech by a politician, a document written by a university official, or an interview with a celebrity and examine the kind of doublespeak they use. What effect does their speech or writing have on the intended audience? Why?

George Orwell
Politics and the English Language

Best known for his allegorical novella *Animal Farm* (Secker and Warburg, 1945) and his dystopian novel *Nineteen Eighty-Four* (Secker and Warburg, 1949), George Orwell (1903–1950) was born Eric Arthur Blair in India and educated in England. Blair adopted the pen name "George Orwell" in 1933, just before he published his first book, *Down and Out in Paris and London*. "Politics and the English Language" was first published in London in 1946, at a time of great hardship and political turmoil following World War II. In his essay Orwell criticizes the use of "ugly" language, noting two particular qualities of ugliness: staleness of imagery and lack of precision. In the end, he advocates plain speech, noting that language should be used as an "instrument of expression" and not as an instrument for "concealing or preventing thought"—a concern to which he gave infamously chilling expression in *Nineteen Eighty-Four* and the "doublethink" of its imaginary, yet hauntingly familiar, totalitarian regime.

How does the language of certain characters in dystopian literature and films, such as *The Hunger Games* series, reflect their manipulative or even sinister motivations?

Most people who bother with the matter at all would admit that the English language is in a bad way, but it is generally assumed that we cannot by conscious action do anything about it. Our civilization is decadent and our language—so the argument runs—must inevitably share in the general collapse. It follows that any struggle against the abuse of language is a sentimental archaism, like preferring candles to electric light or hansom cabs to aeroplanes. Underneath this lies the half-conscious belief that language is a natural growth and not an instrument which we shape for our own purposes.

Now, it is clear that the decline of a language must ultimately have political and economic causes: it is not due simply to the bad influence of this or that individual writer. But an effect can become a cause, reinforcing the original cause and producing the same effect in an intensified form, and so on indefinitely. A man may take to drink because he feels himself to be a failure, and then fail all the more completely because he drinks. It is rather the same thing that is happening to the English language. It becomes ugly and inaccurate because our thoughts are foolish, but the slovenliness of our language makes it easier for us to have foolish thoughts. The point is that the process is reversible. Modern English, especially written English, is full of bad habits, which spread by imitation and which can be avoided if one is willing to take the necessary trouble. If one gets rid of these habits one can think more clearly, and to think clearly is a necessary first step towards political regeneration: so that the fight against bad English is not frivolous and is not the exclusive concern of professional writers. I will come back to this presently, and I hope that by that time the meaning of what I have said here will have become clearer. Meanwhile, here are five specimens of the English language as it is now habitually written.

These five passages have not been picked out because they are especially bad—I could have quoted far worse if I had chosen—but because they illustrate various of the mental vices from which we now suffer. They are a little below the average, but are fairly representative samples. I number them so that I can refer back to them when necessary:

1. I am not, indeed, sure whether it is not true to say that the Milton who once seemed not unlike a seventeenth-century Shelley had not become, out of an experience ever more bitter in each year, more alien [*sic*] to the founder of that Jesuit sect which nothing could induce him to tolerate.
   Professor Harold Laski
   (Essay in *Freedom of Expression*).

2. Above all, we cannot play ducks and drakes with a native battery of idioms which prescribes such egregious collocations of vocables as the Basic *put up with* for *tolerate* or *put at a loss* for *bewilder*.
   Professor Lancelot Hogben (*Interglossa*).

3. On the one side we have the free personality: by definition it is not neurotic, for it has neither conflict nor dream. Its desires, such as they are, are transparent, for they are just what institutional approval keeps in the forefront of consciousness; another institutional pattern would alter their number and intensity; there is little in them that is natural, irreducible, or culturally dangerous. But *on the other side,* the social bond itself is nothing but the mutual reflection of these self-secure integrities. Recall the definition of love. Is not this the very picture of a small academic? Where is there a place in this hall of mirrors for either personality or fraternity?

   Essay on psychology in *Politics* (New York).

4. All the "best people" from the gentlemen's clubs, and all the frantic fascist captains, united in common hatred of Socialism and bestial horror of the rising tide of the mass revolutionary movement, have turned to acts of provocation, to foul incendiarism, to medieval legends of poisoned wells, to legalize their own destruction of proletarian organizations, and rouse the agitated petty-bourgeoisie to chauvinistic fervor on behalf of the fight against the revolutionary way out of the crisis.

   Communist pamphlet.

5. If a new spirit *is* to be infused into this old country, there is one thorny and contentious reform which must be tackled, and that is the humanization and galvanization of the B.B.C. Timidity here will bespeak canker and atrophy of the soul. The heart of Britain may be sound and of strong beat, for instance, but the British lion's roar at present is like that of Bottom in Shakespeare's *Midsummer Night's Dream*—as gentle as any sucking dove. A virile new Britain cannot continue indefinitely to be traduced in the eyes, or rather ears, of the world by the effete languors of Langham Place, brazenly masquerading as "standard English." When the Voice of Britain is heard at nine o'clock, better far and infinitely less ludicrous to hear aitches honestly dropped than the present priggish, inflated, inhibited, school-ma'amish arch braying of blameless bashful mewing maidens!

   Letter in *Tribune.*

   Each of these passages has faults of its own, but, quite apart from avoidable ugliness, two qualities are common to all of them. The first is staleness of imagery; the other is lack of precision. The writer either has a meaning and cannot express it, or he inadvertently says something else, or he is almost indifferent as to whether his words mean anything or not.

5   This mixture of vagueness and sheer incompetence is the most marked characteristic of modern English prose, and especially of any kind of political writing. As soon as certain topics are raised, the concrete melts into the abstract and no one seems able to think of turns of speech that are not hackneyed: prose consists less and less of *words* chosen for the sake of their meaning, and more and more of *phrases* tacked together like the sections of a prefabricated hen-house. I list below, with notes and examples, various of the tricks by means of which the work of prose-construction is habitually dodged:

DYING METAPHORS. A newly invented metaphor assists thought by evoking a visual image, while on the other hand a metaphor which is technically "dead" (e.g. *iron resolution*) has in effect reverted to being an ordinary word and can generally be used without loss of vividness. But in between these two classes there is a huge clump of worn-out metaphors which have lost all evocative power and are merely used because they save people the trouble of inventing phrases for themselves. Examples are: *Ring the changes on, take up the cudgels for, toe the line, ride roughshod over, stand shoulder to shoulder with, play into the hands of, no axe to grind, grist to the mill, fishing in troubled waters, on the order of the day, Achilles' heel, swan song, hotbed.* Many of these are used without knowledge of their meaning (what is a "rift," for instance?), and incompatible metaphors are frequently mixed, a sure sign that the writer is not interested in what he is saying. Some metaphors now current have been twisted out of their original meaning without those who use them even being aware of the fact. For example, *toe the line* is sometimes written *tow the line.* Another example is *the hammer and the anvil,* now always used with the implication that the anvil gets the worst of it. In real life it is always the anvil that breaks the hammer, never the other way about: a writer who stopped to think what he was saying would be aware of this, and would avoid perverting the original phrase.

OPERATORS or VERBAL FALSE LIMBS. These save the trouble of picking out appropriate verbs and nouns, and at the same time pad each sentence with extra syllables which give it an appearance of symmetry. Characteristic phrases are *render inoperative, militate against, make contact with, be subjected to, give rise to, give grounds for, have the effect of, play a leading part (role) in, make itself felt, take effect, exhibit a tendency to, serve the purpose of,* etc., etc. The keynote is the elimination of simple verbs. Instead of being a single word, such as *break, stop, spoil, mend, kill,* a verb becomes a *phrase,* made up of a noun or adjective tacked on to some general-purposes verb such as *prove, serve, form, play, render.* In addition, the passive voice is wherever possible used in preference to the active, and noun constructions are used instead of gerunds (*by examination of* instead of *by examining*). The range of verbs is further cut down by means of the *-ize* and deformations, and the banal statements are given an appearance of profundity by means of the *not un-*formation. Simple conjunctions and prepositions are replaced by such phrases as *with respect to, having regard to, the fact that, by dint of, in view of, in the interests of, on the hypothesis that;* and the ends of sentences are saved from anticlimax by such resounding common places as *greatly to be desired, cannot be left out of account, a development to be expected in the near future, deserving of serious consideration, brought to a satisfactory conclusion,* and so on and so forth.

PRETENTIOUS DICTION. Words like *phenomenon, element, individual* (as noun), *objective, categorical, effective, virtual, basic, primary, promote, constitute, exhibit, exploit, utilize, eliminate, liquidate* are used to dress up simple statement and give an air of scientific impartiality to biased judgments. Adjectives like *epoch-making, epic, historic, unforgettable, triumphant, age-old, inevitable, inexorable, veritable,* are used to dignify the sordid processes of international politics, while writing that aims at glorifying war usually takes on an archaic color, its characteristic words being: *realm, throne, chariot, mailed fist, trident, sword, shield, buckler, banner, jackboot, clarion.* Foreign words and expressions such as *cul de sac, ancien régime, deus ex machina, mutatis mutandis, status quo, gleichschaltung, Weltanschauung,* are used to give an air of culture and elegance. Except for the useful abbreviations *i.e., e.g.,* and *etc.,* there is no real need for any of the hundreds of foreign phrases now current in English. Bad writers, and especially scientific, political and sociological writers, are nearly always haunted by the notion that Latin or Greek words are grander than Saxon ones, and unnecessary words like *expedite, ameliorate, predict, extraneous, deracinated, clandestine, subaqueous* and hundreds of others constantly gain ground from their Anglo-Saxon opposite numbers.[1] The jargon peculiar to Marxist writing (*hyena, hangman, cannibal, petty bourgeois, these gentry, lacquey, flunkey, mad dog, White Guard,* etc.) consists largely of words and phrases translated from Russian, German or French; but the normal way of coining a new word is to use a Latin or Greek root with the appropriate affix and, where necessary, the *-ize* formation. It is often easier to make up words of this kind (*deregionalize, impermissible, extramarital, non-fragmentary* and so forth) than to think up the English words that will cover one's meaning. The result, in general, is an increase in slovenliness and vagueness.

MEANINGLESS WORDS. In certain kinds of writing, particularly in art criticism and literary criticism, it is normal to come across long passages which are almost completely lacking in meaning.[2] Words like *romantic, plastic, values, human, dead, sentimental, natural, vitality,* as used in art criticism, are strictly meaningless, in the sense that they not only do not point to any discoverable object, but are hardly ever expected to do so by the reader. When one critic writes, "The outstanding feature of Mr. X's work is its living quality," while another writes, "The immediately striking thing about Mr. X's work is its peculiar deadness," the reader accepts this as a simple difference of opinion. If words like *black* and *white* were involved, instead of the jargon words *dead* and *living,* he would see at once that language was being used in an improper way. Many political words are similarly abused. The word *Fascism* has now no meaning except in so far as it signifies "something not desirable." The words *democracy, socialism, freedom, patriotic, realistic, justice,* have each of them several different meanings which cannot be reconciled with one another. In the case of a word like *democracy,* not only is there no agreed definition, but the attempt to make one is resisted from all sides. It is almost universally felt that when we call a country democratic we are praising it: consequently the defenders of every kind of regime claim that it is a democracy, and fear that they might have to stop using the word if it were tied down to any one meaning. Words of this kind are often used in a consciously dishonest way. That is, the person who uses them has his own private definition, but allows his hearer to think he means something quite different. Statements like *Marshal Petain was a true patriot, The Soviet Press is the freest in the world, The Catholic Church is opposed to persecution,* are almost always made with intent to deceive. Other words used in variable meanings, in most cases more or less dishonestly, are: *class, totalitarian, science, progressive, reactionary, bourgeois, equality.*

10   Now that I have made this catalogue of swindles and perversions, let me give another example of the kind of writing that they lead to. This time it must of its nature be an imaginary one. I am going to translate a passage of good English into modern English of the worst sort. Here is a well-known verse from *Ecclesiastes:*

> I returned and saw under the sun, that the race is not to the swift,
> nor the battle to the strong, neither yet bread to the wise, nor yet

> riches to men of understanding, nor yet favour to men of skill; but time and chance happeneth to them all.

Here it is in modern English:

> Objective consideration of contemporary phenomena compels the conclusion that success or failure in competitive activities exhibits no tendency to be commensurate with innate capacity, but that a considerable element of the unpredicable must invariably be taken into account.

This is a parody, but not a very gross one. Exhibit (3), above, for instance, contains several patches of the same kind of English. It will be seen that I have not made a full translation. The beginning and ending of the sentence follow the original meaning fairly closely, but in the middle the concrete illustrations—race, battle, bread—dissolve into the vague phrase "success or failure in competitive activities." This had to be so, because no modern writer of the kind I am discussing—no one capable of using phrases like "objective consideration of contemporary phenomena"—would ever tabulate his thoughts in that precise and detailed way. The whole tendency of modern prose is away from concreteness. Now analyse these two sentences a little more closely. The first contains forty-nine words but only sixty syllables, and all its words are those of everyday life. The second contains thirty-eight words of ninety syllables: eighteen of its words are from Latin roots, and one from Greek. The first sentence contains six vivid images, and only one phrase ("time and chance") that could be called vague. The second contains not a single fresh, arresting phrase, and in spite of its ninety syllables it gives only a shortened version of the meaning contained in the first, Yet without a doubt it is the second kind of sentence that is gaining ground in modern English. I do not want to exaggerate. This kind of writing is not yet universal, and outcrops of simplicity will occur here and there in the worst-written page. Still, if you or I were told to write a few lines on the uncertainty of human fortunes, we should probably come much nearer to my imaginary sentence than to the one from *Ecclesiastes*.

As I have tried to show, modern writing at its worst does not consist in picking out words for the sake of their meaning and inventing images in order to make the meaning clearer. It consists in gumming together long strips of words which have already been set in order by someone else, and making the results presentable by sheer humbug. The attraction of this way of writing is that it is easy. It is easier—even quicker, once you have the habit—to say *In my opinion it is not an unjustifiable assumption that* than to say *I think*. If you use readymade phrases, you not only don't have to hunt about for words; you also don't have to bother with the rhythms of your sentences, since these phrases are generally so arranged as to be more or less euphonious. When you are composing in a hurry—when you are dictating to a stenographer, for instance, or making a public speech—it is natural to fall into a pretentious, Latinized style. Tags like *a consideration which we should do well to bear in mind* or *a conclusion to which all of us would readily assent* will save many a sentence from coming down with a bump. By using stale metaphors, similes and idioms, you save much mental effort, at the cost of leaving your meaning vague, not only for your reader but for yourself. This is the significance of mixed metaphors. The sole aim of a metaphor is to call up a visual image. When these images clash—as in *The Fascist octopus has sung its swan song, the jackboot is thrown into the melting pot*—it can be taken as certain that the writer is not seeing a mental image of the objects he is naming; in other words he is not really thinking. Look again at the examples I gave at the beginning of this essay. Professor Laski (1) uses five negatives in fifty-three words. One of these is superfluous, making nonsense of the whole passage, and in addition there is the slip *alien* for akin, making further nonsense, and several avoidable pieces of clumsiness which increase the general vagueness. Professor Hogben (2) plays ducks and drakes with a battery which is able to write prescriptions, and, while disapproving of the everyday phrase *put up with,* is unwilling to look *egregious* up in the dictionary and see what it means; (3), if one takes an uncharitable attitude towards it, is simply meaningless: probably one could work out its intended meaning by reading the whole of the article in which it occurs. In (4), the writer knows more or less what he wants to say, but an accumulation of stale phrases chokes him like tea leaves blocking a sink. In (5), words and meaning have almost parted company. People who write in this manner usually have a general emotional meaning—they dislike one thing and want to express solidarity with another—but they are not interested in the detail of what they are saying. A scrupulous writer, in every sentence that he writes, will ask himself at least four questions, thus: What am I trying to say? What words will express it? What image or idiom will make it clearer? Is this image fresh enough to have an effect? And he will probably ask himself two more: Could I put it more shortly? Have I said anything that is avoidably ugly? But you are not obliged to go to all this trouble. You can shirk it by simply throwing your mind open and letting the ready-made phrases come crowding in. They will construct your sentences for you—even think your thoughts for you, to a certain extent—and at need they will perform the important service of partially concealing your meaning even from yourself. It is at this point that the special connection between politics and the debasement of language becomes clear. In our time it is broadly true that political writing is bad writing. Where it is not true, it will generally be found that the writer is some kind of rebel, expressing his private opinions and not a "party line." Orthodoxy, of whatever color, seems to demand a lifeless, imitative style. The political dialects to be found in pamphlets, leading articles, manifestos, White Papers and the speeches of under-secretaries do, of course, vary from party to party, but they are all alike in that one almost never finds in them a fresh, vivid, home-made turn of speech. When one watches some tired hack on the platform mechanically repeating the familiar phrases—*bestial atrocities, iron heel, bloodstained tyranny, free peoples of the world, stand shoulder to shoulder*—one often has a curious feeling that one is not watching a live human being but some kind of dummy; a feeling which suddenly becomes stronger at moments when the light catches the speaker's spectacles and turns them into blank discs which seem to have no eyes behind them. And this is not altogether fanciful. A speaker who uses that kind of phraseology has gone some distance towards turning himself into a machine. The appropriate noises are coming out of his larynx, but his brain is not involved as it would be if he were choosing his words for himself. If the speech he is making is one that he is accustomed to make over and over again, he may be almost unconscious of what he is saying, as one is when one utters the responses in church. And this reduced state of consciousness, if not indispensable, is at any rate favorable to political conformity.

In our time, political speech and writing are largely the defence of the indefensible. Things like the continuance of British rule in India, the Russian purges and deportations, the dropping of the atom bombs on Japan, can indeed be defended, but only by arguments which are too brutal for most people to face, and which do not square with the professed aims of political parties. Thus political language has to consist largely of euphemism, question-begging and sheer cloudy vagueness. Defenceless villages are bombarded from the air, the inhabitants driven out into the countryside, the cattle machine-gunned, the huts set on fire with incendiary bullets: this is called *pacification*. Millions of peasants are robbed of their farms and sent trudging along the roads with no more than they can carry: this is called *transfer of population* or *rectification of frontiers*. People are imprisoned for years without trial, or shot in the back of the neck or sent to die of scurvy in Arctic lumber camps: this is called *elimination of unreliable elements*. Such phraseology is needed if one wants to name things without calling up mental pictures of them. Consider for instance some comfortable English professor defending Russian totalitarianism. He cannot say outright, "I believe in killing off your opponents when you can get good results by doing so." Probably, therefore, he will say something like this:

> While freely conceding that the Soviet regime exhibits certain features which the humanitarian may be inclined to deplore, we must, I think, agree that a certain curtailment of the right to political opposition is an unavoidable concomitant of transitional periods, and that the rigors which the Russian people have been called upon to undergo have been amply justified in the sphere of concrete achievement.

15   The inflated style is itself a kind of euphemism. A mass of Latin words falls upon the facts like soft snow, blurring the outlines and covering up all the details. The great enemy of clear language is insincerity. When there is a gap between one's real and one's declared rums, one turns as it were instinctively to long words and exhausted idioms, like a cuttlefish squirting out ink. In our age there is no such thing as "keeping out of politics." All issues are political issues, and politics itself is a mass of lies, evasions, folly, hatred and schizophrenia. When the general atmosphere is bad, language must suffer. I should expect to find—this is a guess which I have not sufficient knowledge to verify—that the German, Russian and Italian languages have all deteriorated in the last ten or fifteen years, as a result of dictatorship.

But if thought corrupts language, language can also corrupt thought. A bad usage can spread by tradition and imitation, even among people who should and do know better. The debased language that I have been discussing is in some ways very convenient. Phrases like *a not unjustifiable assumption, leaves much to be desired, would serve no good purpose, a consideration which we should do well to bear in mind,* are a continuous temptation, a packet of aspirins always at one's elbow. Look back through this essay, and for certain you will find that I have again and again committed the very faults I am protesting against. By this morning's post I have received a pamphlet dealing with conditions in Germany. The author tells me that he "felt impelled" to write it. I open it at random, and here is almost the first sentence that I see: "[The Allies] have an opportunity not only of achieving a radical transformation of Germany's social and political structure in such a way as to avoid a nationalistic reaction in Germany itself, but at the same time of laying the foundations of a cooperative and unified Europe." You see, he "feels impelled" to write—feels, presumably, that he has something new to say—and yet his words, like cavalry horses answering the bugle, group themselves automatically into the familiar dreary pattern. This invasion of one's mind by ready-made phrases (*lay the foundations, achieve a radical transformation*) can only be prevented if one is constantly on guard against them, and every such phrase anaesthetizes a portion of one's brain.

I said earlier that the decadence of our language is probably curable. Those who deny this would argue, if they produced an argument at all, that language merely reflects existing social conditions, and that we cannot influence its development by any direct tinkering with words and constructions. So far as the general tone or spirit of a language goes, this may be true, but it is not true in detail. Silly words and expressions have often disappeared, not through any evolutionary process but owing to the conscious action of a minority. Two recent examples were *explore every avenue* and *leave no stone unturned,* which were killed by the jeers of a few journalists. There is a long list of flyblown metaphors which could similarly be got rid of if enough people would interest themselves in the job; and it should also be possible to laugh the *not un-*formation out of existence,[3] to reduce the amount of Latin and Greek in the average sentence, to drive out foreign phrases and strayed scientific words, and, in general, to make pretentiousness unfashionable. But all these are minor points. The defence of the English language implies more than this, and perhaps it is best to start by saying what it does *not* imply.

To begin with it has nothing to do with archaism, with the salvaging of obsolete words and turns of speech, or with the setting up of a "standard English" which must never be departed from. On the contrary, it is especially concerned with the scrapping of every word or idiom which has outworn its usefulness. It has nothing to do with correct grammar and syntax, which are of no importance so long as one makes one's meaning clear, or with the avoidance of Americanisms, or with having what is called a "good prose style." On the other hand it is not concerned with fake simplicity and the attempt to make written English colloquial. Nor does it even imply in every case preferring the Saxon word to the Latin one, though it does imply using the fewest and shortest words that will cover one's meaning. What is above all needed is to let the meaning choose the word, and not the other way about. In prose, the worst thing one can do with words is to surrender to them. When you think of a concrete object, you think wordlessly, and then, if you want to describe the thing you have been visualizing you probably hunt about till you find the exact words that seem to fit it. When you think of something abstract you are more inclined to use words from the start, and unless you make a conscious effort to prevent it, the existing dialect will come rushing in and do the job for you, at the expense of blurring or even changing your meaning. Probably it is better to put off using words as long as possible and get one's meaning as clear as one can through pictures or sensations. Afterwards one can choose—not simply *accept*—the phrases that will best cover the meaning, and then switch round and decide what impression one's words are likely to make on another person. This last effort of the mind cuts out all stale or mixed images, all prefabricated phrases, needless repetitions, and humbug and vagueness generally. But one can often be in doubt about the effect of a word or a phrase, and one needs rules that one can rely on when instinct fails. I think the following rules will cover most cases:

i. Never use a metaphor, simile or other figure of speech which you are used to seeing in print.
ii. Never use a long word where a short one will do.
iii. If it is possible to cut a word out, always cut it out.
iv. Never use the passive where you can use the active.
v. Never use a foreign phrase, a scientific word or a jargon word if you can think of an everyday English equivalent.
vi. Break any of these rules sooner than say anything outright barbarous.

These rules sound elementary, and so they are, but they demand a deep change in attitude in anyone who has grown used to writing in the style now fashionable. One could keep all of them and still write bad English, but one could not write the kind of stuff that I quoted in those five specimens at the beginning of this article.

I have not here been considering the literary use of language, but merely 20
language as an instrument for expressing and not for concealing or preventing thought. Stuart Chase and others have come near to claiming that all
abstract words are meaningless, and have used this as a pretext for advocating a kind of political quietism. Since you don't know what Fascism is, how
can you struggle against Fascism? One need not swallow such absurdities as
this, but one ought to recognize that the present political chaos is connected
with the decay of language, and that one can probably bring about some
improvement by starting at the verbal end. If you simplify your English, you
are freed from the worst follies of orthodoxy. You cannot speak any of the
necessary dialects, and when you make a stupid remark its stupidity will be
obvious, even to yourself. Political language—and with variations this is
true of all political parties, from Conservatives to Anarchists—is designed
to make lies sound truthful and murder respectable, and to give an appearance of solidity to pure wind. One cannot change this all in a moment, but
one can at least change one's own habits, and from time to time one can
even, if one jeers loudly enough, send some worn-out and useless phrase—
some *jackboot, Achilles' heel, hotbed, melting pot, acid test, veritable inferno* or
other lump of verbal refuse—into the dustbin where it belongs.

NOTES

1 An interesting illustration of this is the way in which the English flower names
which were in use till very recently are being ousted by Greek ones, *snapdragon*
becoming *antirrhinum, forget-me-not* becoming *myosotis,* etc. It is hard to see
any practical reason for this change of fashion: it is probably due to an instinctive turning-away from the more homely word and a vague feeling that the
Greek word is scientific.

2 Example: "Comfort's catholicity of perception and image, strangely Whitman-
esque in range, almost the exact *opposite* in aesthetic compulsion, continues to
evoke that trembling atmospheric accumulative hinting at a cruel, an inexorably
serene timelessness. . . . Wrey Gardiner scores by aiming at simple bull's-eyes
with precision. Only they are not so simple, and through this contented sadness
runs more than tile surface bitter-sweet of resignation." *(Poetry Quarterly.)*

3 One can cure oneself of the *not un-* formation by memorizing this sentence:
A not unblack dog was chasing a not unsmall rabbit across a not ungreen field.

Analyze

1. How convinced are you by Orwell's claim that "the decline of a
   language must ultimately have political and economic causes?" Why?

2. What is "pretentious diction"? Examine some of the examples from the essay and explain what makes them "pretentious." Can you think of other examples that would fall into this category?
3. Summarize some of Orwell's main ideas about language use and reflect on how relevant they might be in today's society.

Explore

1. Now that you've read his essay, can you think of times you used the types of prose that Orwell warns us against? Which kinds of writing are you most guilty of practicing? Did you feel forced to write this way? Why?
2. Orwell claims that "political writing is bad writing" because it rarely contains "a fresh, vivid, homemade turn of speech." Do you agree with this view? Select at least two political speeches that are of interest to you and analyze the kind of language that is used in them. Do these speeches confirm Orwell's position? Why or why not?
3. Does the genre of writing—whether it is an email, tweet, Facebook update, or a scientific paper, academic essay, or formal speech—dictate the forms of language that the writer uses? Find a scholarly article written in the discipline you are (or plan to be) majoring in and examine how the author conveys his or her ideas. What would Orwell say about this type of writing? How would you respond to his evaluation?

Alexis Madrigal
Why Are Spy Researchers Building a "Metaphor Program"?

Alexis Madrigal is a senior editor at *The Atlantic*, where he oversees the Technology channel. He cofounded *Longshot* magazine, a high-speed media experiment that garnered attention from *The New York Times*, *The Wall Street Journal*, and the BBC, and also made *Wired Science* one of the most popular blogs in the world. The following piece appeared in *The Atlantic*, an American magazine founded in 1857 in Boston. For more than 150 years, it has published important commentary from leading thinkers on issues in contemporary politics. In the piece that follows, Madrigal introduces readers to the federal Metaphor Program, designed explicitly to examine what individuals' pervasive use of metaphors in everyday speech can reveal about their worldviews and belief systems.

Madrigal notes that the study of metaphors can open our eyes up to the "deep and fundamental way that humans make sense of the world." To what extent do you think this statement is true or not true?

A small research arm of the U.S. government's intelligence establishment wants to understand how speakers of Farsi, Russian, English, and Spanish see the world by building software that automatically evaluates their use of metaphors.

That's right, metaphors, like Shakespeare's famous line, "All the world's a stage," or more subtly, "The darkness pressed in on all sides." Every speaker in every language in the world uses them effortlessly, and the Intelligence Advanced Research Projects Activity wants know how what we say reflects our worldviews. They call it The Metaphor Program, and it is a unique effort within the government to probe how a people's language reveals their mindset.

"The Metaphor Program will exploit the fact that metaphors are pervasive in everyday talk and reveal the underlying beliefs and worldviews of members of a culture," declared an open solicitation for researchers released last week. A spokesperson for IARPA declined to comment at the time.

IARPA wants some computer scientists with experience in processing language in big chunks to come up with methods of pulling out a culture's relationship with particular concepts. "They really are trying to get at what people think using how they talk," Benjamin Bergen, a cognitive scientist at the University of California, San Diego, told me. Bergen is one of a dozen or so lead researchers who are expected to vie for a research grant that could be worth tens of millions of dollars over five years, if the team can show progress towards automatically tagging and processing metaphors across languages.

"IARPA grants are big," said Jennifer Carter of Applied Research 5 Associates, a 1,600-strong research company that may throw its hat in the Metaphor ring after winning a lead research spot in a separate IARPA solicitation. While no one knows the precise value of the rewards of the

IARPA grants and the contracts are believed to vary widely, they tend to support several large teams of multidisciplinary researchers, Carter said. The awards, which would initially go to several teams, could range into the five digits annually. "Generally what happens . . . there will be a 'downselect' each year, so maybe only one team will get money for the whole program," she said.

All this to say: The Metaphor Program may represent a nine-figure investment by the government in understanding how people use language. But that's because metaphor studies aren't light or frilly and IARPA isn't afraid of taking on unusual sounding projects if they think they might help intelligence analysts sort through and decode the tremendous amounts of data pouring into their minds.

In a presentation to prospective research "performers," as they're known, The Metaphor Program's manager, Heather McCallum-Bayliss gave the following example of the power of metaphors in political discussions. Her slide reads:

> Metaphors shape how people think about complex topics and can influence beliefs. A study presented participants with a report on crime in a city; they were asked how crime should be addressed in the city. The report contained statistics, including crime and murder rates, as well as one of two metaphors, CRIME AS A WILD BEAST or CRIME AS A VIRUS. The participants were influenced by the embedded metaphor . . .

McCallum-Bayliss appears to be referring to a 2011 paper published in the *PLoS ONE*, "Metaphors We Think With: The Role of Metaphor in Reasoning," lead authored by Stanford's Paul Thibodeau. In that case, if people were given the crime-as-a-virus framing, they were more likely to suggest social reform and less likely to suggest more law enforcement or harsher punishments for criminals. The differences generated by the metaphor alternatives were "were larger than those that exist between Democrats and Republicans, or between men and women," the study authors noted.

Every writer (and reader) knows that there are clues to how people think and ways to influence each other through our use of words. Metaphor researchers, of whom there are a surprising number and variety, have formalized many of these intuitions into whole branches of cognitive linguistics using studies like the one outlined above (more on that later). But what IARPA's project calls for is the deployment of spy resources against an entire language. Where you or I might parse a sentence, this project wants to parse, say, all the pages in Farsi on the Internet looking for hidden levers into the consciousness of a people.

"The study of language offers a strategic opportunity for improved coun-   10
terterrorist intelligence, in that it enables the possibility of understanding of the Other's perceptions and motivations, be he friend or foe," the two authors of *Computational Methods for Counterterrorism* wrote. "As we have seen, linguistic expressions have levels of meaning beyond the literal, which it is critical to address. This is true especially when dealing with texts from a high-context traditionalist culture such as those of Islamic terrorists and insurgents."

In the first phase of the IARPA program, the researchers would simply try to map from the metaphors a language used to the general affect associated with a concept like "journey" or "struggle." These metaphors would then be stored in the metaphor repository. In a later stage, the Metaphor Program scientists will be expected to help answer questions like, "What are the perspectives of Pakistan and India with respect to Kashmir?" by using their metaphorical probes into the cultures. Perhaps, a slide from IARPA suggests, metaphors can tell us something about the way Indians and Pakistanis view the role of Britain or the concept of the "nation" or "government."

The assumption is that common turns of phrase, dissected and reassembled through cognitive linguistics, could say something about the views of those citizens that they might not be able to say themselves. The language of a culture as reflected in a bunch of text on the Internet might hide secrets about the way people think that are so valuable that spies are willing to pay for them.

More Than Words

ARPA is modeled on the famed DARPA—progenitors of the Internet among other wonders—and tasked with doing high-risk, high-reward research for the many agencies, the NSA and CIA among them, that make up the American intelligence-gathering force. IARPA is, as you might expect, a low-profile organization. Little information is available from the organization aside from a couple of interviews that its administrator, Lisa Porter, a former NASA official, gave back in 2008 to *Wired* and *IEEE Spectrum*. Neither publication can avoid joking that the agency is like James Bond's famous research crew, but it turns out that the place is more likely to use "cloak-and-dagger" in a sentence than in actual combat with supervillainy.

A major component of the agency's work is data mining and analysis. IARPA is split into three program offices with distinct goals: Smart Collection "to dramatically improve the **value** of collected data from all sources"; Incisive Analysis "to maximize **insight** from the information we collect, in a **timely** fashion"; and Safe & Secure Operations "to counter new capabilities implemented by our adversaries that would threaten our ability to operate freely and effectively in a **networked** world." The Metaphor Program falls under the office of Incisive Analysis and is headed by the aforementioned McCallum-Bayliss, a former technologist at Lockheed Martin and IBM, who co-filed several patents relating to the processing of names in databases.

15   Incisive Analysis has put out several calls for other projects. They range widely in scope and domain. The Babel Program seeks to "demonstrate the ability to generate a speech transcription system for any new language within one week to support keyword search performance for effective triage of massive amounts of speech recorded in challenging real-world situations." ALADDIN aims to create software to automatically monitor massive amounts of video. The FUSE Program is trying to "develop automated methods that aid in the systematic, continuous, and comprehensive assessment of technical emergence" using the scientific and patent literature.

All three projects are technologically exciting, but none of those projects has the poetic ring nor the smell of humanity of The Metaphor Program. The Metaphor Program wants to understand what human beings mean through the unvoiced emotional inflection of our words. That's normally the work of an examined life, not a piece of spy software.

There is some precedent for the work. It comes from two directions: cognitive linguistics and natural language processing. On the cognitive linguistic side, George Lakoff and Mark Johnson of the University of California, Berkeley did the foundational work, notably in their 1980 book, *Metaphors We Live By*. As summarized recently by Zoltán Kövecses in his book, *Metaphor: A Practical Introduction*, Lakoff and Johnson showed that metaphors weren't just the devices of writers but rather "a valuable cognitive tool without which neither poets nor you and I as ordinary people could live."

In this school of cognitive linguistics, we need to use more embodied, concrete domains in order to describe more abstract ones. Researchers assembled the linguistic expressions we use like "That class gave me food for thought" and "His idea was half-baked" into a construct called a "conceptual category." These come in the form of awesomely simple sentences like "Ideas Are Food." And there are whole great lists of them. (My favorites: Darkness Is a Solid; Time Is Something Moving Toward You; Happiness Is Fluid In a Container; Control Is Up.) The conceptual categories show that humans use one domain ("the source") to describe another ("the target"). So, take Ideas Are Food: thinking is preparing food and understanding is digestion and believing is swallowing and learning is eating and communicating is feeding. Put simply: We import the logic of the source domain into the target domain.

The main point here is that metaphors, in this sense, aren't soft or literary in any narrow sense. Rather, they are a deep and fundamental way that humans make sense of the world. And unfortunately for spies who want to filter the Internet to look for dangerous people, computers can't make much sense out of sentences like, "We can make beautiful music together," which Google translates as something about actually playing music when, of course, it really means, "We can be good together." (Or as the conceptual category would phrase it: "Interpersonal Harmony Is Musical Harmony.")

While some of the underlying structures of the metaphors—the conceptual categories—are near universal (e.g. Happy Is Up), there are many variations in their range, elaboration, and emphasis. And, of course, not every category is universal. For example, Kövecses points to a special conceptual category in Japanese centered around the hara, or belly, "Anger Is (In The) Hara." In Zulu, one finds an important category, "Anger Is (Understood As Being) In the Heart," which would be rare in English. Alternatively, while many cultures conceive of anger as a hot fluid in a container, it's in English that we "blow off steam," a turn of phrase that wouldn't make sense in Zulu.

These relationships have been painstakingly mapped by human analysts over the last 30 years and they represent a deep culturolinguistic knowledge base. For the cognitive linguistic school, all of these uses of language reveal something about the way the people of a culture understand each other and the world. And that's really the target of the metaphor program, and what makes it unprecedented. They're after a deeper understanding of the way people use words because the deep patterns encoded in language may help intelligence analysts understand the people, not just the texts.

For Lakoff, it's about time that the government started taking metaphor seriously. "There have been 30 years of neglect of current linguistics in all government-sponsored research," he told me. "And finally there is somebody in the government who has managed to do something after many years of trying."

UC San Diego's Bergen agreed. "It's a totally unique project," he said. "I've never seen anything like it."

But that doesn't mean it's going to be easy to create a system that can automatically deduce what Americans' biases about education are from a statement like "The teacher spoon-fed the students."

25   Lakoff contends that it will take a long, sustained effort by IARPA (or anyone else) to complete the task. "The quick-and-dirty way" won't work, he said. "Are they going to do a serious scientific account?"

Building a Metaphor Machine

The metaphor problem is particularly difficult because we don't even know what the right answers to our queries are, Bergen said.

"If you think about other sorts of automation of language processing, there are right answers," he said. "In speech recognition, you know what the word should be. So you can do statistical learning. You use humans, tag up a corpus and then run some machine learning algorithms on that. Unfortunately, here, we don't know what the right answers are."

For one, we don't really have a stable way of telling what is and what is not metaphorical language. And metaphorical language is changing all the time. Parsing text for metaphors is tough work for humans and we're made for it. The kind of intensive linguistic analysis that's made Lakoff and his students (of whom Bergen was one) famous can take a human two hours for every 500 words on the page.

But it's that very difficulty that makes people want to deploy computing resources instead of human beings. And they do have some directions that they could take. James Martin of the University of Colorado played a key role in the late 1980s and early 1990s in defining the problem and

suggesting a solution. Martin contended "the interpretation of novel metaphors can be accomplished through the systematic extension, elaboration,
and combination of knowledge about already well-understood metaphors,"
in a 1988 paper.

What that means is that within a given domain—say, "the family" in   30
Arabic—you can start to process text around that. First you'll have humans
go in and tag up the data, finding the metaphors. Then, you'd use what they
learned about the target domain "family" to look for metaphorical words
that are often associated with it. Then, you run permutations on those
words from the source domain to find other metaphors you might not have
before. Eventually you build up a repository of metaphors in Arabic around
the domain of family.

Of course, that's not exactly what IARPA's looking for, but it's where the
research teams will be starting. To get better results, they will have to start
to learn a lot more about the relationships between the words in the metaphors. For Lakoff, that means understanding the frames and logics that
inform metaphors and structure our thinking as we use them. For Bergen,
it means refining the rules by which software can process language. There
are three levels of analysis that would then be combined. First, you could
know something about the metaphorical bias of an individual word. Cross-
roads, for example, is generally used in metaphorical terms. Second, words
in close proximity might generate a bias, too. "Knockout in the same clause
as 'she' has a much higher probability of being metaphorical if it's in close
proximity to 'he,'" Bergen offered as an example. Third, for certain topics,
certain words become more active for metaphorical usage. The economy's
movement, for example, probably maps to a source domain of motion
through space. So, accelerate to describe something about the economy is
probably metaphorical. Create a statistical model to combine the outputs of
those three processes and you've got a brute-force method for identifying
metaphors in a text.

In this particular competition, there will be more nuanced approaches
based on parsing the more general relationships between words in text:
sorting out which are nouns and how they connect to verbs, etc. "If you
have that information, then you can find parts of sentences that don't look
like they should be there," Bergen explained. A classic kind of identifier
would be a type mismatch. "If I am the verb 'smile,' I like to have a subject
that has a face," he said. If something without a face is smiling, it might be
an indication that some kind of figurative language is being employed.

From these constituent parts—and whatever other wild stuff people cook up—the teams will try to build a metaphor machine that can convert a language into underlying truths about a culture. Feed text in one end and wait on the other end of the Rube Goldberg software for a series of beliefs about family or America or power.

We might never be able to build such a thing. Indeed, I get the feeling that we can't, at least not yet. But what if we can?

35   "Are they going to use it wisely?" Lakoff posed. "Because using it to detect terrorists is not a bad idea, but then the question is: Are they going to use it to spy on us?"

I don't know, but I know that as an American I think through these metaphors: Problem Is a Target; Society Is a Body; Control Is Up.

Analyze

1. What, according to the article, is the motive behind IARPA's project "The Metaphor Program?" What goals would the project accomplish?
2. Would you agree that the Metaphor Program is not spy software but something more human? Why or why not?
3. Analyze some of the examples provided in this article as you explain the difference between a "source domain" and a "target domain." What is the relationship between these two domains?

Explore

1. Make a list of some common metaphors you could build around concepts such as "love," "family," or "work." What do these metaphors reveal about the culture to which you belong?
2. Write a letter to a local politician arguing for or against The Metaphor Program. Refer to Madrigal's article as you examine the effect that the creation of a "machine that can convert a language into underlying truths about a culture" may have on our lives.
3. Technological advancements have certainly made our lives easier, but they often come at a price. What happens when we rely on machines with human-like capacity for directions (GPS), for information (iPhone's Siri) or for scoring student writing (Accuplacer)? Write a research paper on one of these topics by examining the views of published scholars.

Neal Whitman
"Kinetic" Connections

Neal Whitman is a blogger at *Literal-Minded*, where he writes about linguistics in everyday life from the point of view of a husband and father. He has published articles in *Language, Journal of Linguistics,* and other publications. The following selection appeared on the website *Visual Thesaurus* on May 4, 2011. *Visual Thesaurus* is "an interactive dictionary and thesaurus which creates word maps that blossom with meanings and branch to related words." In the following selection, Whitman examines the use of the word "kinetic" in an article explaining how U.S. forces managed to locate and kill Osama bin Laden. He later recognizes how pervasive the word *kinetic* has actually become in military language, from *kinetic warfare* to *kinetic targeting.*

What other examples of military language have you noticed recently in either the news online, in the papers, or on television?

I stayed up late on the night of May 1 to hear President Obama's stunning announcement: A special-forces mission, which could have gone humiliatingly wrong, had instead succeeded in killing Osama bin Laden, the man behind the worst terrorist attack on American soil. I watched until the news reporters ran out of things to say, when they began to fill airtime by repeating things and asking the opinions of people in the streets while waiting for something else to happen.

I had to wait until the next morning to read more about how US forces had actually managed to achieve this victory, when I read this article in the *National Journal* online. The team of Navy SEALs that carried out the mission, I learned, were part of a special group of special-missions units and task forces known as the Joint Special Operations Command. The article went on to explain some more about JSOC, saying:

> Recently, JSOC built a new Targeting and Analysis Center in Rosslyn, Va. Where the National Counterterrorism Center tends to focus on threats to the homeland, TAAC, whose existence was first

disclosed by the Associated Press, focuses outward, on active "kinetic"—or lethal—counterterrorism missions abroad.

The definition of *kinetic* caught my eye. It was in quotation marks, followed by a gloss to explain its meaning. Apparently the author, Mark Ambinder, didn't expect his readers to be familiar with this specialized meaning of *kinetic*. But people have been getting familiar with it for several months now. My introduction to it was during the annual meeting of the American Dialect Society in January, when the term *kinetic event* won the "Most Euphemistic" category in the ADS's 2010 Word of the Year vote. A kinetic event is "a violent action in the field of battle," according to the definition Ben Zimmer is writing in the "Among the New Words" column in next month's issue of *American Speech*, the journal of the ADS. The term had been in the news from Afghanistan in reports like this one from September (to appear in Ben's entry):

> The coalition is reporting . . . that in August, just last month, there were more than 4,900 kinetic events. That's an attack, mortars, rockets, small arms, IEDs.

In March, the public awareness of this new sense of *kinetic* was raised further by the phrase *kinetic military action,* the widely ridiculed term used by Ben Rhodes, the Deputy National Security Advisor in describing the United States' role in the ongoing conflict in Libya. Jonathan Allen wrote an article on *Politico.com*:

> Police action, conflict, hostilities and now "kinetic military action." They're all euphemisms for that word that this White House and many before it have been so careful not to say: War.
>
> Administration officials told congressional aides in a closed briefing earlier this week that the United States is not at war with Libya, and Deputy National Security Adviser Ben Rhodes danced around the question in a Wednesday exchange with reporters aboard Air Force One.
>
> "I think what we are doing is enforcing a resolution that has a very clear set of goals, which is protecting the Libyan people, averting a humanitarian crisis, and setting up a no-fly zone," Rhodes said.

"Obviously that involves kinetic military action, particularly on the front end. But again, the nature of our commitment is that we are not getting into an open-ended war, a land invasion in Libya."

Although the military sense of *kinetic* seeped into public consciousness   5
in 2010 and 2011, as with many seemingly new words, it turns out to have
spent a number of years paying its dues before getting its big break.

The euphemistic feel of *kinetic* comes from its association with scientific
inquiry. Unless you're a teacher (who deals with visual, auditory, and kines-
thetic learning styles) or an artist (who might create kinetic sculptures), the
word *kinetic* probably brings to mind high-school physics class, and lectures
about potential and kinetic energy. In fact, in its first uses relating to the
military or national defense, *kinetic* did mean "relating to kinetic energy."
In the 1978 edition of the *Code Name Handbook: Aerospace Defense Technology* the acronym *SKEW* is defined as a "shoulder-fired kinetic energy
weapon". A kinetic-energy weapon, as opposed to a chemical-energy
weapon, is one that does its damage with the simple kinetic energy of the
projectiles it fires. A gun with ordinary, non-exploding bullets would be
one example of a kinetic energy weapon.

Alternatively, a kinetic energy weapon could be a missile or other heavy
object hurled from space, as long as it isn't equipped with, say, a nuclear
warhead. A 1983 article in the *Boston Globe* quotes a brochure for a weapons conference as mentioning missiles as kinetic energy weapons. One part
of Ronald Reagan's proposed Strategic Defense Initiative/"Star Wars" mis-
sile-defense system was the "kinetic kill vehicle" (KKV). The term starts
appearing in news reports from 1985, and continues to do so even now,
though these days the focus is more on destroying Chinese rather than
Russian missiles or satellites.

A year after the proposal of SDI, the phrase *kinetic energy penetrator*
as a synonym/euphemism for *bullet* was in circulation, and five years
after that, it got a real workout during Operation Desert Storm, when US
tanks were equipped with kinetic energy penetrators made of depleted
uranium—a good conveyor of kinetic energy because of its high density.
(I have to say, though, that using DU as a weapon by turning it into a really
heavy piece of ammunition is like using a barometer to determine the
height of a building by throwing it over the edge and timing how long it
takes to hit the ground.)

These uses of *kinetic* seem to have paved the way toward its broader meaning of military attacks, which had become well-established by the time of the September 11 terrorist attacks. In a 2002 article in Slate, Timothy Noah introduces his readers to the term *kinetic warfare*:

> "Retronym" is a word coined by Frank Mankiewicz, George Mc-Govern's campaign director, to delineate previously unnecessary distinctions. Examples include "acoustic guitar," "analog watch," "natural turf," "two-parent family," and "offline publication." Bob Woodward's new book, *Bush at War*, introduces a new Washington retronym: "kinetic" warfare.

10   Noah then quotes from page 150 of *Bush at War,* in which President Bush and his advisors talk about "going kinetic" against al Qaeda after 9/11. Noah continues:

> In common usage, "kinetic" is an adjective used to describe motion, but the Washington meaning derives from its secondary definition, "active, as opposed to latent." Dropping bombs and shooting bullets—you know, killing people—is kinetic. But the 21st-century military is exploring less violent and more high-tech means of warfare, such as messing electronically with the enemy's communications equipment or wiping out its bank accounts. These are "non-kinetic." . . . Asked during a January [2002] talk at National Defense University whether "the transformed military of the future will shift emphasis somewhat from kinetic systems to cyber warfare," Donald Rumsfeld answered, "Yes!" (Rumsfeld uses the words "kinetic" and "non-kinetic" all the time.)

In addition to *kinetic warfare* and *kinetic systems*, there is a host of other 21st-century *kinetic* terms, including *kinetic operations, kinetic capability, kinetic engagements, kinetic strike, kinetic activity,* and *kinetic targeting,* i.e. bombing. These days the bombs don't have to be non-explosive; the opposite of kinetic targeting is *soft targeting*: dropping leaflets. Areas where fighting is going on are *kinetic areas. Kinetic* can be a predicate adjective, too, i.e., one that comes after a linking verb. An army unit might *go kinetic,* and an article from 2006 tells how British soldiers in Iraq believed their American counterparts were "too kinetic." (Kinetic Yankees, if you will.) There is even an adjective, *post-kinetic*, to describe reconstruction, or places where battles have taken place.

Commander Philip Thrash, an old high-school friend and former field artillery officer in the US Army, served in Afghanistan in 2007–2008. He confirms that it isn't just the top brass who use *kinetic*. He started to hear it among his superiors in 2003 or 2004, and during his service, he and his peers and subordinates used it often. As he explained: You hear your superiors use it, and if you want to communicate effectively with them, you use the words they use, and then it just becomes part of your lexicon. *Kinetic* is useful because it can cover a lot of more specific verbs, such as *engage*, *acquire (a target)*, *move to contact*, *destroy*, *neutralize*. Summing up, Philip used an unsettling but soberingly accurate turn of phrase that has been in print since at least the late 1970s, and that some veterans remember from the Vietnam War. Basically, he said, *kinetic* is "a polite way of saying 'kill people and break things.'"

Analyze

1. Why, according to Whitman, does the word *kinetic* have a "euphemistic feel"? Do you agree that it is a euphemism? Why or why not?
2. What is a "retronym" and why would "kinetic" warfare be considered a retronym?
3. What is Whitman's purpose in writing this article? Refer to specific parts of his essay as you respond.

Explore

1. Does a word like "kinetic" hide or highlight how countries operate during war time? Write a brief response to the different ways the word can be used and what it tells you about the language of war.
2. Examine some of the retronyms Whitman mentions in this article. What cultural changes do terms reflect and why are they important today?
3. What is the function of euphemisms in our society? Look into the history of popular words and phrases that are considered to be euphemisms, and refer to scholarly articles by language experts to support your argument.

Julie Sedivy
Are You a Mac or a Mac User? How the Language of Identity Persuades

Cognitive scientist Julie Sedivy has taught at Brown University and the University of Calgary. The following excerpt from Sedivy's book, *Sold on Language: How Advertisers Talk to You and What This Says About You* (Wiley, 2011), was posted to *Psychology Today* (the website for the magazine of the same name) in August 2011. *Psychology Today* features articles and blogs by renowned academics and clinicians who write about psychology for a general readership. In this excerpt, Sedivy examines strategies of verbal persuasion used by advertisers, and how consumers tend to rely on advertising language as a way of self-identifying. She notes, "I've witnessed . . . how compelling the need can be to align consumer behavior with a sense of self, and how this need can override even the most careful deliberation."

Have you ever used a brand name to describe the type of person you are—or have you ever had a brand name applied to you, in either a complimentary or derogatory fashion?

Do you think of yourself as a beer-drinker, or do you merely drink beer? Are you a Volkswagen driver or a Democrat, or do you just drive a Volkswagen or vote for Democratic candidates? The difference in how these notions are worded involves more than just splitting linguistic hairs. Phrases like *drive a Volkswagen* or *vote for Democrats* simply describe behaviors that you take part in. But if you assert that you're a Volkswagen driver or a Democrat, you're expressing something fundamental about *who you are*. Wielding the right language to tap into people's sense of identity, as it turns out, can make for potent persuasion.

Every now and then, though, someone makes it clear that covert techniques of persuasion can be used for the public good and not just for nefarious purposes. For example, one recent study shows that tweaking language to focus on identity can drive people to the voting booths. Christopher Bryan and several colleagues from Stanford and Harvard Universities recruited citizens who were registered to vote in the 2008 presidential election and gave them a short "election survey" less than 24 hours before the election. Some people saw questions such as *"How important is it to you to vote in the upcoming election?"* Others instead answered questions like *"How important is it to you to be a voter in the upcoming election?"* Subtle difference in wording, no? A mere flick of the linguistic wrist. But guess what? It had a massive effect on actual voter turnout. About 82% of the people who were asked the first question later turned up at the polls, just slightly above the national average for registered voters (79%). In contrast, the voter rate after the second question (which prompted people to think of themselves as either voters or non-voters) was a staggering 95.5%. A second study of the 2009 gubernatorial election in New Jersey yielded an effect that was just slightly smaller—a 10% difference due to questionnaire wording.

According to the authors, these findings are "among the largest experimental effects ever observed on objectively measured voter turnout." To put them into perspective, the researchers also measured the impact of age, gender, ethnicity, level of education, political knowledge, and even interest in politics—*none of which* showed any statistically reliable effects on voter turnout for their sample of registered voters. (Though perhaps they should also have studied the impact of supplying donuts at the polling stations.)

As the study by Bryan and colleagues suggests, we humans appear to resonate like plucked strings to messages that appeal to our self-concept. On the more commercial side of things, marketers have of late been putting more emphasis on telling us about who are and less on what their products can do for us. Techniques of identity marketing range from linking brands with certain symbols or spokespersons to choosing regional linguistic dialects in commercials. But no one has raised the practice to quite the same explicit level as Apple with its *Mac vs. PC* ad campaign, in which stereotyped characters were offered up as the very embodiment of competing computer brands. Remember how each ad began with the words "I'm a Mac" and "I'm a PC"? You don't get identity marketing much clearer than that. (And the central message was equally clear: to avoid being fatally dorky, get a Mac.)

Consumers, incidentally, jump at the opportunity to use products as a way of defining and broadcasting their personal identities, as documented by Rob Walker in his interesting book *Buying in: What We Buy and Who We Are.* These days, to drink Pabst beer rather than Heineken or to use   5

French's yellow mustard over Dijon-style is more than just a matter of personal taste. It says something about who we are, and we thank the makers of beer and mustard for giving us the tools with which to say it.

Maybe I shouldn't have been as startled as I was by the whopping size of the effect of identity-based language on voter turnout. After all, I've recently witnessed an example of how compelling the need can be to align consumer behavior with a sense of self, and how this need can override even the most careful deliberation. Some close friends of mine were in the market for a new car. They're thorough, thoughtful types, and did a lot of research before ever setting foot in a dealership. They narrowed the field down to two station wagons they were interested in: the Volkswagen Passat and the Subaru Outback. Over dinner one evening, they reported that they'd made a list of the features they wanted in a car and had pored over consumer reports. They were going to test-drive both cars, but their research already suggested that the Passat had the greatest number of their desired features at a better price. Two weeks later, they pulled up in their shiny new Subaru. "What happened to the Passat?" I asked. The husband looked sheepish. "When it comes down to it," he explained, "We're just not Passat people."

NOTES

1 I first learned of this interesting paper in a blog post by linguist David Beaver. In his post on the Language Log blog, Beaver addresses some more subtle linguistic points than I have talked about here.

2 To read the paper on identity-based language and voter turnout:
Bryan, C. J., Walton, G. M., Rogers, T. & Dweck, C. S. 2011. Motivating voter turnout by invoking the self. *Proceedings of the National Academy of Science, 108*, 12653–12656.

Analyze

1. Why did the phrase "to be a voter" have such a big effect on people's voting practice? Explain the differences implied by the phrases "to vote" and "to be a voter."

2. Sedivy states that "humans appear to resonate like plucked strings to messages that appeal to our self-concept" but doesn't explain why. Think about some of the reasons why our sense of identity is so closely tied to the choices we make as consumers.

3. Do you agree with the interpretation that PC users are "fatally dorky"? Discuss how the image associated with an Apple product is different from that of a Microsoft product and explain what accounts for this difference.

Explore

1. Are you loyal to certain brands of products because of the way these products—and their advertising—appeal to your identity? Write a narrative essay in which you describe at least two such products and reflect on what they say about you.

2. Sedivy ends with an intriguing story about friends who think of themselves as "Subaru people" rather than "Passat people." Can people actually be defined by the type of car they drive? Analyze a television commercial for a popular brand of car by first describing the exactly what you see in the advertisement and then interpreting its message. What type of personality and lifestyle (a "demographic") would this type of car-owner have? If you think the advertisement is specifically aimed at your demographic, do you find its depiction appealing—or off-base?

3. Sedivy's essay forces us to consider the power of words, images, and ideas often associated with consumer products. In a carefully re-searched essay in which you cite media critics and analysts, consider the advertising strategies companies use to create and market products and the effect it has on the consumer.

Forging Connections

1. All of the selections in this chapter reflect how powerful institutions (e.g., the government and media) commonly rely on the clever and creative use of language to manipulate, coerce, convince, and even confuse. However, is it possible for people without access to power to benefit from such language? What might these benefits be? Refer to the ideas from at least two readings in this chapter as you develop your argument.

2. Madrigal and Lutz's articles show how metaphors and euphemisms can offer insights about cultural patterns and thought. Analyze some of the examples the authors provide in their essays and discuss their meaning and relevance.

Looking Further

1. The media is the driving engine of publicity. We see advertisements every-where we look—on television, billboards, websites, and in magazines—and their sole aim is to convince us to buy products. Do advertisements always tell us the truth about these products or do they use language that, as William Lutz notes in his essay "The World of Doublespeak," make "the bad seem good, the negative appear positive"? Analyze an advertisement that you believe employs persuasive but perhaps mislead-ing language to promote its product. Refer to Lutz's definition of double-speak as you explain how the advertisement uses particular words and phrases to accomplish its goal.

2. Are our perception of politicians and world leaders tied to the way they express themselves? Examine how a famous politician uses the power of words to convey his or her ideas and beliefs and how this shapes your impression of the person. Does the person's race or gender influence the language that is used? How? Refer to at least one selection from Chapter 5, "Language and Gender," or Chapter 6, "Language and Race," to inform your argument.

8 Fighting Words

You might have heard the common saying, "Sticks and stones may break my bones but words can never hurt me." Well, the authors of the selections in this chapter provide ample evidence to the contrary. They go to great lengths to argue that although certain words and phrases might have innocent origins, the ways they have come to be used have forever changed their meaning and impact. Whether they are phrases that are skillfully conjured to offend, hurt, and discriminate, or seemingly benign words that somehow became weapons hurled at vulnerable populations, there is no doubt that words have the power not only to express certain values but also to influence the way these values get attached to a target population.

Authors in this chapter argue that the battle against violence, hatred, and bigotry is, at least partially, a battle against the language that fosters such beliefs and behaviors. The question, then, is whether or not a shift in the language itself can elicit a change in harmful perceptions and attitudes toward others. Is it possible that in the 21st century the very mechanisms that enable quick and efficient dissemination of hate speech (e.g., texts, Twitters, emails, and Facebook posts) might also help in reversing its effects by making it just as easy to condemn such offensive words and phrases? Ultimately, who should take responsibility for the spread of "loaded" terms—the media, the individual, or language itself?

Activist and writer Rebecca Solnit argues in "When the Media Is the Disaster" that the media's consistent and thoughtless use of words such as "looting" can have a far more disastrous effect on already weakened populations, like the earthquake-ravaged people of Haiti, than the disaster itself. She compares such language to crimes against humanity. In "Words as Weapons," Susan Benesch, Professor and Director of the World Policy Institute's Dangerous Speech Project, demonstrates how the ghost of a violent, oppressive past still haunts South Africa as it struggles to deal with its linguistic legacy. Although the *Journal of Animal Ethics* might have good intentions, Julie Sedivy points out in "Politically Correct Animal Language" that replacing commonplace terms used to refer to animals with more neutral-sounding words might not have the effect animal ethicists expect. In "The Dirtiest of Words on Capitol Hill: 'Racism',' Shani O. Hilton, a Washington, DC correspondent for the website *Colorlines*, makes a list of the most racially charged words used in Congress and offers us a glimpse into how these words break down by party line. In the article "'Anchor Baby' Added to New American Heritage Dictionary" and "American Heritage Dictionary Redefines 'Anchor Baby' Term as 'Offensive' and 'Disparaging'," Director of the Immigration Policy Center Mary Giovagnoli is at first disappointed at how dictionaries fail to be precise when defining politically charged words such as "anchor baby" and then, after noting a reversal in the definition, discusses how a thoughtful review of language might lead to immigration reform. Finally, *Boston Globe* columnist Mark Peters, in his essay "Why Personhood Is Powerful," traces the history of the term "personhood," notes it's more recent and controversial applications, and alerts us to the challenges it will pose in the future.

Rebecca Solnit
When the Media Is the Disaster

Rebecca Solnit is a San Francisco-based writer, historian, and activist. Her book *River of Shadows, Eadweard Muybridge and the Technological Wild West* (Penguin Books, 2004) received a Guggenheim fellowship, the National Book Critics Circle Award in criticism, and the Lannan Literary Award. She is a contributing editor to *Harper's Magazine* as well as a frequent editor to *Tomdispatch*, a website that features global voices and perspectives not heard in the mainstream media. The following post appeared in January 2010 in *Guernica*, an award-winning, bimonthly online magazine of ideas, art, poetry, and fiction.

Is it reasonable to expect journalists to remain cautious and impartial when covering breaking news, especially on the scale of a natural disaster or civil war? What is your responsibility as a consumer of journalism to consider alternate viewpoints?

Soon after almost every disaster the crimes begin: ruthless, selfish, indifferent to human suffering, and generating far more suffering. The perpetrators go unpunished and live to commit further crimes against humanity. They care less for human life than for property. They act without regard for consequences.

I'm talking, of course, about those members of the mass media whose misrepresentation of what goes on in disaster often abets and justifies a second wave of disaster. I'm talking about the treatment of sufferers as criminals, both on the ground and in the news, and the endorsement of a shift of resources from rescue to property patrol. They still have blood on their hands from Hurricane Katrina, and they are staining themselves anew in Haiti.

Within days of the Haitian earthquake, for example, the *Los Angeles Times* ran a series of photographs with captions that kept deploying the word "looting." One was of a man lying face down on the ground with this caption: "A Haitian police officer ties up a suspected looter who was carrying a bag of evaporated milk." The man's sweaty face looks up at the camera, beseeching, anguished.

Another photo was labeled: "Looting continued in Haiti on the third day after the earthquake, although there were more police in downtown Port-au-Prince." It showed a somber crowd wandering amid shattered piles of concrete in a landscape where, visibly, there could be little worth taking anyway.

5   A third image was captioned: "A looter makes off with rolls of fabric from an earthquake-wrecked store." Yet another: "The body of a police officer lies in a Port-au-Prince street. He was accidentally shot by fellow police who mistook him for a looter."

People were then still trapped alive in the rubble. A translator for Australian TV dug out a toddler who'd survived 68 hours without food or water, orphaned but claimed by an uncle who had lost his pregnant wife. Others were hideously wounded and awaiting medical attention that wasn't arriving. Hundreds of thousands, maybe millions, needed, and still need, water, food, shelter, and first aid. The media in disaster bifurcates. Some step out of their usual "objective" roles to respond with kindness and practical aid. Others bring out the arsenal of clichés and pernicious myths and begin to assault the survivors all over again.

The "looter" in the first photo might well have been taking that milk to starving children and babies, but for the news media that wasn't the most urgent problem. The "looter" stooped under the weight of two big bolts of fabric might well have been bringing it to now homeless people trying to shelter from a fierce tropical sun under improvised tents.

The pictures do convey desperation, but they *don't* convey crime. Except perhaps for that shooting of a fellow police officer—his colleagues were so focused on property that they were reckless when it came to human life, and a man died for no good reason in a landscape already saturated with death.

In recent days, there have been scattered accounts of confrontations involving weapons, and these may be a different matter. But the man with the powdered milk? Is he really a criminal? There may be more to know, but with what I've seen I'm not convinced.

What Would You Do?

10   Imagine, reader, that your city is shattered by a disaster. Your home no longer exists, and you spent what cash was in your pockets days ago. Your credit cards are meaningless because there is no longer any power to run

credit-card charges. Actually, there are no longer any storekeepers, any banks, any commerce, or much of anything to buy. The economy has ceased to exist.

By day three, you're pretty hungry and the water you grabbed on your way out of your house is gone. The thirst is far worse than the hunger. You can go for many days without food, but not water. And in the improvised encampment you settle in, there is an old man near you who seems on the edge of death. He no longer responds when you try to reassure him that this ordeal will surely end. Toddlers are now crying constantly, and their mothers infinitely stressed and distressed.

So you go out to see if any relief organization has finally arrived to distribute anything, only to realize that there are a million others like you stranded with nothing, and there isn't likely to be anywhere near enough aid anytime soon. The guy with the corner store has already given away all his goods to the neighbors. That supply's long gone by now. No wonder, when you see the chain pharmacy with the shattered windows or the supermarket, you don't think twice before grabbing a box of PowerBars and a few gallons of water that might keep you alive and help you save a few lives as well.

The old man might not die, the babies might stop their squalling, and the mothers might lose that look on their faces. Other people are calmly wandering in and helping themselves, too. Maybe they're people like you, and that gallon of milk the fellow near you has taken is going to spoil soon anyway. You haven't shoplifted since you were 14, and you have plenty of money to your name. But it doesn't mean anything now.

If you grab that stuff are you a criminal? Should you end up lying in the dirt on your stomach with a cop tying your hands behind your back? Should you end up labeled a looter in the international media? Should you be shot down in the street, since the overreaction in disaster, almost *any* disaster, often includes the imposition of the death penalty without benefit of trial for suspected minor property crimes?

Or are you a rescuer? Is the survival of disaster victims more important than the preservation of everyday property relations? Is that chain pharmacy more vulnerable, more a victim, more in need of help from the National Guard than you are, or those crying kids, or the thousands still trapped in buildings and soon to die?

It's pretty obvious what my answers to these questions are, but it isn't obvious to the mass media. And in disaster after disaster, at least since the

San Francisco earthquake of 1906, those in power, those with guns and the force of law behind them, are too often more concerned for property than human life. In an emergency, people can, and do, die from those priorities. Or they get gunned down for minor thefts or imagined thefts. The media not only endorses such outcomes, but regularly, repeatedly, helps prepare the way for, and then eggs on, such a reaction.

If Words Could Kill

We need to banish the word "looting" from the English language. It incites madness and obscures realities.

> "We need to banish the word 'looting' from the English language."

"Loot," the noun and the verb, is a word of Hindi origin meaning the spoils of war or other goods seized roughly. As historian Peter Linebaugh points out, "At one time loot was the soldier's pay." It entered the English language as a good deal of loot from India entered the English economy, both in soldiers' pockets and as imperial seizures.

After years of interviewing survivors of disasters, and reading first-hand accounts and sociological studies from such disasters as the London Blitz and the Mexico City earthquake of 1985, I don't believe in looting. Two things go on in disasters. The great majority of what happens you could call emergency requisitioning. Someone who could be you, someone in the kind of desperate circumstances I outlined above, takes necessary supplies to sustain human life in the absence of any alternative. Not only would I not call that looting, I wouldn't even call that theft.

20   Necessity is a defense for breaking the law in the United States and other countries, though it's usually applied more to, say, confiscating the car keys of a drunk driver than feeding hungry children. Taking things you don't need is theft under any circumstances. It is, says the disaster sociologist Enrico Quarantelli, who has been studying the subject for more than half a century, vanishingly rare in most disasters.

Personal gain is the last thing most people are thinking about in the aftermath of a disaster. In that phase, the survivors are almost invariably more altruistic and less attached to their own property, less concerned with the long-term questions of acquisition, status, wealth, and security, than just about anyone not in such situations imagines possible. (The best accounts from Haiti of how people with next to nothing have patiently tried to share the little they have and support those in even worse shape than them only emphasize this disaster reality.) Crime often drops in the wake of a disaster.

The media are another matter. They tend to arrive obsessed with property (and the headlines that assaults on property can make). Media outlets often call everything looting and thereby incite hostility toward the sufferers as well as a hysterical overreaction on the part of the armed authorities. Or sometimes the journalists on the ground do a good job and the editors back in their safe offices cook up the crazy photo captions and the wrong-headed interpretations and emphases.

They also deploy the word *panic* wrongly. Panic among ordinary people in crisis is profoundly uncommon. The media will call a crowd of people running from certain death a panicking mob, even though running is the only sensible thing to do. In Haiti, they continue to report that food is being withheld from distribution for fear of "stampedes." Do they think Haitians are cattle?

The belief that people in disaster (particularly poor and nonwhite people) are cattle or animals or just crazy and untrustworthy regularly justifies spending far too much energy and far too many resources on control—the American military calls it "security"—rather than relief. A British-accented voiceover on CNN calls people sprinting to where supplies are being dumped from a helicopter a "stampede" and adds that this delivery "risks sparking chaos." The chaos already exists, and you can't blame it on these people desperate for food and water. Or you can, and in doing so help convince your audience that they're unworthy and untrustworthy.

Back to looting: of course you can consider Haiti's dire poverty and failed 25 institutions a long-term disaster that changes the rules of the game. There might be people who are not only interested in taking the things they need to survive in the next few days, but things they've never been entitled to own or things they may need next month. Technically that's theft, but I'm not particularly surprised or distressed by it; the distressing thing is that even before the terrible quake they led lives of deprivation and desperation.

In ordinary times, minor theft is often considered a misdemeanor. No one is harmed. Unchecked, minor thefts could perhaps lead to an environment in which there were more thefts and so forth, and a good argument can be made that, in such a case, the tide needs to be stemmed. But it's not particularly significant in a landscape of terrible suffering and mass death.

A number of radio hosts and other media personnel are still upset that people apparently took TVs after Hurricane Katrina hit New Orleans in August 2005. Since I started thinking about, and talking to people about, disaster aftermaths I've heard a lot about those damned TVs. Now, which matters more to you, televisions or human life? People were dying on rooftops and in overheated attics and freeway overpasses, they were stranded in all kinds of hideous circumstances on the Gulf Coast in 2005 when the mainstream media began to obsess about looting, and the mayor of New Orleans and the governor of Louisiana made the decision to focus on protecting property, not human life.

A gang of white men on the other side of the river from New Orleans got so worked up about property crimes that they decided to take the law into their own hands and began shooting. They seem to have considered all black men criminals and thieves and shot a number of them. Some apparently died; there were bodies bloating in the September sun far from the region of the floods; one good man trying to evacuate the ruined city barely survived; and the media looked away. It took me months of nagging to even get the story covered. This vigilante gang claimed to be protecting property, though its members never demonstrated that their property was threatened. They boasted of killing black men. And they shared values with the mainstream media and the Louisiana powers that be.

Somehow, when the Bush administration subcontracted emergency services—like providing evacuation buses in Hurricane Katrina—to cronies who profited even while providing incompetent, overpriced, and much delayed service at the moment of greatest urgency, we didn't label that looting. Or when a lot of wealthy Wall Street brokers decide to tinker with a basic human need like housing . . . Well, you catch my drift.

30

Woody Guthrie once sang that "some will rob you with a six-gun, and some with a fountain pen." The guys with the six guns (or machetes or sharpened sticks) make for better photographs, and the guys with the fountain pens not only don't end up in jail, they end up in McMansions with four-car garages and, sometimes, in elected—or appointed—office.

Learning to See in Crises

Last Christmas a priest, Father Tim Jones of York, started a ruckus in Britain when he said in a sermon that shoplifting by the desperate from chain stores might be acceptable behavior. Naturally, there was an uproar. Jones told the Associated Press: "The point I'm making is that when we shut down every socially acceptable avenue for people in need, then the only avenue left is the socially unacceptable one."

The response focused almost entirely on why shoplifting is wrong, but the claim was also repeatedly made that it doesn't help. In fact, food helps the hungry, a fact so bald it's bizarre to even have to state it. The means by which it arrives is a separate matter. The focus remained on shoplifting, rather than on why there might be people so desperate in England's green and pleasant land that shoplifting might be their only option, and whether unnecessary human suffering is itself a crime of sorts.

Right now, the point is that people in Haiti need food, and for all the publicity, the international delivery system has, so far, been a visible dud. Under such circumstances, breaking into a U.N. food warehouse—food assumedly meant for the poor of Haiti in a catastrophic moment—might not be "violence," or "looting," or "law-breaking." It might be logic. It might be the most effective way of meeting a desperate need.

Why were so many people in Haiti hungry before the earthquake? Why 35 do we have a planet that produces enough food for all and a distribution system that ensures more than a billion of us don't have a decent share of that bounty? Those are not questions whose answers should be long delayed.

Even more urgently, we need compassion for the sufferers in Haiti and media that tell the truth about them. I'd like to propose alternative captions for those *Los Angeles Times* photographs as models for all future disasters:

Let's start with the picture of the policeman hogtying the figure whose face is so anguished: "Ignoring thousands still trapped in rubble, a policeman accosts a sufferer who took evaporated milk. No adequate food distribution exists for Haiti's starving millions."

And the guy with the bolt of fabric? "As with every disaster, ordinary people show extraordinary powers of improvisation, and fabrics such as these are being used to make sun shelters around Haiti."

For the murdered policeman: "Institutional overzealousness about protecting property leads to a gratuitous murder, as often happens in crises. Meanwhile countless people remain trapped beneath crushed buildings."

And the crowd in the rubble labeled looters? How about: "Resourceful 40 survivors salvage the means of sustaining life from the ruins of their world."

That one might not be totally accurate, but it's likely to be more accurate than the existing label. And what is absolutely accurate, in Haiti right now, and on Earth always, is that human life matters more than property, that the survivors of a catastrophe deserve our compassion and our understanding of their plight, and that we live and die by words and ideas, and it matters desperately that we get them right.

Analyze

1. Are you convinced by Solnit's interpretation of the word "looting"? Summarize her main argument by referring to the key points she makes in her essay.
2. What point about media representation of disaster does Solnit's discussion of the *Los Angeles Times* photographs reveal to you?
3. How would you characterize the voice Solnit employs in her essay? What does it tell you about her intentions as a writer?

Explore

1. The author believes that the word "looting" should be removed from the English language because "it incites madness and obscures realities." Do you agree with her? Would simply eliminating certain words from our language help in getting rid of ideas associated with them? Why?
2. Find images of "looting" from disasters such as Hurricane Katrina, the Haitian earthquake, or the Los Angeles riots that have been published in the media. Describe what you see in these images. If there are captions, do you feel they are accurate—or even adequate? Write an essay in which you analyze two such images by referring to Solnit's ideas about the moral implications of the acts reflected in the photographs. Develop a clear argument about the responsibility that journalists have when covering disasters.
3. Solnit argues that it is only logical for starving Haitians to break into the U.N. food warehouse because it is the "most effective way of meeting a desperate need." Write a letter to the U.N. Secretary General in which you address the problem of food supply to disaster-ridden countries like Haiti. Refer back to Solnit's argument as you make suggestions for improving the ways in which the media and relief organizations can work together to convey an accurate, compassionate portrayal of people in a disaster zone whose needs are not being met.

Susan Benesch
Words as Weapons

Susan Benesch directs the World Policy Institute's Dangerous Speech project and teaches advanced international human rights at American University's School of International Service. A human rights lawyer, she has also worked for the Center for Justice and Accountability, Amnesty International, and the Lawyers Committee for Human Rights (now Human Rights First). The following selection was published in the Spring 2012 "Speaking in Tongues" issue of *World Policy Journal*. The journal provides a forum for solution-focused, accessible policy analysis and public debate. In her essay Benesch questions the permissibility of certain speech, especially speech that can potentially incite violence in politically fragile developing nations.

Is "freedom of speech" a luxury only for politically stable and wealthy societies? Should oppressed people, who have no other weapons with which to fight, be allowed to use potentially inflammatory speech in their struggles for freedom?

A mong friends and fans at his boozy 29th birthday party in March 2010, the South African youth leader Julius Malema cocked his right thumb, pointed his finger like a pistol and chanted "Dubulu iBhunu" (shoot the Boer). The crowd sang along merrily.

Malema sang Dubulu iBhunu again a few days later at a rally at the University of Johannesburg, but this time it was aired on television and translated into Afrikaans, in which 'Boer' originally meant 'farmer' and is now a derogatory term for Afrikaner. Hundreds of agitated whites filed formal protests and a judge ordered Malema to stop singing Dubulu iBhunu until the matter could be decided in court. He went on anyway, saying he was only preserving an old anthem from the anti-apartheid struggle—a piece of cultural heritage not to be taken literally. He was singing about the Afrikaner-designed apartheid system, he said, not encouraging his listeners to shoot people.

A hailstorm of debate followed in South Africa, especially on the Internet. Whites especially feared that the song was inspiring black South Africans to kill Afrikaner farmers. In recent years, hundreds of white farm owners and managers had been murdered, mostly in connection with robberies, but often with gruesome violence, and sometimes with their wives or children. But the ruling African National Congress defended Malema, then head of its Youth League, and the song. Party spokesman Jackson Mthembu took responsibility for it on behalf of the ANC, saying it "was sung for many years even before Malema was born," and must be understood in the context of the anti-apartheid struggle. South Africa's minister of arts and culture, Lulu Xingwana, and other politicians joined in defying the judge by chanting the song on the 31st anniversary of an anti-apartheid fighter's hanging.

The controversy was still raging months later, in February 2011, when U2's Bono went on tour in South Africa. Asked about Dubulu iBhunu, he compared it to Irish Republican Army songs he had sung with his uncles as a child. "It's about where and when you sing those songs," Bono said. Indeed, speech and song can be powerful catalysts for human action of all kinds, but their meaning and impact depend tremendously on context and on who's speaking and listening.

5   Afriforum, an Afrikaner civil rights group, took Malema to court over his song, and in September 2011, Judge Collin Lamont banned it under South African law prohibiting speech that demonstrates a clear intention to be hurtful, to incite harm, or to promote hatred. Minutes after the judge finished reading his thoughtful, hour-long verdict, a knot of Malema's young supporters belted out Dubulu iBhunu a few feet away from the courthouse door, just as he had warned they would. The singers had a live audience—a row of police standing rigid in their riot helmets. Neither judge nor police could stop a song.

In his courtroom defense, Malema said the fault lay not with him but with journalists who had made Afrikaners aware of the song by translating its words. He failed to convince the judge, but unwittingly put his finger on a deep change taking place in communications worldwide, which demands new policy, especially since law is inadequate to deal with it alone.

Teaching Fear & Hatred

People are increasingly privy to communication that they would not have heard (or read or seen) in the past, namely the internal language of other, disparate cultural communities—the songs that members of a group sing together, the jokes they tell to one another, and the words their leaders use to rally supporters, to teach fear and hatred of others outside the group, or to inspire violence.

Muslims from Afghanistan to Saudi Arabia learn that the prophet Mohammed has been lampooned (and to them, defiled) by cartoonists at a provincial Danish newspaper, feminists discover Facebook pages where men gather to trade rape jokes among themselves, and rural Afrikaners hear of a Zulu song that they fear may be catalyzing violence against them in the racially charged atmosphere of present-day South Africa.

Several factors have converged to influence diverse audiences and raise the stakes in many linguistic battlegrounds. In South Africa, a prime factor was the fall of apartheid, as Judge Lamont noted in his Dubulu iBhunu ruling. Since Nelson Mandela became president in 1994, blacks and whites in South Africa have been forced to hear one another, literally and figuratively, as never before. People who "were not accustomed to each other in any way commenced associating and interacting with each other" sometimes producing "extreme social conflict," the judge observed. In a number of other countries, struggles against authoritarian regimes and sometimes, their fall, have broken walls between culturally or religiously disparate groups. This can cause greater understanding, as in the case of some Han Chinese netizens who have learned to listen to the grievances of Tibetans for the first time. Or it can lead to terror, as it did for Coptic Christians in Egypt.

Moreover, mass migration and shifting boundaries have moved cultur-   10
ally far-flung communities within earshot of one another, since they now share the same nationality—transforming once largely homogeneous societies into stewpots of diversity. The Danish Muslim community that reacted with outrage to the cartoons published in 2005, for example, hardly existed a few decades earlier. And worldwide, the Internet, text messaging, and social media are perhaps the greatest engines of audience diversification, since they allow communities to listen in to one another as never before. Not only do words and images travel faster and further, they hop lightly and quickly over historic boundaries between human communities.

Even language barriers are surmounted by means of technology. Though at times dangerously imprecise, translation can now be automatic and rapid.

It is difficult to overstate the importance of this shift. Since our primitive ancestors learned to speak, it has been a universal and common human practice to gather in a group and listen to a speaker—family elder, religious leader, military commander, or politician. Speaker and audience share a unique body of cultural knowledge and beliefs that shape their understanding of the language that passes between them, whether it is a song, cartoon, or a shouted phrase. When communicating within a group, speakers choose language familiar to their own people, not the "others"—feminists, blacks or whites, the other tribe, another party, or adherents of another religion. The speaker knows the audience's particular fears, grievances, historical references—and uses that knowledge to make the speech powerful.

Since language travels so easily between communities, it is increasingly unusual for leaders to speak to their own people and not be heard by others. Some, like the Danish cartoonists, are surprised by the outraged and sometimes violent responses they provoke. Others seem indifferent or cravenly satisfied, like Malema or Terry Jones, the pastor who burned the Quran in Gainesville, Florida, in March 2011, ostensibly to "punish" the holy book. Jones persisted even after General David Petraeus, then the American commander in Afghanistan, as well as the U.S. State Department, and the White House asked him to refrain. The news immediately reached Afghanistan and all too predictably, 22 people including seven foreign UN workers were killed by an enraged mob in Mazar-i-Sharif.

Broader Audiences

With each well-publicized case, producers of speech—whether preachers, cartoonists, or singers—are increasingly on notice that their words or images are likely to reach audiences of different cultural backgrounds and will be judged by varied standards. As Judge Lamont wrote, after Dubulu iBhunu was the subject of such a widespread furor in South Africa, it "would never be innocuous again."

15   Some speakers can be induced to be more careful with their words when they know they will be heard by a wider group, which presents opportunities for new policy and advocacy. Where the audience is not already broadened, it can be useful to diversify it intentionally. This is an alternative to prohibiting certain kinds of speech, which is a bad option since it can impinge on freedom of expression and often fails in practice.

Kenya saw months of mounting inflammatory speech in 2007 when political leaders incited their own tribes against other tribes—too often using vernacular or tribal languages. In a country with 43 distinct ethnic groups, almost everyone speaks a "mother tongue," usually in addition to Swahili or English, but no one can understand them all. At the end of 2007, after a disputed presidential election, parts of the country exploded into violence. More than 1,000 people were killed, some 500,000 displaced. Now, as Kenya is preparing for its next presidential election, its KTN television network has been experimenting with an audience-diversification technique.

When Kenyan politicians give inflammatory speeches to their own flocks in their own languages, speaking in terms that they would hesitate to use before a wider audience, KTN sometimes broadcasts such clips on national television, subtitled in Swahili or English. The network has chosen to diversify the audience as a way of discouraging or embarrassing those who would use inflammatory speech in their own narrow circles. KTN news director Linus Kaikai says of politicians who use more incendiary language when they speak to their own ethnic groups in their own mother tongues, "It makes them mind what they say. It tends to sanitize their language."

This technique is related to the standard human rights advocacy technique of naming and shaming. True rogues may not be deterred by attempts to shame them, but some speakers can be influenced, even brought into line by members of their own community. The ANC, for example, expelled Malema from the party at the end of February. He had given the ANC many other reasons to discipline him, including personal corruption and his public criticisms of President Jacob Zuma. But the song, too, had embarrassed the ANC leadership.

And Then There's Law

Law, although blunt and unwieldy for this task, is the main tool to rein in dangerous speech without trampling on freedom of expression. In the past 15 years, international courts have convicted more than a dozen defendants, most of them Rwandan, for incitement to genocide, and accepted several guilty pleas. The International Criminal Court investigated Kenya's 2007–2008 violence and is now prosecuting just four Kenyans for crimes against humanity, including a radio broadcaster whose role was limited to speech—a clear indication that the ICC is convinced of the importance of speech in catalyzing mass violence.

20   Joshua arap Sang, the broadcaster, is accused of inciting violence during his morning call-in show on KASS FM, a Kalenjin-language radio station that remains influential among members of Kenya's Kalenjin ethnic group. If Sang is convicted, and perhaps even if he is acquitted, his case will become a landmark in international law on criminal speech.

The ICC alone could not possibly deal with the large universe of speech that inflames tension and may spark violence. In addition, most such speech does not rise to the level of the grave international crimes to which the ICC's jurisdiction is limited. A policymaking tool is needed to draw the line between speech that should be sanctioned and speech that must be tolerated in the name of freedom of expression, no matter how ugly it may be.

Diverse communities will never agree on which speech is inherently offensive. Is a drawing depicting Mohammed merely provocative, even amusing, or unbearably offensive? International law and policy should focus on a narrow but notable subset—inflammatory speech that precedes violence, especially outbreaks of mass violence like genocide. Before such outbreaks, leaders address their own group with language calculated to dehumanize another target group. Nazi propagandists referred to Jews as vermin and pests, Hutu propagandists spoke of cockroaches, meaning Tutsi people, Slobodan Milosevic described Muslims as black crows. In case after case, such speech is a precursor to mass violence, especially violence against defenseless civilian populations.

The Dangerous Speech Project has gathered typical hallmarks of speech that seems to catalyze just such mass violence and has developed guidelines for analyzing the level of danger posed by a particular turn of phrase: how likely it is to lead to violence in a specific context. This analysis can be applied to any form of expression—a drawing, photograph, or film—not just words.

Which Words Spark

One can estimate the likelihood that speech will spark violence in any given situation using just these five criteria: the speaker, the audience, the speech itself, the social and historical context, and the means of dissemination.

25   In each case, one or more of these criteria may be especially important. A speaker can have great influence over a particular audience, while certain

audiences may be especially vulnerable, because of economic hardship, fear, or existing grievances. Certain language-related events—defined broadly to include such acts of expression as burning a book—can be particularly powerful. In some cases, it is the last criterion, the mode of dissemination, that is of paramount importance, especially when it is a form of new media. Text messaging is used increasingly to organize riots and massacres in many countries. For youths in developing nations, whose cell phones link them to the wider world and give them a sense of agency and power, a message may pop up on their screens like this one from the 2007, when ethnic violence broke out in Kenya:

> "No more innocent Kikuyu blood will be shed. We will slaughter them right here in the capital city. For justice, compile a list of Luo's you know . . . we will give you numbers to text this information."

In such a case, the mode of dissemination may be as influential as the content.

In the case of Dubulu iBhunu, Malema was an influential leader chanting his song to young followers who are suffering widespread economic hardship and are still disadvantaged compared to white South Africans. Some of the words of the song compare Boers to dogs, dehumanizing them. So it is hard not to construe the refrain, especially with the hand gestures Malema uses, as a call to attack.

A few months after Judge Lamont banned the song, in April 2011, Tokelo Nhlapo, a youth league member and student leader at the University of the Witwatersrand, told a gathering, "I am tempted to sing this song," and then began chanting the banned song with a new refrain: "Dubulu Lekgoa" or "shoot the whites," accompanied by his enthusiastic student audience, all on their feet.

Analyze

1. Why does Benesch begin and end her essay with the Malema case? What particular point does the case illustrate?
2. Do you agree with Benesch's point that "language travels so easily between communities" because of the rise of technology? Analyze the examples she provides in the essay as you respond.
3. What is the Dangerous Speech Project? Why do you think it was created?

Explore

1. Write about a time when you or someone you know was the target of hate speech. What sort of language was used against you? Why? What was your reaction?

2. According to the author, it is possible for "any form of expression—a drawing, photograph, or film—not just words" to incite violence and acts of aggression. Choose a particular case where such an expression of hatred led to protest and violence. Apply Benesch's five criteria— "the speaker, the audience, the speech itself, the social and historical context, and the means of dissemination"—to analyze the case.

3. Write a research paper in which you examine how advances in media and technology—what Benesch calls "means of dissemination"—have led to an increase in incidents related to offensive speech. How are the Internet, cell phones, Twitter, and social media such as Facebook being used by certain groups to provoke others? Do such incidents violate the right to freedom of speech? Why or why not? Look to the opinions of legal experts as you write your essay.

Julie Sedivy
Politically Correct Animal Language

Cognitive scientist Julie Sedivy has taught at Brown University and the University of Calgary. The following article was posted to *Psychology Today* website on May 14, 2011. *Psychology Today* features articles and blogs by renowned academics and clinicians who write about psychology for a general readership. Here, Sedivy observes the importance of word choice—not just because of the associations the words conjure up, but also because of what those words say about a speaker's motives.

Consider your own word choices—to what extent do you carefully choose your words? Do you think word choice matters in all contexts?

Lately I've read a number of sarcastic comebacks to a proposal made by the editors of the *Journal of Animal Ethics* pleading for greater mindfulness in language about animals. The journal argues for dropping out of our vocabulary words and phrases such as "vermin," "beasts," or "eat like a pig." The editors suggest that even words like "pet," "wildlife" or "animal" carry negative associations—perhaps, they hint, we could instead refer to them respectively (and respectfully) as "companion animals," "free-living animals" or "differentiated entities."

Many of the commentaries I've read poke fun at the notion that poor Fido will feel miffed if we refer to him by the derogatory word "pet." Erin Skarda, writing for *Time*, snickers "We're pretty sure that your dog doesn't mind being called a 'pet' just as long as you keep up with the tasty food, belly scratches and long walks around the neighborhood." Bottom of Form Amusing copy, but hardly the point.

What the editors of *JAE* are after, obviously, is the attitudes of the *human* variety of animals. The hope is that avoiding language with negative baggage will help nudge our culture away from views of animals as mere property, resources or threats. Snarky editorials aside: would this strategy of language reform work?

The idea that people's attitudes or behavior can be tweaked by language is certainly not a crazy one. Before politicians propose a new policy, they'll often spend good money taking words out for a test drive with the voting public. Want to propose *oil drilling* or do you want to call it *energy exploration*? Turns out it matters. Want to know how the public feels about gays in the military? Depends on the question. A CBS poll conducted in 2010 showed that 51% of respondents "strongly favored" allowing "gay men and lesbians" to serve in the military, while only 34% felt the same way about "homosexuals."

In December 2010, *Media Matters* reported a leaked memo by Fox   5
News editor Bill Sammon to journalists instructing them to use the phrase "government run option" instead of "public option" when referring to the Democratic health care reform. Why? Apparently, Republican pollster Frank Luntz had pointed out that "if you call it a 'public option,' the American people are split," but that "if you call it the 'government option,' the public is overwhelmingly against it."

And if language didn't matter, why are liberals so eager to re-brand themselves as "progressives"? The use of a word fires up not only its meaning, but also memories of the contexts in which that word has been used, and the derogatory "feel" of words like "liberal" and "homosexual" comes not from their meanings, but from the fact that they've been wielded as terms of loathing. Incidentally, as linguist Geoff Nunberg points out in his book *Talking*

Right, there was a time in history when it was the word "conservative" that was tainted, as revealed by the following quote from a 1949 editorial:

> *"If a man is described as a 'conservative' in politics . . . he is likely to be suspected of wanting to cheat widows and orphans and generally to be a bad fellow who associates with other bad fellows. Consequently, very few people will admit they are conservatives and if they are accused they will go to great lengths to prove otherwise."*

Times change.

But language can only work as a lever for attitude change if it's expertly applied. And it's in the execution, not the intentions, that the editors of *JAE* fail.

For one thing, they argue that "pet" is pejorative because it activates the mental construct that animals are owned and regarded as nothing but property. But I doubt that this is the dominant association with the word. Before ditching it, one would actually want to check. With empirical evidence, Frank Luntz-style. The fact that the word is used as a term of endearment and gets co-opted in expressions like "pet project," or "teacher's pet" suggests to me that it mostly activates mental constructs of affection and favoritism.

And I have my reservations about the term "free-living" instead of "wildlife." The editors claim that "'wildness' is synonymous with uncivilized, unrestrained, barbarous existence." But to me at least, "wildlife," like "wilderness," is something to be cherished rather than eliminated, and "free-living" mostly activates thoughts of hippie communes—an association that I suspect would alarm the staff at Banff National Park, who have the utmost respect for grizzly bears, but do their best to dissuade the local tourist population from treating them as photo props.

But terms like "animal companion" or "differentiated entity" are especially clumsy. Word choice matters not just because of its associations, but also because it can say something about the speaker's motives for using the language he did. Hearers automatically (and subconsciously) ask themselves: "Why is he saying this? And why is he saying it *in these words?*"

For example: it turns out that anti-drug programs that go to great lengths to train teenagers to assertively "just say no" to drugs by running them through various role-playing scenarios can actually increase the likelihood of drug use. Why? Because the kids wonder "Why are they spending so much time teaching me this?" and wind up concluding that it's because *everyone* is doing drugs, and dealers lurk around every corner. The training inadvertently folds in an implicit form of peer pressure. Good intentions, road to hell.

A convoluted phrase like "differentiated entity" used instead of "animal" doesn't exactly slip under the radar. A normal person will wonder: Why all this linguistic beating around the bush? Two conclusions are likely. One, that the speaker is using the phrase to try to mold attitudes. (And since no one likes to be instructed how to think, this predictably leads to all the ridicule about "politically correct" language.) And second, that there's something unseemly about animals, so much so that they can't be referred to directly in polite company—a bit like saying you're going to powder your nose when you really mean you need to urinate. Not using the obvious word can signal that there's something taboo about the whole concept.

The *JAE* editors have the best of intentions, and there's nothing wrong with their starting assumptions. But they could have used the expertise and linguistic finesse of someone like Frank Luntz in crafting their guidelines.

Analyze

1. Explain the position that the *Journal of Animal Ethics* takes with regard to language used to describe animals. What reasons might they have for taking this position?
2. Are you convinced by Sedivy's analysis of *JAE*'s suggested terminology? Why or why not?
3. What is Sedivy's purpose in writing this essay? How can you tell?

Explore

1. What does the term "animal ethics" mean to you? Write about a personal experience with pets (or other animals) that explains your views on the ethical treatment of animals.
2. What exactly does *JAE*'s recommendation of new terms tell you about treating animals ethically? Will new words and phrases like the ones *JAE* is suggesting naturally lead to better, more humane treatment of animals? Why or why not?

3. Whereas house pets such as dogs and cats are often treated like beloved companions in the developed world, populations of endangered wild animals (e.g., elephants, rhinos, and tigers) in certain nonindustrialized nations are being poached to the point of extinction. Write a research paper that examines how two different nonprofit animal advocacy groups disseminate information about this problem, and then compare those appeals to a news organization's coverage of the same poaching problem. Is the goal of either advocacy group to raise awareness, to raise money, or both? What kinds of language does each group use to appeal to its audience? How is that language different from a journalistic perspective on the problem?

Shani O. Hilton
The Dirtiest of Words on Capitol Hill: "Racism"

Shani O. Hilton is associate editor for *Campus Progress*, the website for the organization that promotes the involvement of young people in progressive political issues. She is also the Washington, DC correspondent for *Colorlines*, a news site known for its award-winning investigative reporting and analysis of racial justice issues. A native of central California, Hilton earned a degree in journalism from Howard University. Her writing has appeared in *The American Prospect*, *The Atlantic*, *The Root*, and other publications. She also maintains a personal blog where she muses on pop culture, race, and feminism. Wanting a more intimate window into how Congress thinks, and what elected officials are saying about racial justice issues, Hilton scoured the *Capitol Words* project—a catalog of every word ever spoken on the House and Senate floors. She lists a handful of the most popular words spoken, and the contexts in which they are used, in the following entry posted on *Colorlines* in January 2012.

What "code words" for racially sensitive topics do you hear from politicians, on the news, or from campus groups?

Campaign season officially kicks off tonight as Iowa Republicans caucus over who will be the party's presidential nominee. We've already heard a lot of talking—in scores of debates, a torrent of press releases and a cacophony of press coverage. But we'll be hearing much, much more over the next 11 months. So, *Colorlines.com* figured it was a good time to take a look at what our existing elected officials are already saying about some crucial racial justice issues—or, more specifically, to look at *how* they're saying it. To do so, I turned to the neat *Capitol Words* tool from the Sunlight Foundation.

In scouring *Capitol Words*—a project that catalogues all the words recorded on the House and Senate floors—it's not a surprise that 90 percent of the politicians who use the phrase "undocumented immigrant" are Democrats, while only 11 percent use "illegal aliens." But charting the popularity of words that stand-in for a frank conversation about race is an interesting experiment that doesn't always yield expected results.

Since 1996, for instance, "immigration" has typically been mentioned by Republicans slightly more often than Democrats. The three members of Congress who have brought it up the most frequently are Colorado Republican Tom Tancredo, Alabama Republican Jeff Sessions and Texas Democrat Sheila-Jackson Lee. But in the last two years, both parties have used the word at about the same rates—a reminder that immigration has become a key political battleground. Since 2009, Iowa Republican Steve King, an anti-immigration hardliner, has been the most frequent user of the word, followed by two Democrats: California's Dianne Feinstein and Colorado's Jared Polis. (Relatedly: King's third most favorite word to use on the House floor is the pejorative "illegals.")

Here are a handful of other words that offer a window into how Congress thinks.

"Urban"

"Urban" is a euphemism best known to be thrown around in any 5
discussion of largely poor and black parts of the United States. Not a surprise, since outside of the South, the country's black population centers tend to be in cities. This term is far more popular among Democrats than Republicans—61 percent of Dems use the term versus 37 percent of

Republicans. "Rural," a term which tends to mean "poor and white," actually gets more play.

"Outsourcing"

The fear of foreign workers "taking our jobs" manifests in the word "outsourcing." And while 10 years ago, the phrase hardly crossed the lips of any members of Congress, 2004 saw a spike after a North Dakota Democrat introduced the "Increasing Notice of Foreign Outsourcing Act," a bill that, yes, took notice of an increase in foreign outsourcing. While it died in committee, Democrats have not let the word go, and 71 percent of occurrences of the word come from them. Meanwhile the phrase "our jobs" has a more equitable usage: 54 percent of Democrats and 43 percent of Republicans use it.

"Racial Preference"

Much like "undocumented" versus "illegal," the terms "affirmative action" and "racial preference" ostensibly mean the same thing—except the latter terms are both derisive. It's not a surprise that only 12 percent of people using the term "racial preference" are Democrats, while Republicans make up 88 percent of the people who say it. Interestingly, of the three Republicans who use it the most, two come from mostly white states—Kentucky's Mitch McConnell and Utah's Orrin Hatch. Only Alabama's Jeff Sessions comes from a state with a large black population; more than 1 in 4 Alabama residents are black.

"Profiling"

Last month, "profiling" got a boost after Michigan's John Conyers introduced the End Racial Profiling Act. But since 1996, three out of four times the word is being used it's uttered by Democrats. And there's no straight analog for the word coming out of the Republican party—a sign that very few believe that profiling is a policy worth discussing.

Ethnicity Descriptors

S earch for the words "black," "African," "Asian," "Hispanic," "Latino," "Native American," and you'll find that Democrats are the ones using them three times as much as Republicans (though "Muslim" is equally popular). Republicans might take this as proof that that Democrats are obsessed with race—but conservatives' inability to discuss race in a formal setting reinforces how out of touch they can be with the reality of racial injustice.

"Racism"

G ranted, no one really wants to talk about racism aside from members of   10 the Congressional Black Caucus. Immediately after Sept. 11, the word "racism" was used fairly frequently—at least compared to now—likely in an attempt to quell anti-Muslim sentiment. But these days it's become the dirtiest of words. Members of Congress said the word only 46 times this year. In the month of September 2001 alone, it was mentioned 50 times.

Analyze

1. The terms "undocumented immigrant" and "illegal alien" are often used interchangeably to refer to those who do not have the necessary legal status to live or work in the United States. How do these terms differ and what does each imply?
2. As she lists the most common "racial justice" terms used by Congress, Hilton notes who is apt to use them more, Democrats or Republicans. What is she trying to get at? Why?
3. What is *Capitol Words*? What is its significance, and who do you think benefits from the work of such a project?

Explore

1. Select two of the "dirty" terms Hilton lists in her article. What, in your opinion, do these terms mean? Would Democrats agree with you? Would Republicans? Why or why not?

2. Do you think that the way politicians talk about racial justice issues—particularly the language they use—has any impact on how the general public views these issues? What differences in opinion might there be between politicians and citizens? Explain your ideas in a short analytical essay by referring to and using specific evidence from Hilton's essay.

3. Racial profiling and outsourcing are controversial issues that have social and economic implications not just for Americans but for citizens of other countries as well. Examine one of these topics in a research paper. Describe the issue, use scholarly articles to explain the problems associated with it, and develop a clear argument that expresses how complex it can be and why.

Mary Giovagnoli

"'Anchor Baby' Added to New American Heritage Dictionary" and "American Heritage Dictionary Redefines 'Anchor Baby' Term as 'Offensive' and 'Disparaging'"

Mary Giovagnoli is the Director of the Immigration Policy Center (IPC). Prior to joining the IPC, Giovagnoli served as Senior Director of Policy for the National Immigration Forum and practiced law with the Departments of Justice and Homeland Security, specializing in asylum and refugee law. In 2005, as a recipient of the Congressional Fellowship, she served in Senator Edward M. Kennedy's office working on comprehensive immigration reform and refugee issues. The following two blog posts appeared in December 2011 on *ImmigrationImpact*, a site launched in 2008 to help shape and develop comprehensive and achievable immigration policy reform. In these posts, Giovagnoli emphasizes the importance—and responsibility—of dictionaries to use neutral language in their definitions, or to identify when loaded language is being used. As she observes with "anchor baby," a phrase newly added to the *New American Heritage Dictionary*, not only does the definition reflect anti-immigration rhetoric, it also implies an acceptance of the term's derogatory usage.

Do you think it matters whether dictionary terms are defined without bias? Why or why not?

The degree to which the immigration debate has coarsened over the last few years is no more evident than in the pages of the recently released fifth edition of the New American Heritage Dictionary. Among the new entries is the term "anchor baby." You might think that the definition would read something like: slang, a pejorative description of a child born in the United States to parents without legal status, implying that the parents intend to leverage the child's citizenship to "anchor" their own presence in the U.S. You would be wrong.

Instead, the definition reads:

anchor baby *n.*

A child born to a noncitizen mother in a country that grants automatic citizenship to children born on its soil, especially such a child born to parents seeking to secure eventual citizenship for themselves and often other members of their family.

According to the dictionary's executive editor, the trick to defining new words is to "to define them objectively without taking sides and just presenting what it is. And, in some cases up, you know, anchor baby is definitely a very charged, politically charged word."

Although the politically charged nature of the word made defining it difficult, the editors ultimately felt it was best to put the word in with no commentary, claiming "it falls into a gray area where we felt it was better just to state what it was, and then people can filter their own life experiences through the word and judgments on it as they see fit."

The trouble with this philosophy is that "anchor baby" is not a neutral 5 term, nor from what we have been able to find, has it ever been. First, it appears to be a wholly American term, one mired in the politics of anti-immigrant rhetoric. Those who use it are not in the business of clinically describing some sort of sociological phenomena. They are instead intent on suggesting that people come to the country illegally and deliberately have babies in order to use their children's citizenship to acquire legal status of their own.

Second, the New American Heritage Dictionary's definition ignores the very specific intent of the term and, in fact, gives it more credibility by treating it as some sort of universal description of children who acquire citizenship at birth. This masks the poisonous and derogatory nature of the term, a term which demeans both parent and child and in the process suggests that it is acceptable to call a child born in the U.S.—i.e. an American citizen—an "anchor baby."

What is particularly disturbing about this new definition is that it confuses popularity of a term with neutrality. While the term anchor baby has skyrocketed in usage in the last decade, that usage appears to be spurred by the general explosion of anti-immigrant rhetoric, blogs, and other media outlets. Objective reporters tend to put the phrase in quotations, to indicate that the term is a loaded one.

In fact, back in 2006, Chicago Tribune columnist Eric Zorn received complaints about his reference to the child of an illegal immigrant seeking sanctuary in a Chicago church as an "anchor baby." Zorn found that the term isn't a neutral descriptor, but instead, according to one of his sources, it's a way to dehumanize the children of undocumented immigrants. Upon reflection, Zorn said that the complaints he received were a "good enough reason to regret having used it and to decide not to use it in the future. Sound arguments don't need loaded language."

And loaded language needs to be identified as such in the dictionary. The New American Heritage Dictionary acknowledges the derogatory nature of hundreds of terms. By failing to do so with the term "anchor baby," however, the dictionary implies that the term is acceptable in common usage and misleads the public by insinuating that giving birth to a child in the United States necessarily carries with it the intention of using that child for immigration status.

10   In an era where politicians and pundits have no qualms about being imprecise, dictionary editors need to be—even if that means calling a term "highly charged," "political," or down right nasty. While dictionaries may be neutral, language isn't. "Anchor baby" is a term that epitomizes the way words reflect and reframe a debate.

American Heritage Dictionary Redefines "Anchor Baby" Term as "Offensive" and "Disparaging"

The firestorm around the inclusion of the term "anchor baby" in the new edition of the American Heritage Dictionary has led to a dramatic reversal in the definition. Not only did the executive editor, Steven Kleinelder, emphatically apologize for the initial definition, he promised swift action to change it. By Monday morning, the term was labeled as "offensive." By Monday afternoon, a new definition appeared online, one that was crafted to reflect more accurately just how artificial a term it really is:

anchor baby *n. Offensive*
    Used as a disparaging term for a child born to a noncitizen mother in a country that grants automatic citizenship to children born on its soil, especially when the child's birthplace is thought to have been chosen in order to improve the mother's or other relatives' chances of securing eventual citizenship.

This is the kind of controversy that doesn't fade away quickly, and many argue that the term is so offensive that it shouldn't appear in the dictionary at all. I understand but disagree with that position, largely because the term, however offensive, exists as a political and practical reality. I think the new definition validates what many outraged voices in blogs, on Twitter, and in the press have been saying all along: "anchor baby" is a term that shouldn't exist but does because immigration restrictionists are really good at creating words that generate fear.

While the origins are not reflected in the definition, characterizing the term as both "offensive" and "disparaging" says volumes about how it is used in real life. I would much rather have a curious student or citizen have the ability to look up the term in the dictionary and find this definition than to find no guidance and accept the meaning and agenda of restrictionists who used it.

And of course, that agenda is the repeal or amendment of the Fourteenth Amendment to eliminate citizenship at birth. The Immigration Policy Center has published numerous articles on the legal and practical problems inherent in that position. This position, in turn, arises from the misplaced notion that the problems plaguing our current immigration

system would somehow be eliminated if only we could prevent persons here
without legal status from having children.

5   It's not solely the dictionary's job to lay out the politics behind words. It
is the job of advocates and scholars, policy-makers and politicians, community leaders, people of faith, and everyone else who values a constructive
solution to immigration reform.

We must not only monitor how terms are used and defined, but must
work to make hateful terms archaic. If we challenge the people who prefer
fear to solutions, and direct our energies affirmatively towards an immigration system that is thoughtful, fair and reflects our country's needs as
well as our values, then hateful terms like "anchor baby" can become part
of the past.

Analyze

1. Explain the reasons why Giovagnoli thinks that "anchor baby" is not a
   neutral term. Do you agree with her views?
2. What is "loaded language" and should dictionaries be responsible for
   identifying them as such? Why or why not?
3. Compare the *New American Heritage Dictionary*'s revised definition
   of the term "anchor baby" with its original definition. What differences do you notice and how do these differences affect the meaning of
   the term?

Explore

1. Is it possible for hateful terms to become archaic, that is, to lose popularity and no longer be part of common usage? Can you think of
   demeaning or offensive words that are no longer in use? What do you
   think caused their decline?
2. Who are "immigration restrictionists" and what is their agenda? Investigate the term by searching for it in your library database. Are there
   other words that can or should be used to describe this group of people?
   Could the term be just as loaded as "anchor baby"? Why or why not?
3. To what extent are solutions to immigration reform dependent on the
   language used to define, describe, and discuss the problems associated
   with immigration? How can such a hotly debated issue be discussed
   with neutral language?

Mark Peters
Why Personhood Is Powerful

Mark Peters is a language columnist and freelance writer whose work has appeared in various media outlets, including his own blog, *markwordlustpeters* *.tumblr.com.* "Why Personhood Is Powerful" was published in November 2011 in the *Boston Globe.* Peters presents a history of the word "personhood" in an attempt to explain controversial recent attempts to extend its meaning to nonhuman entities. Regardless of the context in which it is being used— whether in reference to human beings, animals, corporations, or aliens— Peters asserts that "the quest for personhood is the quest for rights."

Peters notes that, when fighting for acceptance, the word "person" becomes especially crucial and important. Why do you think this is?

What is a person? For one thing, it's a battlefield. The latest skirmish over the scope of the word, galvanizing some and outraging others, occurred in Mississippi, where a failed amendment to the state constitution would have granted legal personhood to fertilized eggs.

At the same time, some—say, many of those occupying Wall Street—are dismayed that corporations are considered persons in a legal sense. Animal advocates argue for the personhood of animals, especially the most intelligent animals, such as dolphins and chimpanzees. Scholars such as Christopher D. Seps claim that pets should be treated as persons, at least in certain legal situations. There are more than 7 billion humans in the world, but a lot more potential persons.

Why so much controversy over a word? Why have some found it vitally important to extend *person* to include not-exactly-human things, while others find it grotesque and overreaching? Partly it's because we think of *person* as meaning human. But the word isn't that simple: There's a long history of *person* being used in other ways, including definitions that mean both less and more than being a member of the human race.

Person has led a double life in English since the early 1200s, according to the Oxford English Dictionary, meaning both a human and a type of role, especially the theatrical kind. This theatricality goes all the way to the word's roots, in the Latin *persona*—a type of mask used by an actor. (That word, too, survives in English, meaning an alias, disguise, or character.) The etymological origins of personhood, then, are all about the mask, not about who's wearing it.

5   From the beginning, personhood was flexible and adaptable. The idea that corporations have some of the rights of persons, for example, is centuries old. As William S. Laufer has written in "Corporate Bodies and Guilty Minds: The Failure of Corporate Criminal Liability," the seeds of corporate personhood were sown in the 1300s under King Edward III, when corporations attained some property rights. This example from the Common Laws of England in 1765 lays out the distinction that still vexes us: "Natural persons are such as the God of nature formed us; artificial are such as are created and devised by human laws for the purposes of society and government; which are called corporations or bodies politic." Then as now, corporate personhood granted a business privileges while sparing the members from blame.

Older idioms such as "put on a person" highlight the artificiality of personhood, as in this example from 1653: "No man can long put on a person and act a part, but his evill manners will peep through the corners of the white robe." Many uses of *person* still carry this sense of role playing. It's no accident that giving an inanimate object human characteristics is called personification, not humanification.

On the other hand, since at least 1390, *person* has been used to mean someone's physical self or body, a meaning still evident in phrases such as "in person" and "concealed on his person." Sometimes this sense is narrowed to mean genitals, especially the male variety, producing some amusingly euphemistic statements such as this prohibition from the British Vagrancy Act of 1824: "Every Person wilfully, openly, lewdly and obscenely exposing his Person in any Street or in any place of public Resort, with intent to insult any Female, shall be deemed a Rogue and Vagabond."

Even as these lighter sides of *person* live on, the word carries another, more serious meaning: "an individual regarded as having human rights, dignity, or worth," to quote the OED. Personhood, then, means a corporation can claim the right of free speech—in the form of campaign contributions. Animal-rights advocates want animals to have personhood so they will be treated as worthy, dignified beings who deserve protection from poaching, experimentation, and other harms. The quest for personhood is the quest for rights.

So when a group is fighting for acceptance, *person* becomes a crucial and useful term. During the height of the feminist movement, women used it to claim a better role in society, as seen in this 1970 usage in the OED: "Women are at last becoming persons first and wives second."

Given that personhood confers such power and security, it's no wonder that advocates seek to extend the label to the corporations, pets, primates, and fertilized eggs we want to shelter. But since America hasn't always recognized the rights of certain classes of genuine human beings, it's understandable that many would be alarmed by the extension of personhood to corporations, poodles, or embryos. These attempts can seem outright demeaning, as in the case of a recent suggestion by PETA that the slavery-abolishing 13th amendment should apply to killer whales at SeaWorld.

Still, it's possible that our current struggles over the meaning of *person* will seem tame compared to what lies ahead. Since the beginning of the field of robotics, scientists have wondered if a robot will ever achieve enough autonomy to be considered a person. If we ever encounter an alien race, they sure won't be humans, but they'll probably be persons. Is a human clone a person? Personally, I would think so; I bet many won't agree. But then, arguing over who's a person and who's not may be part of what makes us human.

Analyze

1. What distinction does Peters draw between "humans" and "persons" as he opens his essay? Is this a reasonable or useful distinction? Why or why not?
2. What is the origin and history of the word personhood? Has its meaning changed at all? How so?
3. What is Peters's purpose in writing this essay? How can you tell?

Explore

1. Read the 13th amendment to the U.S. Constitution and summarize its meaning in your own words. Then write a letter to PETA responding to their claim that this amendment should be applied to killer whales that perform at SeaWorld. Would you support PETA on this? Why or why not?
2. Write an analytical essay that examines the phenomenon of corporate personhood. How do corporations benefit from this status and how does it affect the consumer?

3. In a research essay that delves into ethical issues of personhood, examine whether nonhumans such as robots, pets, primates, or fertilized eggs deserve the status of "person." Be sure to look at arguments both in favor of and against the granting of personhood and to discuss the motives behind such arguments.

Forging Connections

1. In her essay Solnit blames the media for using the word "looter" to spread "clichés and pernicious myths" that further hurt the victims of disasters, whereas Benesch touches on the importance of the "mode of dissemination" of offensive language given the rise of new media. What do these two authors tell us about the role of media in spreading offensive or inflammatory speech? Should regular citizens bear just as much responsibility as journalists when they use "loaded" words and language? Why or why not?

2. Look into the Dangerous Speech Project referred to in Benesch's article and the Capitol Words project mentioned in Hilton's essay. What makes these projects unique? What particular purpose do you think they serve?

Looking Further

1. Rebecca Solnit ("When the Media Is the Disaster") blames the mass media for perpetuating a particular view of the postearthquake population of Haiti through overuse—or perhaps abuse—of words such as "looter." Can you think of words that are associated with racial and minority groups—words Shani O. Hilton ("The Dirtiest of Words on Capitol Hill: 'Racism'") or Bassey Ikpi ("Why the Whole 'Poor Africa' Thing Isn't Cool," Chapter 6) might bring to Solnit's attention—that have a similar negative effect on public perception? How and by whom are these words employed? What effect does it have on the intended population?

2. If Mary Giovagnoli and Shani O. Hilton were to have a conversation, how would they go about defining and redefining some of the terms Hilton lists in her essay? Write an essay in which you take up some of Hilton's words and phrases and, with reference to any of the selections in Chapter 7 ("Language and Politics"), discuss why they need to be redefined and state what those new definitions might look like and why.

9 The Language of Globalization

Although the terms "Globish" and "glocal" sound like strange and awkward variations of the word "global," they are an accurate reminder of how language adapts to needs of the times and reflects the realities of our lives today. As traditional "standard" English is replaced by varieties of "Englishes" spoken all over the world, there is a demand for a simpler, and more easily communicable, English known as "Globish." And "glocal" is a compressed term that represents global and local realities simultaneously. At the same time, formal and "proper" English is not just a language but a marketable commodity that is the driving engine at educational institutions. This push and pull of language that speakers are experiencing across the globe is a sign that although English is ubiquitous, it might not be recognizable as the English of yesteryear—or even yesterday. As the authors in this chapter make clear, there is no doubt that as a language English is paradoxically both in demand and in decline.

In his article "'Conquer English to Make China Strong': The Globalization of English" author, newspaper and magazine contributor, and the theater critic for the *London Evening Standard*, Henry Hitchings eloquently argues that English, historically a language of conquest and conversion, is now taking on local flavors as it gets adopted—and adapted—by non-native speakers around the world. Freelance writer Julie Traves picks up on this idea of adoption in her essay "The Church of Please and Thank You" as she describes how despite a growing demand for English, students and teachers around the world are increasingly aware of the cultural effects of English language learning. In "Operation Mind Your Language," Pallavi Polanki shows how English is the language of hope and optimism for Afghanis who are determined, against all odds, to become qualified English teachers. On a different note, Shehzad Nadeem, professor of urban and global sociology at Lehman College in New York City, demonstrates in his essay "Accent Neutralisation and a Crisis of Identity in India's Call Centres" that it is hard to avoid the identity crisis that arises when a neutral accent is imposed on call center workers in India. In her article "Investigating 'Globish'," Gloria Gibbons, a health care and communications expert, acknowledges that Globish is becoming trendy in the advertising world but also sounds a warning against its limitations. Finally, in "'Oh My Lady Gaga! This Is So Geilivable!': Chinglish Entering Globish?" blogger Jin Zhao lays out the perils and promise of hybridized languages as she describes the rise of "Chinglish"—words popularized by Chinese cyberenthusiasts.

Henry Hitchings
"'Conquer English to Make China Strong': The Globalization of English"

Author, reviewer, and critic Henry Hitchings specializes in narrative nonfiction, with a particular focus on language and cultural history. Author of four books, his second, *The Secret Life of Words: How English Became English* (Picador, 2009) won the 2008 John Llewellyn Rhys Prize. In the following piece, excerpted from his book *The Language Wars: A History of Proper English* (Farrar, Straus and Giroux, 2011), Hitchings reflects on the propagation of English around the globe—and what this means for non-English languages and other cultures.

What do you think are the consequences of English becoming the primary spoken language around the world?

No language has spread as widely as English, and it continues to spread. Internationally the desire to learn it is insatiable. In the twenty-first century the world is becoming more urban and more middle class, and the adoption of English is a symptom of this, for increasingly English serves as the lingua franca of business and popular culture. It is dominant or at least very prominent in other areas such as shipping, diplomacy, computing, medicine and education. A recent study has suggested that among students in the United Arab Emirates "Arabic is associated with tradition, home, religion, culture, school, arts and social sciences", whereas English "is symbolic of modernity, work, higher education, commerce, economics and science and technology".[1] In Arabic-speaking countries, science subjects are often taught in English because excellent textbooks and other educational resources are readily available in English. This is not something that has come about in an unpurposed fashion; the propagation of English is an industry, not a happy accident.

English has spread because of British colonialism, the technological advances of the Industrial Revolution, American economic and political ascendancy, and further (mostly American) technological developments in the second half of the twentieth century. Its rise has been assisted by the massive exportation of English as a second language, as well as by the growth of an English-language mass media. The preaching of Christianity, supported by the distribution of English-language Bibles, has at many times and in many places sustained the illusion, created by Wyclif and Tyndale and Cranmer, that English is the language of God.

The history of English's global diffusion is littered with important dates: the planting of the Jamestown colony in 1607; Robert Clive's victory at the

Battle of Plassey in 1757, which ushered in the dominion of the British East India Company; the creation of the first penal colony in Australia in 1788; the British settlement at Singapore in 1819 and establishment of a Crown Colony in Hong Kong in 1842; the formal beginning of British administration in Nigeria in 1861; the foundation of the BBC in 1922 and the United Nations in 1945; the launch by AT&T of the first commercial communications satellite in 1962. This list is condensed. It takes no account, for instance, of the various waves of Anglomania that swept much of Europe in the eighteenth century. But it will be apparent that the diffusion of English has had a lot to do with material reward, the media, and its use as a language of instruction. A fuller list might intensify the impression of a whiff of bloodshed.

Wherever English has been used, it has lasted. Cultural might outlives military rule. In the colonial period, the languages of settlers dominated the languages of the peoples whose land they seized. They marginalized them and in some cases eventually drove them to extinction. All the while they absorbed from them whatever local terms seemed useful. The colonists' languages practised a sort of cannibalism, and its legacy is still sharply felt. English is treated with suspicion in many places where it was once the language of the imperial overlords. It is far from being a force for unity, and its endurance is stressful. In India, while English is much used in the media, administration, education and business, there are calls to curb its influence. Yet even where English has been denigrated as an instrument of colonialism, it has held on—and in most cases grown, increasing its numbers of speakers and functions.

5   In the early decades of the twentieth century, H. G. Wells imagined what would become known as World English.[3] That term for the concept of English as an international language, a global second language, an intellectual and commercial lubricant, even an instrument of foreign policy on the part of the major English-speaking nations, grew common only in the 1960s. It has circulated since the 1920s, though, and the idea was touched upon earlier, not just by Wells, but also by Alexander Melville Bell, who had in 1888 presented *World-English,* a scheme of revised spellings intended to help learners acquire the language that, as he saw it, exceeded all others "in general fitness to become the tongue of the World".[4] Robert Nares, writing in 1784, presented with no little relish a vision of English extending prodigiously around the globe. Even before that, John Adams had prophesied that it would become the most widely spoken and read language—and "the most respectable".[5]

The term World English is still in use, but is contested by critics who believe it strikes too strong a note of dominance. Today World English is known by several names, perhaps the most catchy of which is Globish (though personally I think this sounds silly), a term popularized by Jean-Paul Nerrière, in his book *Don't Speak English, Parlez Globish* (2004). Globish, as conceived by Nerrière, is a pragmatic form of English consisting of 1,500 words, intended to make it possible for everyone in the world to understand everyone else. It is reminiscent of C. K. Ogden's Basic English. To give a flavour of it, I shall list all the words it contains that begin with y: *year, yellow, yes, yesterday, yet, you, young, your, yours.* We may not miss *yeoman* or *yodel,* but what about *yawn, yell* and *youth?* Nerrière is a former vice-president of marketing at IBM, and has branded Globish a "decaffeinated" form of English. Humour and metaphor are out. Short sentences are in. The late Palestinian leader Yasser Arafat is held up as an excellent exponent of the form. Nerrière also argues, less than convincingly, that the rise of Globish will help preserve French by minimizing the influence of caffeine-loaded English. The opposite view has been put forward by Claude Duneton, whose book *La Mort du français* (1999) predicts that French will disappear by 2050.

For Jean-Paul Nerrière the decaffeination of English is virtuous, but in the same phenomenon Edward Said has found cause for alarm. In his book *Culture and Imperialism* Said recalls his experience of visiting the English department at a university in "one of the Persian Gulf States" in 1985. "In sheer numerical terms English attracted the largest number of young people of any department in the university", but although the students "dutifully read Milton, Shakespeare, Wordsworth, Austen, and Dickens" their purpose in doing so was to become expert in the lingua franca of international business. "This," writes Said, "all but terminally consigned English to the level of a technical language stripped of expressive and aesthetic characteristics and denuded of any critical or self-conscious dimension."[6] Such an approach makes the use of English a mechanical act; it enables the basic transmission and deciphering of information, but it is intellectually stunting rather than empowering.

Nerrière's Globish is not alone. Madhukar Gogate, a retired Indian engineer, has independently come up with an idea for something he too calls Globish. It would use phonetic spellings to create what he considers a neater form of English. This could become a global language enabling links between people from different cultures. Meanwhile Joachim Grzega, a German linguist, is promoting Basic Global English, which has a mere twenty grammatical rules and a vocabulary comprising 750 words that learners are expected to supplement with an additional 250 words relevant to their individual needs.

Although these schemes may be intended in a different spirit, promoting a neutral form of English rather than one freighted with "Anglo" values, they are part of a larger, often invisible project: to establish a community, without territorial boundaries, of people who use English; to make its use seem not just normal, but also prestigious; and to market it as a language of riches, opportunity, scholarship, democracy and moral right. This is supported economically, politically, in education and the media, and sometimes also by military force. Much of the endorsement happens covertly.[7] And as English continues to spread, it seems like a steamroller, squashing whatever gets in its way. True, it is often used along-side local languages and does not instantly replace them. Yet its presence shifts the cultural emphases in the lives of those who adopt it, altering their aspirations and expectations. English seems, increasingly, to be a second first language. It is possible to imagine it merely coexisting with other languages, but easy to see that coexistence turning into transcendence. As English impinges on the spaces occupied by other languages, so linguists are increasingly finding that they need to behave like environmentalists: instead of being scholars they have to become activists.

> "English seems, increasingly, to be a second first language."

10   There have been attempts to create an artificial language for use by all the world. In the second half of the nineteenth century and then especially in the early years of the twentieth, schemes to construct new languages were numerous. Most of these are now forgotten: who remembers Cosmoglossa, Spokil, Mundolingue, Veltparl, Interlingua, Romanizat, Adjuvilo or Molog? Some of the innovators sound like remarkably odd people. Joseph Schipfer, developer of Communicationssprache, was also known for promoting means of preventing people from being buried alive. Etienne-Paulin Gagne, who devised Monopanglosse, proposed that in time of famine Algerians help their families and friends by exchanging their lives or at least some of their limbs for food, and was willing if necessary to give up his own body to the needy.

Only two schemes enjoyed success. In 1879 a Bavarian pastor, Johann Martin Schleyer, devised Volapük. It was briefly very popular: within ten years of its invention, there were 283 societies to promote it, and guides to Volapük were available in twenty-five other languages. As Arika Okrent observes in her book *In the Land of Invented Languages,* Volapük is a gift to people with a puerile sense of humour: "to speak" is *pükön,* and "to succeed" is *plöpön.*[8] More famous and less daft-sounding were the efforts of Ludwik Zamenhof, a Polish ophthalmologist of Lithuanian Jewish descent, who in the 1870s began work on creating Esperanto, a language without irregularities. He published his first book on the subject in 1887, summing up the language's grammar in sixteen rules and providing a basic vocabulary. Zamenhof's motives were clear; he had grown up in the ghettos of Bialystok and Warsaw, and, struck by the divisiveness of national languages, he dreamt of uniting humanity.[9] Esperanto is certainly the most successful of modern invented languages, but although it still has enthusiastic supporters there is no prospect of its catching on as Zamenhof once hoped.

Readers of this book are more likely to have heard Klingon, which was originated by Marc Okrand for the *Star Trek* films, and the Elvish languages— notably Quenya and Sindarin, modelled on Finnish and Welsh respectively— devised by J. R. R. Tolkien and faithfully used in Peter Jackson's films of *The Lord of the Rings.* A more recent example of a new artificial language is the one conceived by Paul Frommer that is spoken by the blue-skinned Na'vi in James Cameron's 2009 film *Avatar.* Where once they embodied political hopefulness in the real world, invented languages have become accessories of art and entertainment.

Today it is English, rather than any created alternative, that is the world's auxiliary tongue. There are more people who use English as a second language than there are native speakers. Estimates of the numbers vary, but even the most guarded view is that English has 500 million second-language speakers. Far more of the world's citizens are eagerly jumping on board than trying to resist its progress. In some cases the devotion appears religious and can involve what to outsiders looks a lot like self-mortification. According to Mark Abley, some rich Koreans pay for their children to have an operation that lengthens the tongue because it helps them speak English convincingly.[10] The suggestion is that it enables them to produce *r* and *l* sounds, although the evidence of the many proficient English-speakers among Korean immigrants in America and Britain makes one wonder whether the procedure is either necessary or useful. Still, it is a powerful example of the lengths people will go to in order to learn English, seduced by the belief that linguistic capital equals economic capital.

In places where English is used as a second language, its users often perceive it as free from the limitations of their native languages. They associate it with power and social status, and see it as a supple and sensuous medium for self-expression. It symbolizes choice and liberty. But while many of those who do not have a grasp of the language aspire to learn it, there are many others who perceive it as an instrument of oppression, associated not only with imperialism but also with the predations of capitalism and Christianity. (It is mainly thanks to Lenin's 1917 pamphlet about imperialism and capitalism that the two words have come to be pretty much synonymous.) The Australian scholar Alastair Pennycook neatly sums up English's paradoxical status as "a language of threat, desire, destruction and opportunity".[11] Its spread can be seen as a homogenizing (some would say, Americanizing) force, eroding the integrity of other cultures. Yet it is striking that the language is appropriated locally in quite distinct ways. Sometimes it is used against the very powers and ideologies it is alleged to represent. Listening to Somali or Indonesian rappers, for instance, it seems sloppy to say that the use of English in their lyrics is a craven homage to the commercial and cultural might of America.

15   In his book *Globish* (2010), Robert McCrum diagnoses English's "subversive capacity to run with the hare and hunt with the hounds, to articulate the ideas of both government and opposition, to be the language of ordinary people as well as the language of power and authority, rock'n'roll *and* royal decree". He considers it "contagious, adaptable, populist", and identifies the fall of the Berlin Wall in 1989 as the symbolic moment that signalled the beginning of "a new dynamic in the flow of information".[12] McCrum sees English as performing a central role in what Thomas L. Friedman has catchily called "the flattening of the world", the new "single global network".[13]

There are challenges to the position of English as the dominant world language in the twenty-first century. The main ones seem likely to come from Spanish and Mandarin Chinese. Both have more first-language users than English. But at present neither is much used as a lingua franca. The majority of speakers of Mandarin Chinese live in one country, and, excepting Spain, most Spanish-speakers are in the Americas. There is an argument that the revitalization of minority languages is good for English, because it weakens English's large rivals and thus removes obstacles to the language's spread. So, for instance, the resurgence of Catalan, Basque and Galician weakens Castilian Spanish, making it a less powerful rival to English.[14] Apologists for English invert this argument, claiming that the advance of English is good for minority languages. The inversion is spurious.

Nicholas Ostler, a linguist whose insights are often brilliantly surprising, observes that "If we compare English to the other languages that have achieved world status, the most similar—as languages—are Chinese and Malay". All three have subject-verb-object word order, and their nouns and verbs display few inflections. Moreover, "the peculiarly conservative, and hence increasingly anti-phonetic, system is another facet of English that bears a resemblance to Chinese", and "as has happened with Chinese . . . the life of English as it is spoken has become only loosely attached to the written traditions of the language".[15] It's an intriguing link, but hardly a guide to what will happen next.

The main challenges to English may come from within. There is a long history of people using the language for anti-English ends—of creative artists and political figures asserting in English their distance from Englishness or Britishness or American-ness. For instance, many writers whose first language has not been English have infused their English writing with foreign flavours; this has enabled them to parade their heritage while working in a medium that has made it possible for them to reach a wide audience.

Two challenges stand out. I have mentioned India already; English is important to its global ambitions. The language's roots there are colonial, but English connects Indians less to the past than to the future. Already the language is used by more people in India than in any other country, the United States included. Meanwhile in China the number of students learning the language is increasing rapidly. The entrepreneur Li Yang has developed Crazy English, an unorthodox teaching method. It involves a lot of shouting. This, Li explains, is the way for Chinese to activate their "international muscles". His agenda is patriotic. Kingsley Bolton, head of the English department at the City University of Hong Kong, calls this "huckster nationalism".[16] It certainly has a flamboyant quality; one of Li's slogans is "Conquer English to Make China Strong". A few dissenting voices suggest that he is encouraging racism, but the enthusiasm for his populist approach is in no doubt, and it is a symptom of China's English Fever: the ardent conviction that learning English is the essential skill for surviving in the modern world.

20   The embrace of English in the world's two most populous countries means that the language is changing. Some of the changes are likely to prove disconcerting for its native speakers. The "Englishness" of English is being diluted. So, more surprisingly, is its American flavour. English's centre of gravity is moving; in fact, in the twenty-first century the language has many centres. As this continues, native English-speakers may find themselves at a disadvantage. Native speakers freight their use of the language with all manner of cultural baggage. An obvious example is the way we use sporting metaphors. If I say to a Slovakian associate, "you hit that for six", she probably won't have a clue what I am on about. Nor will an American. An Indian very likely will (the image is from cricket), but really I should choose my words with greater care. The trouble is, often I and many others like me do not exercise much care at all. To non-native speakers, quirks and elaborations of this kind are confusing. Non-native speakers of English often comment that they find conversing with one another easier than sharing talk with native speakers. Already many people who learn English do so with little or no intention of conversing with its native users. If I join their conversations, my involvement may prove unwelcome.

At the same time, native speakers of English tend to assume that their ability in this potent language makes it unimportant to learn other languages. The reality is different. British companies often miss out on export opportunities because of a lack of relevant language skills.[17] Moreover, there is a chance that a command of English will within twenty or thirty years be regarded as a basic skill for business, and native speakers of the language will no longer enjoy any competitive advantage. When polled in 2005, more than 80 per cent of people in the Netherlands, Denmark and Sweden claimed to be able to speak English. The figure was around 60 per cent in Finland, 50 per cent in Germany, 30 per cent in France and Italy, and 20 per cent in Spain and Turkey.[18] These figures can safely be assumed to have increased. They come from a study published in 2006 by the British Council, an organization set up in 1934 and today operating as an "international cultural relations body" in more than a hundred countries. In 1989 its Director General, Sir Richard Francis, stated that "Britain's real black gold is not North Sea oil, but the English language".[19] That view is often played down, but the role of the British Council in promoting British English ties in with British corporate interests. Large companies such as British Petroleum (now BP Amoco) have worked with the British Council, funding educational schemes to encourage foreign nationals to learn English. This is not exactly an act of altruism. As Robert Phillipson punchily says, "English for business is business for English."[20] But while English is being pushed, it is also being pulled; it is the language, more than any other, that people want to learn.

The consequences are complex. Some, it would seem, are not as intended. Even as vast amounts are spent on spreading British English, the reality is that English is taking on more and more local colour in the different places where it is used. Accordingly, while the number of languages in the world is diminishing, the number of Englishes is increasing.

NOTES

1 See Salah Troudi, "The Effects of English as a Medium of Instruction", in Adel Jendli, Salah Troudi and Christine Coombe (eds), *The Power of Language: Perspectives from Arabia* (Dubai: TESOL Arabia, 2007), 6.

2 H. G. Wells, *A Modern Utopia* (London: Chapman & Hall, 1905), 17, 21–2.

3 H. G. Wells, *The World Set Free* (London: Macmillan, 1914), 215, 217–18.

4 Alexander Melville Bell, *World-English: The Universal Language* (New York: N. D. C. Hodges, 1888), 7.

5 Quoted in Braj B. Kachru, "American English and other Englishes", in Charles A. Ferguson and Shirley Brice Heath (eds), *Language in the USA* (Cambridge: Cambridge University Press, 1981), 39.

6 Edward W. Said, *Culture and Imperialism* (London: Chatto & Windus, 1993), 368–9.

7 The subject is discussed at some length in Robert Phillipson, "Lingua franca or lingua frankensteinia? English in European integration and globalization", *World Englishes* 27 (2008), 250–84.

8 Arika Okrent, *In the Land of Invented languages* (New York: Spiegel & Grau, 2009), 106.

9 Louis-Jean Calvet, *Language Wars and Linguistic Politics,* trans. Michael Petheram (Oxford: Oxford University Press, 1998), 197–8.

10 Mark Abley, *Spoken Here: Travels Among Threatened Languages* (London: Arrow, 2005), 90.

11 Alastair Pennycook, *Global English and Transcultural Flows* (Abingdon, UK: Routledge, 2007), 5.

12 Robert McCrum, *Globish: How the English Language Became the World's Language* (London: Viking, 2010), 213–16.

13 Thomas L. Friedman, *The World is Flat: A Brief History of the Globalized World in the Twenty-first Century* (London: Allen Lane, 2005), 8.

14 This question is explored in Jacques Maurais and Michael A. Morris (eds), *Languages in a Globalising World* (Cambridge: Cambridge University Press, 2003).

15 Nicholas Ostler, *Empires of the Word: A Language History of the World* (London: HarperCollins, 2005), 476.

16 See Evan Osnos, "Crazy English", *New Yorker*, 28 April 2008.

17 See, for instance, Simon Caulkin, "English, language of lost chances", *Observer*, 24 July 2005.

18 David Graddol, *English Next* (London: The British Council, 2006), 93.

19 Quoted in William Greaves, "Selling English by the Pound", *The Times*, 24 October 1989.

20 Phillipson, *English-Only Europe?*, 78.

Analyze

1. Summarize Hitchings's discussion of the rise of English as a global language. What strikes you most about his ideas?

2. What does the author mean when he calls English a "second first language"? Examine the reasoning he provides for this claim.

3. What, according to Hitchings, are some of the challenges faced by the English language? Do you agree with his views?

Explore

1. Hitchings notes that despite its imperialist history, today there is a greater desire among non-native speakers to learn English than ever before. What are some of the reasons for this? Reflect on your own experiences as a language learner—even if English is your first or native language—as you explore the continued popularity of the language.

2. Write an essay in which you examine some of the ways that speakers of other languages are infusing their speech, music, or writing with English. What does this combination of languages tell you about the culture we live in today? Would you consider these new forms of language "Englishes"? Why or why not?

3. Hitchings points out that the term "Globish" is gaining popularity among those who want to see a "neater form of English." How exactly is Globish different from traditional English? What are some of the advantages? What are its drawbacks? Refer to scholarly articles by linguists and other language experts.

Julie Traves
The Church of Please and Thank You

Julie Traves is the deputy arts editor for the Toronto newspaper *The Globe and Mail*. She is also a freelance writer whose work on arts, society, and ideas has appeared in *Canadian Business*, the *Toronto Star*, and the *National Post*. "The Church of Please and Thank You" was published in the March–April 2005 edition of *This Magazine*, one of Canada's longest publishing alternative journals on Canadian politics, pop culture, and the arts. In her article, Traves examines what has been identified as the "linguistic imperialism" of English. Rather than supplanting other languages as some critics have noted, Traves sees the new, emerging global English as "a bridge language between cultures," and its students and teachers as ambassadors for a more "egalitarian English."

What do you think Traves means by the phrase "egalitarian English?" Can such a language exist in a globalizing world?

Michelle Szabo smiles encouragingly as a young businessman talks about his hobbies in broken English. She is a Canadian teacher at Aeon's language school in Kawagoe, Japan. He is a prospective student she's charged to recruit as part of her job. The two meet in a drab five-storey office building outside the train station. The room is so small it fits only a table and two chairs. But making the sell to would-be learners has little to do with décor. What counts is Szabo's final handshake.

More than contact with an attractive young woman, her personal touch symbolizes a grasp on a better life. In the competitive marketplace of Japan, English test scores make or break job applications. Getting ahead means getting into classes with teachers like Szabo. "I would ask so many people, 'do you expect to use English in your life?' And most people would say 'No, no, no, I just need this test score,'" says Szabo. "I think it's sort of a given for all families—it's like food, shelter, English." Some sarariiman (salarymen) were so excited they trembled when they took her hand.

In addition to the 380 million people worldwide who use English as their first language, it's estimated there are 350 million to 500 million speakers of English as a foreign language (EFL)—and the number is growing. For people from affluent and developing nations alike, it is clear that the secret passwords to safety, wealth and freedom can be whispered only in English. Even 66 percent of French citizens, linguistic protectionists *par excellence*, agreed they needed to speak English in a 2001 Eurobarometer poll. While thinkers such as John Ralston Saul proclaim the death of globalization, locals from countries around the world are clamouring for English training.

Enter thousands of Westerners who spread the English gospel overseas each year. Like the Christian missionaries who came before them, many are young, have a blind faith in the beliefs they've grown up with and are eager to make their mark on the world. Unlike the 19- to 26-year-olds who proselytize for the Latter-day Saints, however, these new missionaries are also out for adventure, good times—and hard cash. Part of a $7.8-billion industry, instructors can earn $400 a month plus room and board in China and up to $4,000 a month in Japan. That's a lot more than a McJob back home.

5   But students expect more than lessons in syntax and style. EFL teachers are also hired to share Western customs and values. "'Let's have lunch sometime' doesn't mean stop by my office tomorrow and we'll go out and have lunch. It means something more general, like 'It's been nice talking to you and maybe at some point I'd like to continue the conversation,'" says Diane Pecorari, a senior lecturer at the University of Stockholm. "When you're teaching formulae like 'Please,' 'Thank you,' 'Can I split the cheque?' you also have to teach the context in which they come up. That means teaching culture."

But what is the effect of that culture on students' dialects, customs—their very identity? Ian Martin, an English professor at York University's Glendon College in Toronto, points to a troubling precedent for the current explosion of EFL. "One of the big moments in the spread of English took place in India in 1835. [British politician] Thomas Babington Macaulay proposed that English be used to create a class of Indian middlemen who would be sympathetic to British interests, without the necessity of large numbers of British citizens coming out and running the show." Instead of invading India at great economic and human cost,

English allowed the British to transform the country from within. With English on the tip of their tongues, Indians could much more easily swear allegiance to England.

Today's linguistic imperialism has a similar goal. Where once English facilitated the staffing of colonial offices, now it helps fill the cubicles of multinational corporations. Teaching locals Western speech and when it's appropriate to use it no longer transforms them into perfect Englishmen, it makes them into perfect businessmen and women. The politics of English haven't changed—the language simply serves a new corporate master.

To be sure, even those who are fascinated by the countries where they teach sometimes can't help transforming "the natives" as part of their work abroad. Canadian Michael Schellenberg, who taught in Japan more than a decade ago, loved learning about Japanese customs but also sheepishly admits he urged students to express themselves—quite against the Japanese grain. "One of the sayings in Japan is that the nail that sticks up will get pounded down. They wanted people to conform," he says. "I remember classes where I'd be like, 'Just be yourself!' As someone in my early 20s, I had a pretty good sense of how I thought the world should be. I felt pretty confident being forthright about that."

Teaching materials subtly suggest the superiority of Western values. Produced primarily in the US and UK, textbooks propagate the advantages of materialism, individualism and sexual liberation. For example, Ian Martin recalls an Indian friend's reaction to one textbook that showed Jack and Jane meeting in lesson one and dancing alone together by lesson three. "Where are the parents?" his friend wondered.

Some newer textbooks are more culturally sensitive. But in many of the books currently in circulation, says Martin, "there's nothing about environmentalism, nothing about spirituality, nothing about, say, respecting nonnative [English] speakers. And there's very little realism in any of the language learning material that I've seen. It's this mythic world of dream fulfillment through consumerism and Westernization." The Aeon language franchise in Japan uses Cameron Diaz and Celine Dion as its poster girls.

Of course, not all teachers aggressively peddle a mythic world—some have their soapbox thrust upon them. In her book *The Hemingway Book*

Club of Kosovo, California writer Paula Huntley chronicles her experience teaching English to the survivors of the area's brutal ethnic clashes. Huntley doesn't believe her language and culture are better than any other. She wants to learn from the Kosovars as much as they want to learn from her. It's her students who are convinced that the American way is the way forward, that English is the true language of progress.

Before leaving for Kosovo, Huntley crams for four weeks to complete an English as a second language instructors' certificate. But this is not what impresses the owner of the Cambridge School in Kosovo, a man named Ahmet whose house and library of 5,000 books were destroyed by the Serbs. Barely looking at her CV, he tells her she's hired. "'You are an American,'" he says. "'So you can teach our students more than English. You can teach them how to live together, with others, in peace. You can teach them how to work, how to build a democracy, how to keep trying no matter what the odds.'"

Then there is the conflicted experience of Kathy Lee. She teaches at Guangdong Industry Technical College in China. In a suburb called Nanhai, the school is putting up satellite facilities eight times larger than the main campus. Teaching labs have banks of computers and a plasma screen TV. But like so much of the country, there is such impatience to forge ahead that Lee conducts her three classes a week amid construction because the school is expanding so fast.

Her pupils are equally anxious to take part in the country's massive business boom. Though most of them have been studying English since primary school, their fluency is strained. They tell her: "The world is growing and many people speak English. If I want to do business with them, I must speak English well too!" What students want is a foreign teacher to help them get up to speed. That's why the college has hired the 23-year-old Canadian at 4,000 RMB a month, two to three times the average salary for Chinese teachers.

15   The payoff is more than just monetary for Lee. Born in China but raised in Canada, she accepted the job so she could live in Hong Kong, within a short train ride from her sick grandmother. But now, her feelings have deepened. "When the schools were asking me why I wanted to teach in China, I BS'd and said it's because I wanted to learn about my 'other' culture," she says. "But the more I said it, the more I believed it. Now, I feel that I need to be here and learn what it means to be a Chinese person."

Yet the way of life Lee is trying to understand is challenged by her methodology in the classroom. By the end of term, her students will be well practised in communication modes that are entirely un-Chinese. Lee worries about this—and the general English fever sweeping the country that even includes television programs that aim to teach English.

"I know that if everyone spoke English in the world there would still be cultural differences, but the differences between cultures will become less and less," she says. "Why is China pushing English so hard? [My students] get the sense that their own language is not good enough. To prosper, they need English. What was wrong with the way it was before? Why do you have to be Western to be competitive in business?"

If it is tough for teachers to come to terms with these questions, it is even more complex for students. While some are in what Martin calls a "process of self-assimilation," others are much more ambivalent about the course they are on. These students may be struggling with the political implications of learning English in places where the language is associated with American or British hegemony. Or they may simply recognize that as English proliferates, the survival of their own customs and dialects is under threat.

Take 27-year-old Sanghun Cho of South Korea. He is a graduate student in Toronto and has a Canadian girlfriend. But when he thinks of English he also thinks of the US. "It's a kind of dilemma for Koreans," he says. "I don't like America in Korea because they want to control the Korean government, but to survive in this kind of competitive environment I have to speak English and I have to know what English culture is."

Another South Korean student puts it even more bluntly. Part of a multinational research project Martin has been conducting over the past five years to examine why students study English as a foreign language, the student was asked to draw a picture of his future with English, and describe the picture. He sketched Uncle Sam extending a fishing line from the US across the Pacific Ocean, a hook dangling above the student's open mouth. His description: "English is the bait that Americans are using to catch Koreans in their net."

Marta Andersson is a part of the last generation of Poles forced to learn   20
Russian in school. When she was able to study English after the fall of communism, she was thrilled. On the one hand, it paid off: she got a good job in Poland, is now studying abroad and speaks English at home with her husband. On another level, though, Andersson is aware that using English

is eroding part of what her people fought for. "I have just started to lose the sense of my native language and just wait when it will become moribund," she says, "Yet I cannot imagine my future without the presence of English."

Swede Hélène Elg is also concerned about the fate of her language as English words invade it the way they do in "Chinglish" and "Franglais." "I think it's important to separate the languages in order to 'protect' our own," she says. "I realize that languages evolve, allowing new words to come into use, but we should be aware of that development and be cautious about it. The reason I feel this is because languages are so much more than just words. Words have cultural connotations. As with languages, cultures evolve, but that development should not be about adopting another culture."

Can students fight back? It's arguable that withdrawing from English would exact too high a cost for those who want to be a part of a global economy. Instead, what's changing is how people from around the world use English. Rather than simply conforming to an English steeped in Western values, many students are co-opting the language for themselves.

On an internet discussion board for EFL teachers, one teacher writes: "I feel the need of reminding our students and young colleagues that the purpose of learning English is not for us to 'speak and act' like an English person . . . but to 'speak English' as an educated Indonesian." Similarly, one Cuban who participated in Martin's project drew a picture of a rocket being launched into the sky with the description: "English is the rocket which will allow Cuba to tell its own stories to the world."

A new "global" English is emerging that is a bridge language between cultures, not simply a language that supplants other cultures. As Salman Rushdie is quoted as saying in the best-selling history *The Story of English*, "English, no longer an English language, now grows from many roots; and those whom it once colonized are carving out large territories within the language for themselves. The Empire is striking back." Along with students, many teachers are joining the fight to create a more egalitarian English. They do not want to be cultural colonialists. As David Hill, a teacher in Istanbul, writes in *The Guardian Weekly*: "English is global for highly dubious reasons: colonial, military and economic hegemony, first of the British, now of the US. . . . If we are not to be imperialists then we must help our students to express themselves, not our agenda." To do that, new programs are emerging, like the Certificate in the Discipline of Teaching English as an International Language, which Martin coordinates at Glendon College. It pays close attention to issues of cultural sensitivity and autonomy when training teachers. As Martin says, "We're trying to come to grips with the effect of globalization on language teaching. Do we want a globalization that is going to be assimilationist to Western models of communication only? Or, do we want to help people gain a voice in English?"

Michelle Szabo is one teacher who has tried to give her students a voice.   25
After her stint in Japan, she took a job at Chonbuk National University in South Korea from 2003 to 2004. On one November morning, she recalls encouraging discussion about the power of English. Her hope was to give pause to students who'd never considered the impact of studying English on their lives—as well as a place for those who had thought about it—a rare place to vent.

And there was plenty of venting as students heatedly debated face-to-face from desks arranged in a conversation-friendly horseshoe configuration. "One side was feeling very pressured and resentful," says Szabo, "and one side was saying, 'No, [English is] opening doors for us.'" Szabo tried to "equalize" the class by sitting among the students. She also said little. She wanted a forum that conveyed the message, "I'm not here to change you, to acculturize you, to force my beliefs on you," she says.

But even Szabo's new self-consciousness about what it is she is selling to her students along with English grammar has limits. English has irrevocably changed and acculturated the world already. Even if locals don't want to participate in the global capitalist machine, they need English to truly challenge it. As one of Szabo's students couldn't help but point out during the debate, "Isn't it ironic we're discussing the effect of English—in English?"

Analyze

1. As the teaching of English gains global popularity, what are some of the challenges faced by both teachers and students of English in non-English-speaking countries?

2. What do Traves's references to the two South Korean students tell you about the tension between language and culture? Are they justified in their views? Why or why not?

3. What overall argument does Traves develop in her essay? Refer to specific parts of her text that serve as supporting evidence for her argument.

Explore

1. Traves quotes Helene Elg as saying that "words have cultural connotations." Would you agree that learning English in the United States
   is not just learning a language but also learning a culture? How does
   speaking and writing in English reflect an "American" attitude?

2. In a personal narrative essay consider how the language you are most
   comfortable using reflects the values of the culture to which you
   belong. Analyze the specific words, phrases, and images that are associated with the language and discuss whether—and to what extent—it
   paints a picture of your cultural identity.

3. Is it possible for English to be "egalitarian" and not reflective of any
   Western agenda? Through your library database, search for a newspaper that is published in a non-English-speaking country but printed in
   English. Select a couple of articles of interest to you and examine the
   way the writers express their ideas. Do their words, ideas, and expressions give you any clue of their culture? Why or why not?

Pallavi Polanki
Operation Mind Your Language

Pallavi Polanki is a special correspondent for *Firstpost*, an online news source
that offers thoughtful analysis of news in India and around the world. Polanki
also served as a special correspondent and launch team member for *Open*
magazine, a weekly current affairs and features magazine geared primarily
for the progressive, globally minded Indian reader. "Operation Mind Your Language" appeared in *Open* in May 2010. It describes the enthusiasm and ear-
nestness of young Afghans currently training to be English-language teachers
at the National Council of Education Research and Training in New Delhi,
India. Most of these students, who have been sponsored by the Afghan government, are from Afghanistan's conflict-ridden southern provinces. According to the nation's Ministry of Education "nearly 50 percent of [its] 12,000
public schools are in need of over 20,000 qualified English teachers."

To what extent do you think citizens of any nation can improve life in their
country if they improve their functional knowledge of English?

Aback-bencher wearing a bright purple T-shirt and an even brighter smile raises his hand. "God is busy, may I help you?" says the writing on his T-shirt. Twenty-one-year-old Ehsan, from Wardak, a Pashtun-dominated province in central east Afghanistan, volunteers to explain his government's decision to sponsor 43 students at the National Council of Education Research and Training (NCERT) in New Delhi. Another 39 are in Mysore, at NCERT's Regional Institute of Education (RIE) campus, undergoing a similar 20-month programme.

"I am a student of teacher training for English language here," says Ehsan, before he delivers his kick-ass punchline. "As you know, USA nowadays means United States of Afghanistan. English has become our native language," he quips, making his classmates laugh.

He continues.

"Wherever you go in Afghanistan, you will face Americans. That is why English has gained a very high position there. Before the Americans, there were the Russians. At that time, many of our people learnt the Russian language. God-willing, when we return, we will teach the new generation English."

And so, with the new invasion has come the demand for a new language. Seven years of being the headquarters of the "global war on terror," and the subsequent arrival of 31 different nationalities on their soil, has brought with it a huge linguistic challenge that governments and private organisations, both local and international, are scrambling to address.

Pashto and Dari, Afghanistan's two official languages, now share space with a third language. Go shopping in Kabul, and the labelling on packets will be in three languages. A passport issued today in Afghanistan has text printed in Pashto, Dari and English.

English speakers are highly sought after in the job market. According to the Afghan Ministry of Education's statistics, nearly 50 per cent of the 12,000 public schools are in need of over 20,000 qualified English teachers. The quality of English teaching in schools is regarded as poor, and the proficiency of English teachers, lacking.

"Shortage of qualified teachers in general, and English teachers in particular, is a major national challenge. This challenge is bigger in rural, remote and less secure parts of the country. Since 2005, English is taught as a foreign language from Grade Four (it used to begin from Grade Seven). This change has added more demand on English teachers," says Susan Wardak, director general of the Afghan Ministry of Education's Teacher Education Department, in an email interview.

And so the Afghan government is hard at work trying to strengthen English departments at teacher training colleges, and giving out scholarships to students to be trained as English teachers abroad. "Collaboration on teacher education between Afghanistan and India is part of a broad bilateral agreement between the two governments," adds Wardak.

10   And so the stage was set for Operation Mind Your Language. It is a responsibility the students (the majority of whom belong to Afghanistan's conflict-ridden southern provinces) take very seriously. Shy at first, they take their time to open up. But once they do, their warmth and sincerity, not to mention sense of humour, win you over.

For NCERT, this is a first-of-its-kind collaboration. "This 20-month diploma course on English Language and Teaching of English Language has been specifically planned for Afghan students. Initially, the idea was that students would be given teacher training in various disciplines. But later on, considering the interest in English in Afghanistan and its international importance in creating a niche for its youth, the Afghan Ministry of Education decided to focus on the English language," says Poonam Agrawal, head of the International Relations division of NCERT.

Abdul Hadi Hamdard is from Helmand, a volatile southwestern province that has seen many military operations by Nato-led forces in the last seven years. Abdul, 21, was working at a local radio station when he got the scholarship to study in India. "In the name of Allah, we welcome you to our class. My English speaking power is not very good . . . but I am doing my best. When I was in Afghanistan, I could not speak any English. Now I have improved a lot. It is our responsibility to learn English and go back to our country and teach in our schools."

According to 22-year-old Mehrabuddin Wakman, a student at the Mysore campus who's also from the Helmand region, this is a pathbreaking scholarship for students from Afghanistan's southern provinces: "Majority of the 40-odd students here are from the three-four provinces that are most affected by insurgents. The level of education there, therefore, is very low." English, says Mehrabuddin, is their passport to a job, a good salary and even opportunities abroad.

The students, say faculty members, have made tremendous progress since they first arrived. "Initially, we were speaking to them only in English, and they weren't used to that. But we have somehow managed to bridge the gap, and it happened because they watch Hindi serials back home and so they've picked up a little Hindi . . . Once that language barrier was broken, the classrooms became very lively and interactive. Some Pashto words are very close to Punjabi, and so I would use a typically Punjabi word and they would immediately understand what I meant," says Kirti Kapoor, a member of the faculty at NCERT, Delhi.

For teachers, it's encouraging enough that students have found the confi- 15
dence to converse in English. "They now know that their broken English is acceptable. That is a very big achievement after six months. Their confidence is rising as they interact with more and more people. They are a young and adventurous lot," says Basanti Banerjee, also part of the visiting NCERT faculty.

"They have a kind of innocence that you don't find in our students," observes Prema Raghavan, coordinator of the Mysore batch, "In that sense, they seem far more honest in their interactions with teachers. They pretty much say what they think. It feels more like teaching young children. It is very refreshing."

Little gestures by students outside the class have endeared their teachers to them even more. Professor Raghavan relates an incident that happened when she ran into a group of her students at an ice-cream parlour. She had gone with her family, but the students quietly paid her bill before she could. "When I protested, they said, 'Let us have the honour.' They have these little ways that are very touching."

Hakima Zainul Abedin is one of the three girls studying at RIE, Mysore. Hakima, 24, used to be a school teacher in Helmand province.

Like most other Afghan students, her ideas about India came from watching Hindi movies. Only, she took them a little too seriously. "Before I came here, I thought India was a very dangerous place. I had only seen Bollywood films. But now, I've changed my mind. People of India are quite relaxed and they don't interfere." (So much for Bollywood's soft power . . .)

Hakima says teaching and studying in schools, especially for girls, is very 20
risky in her province. "It is extremely difficult for girls to go to school because of the insurgents," she reports. "So many of our schools have been burnt down. But we are rebuilding our schools. I will go back and teach English there. English is our link to the world, and it is very important for Afghanistan to connect with other countries."

Teaching can be a high-risk job in Afghanistan, and many students have chilling personal stories to tell. Abdul Wahid Karimy says he was shot at by the Taliban when he was working as a teacher in a school. "Three people surrounded me and they wanted to kill me. After they shot me in the stomach a couple of times, I fell unconscious. After that, they went looking for my father and uncle," says Wahid, whose father is a school principal in Helmand, where the incident occurred. Wahid moved to Herat province, which borders Iran, one-and-a-half years ago. He says he wants to study law in India after he has finished his diploma. He has also enrolled for computer classes, which he attends in the evening after finishing his lessons at NCERT. "I won't get this opportunity again, once I go back to Afghanistan. I want to make the most of it. I am already 26," says Wahid, who, unlike the majority of his classmates, belongs to the ethnic community of Hazaras, the third largest group after Pashtuns and Tajiks in Afghanistan.

Twenty-year-old Sayed Khaled Folad's father is a member of Afghanistan's parliament. He speaks about how the government too is now keen on hiring people with English language skills. "There are some jobs that employ Americans to work for the Afghan government. Also, if you are consultant for the government, speaking English is a necessity. Then there are NGOs like US-Aid that employ Americans. So working in the administration requires knowledge of English," says Khaled, who is planning to do a degree in India before he joins the government back home. "The government needs good workers, people who want to serve country. If I am getting a degree, it is not for me. It is for my country."

Though studies and homework seem to dominate the agenda after class and on weekends, students are also learning about a new culture and sharing their own with their hosts. Holi and Diwali were celebrated with much enthusiasm on campus. They say they have the photographs to prove it. For their *navroz* or New Year celebrations, students at the NCERT campus treated the teachers and staff to a music and dance performance. Khaled has been playing cricket with his Indian friends at the hostel. Bollywood movies, of course, continue to be a favourite. Not to forget sightseeing. A visit to the Taj Mahal was accomplished on day two of their arrival in Delhi.

So, Operation Mind Your Language seems to be going rather well. Clearly, there is going to be no dearth of challenges for these newly trained English teachers once they return to their rugged provinces. But there's also no doubt that these young Afghans are intent on doing their government proud.

Analyze

1. What is Operation Mind Your Language and what is its mission?
2. What kind of attitude do the Afghan students have toward learning English in India? How would this attitude be different if they came to the United States to learn English? Why?
3. Polanki interviews both Afghan students and their Indian teachers for this article. What picture does she paint of their relationship?

Explore

1. One of the teachers quoted in the article says that the students "now know that their broken English is acceptable." Write about what you think is generally implied by the term "broken English." Why does the teacher say that such language is "acceptable"? What does she mean?
2. Why do you think the Afghan government chose to send its students to India's NCERT and RIE to study English? What may be some of the advantages of learning English in a country where multiple native languages are spoken alongside English? Use evidence from Polanki's essay as you respond.
3. Although education is a fundamental human right, it seems to be a dangerous pursuit in Afghanistan. Find at least two news articles that focus on the current policies that are in place to protect female students and teachers in Afghanistan, and write a research paper about what the Afghan government is doing to improve their opportunities for teaching and learning.

Shehzad Nadeem
Accent Neutralisation and a Crisis of Identity in India's Call Centres

Shehzad Nadeem, a professor at Lehman College in New York City, teaches courses on urban and global sociology and is the author of *Dead Ringers: How Outsourcing Is Changing the Way Indians Understand Themselves* (Princeton University Press, 2011). His research focuses on the intersection of labor, culture, and globalization. "Accent Neutralisation and a Crisis of Identity In India's Call Centers" was published in February 2011 in *The Guardian*, a British national daily newspaper founded in 1821. *The Guardian* is known for its unique blend of global news, politics, and cultural commentary.

With English emerging as the global language, do you think it matters whether those who speak it do so with a "neutral global accent"? Why or why not? When you speak English, is your own accent "neutral"?

"**A**re you calling from India?"
    "No, I'm calling from Modesto, California."
"Well, you sound Indian."
"I've only been here for two months and haven't got the accent right."

5   Thus transpired a conversation between a potential American customer and a 22-year-old Indian call centre worker. As "Sean" tried to convince his interlocutor to refinance his home mortgage, I noticed that he, like many other Indian telecallers, was rather insecure about his accent. Yet his wavering voice told only a partial lie. True, he was not calling from Modesto but south Delhi. But he has only been at the call centre—his virtual Modesto—for two months and has not had sufficient time to "neutralise" his Indian accent. Unshaven and dressed in a red sweatshirt, white high tops, tartan socks and rumpled jeans, Sean speaks with a tortured Americanised twang. The son of an industrialist, he considers his employment to be short term—in a few years, he and his brother, who is seated at the adjacent workstation, plan to join the family business.

As he introduces himself to me, I ask if Sean is his real name or his work name. He affirms both:

"Sean is my work name, but I go by it now."

"Meaning your family and friends call you Sean as well?" I, the pop-eyed interviewer, inquire.

"Yes," he replies calmly. "Everyone calls me that now."

10   I look over to his brother, who nods slowly in confirmation. In what can be construed as either a remarkable instance of cultural self-alienation or youthful insouciance, Akhil is Sean in and out of the workplace.

Initially, workers in the Indian call centre industry were trained in specifically American and British accents, but the preference is increasingly toward a "neutral" global accent, as it allows workers to be shifted around to serve various markets without additional training. As linguist Claire Cowie notes, "businesses that outsource subscribe to the myth of a truly regionless international English accent." Yet the resulting speech is not so much neutral as measured and devoid of the local inflections that would conspicuously mark it as "Indian" (I should note that many companies say they have dropped the policy of locational masking).

The demand for globalised speech has led to the creation of specialised institutes for accent neutralisation. "Those with extremely good skills don't want to [work in call centres]," says Kiran Desai, a veteran accent trainer. "What you get is a lot of people who don't speak very well and aren't from the best schools in Bombay," she adds, in a crisp British-Indian accent.

Schools do not concentrate on phonetics enough "and so they pick up sounds from their mother tongue. We teach them to get rid of mother-tongue influence." Trainees repeat slippery sentences such as "Sachin's sixes are superb" and practice proper pronunciation ("Ahfrica" not "Afreeka"). They read aloud from Hollywood scripts such as *Saving Private Ryan*, they dissect diphthongs and coo consonants, they rid themselves of Indianisms such as "will do the needful" and, of course, they learn to roll their r's and soften their t's. The complete programme, Desai says, takes three to four weeks to take hold in places such as Bombay and Pune, but can last up to two to three months in the south.

For Desai, these are purely technical issues; she is adamant that these practices do not lead to a "loss of culture." And globalisation-boosters such as Thomas Friedman argue that any cultural displacement workers experience is made up for by relatively hefty paychecks. Yet Desai says, uncomprehendingly, that there is sometimes resistance to training: "They say, 'I'm an Indian and I speak fairly well. Why do I need to change?' I don't know why [they object]."

There is thus more at stake than phony identities and neutered accents. 15 As opposed to physical labour, service work involves "emotional labour", wherein workers are called on to amiably display a particular emotional repertoire. In call centres, management technologies penetrate to the very core of your identity. As I witnessed during training sessions, employees are told that the customer can see their smile and sense their mood through their voice. Workers must be able to "pass" as American or British and maintain their composure in the face of sometimes racist abuse by irate customers; it is simply part of the job.

Compounding the situation, the industry's young employees—who are mostly under 30—work the permanent night shift. As Anil, a Bombay-based booking agent for the British rail system remarks: "We were conditioned to say certain sentences. Otherwise, you're marked down on quality. On top of this, an agent never gets seven or eight hours of undisturbed sleep. But when they come into work tired, they have to be on in terms of accent, quality and timing. You just can't be on every day." The nightly negotiation of accents and language is particularly difficult. "We know Hindi, Marathi and other languages, but agents make grammatical errors and translate into English very literally. It's impossible to keep this up," says Anil.

Thus the animating paradox of their condition: they are reaping the benefits of the corporate search for cut-rate labour but also bearing the burdens. They are upwardly mobile cyber-coolies.

Analyze

1. Why does Nadeem start his essay with a scene in a call center in India? What point is the author trying to make?
2. What kind of an accent are call center employees expected to have nowadays? Why?
3. Look up the word "coolie" in a dictionary. Explain what Nadeem means when he describes call center workers as "upwardly mobile cyber-coolies."

Explore

1. Nadeem uses the term "cultural self-alienation" to describe Akhil's transformation into "Sean." What does that term mean to you? Do you know anyone who has an ethnic name but goes by a Western name? How might the act of taking on a Western name affect a non-Western person's identity?
2. Would you agree that native accent reduction for the purposes of learning Western-sounding English could eventually lead to a "loss of culture"? Why or why not?
3. One of the effects of outsourcing is the rapid growth of call centers in India and other developing countries, but even as these centers provide jobs, they take a toll on the lives of the workers. What kind of pressures

are call center workers exposed to in their workplace? Write a research paper that analyzes both the physical and emotional impact that call center work has had on Indian workers by using articles published in scholarly journals, newspapers, or magazines.

Gloria Gibbons
"Investigating 'Globish'"

Gloria Gibbons, who was appointed as Joint CEO (along with Donna Tuths) of Ogilvy Healthworld in 2009, has worked in public relations, advertising, medical education, and consumer advertising. The following piece appeared in the February 2012 *Marketing Channels* newsletter, a part of the Ogilvy CommonHealth Worldwide (CHWW) website. Ogilvy CHWW is a global health care communications network that serves clients across thirty-six countries. In this article, Gibbons talks about the popularizing of Globish—English in 1,500 key words—as the international business language. She argues that, for branding purposes, simpler language allows for global communication of a corporation's message. In other words, the language of the brand needs to be both understood by and representative of all.

Is anything lost when language is simplified so that the maximum number of people can understand it?

Are we all turning "Globish"? And doing this at the expense of our brands? When some of the trends in international brand marketing are considered, I fear we are. And my mission here is to get your support to change this.

Globish, for those who have not come across the term, is the English language in 1,500 key words. It was developed by non-English natives, led by a Frenchman called Jean-Paul Nerriere, to help make international business communications more effective, in a climate where global business teams increasingly comprise non-English natives and a billion people around the world need a consistent language to conduct effective commercial transactions.

The argument is that the more English becomes an international language, the more it will move away from Anglo-Saxon ownership. We are experiencing "language trickle-down" and the limitations of 1,500 words (rather than the full 260,000 of the English language) can actually be useful in aiding communication and understanding, rather than inhibiting it. There is even a Globish Text Scanner that judges whether text passes the Globish test. Simplicity to aid understanding. Compelling stuff.

And then we are told that the vocabulary of Generation "Y" (the leaders of the future) is shrinking, with some business forums predicting a vocabulary of 1,500 words may even be a mark of eloquence in times to come.

5   Similarly, in the pursuit of simplicity to achieve a global solution for our brands, my fear is that global pharma marketing is in danger of doing for the creative visual language what Globish has done for words: dumb it down.

Unfortunately, for all of us, Globish is not the answer to all things written or verbal. Imagine telling a story or writing a poem with only 1,500 words for reference. I do not think I would want to read that poem, let alone remember it and share it.

I may use Globish for basic business transactions, but not for persuasive selling or creating stories that are remembered and drive behaviour change. Here you need to create communication that is evocative, meaningful and memorable, that effectively cuts through the basic information clutter of our age and gets the customer to act.

And, visually, do we really want only to go the way of the common (lowest?) denominator, working with a reduced colour palette of just a few hundred shades, preferably the reds and the blues, down from the 16 million colours on the Mac spectrum, all in the name of simplicity?

We are in danger of watering down our communication in the name of global democracy, or should that read "in the name of Globish"? So I and others at the Health Communications Council of the European Association of Communications Agencies are on a mission to keep the iconic and effective creative idea alive in global marketing and provide global insights, ideas and resources that build brands and do not just tick Globish boxes.

Worrying Trends

Why do I say this? Because some worrying trends are emerging: 10

- *Our agencies are increasingly being asked to find a symbol, a visual design, that is recognisable the world over—the 100 per cent recognition often being treated as more important than the quality of the idea and how it builds, or otherwise, brand equity with customers. Remember that creative effectiveness is not just about recognition, it is about actively engaging customers' hearts and minds with your brand.*

  What a pharma brand desperately needs is a brand guardian in the global team to fight for it and help it navigate the globe. This should be someone who knows the brand's true equity, what the brand can and should stand for and who will represent strong and appropriate creative leadership for the brand. And this guardian will ensure no creative concept falls short of the brand's total value proposition and that the core creative idea pervades all aspects of the brand communication process, across all channels.

- *Some global brand leaders are passing responsibility to local markets to decide on the creative concept, in the name of democracy. This is often in the form of a Eurovision-type contest, in which how many votes is the name of the game. Plus, these votes are often made in isolation without discussion. This is almost the equivalent of a Globish Visual Scanner—to check if we have passed the Globish test. Or am I being too harsh?*

  Do not misunderstand me; we in network agencies want to work more closely with local market brand leaders to build stronger global brands. But it would be so much more valuable and respectful to get local brand leaders' input early, not at the end stages. Their input is needed before pitch, at the insight and ideation stage, to share their thinking with the insights we have generated via our local teams, rather than having to guess their views at pitch without having heard their opinion. Indeed, many request for proposal (RFP) protocols do not allow any access to the local markets pre-pitch. This wastes the opportunity to get multicultural input to make the brand as strong as possible for its global customers.

- *We are increasingly battling with many-paged requests for information* 15 *(RFIs) and Excel spreadsheets, to explain ourselves and get to the "starting block" for a global brand campaign opportunity. But we are increasingly left with the feeling that we are not being asked the right questions.* The RFIs quite rightly ask about our global strength. But the requests too often focus on where the pins are on the map and their size, with a view to assessing global capabilities for roll-out. However, in reality, we often work only as a global hub office on a campaign, to master only. The multiple pins on the map are rarely bought these days. Increasingly, we are being asked to govern the global brand planning process for strategy, creative and integrated channel communication. So, maybe the RFIs should be asking us other global questions?

Would it not be better to ask how we build global brands, not just how we roll them out? Perhaps ask about our methodologies for brand planning that embrace global and local needs, how we gain the "glocal" insights, how we trend watch, build multicultural creative ideas and how we work with a multinational global team council to embed this idea? In summary, how the agency works upstream for a brand to build it, before we ever get to tactical roll-out.

I would also lobby that RFIs should interrogate the creative ideation process and be sure that all concepts developed are created by international teams, not just English natives in the US or London. This will ensure that all concepts ultimately presented to the local market leaders are innately global from the outset. Teams will then be choosing the best of the best, not the one that may just be adequate.

So, in summary, whether your corporate style is "central command and control" or a more glocal balance of responsibility, your brand needs a global community at the centre that always has a glocal point of view, comprising a mix of your people and ours that brings fresh thinking and insights from over the hill, to enrich the cultural creative pool continually, to best develop the global equity for your brand. The problem with Globish is that it just dumps chlorine in that pool.

And a brand deserves a clear brand champion appointed to every global team to lead the global community and always be fighting for the best and against the compromise solution. The brand champion will ensure we do not just shout ever louder about what we want to sell from our closed gated community, while becoming increasingly deaf to what customers want to buy.

Otherwise we are all in danger of "speaking" a very limited visual Globish, of no interest or desire to stakeholders, whether they are internal local markets, global central teams or external customers, and therefore, ultimately, of little value to your brand.

Analyze

1. What is Globish and what are some of its limitations?
2. How would a "brand guardian" help a global marketing team successfully create and market a brand across the world?
3. Summarize Gibbons's main argument in this essay. What are some of her concerns about the rise of Globish? Are these concerns justified?

Explore

1. Gibbons uses the word "glocal" toward the end of her essay. What do you think she means by this term? What is the relevance of such a term in today's global market?
2. As she discusses brand recognition, Gibbons claims that "creative effectiveness is not just about recognition, it is about actively engaging customers' hearts and minds with your brand." Write an essay in which you discuss whether or not you agree with such a marketing agenda. Should an easily recognizable logo (e.g., Nike's swoosh) also emotionally appeal to customers? Who benefits from such "creative effectiveness"?
3. Analyze an international advertisement for a product that is familiar to you. What cultural differences do you notice and how do these differences make the product successful in the global market? Do you notice any "Globish" being used in the advertisement?

Jin Zhao
"Oh My Lady Gaga! This Is So Geilivable!": Chinglish Entering Globish?

Jin Zhao grew up in Kunming, Southwest China and received her MA in Communication from Georgia State University. Her broad interests range from progressive politics in the United States, globalization issues, and new media, to arts, cultures, and music. She currently lives in New York and works as a web intern, journalist, and producer at the magazine and website *The Nation*. The following post appeared in June 2011 on *Things You Don't Know About China*, Zhao's blog about topics the Chinese are talking about in social media, on alternative news websites, or in online communities. The post features and defines variations of English words known as "Chinglish" (Chinese English), and then questions whether these expressions will become part of the Globish vernacular, the English language of international business.

How far should the evolution of a language go for the sake of building a more global community?

I f you haven't used "**Oh my Lady Gaga**" in your blog or *weibo*, you're definitely an "outman" in China. "Oh my Lady Gaga" is used in blogs, *weibo*, and online communities to express shock, surprise, hilarity, or emphasis, something like "Oh my god!" but with a lot more playfulness. The expression went viral after the hosts of a popular variety show "*Kuaile Dabenying*" or "Happy Headquarter" on Hunan Satellite TV used it in the show. It was the hottest cyber expression of 2010, and even caught the attention of Western media such as *The New York Times* and *Metro* in the U.K.

Extremely popular, "Oh my Lady Gaga" is only one of the most popular "Chinglish" (Chinese English) cyber expressions Chinese netizens have created and used in original ways. The expression mentioned before, "*outman*," is also among this category, meaning someone who is out of fashion or trend. The following are some of these popular expressions:

"**Geilivable**," a word coined from "*geili*" in Chinese, a new cyber expression itself meaning "impressive," "cool," "strong," "exciting," etc. Some also add prefixes to "geilivable" to create more words. With prefix "*hen*," meaning "very" in Chinese, "**hengeilivable**" means "very impressive," "very cool," "very strong," or "very exciting." Similarly, "**ungeilivable**" means "unimpressive," "lame," "weak," or "dull." A word that has similar meaning as "geilible" is "**nuibility**." The word is based on an older Chinese slang, "*niubi*," meaning "impressive." "Nuibility" thus means "impressive" or "impressiveness."

Another Chinglish word is "**antizen**." It refers to college graduates who share a small apartment with several roommates, working hard, yet making little money. With the rocketing housing prices in Chinese cities and increasing living expenses, young people in China are under tremendous pressure. In this expression, a strong sense of irony is created by combining "ant," a minute animal thought to be hardworking yet without individuality, and "citizen," an English word that entails entitlement, civil rights, and liberty. This word is an ingenious expression of the frustration, helplessness, and resilience of Chinese young people.

Of course, not all of the words are of political connotation. For instance, 5 Chinese netizens often use "**foulsball**" to refer to soccer (football). Soccer is the most popular sport in China. Ironically, not only the Chinese soccer team has been a weak team no matter how much money has been spent on building it, but the whole soccer scene in China is often plagued by cheating, bribery, gambling, and other scandals. The word "foulsball" is thus invented by Chinese netizens to express their anger and dissatisfaction about Chinese soccer.

Another word, "**smilence**," means "smiling silently." It's used in a situation where the parties engaged in a conversation understand each other without explicitly saying anything. In a censored public space, although it seems to be a choice when there's no choice, "smilence" can be a powerful way of expression that protects netizens from censorship while still gets the point across. Interestingly, "smilence" reminds me of the stereotype of Chinese people in the U.S., who smile in response to anything others say. I wonder if this term has a bit of self-mocking Chinese humor as well.

As English has becoming "Globish," as Robert McCrum puts it, it has also been changed by non-English speakers across the world. I wonder how much of this Chinglish vocabulary will become part of Globish. With more and more English speaking expatriates living in China, Chinglish words may also be increasingly used outside China. In fact, this might well be happening already (see "Geilivable Stretches," "nuibility" in *Urban Dictionary*). As some conservative Chinese are calling for "clean" Chinese language online, I'm sure some English speakers won't be too thrilled about the non-standard usage of English, let alone the funky "foreign" words that are becoming "English." What do you think?

Analyze

1. Why do you think the term "Oh My Lady Gaga" has gained such popularity among Chinese netizens? And who are "netizens" anyway?

2. Summarize the meaning of the Chinglish word "antizen" as best you can. What other meaning can you attribute to this word?

3. What is Zhao's purpose in writing this article and who do you think might be the target audience?

Explore

1. Respond to the question Zhao poses at the end of the article. What do you think about the rise of Chinglish and its effect on Standard English?
2. What image, or perhaps self-image, does Chinglish reveal about its users? Examine some of the words that Zhao describes in the article and write a brief essay that analyzes the cultural stereotypes that might be embedded within them. What effect do the words have on these stereotypes? Why?
3. Write a research paper that examines the debate in China regarding Chinglish. What arguments are being posed by Chinese conservatives? How is the younger, computer-savvy generation responding to these arguments? What does this debate reveal about the future of Chinglish?

Forging Connections

1. The authors in this chapter address the rise of English as a global language and the effect it is having on both non-English speakers and their native languages. Evaluate the arguments presented by at least two writers as you examine how the English language is changing as it is rapidly replaced by a variety of "Englishes."
2. Polanki and Nadeem's essays illustrate how some non-English-speaking cultures still value a traditional form of English and desire to learn it all costs. How is this view of English different from that presented by Zhao? Does traditional English have a different effect on the speaker than Globish or Chinglish?

Looking Further

1. In "Investigating 'Globish'" Gloria Gibbons writes about the need for marketing companies to "gain 'glocal' insights" to sell their products. Why is "Globish" limiting to Gibbons? How would Stephen Pax Leonard ("Death by Monoculture", Chapter 10) respond to Gibbons's argument? Would he be supportive of "Globish" for Gibbons's purposes? Why or why not? Would Julie Sedivy ("Are You a Mac or a Mac User? How the Language of Identity Persuades," Chapter 7) agree with Gibbons or with Leonard?
2. As the authors of this chapter illustrate, in a globalized world, English (in both its traditional and hybridized forms) is the dominant language,

even if it is not always the preferred choice. It is impossible to escape its influence. What kind of impact do you think the enforced use of English has on the identities of speakers of other languages, such as the call center workers described by Shehzad Nadeem ("Accent Neutralisation and a Crisis of Identity in India's Call Centres")? Why or why not? Consider Jaswinder Bolina, "Writing Like a White Guy" (Chapter 6) and Lera Boroditsky, "How Does Our Language Shape the Way We Think?" (Chapter 1), as you formulate your argument.

10 Endangered Languages

The languages we speak are a product of the culture in which we live, but languages also create culture. Thus the reciprocal relationship between who we are and how we express this identity is at the very core of our existence. We simply could not construct a sense of ourselves and the world we occupy without language. In our globalized world, as certain languages have gained power and prominence, many smaller languages and the ways of knowing they represent are in danger of extinction. Because of economic, environmental, and cultural pressures—and, in many tragic cases, outright persecution—speakers of endangered languages find both their words and their cultures slipping away. Our collective failure to respect, record, and preserve our linguistic diversity results in a significant loss to humanity, in some ways equivalent to the loss suffered by our planet's environment as species both large and small are driven to extinction by the demands of globalization. Still, many authors in this final chapter strike a note of optimism, finding hope in the signs that serious efforts are underway to save little-known tongues (and the cultures they represent) from extinction.

Despite the overall decline of indigenous languages, the rise of digital technology has allowed speakers of some of these languages to connect and preserve their language. Jonathan Amos, science and space correspondent for *BBC News*, describes such efforts in his essay "Digital Tools 'To Save Languages.'" Writer and wildlife activist Joanna Eede is similarly hopeful in her essay "You Can't Google It and Get It Back" that new technology will help revive and sustain endangered languages such as Quechua. Cherokee artist and filmmaker Roy Boney's graphic feature "The Indomitable Language: How the Cherokee Syllabary Went From Parchment to iPad" provides a visual experience of the Cherokee syllabary as it narrates the history of its struggle to survive. In "The Death of an Indian-Born Language," linguist Hugo Cardoso tells a poignant tale of William Rozario, the last fluent speaker of Creole of Cochin, whose death is emblematic of the demise of ancient languages. Anthropological linguist Stephen Pax Leonard's article "Death by Monoculture" sounds a warning note against the eroding effects of consumerism on languages of remote populations like the Polar Eskimos. Finally, in the eloquent and forward-thinking essay "Vanishing Voices", writer and professor Russ Rymer reminds us that, despite the threat of erasure, technology is affording linguists and researchers new ways to understand, record, and preserve languages that would otherwise disappear forever.

Jonathan Amos
Digital Tools "To Save Languages"

Jonathan Amos is a science and space correspondent for *BBC News*, where the following article appeared in February 2012. In this piece, Amos reflects on the effects of globalization on language—and how digital resources such as online social media can potentially save some languages from extinction. According to K. David Harrison, a professor of linguistics quoted in the article, "a positive effect of globalization is that you can have a language that is spoken by only five or 50 people in one remote location, and now through digital technology . . . can achieve a global voice and a global audience."

Amos notes that approximately 7,000 languages are currently spoken around the world today. Do you think it's possible for digital technology to save all these languages from extinction? Why or why not?

O f the 7,000 or so languages spoken on Earth today, about half are expected to be extinct by the century's end.

Globalisation is usually blamed, but some elements of the "modern world", especially digital technology, are pushing back against the tide.

> "Small languages are using social media . . . to expand their voice and their presence."

North American tribes use social media to re-engage their young, for example.

Tuvan, an indigenous tongue spoken by nomadic peoples in Siberia and Mongolia, even has an iPhone app to teach the pronunciation of words to new students.

"Small languages are using social media, YouTube, text messaging and various technologies to expand their voice and expand their presence," said K. David Harrison, an associate professor of linguistics at Swarthmore College and a National Geographic Fellow.

"It's what I like to call the flipside of globalisation. We hear a lot about how globalisation exerts negative pressures on small cultures to assimilate. But a positive effect of globalisation is that you can have a language that is spoken by only five or 50 people in one remote location, and now through digital technology that language can achieve a global voice and a global audience."

Harrison, who travels the world to seek out the last speakers of vanishing languages, has been describing his work here at the annual meeting of the American Association for the Advancement of Science (AAAS).

With National Geographic, he has just helped produce eight talking dictionaries. These dictionaries contain more than 32,000 word entries in eight endangered languages. All the audio recordings have been made by native speakers, some of whom like Alfred "Bud" Lane are among the last fluent individuals in their native tongues.

Mr Lane speaks a language known as Siletz Dee-ni, which is restricted to a small area on the central Oregon coast.

10   "Linguists came in and labelled our language moribund, meaning it was heading for the ash heap of history; and our tribal people and our council decided that wasn't going to happen. So we devised a plan to go forward to start teaching our dialect here in the Siletz Valley," he told the meeting.

Mr Lane has sat down and recorded 14,000 words for the online dictionary. "Nothing takes the place of speakers speaking to other speakers, but this bridges a gap that was just sorely needed in our community and our tribe."

Margaret Noori is an expert in Native American studies at the University of Michigan and a speaker of Anishinaabemowin, which is the sovereign language of over 200 indigenous "nations" in Canada and the US. These communities are heavy users of Facebook.

"What we do with technology is try to connect people," Prof Noori said. "All of it is to keep the language."

Dr Harrison says not all languages can survive, and many inevitably will be lost as remaining speakers die off. But he says the new digital tools do offer a way back from the brink for a lot of languages that seemed doomed just a few years ago.

15   He told *BBC News*: "Everything that people know about the planet, about plants, animals, about how to live sustainably, the polar ice caps, the different ecosystems that humans have survived in—all this knowledge is encoded in human cultures and languages, whereas only a tiny fraction of it is encoded in the scientific literature. "If we care about sustainability and survival on the planet, we all benefit from having this knowledge base preserved."

Analyze

1. What impact does globalization have on the life of "small languages" and how does that affect the life of groups that use such languages?
2. How are tribal populations taking advantage of digital media to preserve their languages?
3. What is a "talking dictionary" and how do you think one would go about using such a dictionary?

Explore

1. Why are languages spoken by tribes and indigenous groups on the decline? Imagine that you speak a language that is native to a small community of users. What you have to do (or not do) to preserve such a language?

2. Write a paper in which you describe two languages that are in danger of disappearing. Who are the speakers of these languages? What factors are responsible for their decline?

3. Do you believe that the use of digital technology is the best way to preserve "vanishing" languages? Write a journal response in which you examine whether electronic means of communication such as email, text messages, tweets, and social media are sufficient for language preservation.

Joanna Eede
You Can't Google It and Get It Back

Writer Joanna Eede's deep passion for the preservation of tribal cultures has led her to explore the subject for various newspapers and magazines, including *National Geographic* and *Survival International*, for which she is the editorial consultant and where "You Can't Google It and Get It Back" appeared in August 2011. She reflects on the fate of tribal languages around the globe—and what their potential loss means for the survival of humanity in a world experiencing ecological and environmental distress. Writes Eede, "Languages are far more than mere words: they amount to what we know, and who we know ourselves to be. Their loss is immeasurable."

Have you ever struggled to find the right words to express a feeling or an experience?

"**Y**ou say laughter and I say larfter," sang Louis Armstrong. The difference is subtle. Across the world, however, from the Amazon to the Arctic, tribal peoples say it in 4,000 entirely different ways.

Sadly, no one now says "laughter" in Eyak, a language from the Gulf of Alaska, whose last fluent speaker died in 2008, or in the Bo language from the Andaman Islands, for its last remaining speaker, Boa Senior, died in 2010. Nearly 55,000 years of thoughts and ideas—the collective history of an entire people—died with her.

Most tribal languages are disappearing faster than they can be recorded. Linguists at the Living Tongues Institute for Endangered Languages believe that on average, a language is disappearing every two weeks. By 2100, more than half of the more than 7,000 languages spoken on Earth—many of them not yet recorded—may disappear. The pace at which they are declining exceeds even that of species extinction.

As tribal peoples are evicted from their lands, as their children are taken away from their communities and forced into education systems that strip away traditional wisdom, as wars, urbanisation, genocide, disease, violent land-grabs and globalisation continue to threaten tribal peoples with extinction, so the world's tribal languages are dying. And with the death of tribes and the extinction of their languages, unique parts of human society become nothing more than memories.

5   In Western Brazil, among the endlessly dry, yellowing soya fields of Rondônia state, where smoke billows on the horizon and the smell of burning wood hangs in the air, there still exist small fragments of lush, intact rainforest. Here the five remaining members of the once-thriving, and isolated, Akuntsu tribe live.

Their diminished population is due to the building of a major highway through Rondônia in the 1970s, which resulted in waves of cattle ranchers, loggers, land speculators and colonists occupying the state. The settlers were hungry for land, at any price. Cattle ranchers bulldozed the forest home of the Akuntsu, tried to hide the destruction, and employed gunmen to murder the inhabitants. The surviving members fled into the forest, where they remained, traumatised, until contact was made in the mid-1990s. Since then, linguists have been working with the tribe in an effort to understand their language. The hope is that one day the Akuntsu will not only be able to recount their tragic story in detail, but will be able to share the knowledge and insights embedded in their words.

The fate of tribal languages is the same across the world. Before Europeans arrived in America and Australia, hundreds of complex languages were spoken in each country. Today, neither the Yurok language of California nor the Yawuru of Western Australia has more than a handful of speakers.

Among the Blackfoot tribes of the northwestern plains of North America, it is rare to find a person under the age of 20 speaking the mother tongue, Siksika; most speakers are dwindling groups of elderly people. When languages become the preserve of the old, the knowledge systems inherent in them become endangered; for the rest of the world, this means that unique ways of adapting to the planet and responding creatively to its challenges go to the grave with the last speakers. In a world of ecological uncertainty, such information is no small loss.

In fact, many of the world's tribal languages are not spoken to children. Preventing a tribe from communicating in its language has long been a policy deliberately adopted by dominant authorities in order to marginalise tribal ways of life. From the 1950s to 1980s, the Soviet authorities in Siberia tried to suppress the traditions of the country's tribal peoples by sending tribal children to schools that did not teach their own languages; some children were even punished for daring to speak them.

In Canada, Inuit children were taken away from their homes, sent to residential schools, and beaten for communicating in their mother tongue. "I didn't expect to get strapped at that time, but I did," said George Gosnell, an Inuit man, "I went to the principal's office and I got strapped for using our languages." In Canada's Innu communities, although some teaching is now carried out through the medium of Innu-aimun, the Innu language, most is conveyed in English or French. "The kids don't understand us these days we when use old Innu words," an Innu man told a Survival International researcher, "and we can't translate, because we don't understand."

Understanding is everything, however, in harsh environments. To un- 10 derstand a language and the knowledge and information held within it is to survive: land, life and language are intimately related for most tribal peoples. Encoded within their vocabularies and passed down the generations are the secrets to surviving in the deserts of Africa, the ice-fields of the Arctic or the rainforests of Papua New Guinea. "I cannot read books," said the Gana Bushman Roy Sesana from Botswana. "But I do know how to read the land and animals. All our children could. If they couldn't, they would have died long ago."

The languages of Bo, Innu-aiman, Penan, Akuntsu, Siksika, Yanomami and Yawuru are rich in the results of thousands of years of observation and discovery and aspects of life that are central to the survival of the community—and the wider world. "The hunter gatherer way of being in the world, their way of knowing and talking about the world, depends on detailed, specific knowledge," says anthropologist Hugh Brody, while linguist K. David Harrison, in his book When Languages Die writes, "When we lose a language, we lose centuries of human thinking about time, seasons, sea creatures, reindeer, edible flowers, mathematics, landscapes, myths, music, the unknown and the everyday."

Most tribal languages, however, cannot be found in books. Or on the Internet. Or for that matter in any form of documentation, because most of them have been orally conveyed. But this, of course, makes them no less valid, or relevant. Oral languages record their own parallel stream of history. "Australia's true history is never read," wrote an Aboriginal poet, "But the black man keeps it in his head"—a thought echoed by the Bushman woman Dicao Oma when she said simply, "We have our own talk."

Similarly, the Bolivian Kallawaya, itinerant healers who are thought to have been the naturopathic healers for Inca Kings, and who still travel through the Andean mountain valleys and highland plateaus in search of traditional herbs, also have their own "talk"; a secret family language that has been handed down from father to son, or grandfather to grandson. Some believe the language, called Machaj Juyai or "folk language," to be the secret language of the Inca Kings, linked to the languages of the Amazonian forest, to which the Kallawaya once travelled to find material for their treatments.

In the age of technology, there is some hope of revival for Kallawaya and other fading languages of the world. One encouraging example is Quecha, the most widely spoken indigenous language in South America. It has long been in slow decline but is being revived after Google launched a search engine in Quechua, Microsoft produced versions of Windows and Office in the language, and the scholar Demetrio Túpac Yupanqui translated Don Quixote into his own mother tongue. Documenting and saving ancient languages is thus entirely possible, and can actually be facilitated by the latest communication technologies: mobile phone texts, social networks and iPhone apps.

15   In the end, the death of tribal languages matters not only for the identity of its speakers—a language is, as the linguist Noam Chomsky said, "a mirror of the mind"—but for all of us, for our common humanity. Tribal languages are languages of the earth, suffused with complex geographical, ecological and climatic information that is rooted in locale, but universally

significant. The very fact that the Inuit people of Canada have no one word for snow, for example, but are able to name many different types, demonstrates just how attuned they are to their environment, and therefore to potential changes in it—a skill that, arguably, many urbanised people have lost now that they are that more removed from the natural world.

But languages are also rich in spiritual and social insights—ideas about what it is to be human; to live, love and die. Just as natural cures to humanity's illnesses are waiting to be found in plants in the rainforest, so many ideas, perceptions and solutions about how humans engage with each other and with the natural world already exist, in the tribal languages of the world. Languages are far more than mere words: they amount to what we know, and who we know ourselves to be. Their loss is immeasurable. In the words of Daniel Everett, linguist, author and Dean of Arts and Sciences at Bentley University, "When we lose tribal knowledge we lose part of our 'force' as Homo sapiens. There is an inestimable loss of expression of humor, knowledge, love, and the gamut of human experience. One ancient tradition, a world of solutions to life is lost forever. You can't Google it and get it back."

"They say our language is simple, that we should give up this simple language of ours and speak your kind of language," wrote Inuit Simon Anaviapik. "But this language of mine, of yours, is who we are and who we have been. It is where we find our stories, our lives, our ancestors; and it should be where we find our future, too."

Analyze

1. What point about the role of language does Eede make by recounting the story of the Akuntsu peoples of Brazil?
2. Gana Bushman Roy Sesana says that he knows "how to read the land and animals." What does such "reading" have to do with the language his tribe speaks and why is it important to preserve this knowledge?
3. What is the function of oral languages? How are they maintained and transmitted?

Explore

1. Eede notes that languages are "rich in spiritual and social insights." Consider how the language(s) you speak allow you—or provide you with—ways of thinking about social or spiritual issues. Pay particular

attention to how the words convey ideas and meanings that are unique to the language in which they are spoken.

2. What is Quechua and where is it spoken today? Explore the history of Quechua and its struggle to survive among its users by referring to scholarly articles that you find through your library database.

3. Eede gives us two examples of the imposition of Western languages on native children. Why were such educational policies adopted and what effect did it have on the native population? How have such policies changed over the years?

Roy Boney, Jr.
The Indomitable Language: How the Cherokee Syllabary Went from Parchment to iPad

As a full-blooded Cherokee, citizen of the Cherokee Nation, and hereditary member of the Deer Clan, Roy Boney, Jr. grew up speaking the Cherokee language. An artist and computer animator, Boney has worked on several documentary films about Native Americans. He is the illustrator on the National Park Service's production, *Trail of Tears*. The following graphic feature appeared in *Indian Country Today Media Network*, a weekly, multimedia news site launched in 2011 that serves as the national source of news for Native Americans in the United States. Boney's graphic narrative depicts the origins, evolution, and survival of the syllabic writing system of the Cherokee nation from its acceptance by the Cherokees in 1821 up to now.

What aspects of our modern society can help preserve ancient language and traditions?

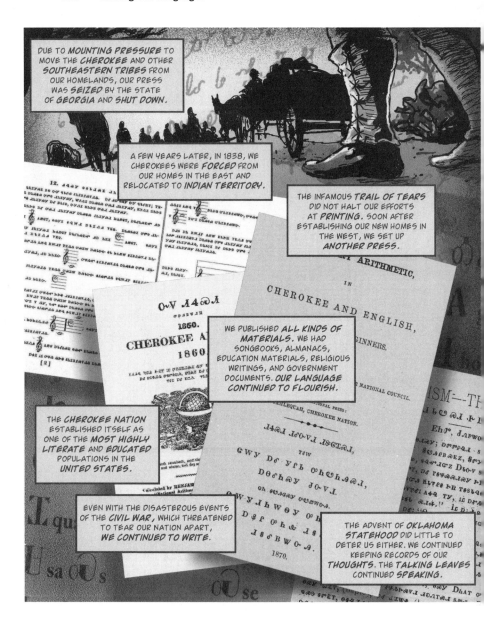

Analyze

1. How successful is Boney in conveying his ideas through the visual medium? Discuss whether his illustrated essay enhances or detracts from the message of his writing.
2. What were "talking leaves" and what was their significance in the Cherokee culture?
3. How did the advent of the printing press, and later computer technology, affect evolution of the Cherokee syllabary?

Explore

1. In an image that represents a literal transformation Boney declares "we can't get much further if we can't adjust." Write about a time when you faced a situation that required you to adapt to a new way of doing things. What difficulties did you face and how did you overcome them? How did you feel about the transition?
2. Find an online copy of the *Cherokee Phoenix* and describe some of the contents of the newspaper. What can you learn about the Cherokee people from this publication? What particular issues seem most crucial to this population?
3. Write a paper in which you analyze the effects of the "Trail of Tears" on the language and culture of Native American peoples. Examine primary sources as well as scholarly articles by historians and scholars of Native American history.

Hugo Cardoso
The Death of an Indian-Born Language

Linguist Hugo Cardoso, who teaches at the University of Macau and the University of Hong Kong, researches the Portuguese-based Creole languages of Asia. "The Death of an Indian-Born Language" is a tribute to William Rozario, the last speaker of the Indo-Portuguese Creole language of Cochin, a major port city located on India's west coast. It was published in October 2010, a few months after Rozario's death, in *Open* magazine. *Open* is a weekly current affairs and features magazine with a progressive, globally minded Indian readership. Creole is a "contact language," which means that several different languages have come into contact with one another by virtue of the space they shared; research in Creole languages helps us understand the cross-cultural interactions that have shaped these spaces. The Creole of Cochin is of particular interest to historians because Cochin is considered one of the world's first globalized cities; its Creole, therefore, is also considered one of the world's first contact languages.

Even if every word of an endangered language is recorded, is it possible to retain the knowledge and perspective of that language once its last native speaker has died?

William Rozario passed away on 20 August 2010, at the age of 87. And with him died the Indo-Portuguese Creole of Cochin. He was the last of its speakers. My first visit to his home in Vypeen, back in 2007, was memorable; he seemed genuinely pleased to learn of my interest in his language.

Creoles are what we call "contact languages", varieties which come about through the contact of several languages sharing the same space. The Indo-Portuguese Creole that Rozario spoke was formed primarily through contact between Malayalam and Portuguese. In other parts of India, however, the equation was different: in the Bombay region, Portuguese interacted with Marathi; in Daman and Diu with Gujarati; and on the southeastern coast of India it interacted with Tamil. At present, Indo-Portuguese Creoles are spoken in very few places. Daman Creole has around 4,000 speakers; that of Korlai, a village in Maharashtra near the old fortress of Chaul, has around 760 speakers; Diu Creole is spoken by some 180 speakers; and the one of Cannanore, only by five.

Researching contact languages like these sheds light on patterns of cultural interaction in the past, and Cochin is of prime interest for historians. It was among the world's first globalised cities, and also the first outpost of the Portuguese in India. It is also for Cochin that we have some of the earliest records of Catholic missionary activities, and of the formation of Eurasian homesteads, two of the main social factors which motivated the appearance of well-defined creolophone communities. Scholars tell us that during the Dutch period, members of the Luso-Asian community of Cochin were highly valued as local mediators because of their cultural and linguistic adaptability. In the period of British domination, they came to be classified as "Anglo-Indians" along with other Eurasians—with whom the community fused to some extent—and this remains unchanged to this day.

The Creole of Cochin was probably one of the first contact languages that sprung up along the coasts of Asia from the outset of European colonial activities there. But it didn't remain in isolation. There has always been population movement in this region, which was probably enhanced by the tendency of Catholics to seek spouses in other Catholic communities. That would explain why, for instance, the Creole of Cochin as spoken by Rozario bears such resemblance to the present-day Creole of Cannanore.

When I met Rozario, drawn by the prospect of recording a language that   5
many believed extinct, he was already retired, and was very generous with his time. From the first day, both he and his family treated me with great warmth. After my first visit, we would write letters to each other every so often, and, when I visited him again later, I felt like an old friend returning home. William Rozario's household is truly one of the most hospitable I've ever come across. The family always insisted I ate with them and we had nice long chats.

Most of the stories Rozario told me had to do with his years growing up on an estate in Wayanad, about how big snakes would sometimes enter the house, or how one of his relatives was an accomplished hunter. As for the language, he said that when he was a child, his entire interaction with the extended family took place in it. Christmas was a time when the family would gather for a party. They played instruments such as the guitar, violin or harmonium, and sang Creole songs. The one he remembered best was *jinjri nona* (by his pronunciation), which scholars know of in a slightly different form, from other Luso-Asian communities in India and Sri Lanka.

Although Rozario had grown up speaking his traditional Creole with other members of the community, the language gradually lost ground in his lifetime. His wife did not speak it, and the younger generation grew up mostly with Malayalam and English. Towards the end of his life, the last person who could converse with him in his mother tongue was his neighbour Francis Paynter, but Paynter passed away a few years ago. In Cochin, some people still remember words, phrases and songs in this language, some may even understand it partially, but William Rozario appeared to be the last fluent speaker. When we met, he seemed happy to be able to speak his language again, even though I had some trouble understanding it at first. I am a native speaker of European Portuguese, and, despite my previous research on the Creole spoken in Diu, I could only pick up Rozario's language in parts at the time.

I heard about Rozario's death through an email sent to me by his daughter-in-law. It was very sad news. Doubly sad, since this meant the death of a friend *and* of a centuries-old language. The Indo-Portuguese Creole of Cochin was the mother tongue of part of the local Catholic community for over four centuries; records from the late 19th-century show that it was still vital at the time. The process of abandonment must have begun around the turn of the 19th century. English or Malayalam gradually took over some of the domains that were previously the precinct of this Creole: religion, home, the neighbourhood and so on. And that is how the present situation came about: Rozario gradually lost interlocutors, and became, in the end, the only Creole speaker left in Cochin.

No matter how much theoretical knowledge an outsider may have gathered beforehand, first contact with these languages always makes an impression. Hearing them makes history almost palpable. To me, it is more striking than looking at a monument. Buildings can last for a while even after they cease to mean much to the people, but it's not the same with spoken language.

10   These Creoles survived because they were important cultural signposts for the communities that spoke them. In the 21st century, however, the world is becoming linguistically and culturally less diverse. It is widely recognised that languages are disappearing faster than ever before, and the processes by which new languages arise cannot keep up.

Analyze

1. What are "contact languages"? Explain why the Creole of Cochin is important in understanding how contact languages function within a culture.
2. What does the story of William Rozario tell you about the process by which languages become endangered? What solutions can you propose that would stem this decline?
3. Cardoso tells us that an encounter with a historic building is different than encountering a historic spoken language. What difference do you think he is referring to?

Explore

1. If you were William Rozario, what would you have done to preserve the Creole of Cochin? What measures is it possible for one to take in a community of dwindling speakers to keep a language alive?

2. Who comprises the Anglo-Indian community in India and what languages do the members of this community speak today?
3. Cardoso says that actually hearing a language "makes history palpable." Apply this idea to a language you are most familiar with. How does this language reflect the history of a people in a particular place at a particular time? If a person of the future heard this language, what kind of a past would he or she see? Why?

Stephen Pax Leonard
Death by Monoculture

Stephen Pax Leonard is a research associate at the Scott Polar Research Institute at the University of Cambridge, England. An anthropological linguist with a range of research interests, Leonard has carried out fieldwork in such places as Iceland, the Faroe Islands, and most recently, Greenland. "Death by Monoculture" appeared in September 2011 in *Research*, Cambridge University's online forum about current research projects. In this report, Leonard describes his one-year stay among the Inghuits, a remote community in northwest Greenland. His fieldwork reveals the endangering effects of "synthetic monoculture" on this group's language and traditions in particular, but in a larger sense, on centuries-old languages, cultures, and traditions worldwide.

If a monoculture is an inevitable consequence of our globalizing world, what—if any—steps should be taken to record and preserve cultural and linguistic diversity? Who should be responsible for taking those actions?

The 21st century is the make-or-break century for cultural and linguistic diversity, and for the future of human civilisation *per se*. An unprecedented and unchecked growth in the world's population, combined with the insistence on exploiting finite resources, will lead to environmental and humanitarian catastrophes as mass urbanisation meets fundamental problems such as the lack of drinking water. The actions that we collectively take over the next fifty years will determine how and if we can overcome such global challenges, and what the shape of the "ethnosphere" or "sum of the world's cultures" is to look like in years to come.

After having spent a year in a remote Arctic community which speaks a vulnerable, minority language and whose cultural foundations are being rocked by climate change, it is clear to me that the link between environmental and cultural vulnerability is genuine and that the two are interwoven. Cultural practices of the Polar Eskimos are based on a history of survival strategies in one of the world's most hostile environments. Their language and "way of speaking" is a representation of that. When the sea ice disappears, their stories will eventually go with it.

We, human beings, rent the world for a period of approximately 80 years. It is our duty to future tenants to leave the house as we found it. The conservation issue goes beyond everything else and should therefore be at the heart of every policy decision. To do otherwise, would be to live in the 20th century. At present, linguists predict that over 50 per cent of the world's languages will no longer be spoken by the turn of the century. Instead of leaving the house in order, we are on the road to the fastest rate of linguistic and cultural destruction in history. Languages die for many reasons, but the current trend is driven by the juggernaut of the homogenising forces of globalisation and consumerism which seems unstoppable and whose language tends to be the new universal tongue, English.

I am a romantic and romantics are nowadays always disillusioned because the world is no longer how they had hoped it to be. I had gone to the top of the world and had wished to find elderly folk sitting around telling stories. Instead, I found adults and children glued to television screens with a bowl of seal soup on their lap, playing exceedingly violent and expletive crammed Hollywoodian video war games. Time and time again, I discovered this awkward juxtaposition of modernity meets tradition. Out in the Arctic wilderness, hunters dressed head to toe in skins would answer satellite phones and check their GPS co-ordinates.

5   Consumerism has now made it to every corner of the world. Some Polar Eskimos may live in tiny, wind-beaten wooden cabins with no running water, but Amazon delivers. Most 8 year-olds who live in Qaanaaq and the remote settlements have the latest smartphones. Media entertainment will, however, never be produced for a language of 770 speakers because it is loss-making. Technology, be it mobile phones, DVDs or video games may support

the top 50 languages maximum, but never more than that. Some languages are not suited to these technologies: Greenlandic words are too long to subtitle and to use in text messaging. Polar Eskimos tend to send text messages in Danish or English because it is easier.

As the world embraces the synthetic monoculture of populism and consumerism, linguistic and cultural diversity risk being erased right across the world. For consumerism to operate efficiently, it requires as few operating languages as possible. That way, the message is consistent and the producer's cost is minimised. This globalised consumerism is the product of a system which is based on an addiction to economic growth. Growth for the sake of growth is the ideology of the cancer cell, and yet it is difficult to hear US presidential candidates or EU officials talk about anything else. Some politicians speak oxymoronically of "sustainable growth" but the combination of a rocketing world population and finite resources is the recipe of "unsustainability" *par excellence*.

Growth has become an abstract imperative that is driving humanity to destroy the ecosystem upon which life depends. If we can shake off the growth habit and focus on the "local" and sustainability for its own sake, minority languages will have a chance to prosper providing they engage with new digital media technologies. The Internet represents surely the best opportunity to help support small or endangered languages and yet 95 per cent of Internet content appears in just 12 languages. The Internet offers also a chance to move away from television which is largely responsible for the spread of a phoney, idiotic form of entertainment culture where production costs are too high to support minority languages.

I have never met anybody who is indifferent to the elimination of biodiversity or the protection of endangered animal species, but linguists and anthropologists are still being asked to defend linguistic and cultural diversity. In doing so, it should be remembered that a language is so much more than a syntactic code or a list of grammar rules. To treat language as such is to reduce it to its least interesting features. When languages die, we do not just lose words, but we lose different ways of conceptually framing things. For the Polar Eskimos, there is no one concept of "ice", but over twenty different ways of referring to various forms of ice. Through different distinctions in meaning, languages provide insights onto how groups of speakers "know the world".

A language is a collection of statements about the world delivered in a multitude of voices set to a background of music. There is a difference between being able to speak a language fluently and to speak a language like a native. The latter requires first and foremost a mastery of the language's paralinguistic features—in the case of Polar Eskimo, a rich and never random repertoire of sighs and groans and a specific mix of intonation patterns and gestures accompanying particular words and phrases. To be able to speak a handful of languages as a native, you have to be able to act and act well, reproducing exactly certain collocations of words to the rhythm, gestures, flow and timbre of its speakers. This is always more important than just having a large vocabulary or putting the verb in the right place. Each language of the world requires a different voice. When we lose a language, we lose an orchestra of voices that permeate the mind. As well as knowledge and perceptions of the world which are built into local language varieties, we lose the music and poetry of words and speech which elicit so much pleasure. There should be no need to defend linguistic diversity. It and the power of language is something to be celebrated. Without it, the world would be utterly dull. After all, who wants to listen to just Beethoven, when you can enjoy Rachmaninov and Shostakovich too? Not that there is any chance of the Polar Eskimos listening to Beethoven, they are too busy indulging in virtual reality Playstation war games whose only poetic content is "fucking pacify him".

Analyze

1. What, according to Leonard, is one of the major reasons for the gradual demise of vulnerable languages?
2. What is the "monoculture" Leonard refers to in his title and how does it affect minority cultures and their languages?
3. Analyze the analogy that Leonard draws between language and music. How is a language like "an orchestra of voices"?

Explore

1. Why is Leonard so disillusioned to see Polar Eskimos behaving like those who live in more modern, developed areas? If you had the opportunity to speak to some of the younger Polar Eskimos about their lifestyle and behaviors, what would you say? Why?
2. How is being able to speak a language fluently different from speaking it like a native? Refer back to Leonard's ideas as you respond.

3. The Polar Eskimos have twenty different words to express the concept of "ice" or "snow." Find translations of these words and write a paper that analyzes the different meanings ascribed to these two concepts. What do these differences in meaning reveal about the Polar Eskimo culture? How would the culture be affected if their language were to disappear?

Russ Rymer
Vanishing Voices

Writer and professor Russ Rymer has contributed to *The New Yorker, Harper's, The Atlantic,* and *National Geographic.* "Vanishing Voices" appeared in *National Geographic* in July 2010. In his report, Rymer poses a deeply philosophical question in the face of a staggering statistic: Although there are approximately 7,000 languages in the world, 78 percent of the world's population speaks only 85 of them—and those 85 represent the largest languages. As the world grows more globalized, the smaller languages spoken in its farthest reaches lose the protection of national boundaries and begin to disappear.

How would you answer Rymer's haunting question: "What is lost when a language goes silent?"

Tuvan: The Compassion of Khoj Özeeri

One morning in early fall Andrei Mongush and his parents began preparations for supper, selecting a black-faced, fat-tailed sheep from their flock and rolling it onto its back on a tarp outside their livestock paddock. The Mongush family's home is on the Siberian taiga, at the edge of the endless steppes, just over the horizon from Kyzyl, the capital of the Republic of Tuva, in the Russian Federation. They live near the geographic center of

Asia, but linguistically and personally, the family inhabits a borderland, the frontier between progress and tradition. Tuvans are historically nomadic herders, moving their *aal*—an encampment of yurts—and their sheep and cows and reindeer from pasture to pasture as the seasons progress. The elder Mongushes, who have returned to their rural aal after working in the city, speak both Tuvan and Russian. Andrei and his wife also speak English, which they are teaching themselves with pieces of paper labeled in English pasted onto seemingly every object in their modern kitchen in Kyzyl. They work as musicians in the Tuvan National Orchestra, an ensemble that uses traditional Tuvan instruments and melodies in symphonic arrangements. Andrei is a master of the most characteristic Tuvan music form: throat singing, or *khöömei.*

When I ask university students in Kyzyl what Tuvan words are untranslatable into English or Russian, they suggest khöömei, because the singing is so connected with the Tuvan environment that only a native can understand it, and also *khoj özeeri,* the Tuvan method of killing a sheep. If slaughtering livestock can be seen as part of humans' closeness to animals, khoj özeeri represents an unusually intimate version. Reaching through an incision in the sheep's hide, the slaughterer severs a vital artery with his fingers, allowing the animal to quickly slip away without alarm, so peacefully that one must check its eyes to see if it is dead. In the language of the Tuvan people, khoj özeeri means not only slaughter but also kindness, humaneness, a ceremony by which a family can kill, skin, and butcher a sheep, salting its hide and preparing its meat and making sausage with the saved blood and cleansed entrails so neatly that the whole thing can be accomplished in two hours (as the Mongushes did this morning) in one's good clothes without spilling a drop of blood. Khoj özeeri implies a relationship to animals that is also a measure of a people's character. As one of the students explained, "If a Tuvan killed an animal the way they do in other places"—by means of a gun or knife—"they'd be arrested for brutality."

Tuvan is one of the many small languages of the world. The Earth's population of seven billion people speaks roughly 7,000 languages, a statistic that would seem to offer each living language a healthy one million speakers, if things were equitable. In language, as in life, things aren't. Seventy-eight percent of the world's population speaks the 85 largest languages, while the 3,500 smallest languages share a mere 8.25 million speakers. Thus, while English has 328 million first-language speakers, and Mandarin 845 million, Tuvan speakers in Russia number just 235,000. Within the next century, linguists think, nearly half of the world's current stock of languages may disappear. More than a thousand are listed as critically or severely endangered—teetering on the edge of oblivion.

In an increasingly globalized, connected, homogenized age, languages spoken in remote places are no longer protected by national borders or natural boundaries from the languages that dominate world communication and commerce. The reach of Mandarin and English and Russian and Hindi and Spanish and Arabic extends seemingly to every hamlet, where they compete with Tuvan and Yanomami and Altaic in a house-to-house battle. Parents in tribal villages often encourage their children to move away from the insular language of their forebears and toward languages that will permit greater education and success.

Who can blame them? The arrival of television, with its glamorized 5 global materialism, its luxury-consumption proselytizing, is even more irresistible. Prosperity, it seems, speaks English. One linguist, attempting to define what a language is, famously (and humorously) said that a language is a dialect with an army. He failed to note that some armies are better equipped than others. Today any language with a television station and a currency is in a position to obliterate those without, and so residents of Tuva must speak Russian and Chinese if they hope to engage with the surrounding world. The incursion of dominant Russian into Tuva is evident in the speaking competencies of the generation of Tuvans who grew up in the mid-20th century, when it was the fashion to speak, read, and write in Russian and not their native tongue.

Yet Tuvan is robust relative to its frailest counterparts, some of which are down to a thousand speakers, or a mere handful, or even one individual. Languages like Wintu, a native tongue in California, or Siletz Dee-ni, in Oregon, or Amurdak, an Aboriginal tongue in Australia's Northern Territory, retain only one or two fluent or semifluent speakers. A last speaker with no one to talk to exists in unspeakable solitude.

Increasingly, as linguists recognize the magnitude of the modern language die-off and rush to catalog and decipher the most vulnerable tongues, they are confronting underlying questions about languages' worth and utility. Does each language have boxed up within it some irreplaceable beneficial knowledge? Are there aspects of cultures that won't survive if they are translated into a dominant language? What unexpected insights are being lost to the world with the collapse of its linguistic variety?

Fortunately, Tuvan is not among the world's endangered languages, but it could have been. Since the breakup of the Soviet Union, the language has stabilized. It now has a well-equipped army—not a television station, yet, or a currency, but a newspaper and a respectable 264,000 total speakers (including some in Mongolia and China). Yet Tofa, a neighboring Siberian language, is down to some 30 speakers. Tuvan's importance to our understanding of disappearing languages lies in another question linguists are struggling to answer: What makes one language succeed while another dwindles or dies?

Aka: The Respect of Mucrow

I witnessed the heartrending cost of broken languages among the Aka people in Palizi, a tiny, rustic hamlet perched on a mountainside in Arunachal Pradesh, India's rugged northeasternmost state. It is reachable by a five-hour drive through palm and hardwood jungles on single-track mountain roads. Its one main street is lined with unpainted board-faced houses set on stilts and roofed with thatch or metal. Villagers grow their own rice, yams, spinach, oranges, and ginger; slaughter their own hogs and goats; and build their own houses. The tribe's isolation has bred a radical self-sufficiency, evidenced in an apparent lack of an Aka word for job, in the sense of salaried labor.

10   The Aka measure personal wealth in mithan, a breed of Himalayan cattle. A respectable bride price in Palizi, for instance, is expressed as eight mithan. The most cherished Aka possession is the precious *tradzy* necklace—worth two mithan—made from yellow stones from the nearby river, which is passed down to their children. The yellow stones for the tradzy necklaces can no longer be found in the river, and so the only way to have a precious necklace is to inherit one.

Speaking Aka—or any language—means immersing oneself in its character and concepts. "I'm seeing the world through the looking glass of this language," said Father Vijay D'Souza, who was running the Jesuit school in Palizi at the time of my visit. The Society of Jesus established the school in part because it was concerned about the fragility of the Aka language and culture and wanted to support them (though classes are taught in English). D'Souza is from southern India, and his native language is Konkani. When he came to Palizi in 1999 and began speaking Aka, the language transformed him.

"It alters your thinking, your worldview," he told me one day in his headmaster's office, as children raced to classes through the corridor outside. One small example: *mucrow.* A similar word in D'Souza's native language would be an insult, meaning "old man." In Aka "mucrow" means something more. It is a term of respect, deference, endearment. The Aka might address a woman as mucrow to indicate her wisdom in civic affairs, and, says D'Souza, "an Aka wife will call her husband mucrow, even when he's young," and do so affectionately.

American linguists David Harrison and Greg Anderson have been coming to Arunachal Pradesh to study its languages since 2008. They are among the scores of linguists worldwide engaged in the study of vanishing languages. Some have academic and institutional affiliations (Harrison and Anderson are both connected with National Geographic's Enduring Voices Project), while others may work for Bible societies that translate Scripture into new tongues. The authoritative index of world languages is *Ethnologue,* maintained by SIL International, a faith-based organization. The researchers' intent may be hands-off, to record a grammar and lexicon before a language is lost or contaminated, or it may be interventionist, to develop a written accompaniment for the oral language, compile a dictionary, and teach native speakers to write.

Linguists have identified a host of language hotspots (analogous to biodiversity hotspots) that have both a high level of linguistic diversity and a high number of threatened languages. Many of these are in the world's least reachable, and often least hospitable, places—like Arunachal Pradesh. Aka and its neighboring languages have been protected because Arunachal Pradesh has long been sealed off to outsiders as a restricted border region. Even other Indians are not allowed to cross into the region without federal permission, and so its fragile microcultures have been spared the intrusion of immigrant labor, modernization—and linguists. It has been described as a black hole of linguistics because its incredible language variety remains so little explored.

Much of public life in Palizi is regulated through the repetition of mythological stories used as forceful fables to prescribe behavior. Thus a money dispute can draw a recitation about a spirit whose daughters are eaten by a crocodile, one by one, as they cross the river to bring him dinner in the field. He kills the crocodile, and a priest promises to bring the last daughter back to life but overcharges so egregiously that the spirit seeks revenge by becoming a piece of ginger that gets stuck in the greedy priest's throat.

Such stories were traditionally told by the elders in a highly formal version of Aka that the young did not yet understand and according to certain rules, among them this: Once an elder begins telling a story, he cannot stop until the story is finished. As with linguistic literacy, disruption is disaster. Yet Aka's young people no longer follow their elders in learning the formal version of the language and the stories that have governed daily life. Even in this remote region, young people are seduced away from their mother tongue by Hindi on the television and English in the schools. Today Aka's speakers number fewer than 2,000, few enough to put it on the endangered list.

One night in Palizi, Harrison, Anderson, an Indian linguist named Ganesh Murmu, and I sat cross-legged around the cooking fire at the home of Pario Nimasow, a 25-year-old teacher at the Jesuit school. A Palizi native, Nimasow loved his Aka culture even as he longed to join the outside world. In his sleeping room in an adjacent hut was a television waiting for the return of electricity, which had been out for many months thanks to a series of landslides and transformer malfunctions. After dinner Nimasow disappeared for a moment and came back with a soiled white cotton cloth, which he unfolded by the flickering light of the cooking fire. Inside was a small collection of ritual items: a tiger's jaw, a python's jaw, the sharp-toothed mandible of a river fish, a quartz crystal, and other objects of a shaman's sachet. This sachet had belonged to Nimasow's father until his death in 1991.

"My father was a priest," Nimasow said, "and his father was a priest." And now? I asked. Was he next in line? Nimasow stared at the talismans and shook his head. He had the kit, but he didn't know the chants; his father had died before passing them on. Without the words, there was no way to bring the artifacts' power to life.

Linguistics has undergone two great revolutions in the past 60 years, on seemingly opposite ends of the discipline. In the late 1950s Noam Chomsky theorized that all languages were built on an underlying universal grammar embedded in human genes. A second shift in linguistics—an explosion of interest in small and threatened languages—has focused on the variety of linguistic experience. Field linguists like David Harrison are more interested in the idiosyncrasies that make each language unique and the ways that culture can influence a language's form. As Harrison points out, some

85 percent of languages have yet to be documented. Understanding them can only enrich our comprehension of what is universal to all languages. Different languages highlight the varieties of human experience, revealing as mutable aspects of life that we tend to think of as settled and universal, such as our experience of time, number, or color. In Tuva, for example, the past is always spoken of as ahead of one, and the future is behind one's back. "We could never say, I'm looking forward to doing something," a Tuvan told me. Indeed, he might say, "I'm looking forward to the day before yesterday." It makes total sense if you think of it in a Tuvan sort of way: If the future were ahead of you, wouldn't it be in plain view?

Smaller languages often retain remnants of number systems that may predate the adoption of the modern world's base-ten counting system. The Pirahã, an Amazonian tribe, appear to have no words for any specific numbers at all but instead get by with relative words such as "few" and "many." The Pirahã's lack of numerical terms suggests that assigning numbers may be an invention of culture rather than an innate part of human cognition. The interpretation of color is similarly varied from language to language. What we think of as the natural spectrum of the rainbow is actually divided up differently in different tongues, with many languages having more or fewer color categories than their neighbors.

Language shapes human experience—our very cognition—as it goes about classifying the world to make sense of the circumstances at hand. Those classifications may be broad—Aka divides the animal kingdom into animals that are eaten and those that are not—or exceedingly fine-tuned. The Todzhu reindeer herders of southern Siberia have an elaborate vocabulary for reindeer; an *iyi düktüg myiys,* for example, is a castrated former stud in its fourth year.

If Aka, or any language, is supplanted by a new one that's bigger and more universally useful, its death shakes the foundations of the tribe. "Aka is our identity," a villager told me one day as we walked from Palizi down the path that wound past the rice fields to the forests by the river. "Without it, we are the general public." But should the rest of the world mourn too? The question would not be an easy one to frame in Aka, which seems to lack a single term for world. Aka might suggest an answer, though, one embodied in the concept of mucrow—a regard for tradition, for long-standing knowledge, for what has come before, a conviction that the venerable and frail have something to teach the callow and the strong that they would be lost without.

Seri: The Wisdom of the Hant Iiha Cöhacomxoj

The ongoing collapse of the world's biodiversity is more than just an apt metaphor for the crisis of language extinction. The disappearance of a language deprives us of knowledge no less valuable than some future miracle drug that may be lost when a species goes extinct. Small languages, more than large ones, provide keys to unlock the secrets of nature, because their speakers tend to live in proximity to the animals and plants around them, and their talk reflects the distinctions they observe. When small communities abandon their languages and switch to English or Spanish, there is a massive disruption in the transfer of traditional knowledge across generations—about medicinal plants, food cultivation, irrigation techniques, navigation systems, seasonal calendars.

25   The Seri people of Mexico were traditionally seminomadic hunter-gatherers living in the western Sonoran Desert near the Gulf of California. Their survival was tied to the traits and behaviors of the species that live in the desert and the sea. An intimate relationship with the plant and animal worlds is a hallmark of the Seris' life and of their language, Cmiique Iitom.

Traditionally the Seris, who refer to themselves as the Comcaac, had no fixed settlements, so their locale of the moment depended on what part of the desert offered the most food, whether the cactus fruit was ripe on the mountainside or the eelgrass was ready to harvest in the bay. Today they reside in two settlements, Punta Chueca and El Desemboque, each a small covey of concrete-block homes set in the vast red, seemingly empty desert beside the gulf. The homes are surrounded by rows of thorny ocotillo canes stuck into the sand, where they've taken root as living fences.

Each day, Armando Torres Cubillas sits in the corner of his open-air, beachside atelier in El Desemboque, his crippled legs curled under him on the sandy ground, carving sea turtles from dark desert ironwood. Occasionally, if he's in the mood, he gazes out over the gulf and eases the artisanship with a song that relates the operatic story of a conversation between the small beach clam *taijitiquiixaz* and the mole crab. The verse is typical of songs of the Seri tribe: a celebration of nature, tinged with loss.

The Seris see their language as a defining characteristic, a seed of their identity. One Seri told me of a "local expression" that says everyone has a flower inside, and inside the flower is a word. A Seri elder, Efraín Estrella Romero, told me, "If one child is raised speaking Cmiique Iitom and another speaking Spanish, they will be different people."

When American linguists Edward Moser and Mary Beck Moser came to live with the Seris in 1951 in El Desemboque, the group's fortunes were at a low ebb—outbreaks of measles and influenza had reduced their numbers to a couple hundred. It was a propitious time for the researchers, though, because the group's culture hadn't yet been co-opted by the majority culture surrounding it. Mary Moser served the tribe as nurse and midwife. After many births, per custom, the families gave her a dried piece of their infants' umbilical cords, which Mary kept protected in a "belly button pot." They also gave her their long, eight-plait braids, markers of Indian identity that the men felt compelled to chop off when they traveled to Mexican towns. The braids were like cultural umbilical cords, severed connections between what was old and what was new, evidence of the broken link.

The Mosers had a daughter, Cathy, who grew up among the Seris in El   30
Desemboque and became a graphic artist and ethnographer. She and her husband, Steve Marlett, a linguist with SIL International and the University of North Dakota, have continued the Mosers' study of the Seri language. Today the community has rebounded to somewhere between 650 and 1,000 speakers. They have managed to hang on to their language, thanks in part to their hostility to the majority culture of Mexico. Steve Marlett diplomatically refers to this in one academic paper as "the general lack of cultural empathy between the Seri population and the Spanish-speaking population." In 1773 they killed a priest who tried to establish a mission. The Vatican did not send a follow-up, and the tribe was never Catholicized.

The Seris maintain to this day a proud suspicion of outsiders—and a disdain for unshared individual wealth. "When the Seris become rich, they will cease to exist" is a Seri saying. Having been nomadic, they tend to regard possessions as burdens. Traditionally, when a Seri died, he was buried with his few personal possessions. Nothing was passed down to relatives except stories, songs, legends, instructions.

What modern luxuries the Seris have adopted are imported without their Spanish names. Automobiles, for instance, have provoked a flurry of new words. A Seri car muffler is called *ihíisaxim an hant yaait,* or into which the breathing descends, and the Seri term for distributor cap associates it with an electric ray that swims in the Gulf of California and gives you a shock. Such words are like ocotillo canes stuck into the sand: The Cmiique Iitom lexicon is alive, and as it grows, it creates a living fence around the culture.

Sitting in the shade of an awning in front of his house, René Montaño told me stories of an ancient race of giants who could step over the sea from their home on Tiburon Island to the mainland in a single stride. He told me of *hant iiha cöhacomxoj,* those who have been told about Earth's possessions, all ancient things. "To be told" entails an injunction: Pass it on. Thanks to that, we have all become inheritors of the knowledge enshrined within Cmiique Iitom. Folk sayings and often even single words encase centuries of close observation of species that visiting scientists have only begun to study in recent decades.

Cmiique Iitom has terms for more than 300 desert plants, and its names for animals reveal behaviors that scientists once considered farfetched. The Seri word for harvesting eelgrass clued scientists in to the sea grass's nutritional merits. (Its protein content is about the same as wheat's.) The Seris call one sea turtle *moosni hant cooit,* or green turtle that descends, for its habit of hibernating on the floor of the sea, where the traditional fishermen used to harpoon it. "We were skeptical when we first learned from the Seri Indians of Sonora, Mexico, that some Chelonia are partially buried on the sea floor during the colder months," stated a 1976 paper in *Science* documenting the behavior. "However, the Seri have proved to be highly reliable informants." The Seris enjoyed eating sea turtles but not leatherbacks, for a simple reason. Leatherbacks, they say, understand their language and are Seri themselves. In 2005 the Seri name for shark, *hacat,* became the official name for a newly discovered species of smooth-hound shark, *Mustelus hacat.* Newly discovered by modern scientists, that is—the Seris had been aware of them for years.

35   The Seri language is what linguists call an isolate, though a better term might be "sole survivor." "The Seris are a window into a lost world of gulf peoples," Steve Marlett says, referring to the extensive family of potentially linguistically linked groups who once inhabited both coasts of the Gulf of California. "Many others are gone," he says, and worse, gone before they could be documented. One remaining key to the nearly vanished cultures is Cmiique Iitom.

One way to preserve a language is to enshrine it in writing and compile a dictionary. Linguists both love and fear the prospect of inventing scripts for languages that are usually verbal only. Fear because the very idea of an alphabet changes the language the alphabet is meant to preserve and converts the linguist from observer to activist. David Harrison and Greg Anderson compiled the first Tuvan-English dictionary and are proud of the excitement the volume elicited from native speakers. Steve and Cathy Marlett worked until 2005 finishing a Cmiique Iitom dictionary begun by her parents in 1951. Steve remembers the day René Montaño asked, "Can I show you how I write?" and demonstrated a way of dividing words that had not occurred to the linguist before. The revelation meant revising years of work. But Marlett was delighted, because the project was enlisting native Seri speakers into diagnosing and defining their own language.

The cataloging of vocabulary and pronunciation and syntax that field linguists do in remote outposts helps keep a language alive. But saving a language is not something linguists can accomplish, because salvation must come from within. The answer may lie in something Harrison and Anderson witnessed in Palizi one day, when a villager in his early 20s came with a friend to perform a song for them. Palizi is far removed from pervasive U.S. culture, so it was something of a surprise to the two linguists when the teenagers launched into a full-bore, L.A.-style rap song complete with gang hand gestures and head bobbing and attitude, a pitch-perfect rendition of an American street art, with one refinement: They were rapping in Aka.

Were the linguists dismayed? I asked. To the contrary, Harrison said. "These kids were fluent in Hindi and English, but they chose to rap in a language they share with only a couple thousand people." Linguistic co-optation and absorption can work both ways, with the small language sometimes acting as the imperialist. "The one thing that's necessary for the revival of a language," Father D'Souza told me one day, "is pride."

Against the erosion of language stands an ineffable quality that can't be instilled from without: someone's insistence on rapping in Aka, on singing in Tuvan, on writing in the recently orthographized Cmiique Iitom. The Mosers' and Marletts' dictionary initiative has given birth to a new profession in Seriland: scribe. Several booklets have been authored by Seris. The Marletts hope the number of volumes will reach 40, one threshold, it is believed, for enticing people to maintain literacy in a language (though some put the number much higher).

The interest is already there. The Marletts had a regular visitor when 40 they were living in El Desemboque, a young boy who would come each day to pore over a Cmiique Iitom booklet. One day he arrived, and the Marletts explained they'd lent it to someone else. "He just burst into uncontrollable tears," Steve remembers.

The spread of global culture is unstoppable. Kyzyl, a capital city that never had a railroad connect it to the rest of Russia, will get one in the next few years. In El Desemboque power lines have been run through the desert to drive an electric pump for a municipal well. And in Arunachal Pradesh a new hydroelectric dam has been completed, ensuring the village of Palizi better access to electricity, refrigeration, and television.

To be involved in the plight of vanishing languages, even just as a journalist, is to contemplate the fragility of tribal life. Since my visits over the past two years to Palizi and Kyzyl and Seriland, Efraín Estrella died of pancreatitis, and young Pario Nimasow, who unwrapped his father's shaman's kit for me and wondered what its contents might mean, was killed in a landslide. A week after I wrote the paragraph describing Armando Torres's daily singing, I received an email from Cathy Marlett. "Sad news," its subject line read. Torres had died of a heart attack at 67, in his place by the beach in El Desemboque.

Their mortality is a reminder of the mortality of their cultures, an intimation that with each speaker's death another vital artery has been severed. Against that—against the possibility that their language could slip away without alarm or notice—stands a proud perseverance, a reverence for the old, an awareness that in important ways a key to our future lies behind us. That, and an insistence that the tongues least spoken still have much to say.

Analyze

1. Why is *khoj özeeri* such a difficult word to translate into English? What intensity of meaning does the word carry?
2. Rymer states "Prosperity, it seems, speaks English." What does he mean by this? Do you agree with his position? Why or why not?
3. What is the central argument of Rymer's essay? How does the organization of the essay guide the reader toward a greater understanding of this argument?

Explore

1. What is the value of small languages such as Aka, Tuva, and Cmiique Iitom? Refer to Rymer's examples of how these languages function as you respond.
2. Write a paper that both describes and evaluates the National Geographic's Enduring Voices Project. Why was this project created? What are some of its goals and how are these goals being achieved?
3. Listen to the audio materials found in the Talking Dictionaries link on the National Geographic's Enduring Voices Project website. In a

brief analytical essay, write about the sounds of the various endangered languages that are captured here. What do these sounds tell you about these languages and their users?

Forging Connections

1. The title of Joanna Eede's essay implies that the Internet in general, and search engines in particular, are of little use when it comes to retrieving lost languages. How would some of the other authors in this chapter who claim that digital technology does have the capacity to revive and strengthen languages spoken by small populations respond to Eede? Is it possible to Google and find information on the Innu language of Canada or the Yurok language of California? What can you find when you do such a search?

2. What contributions could Cherokee graphic artist Roy Boney make to National Geographic's Enduring Voices Project? How could Boney's artistic skills be put to use so that languages such as Aka, Tuva, and Cmiique Iitom become visually available—and therefore alive and accessible—to users beyond the communities in which they are spoken?

Looking Further

1. In discussing the rise of Spanglish, Felipe de Ortego y Gasca ("Regarding Spanglish," Chapter 6) notes that "languages in contact zones fertilize each other." Similarly, Hugo Cardoso ("The Death of an Indian-Born Language") notes that "Creoles are . . . 'contact languages', varieties which come about through the contact of several languages sharing the same space." How are Creoles different from languages like Spanglish or Chinglish? Examine the respective authors' descriptions of these languages, and consult at least one scholarly source for a linguistic definition of "creole," as you discuss the differences and similarities.

2. Stephen Pax Leonard ("Death by Monoculture") and Russ Rymer ("Vanishing Voices") use different metaphors to describe language. What are these metaphors? Which one is more meaningful to you? Why? If these metaphors were to be examined by researchers in the "Metaphor Program" described by Alexis Madrigal ("Why Are Spy Researchers Building a 'Metaphor Program'?," Chapter 7), what conclusions would they reach about the writers?

Researching and Writing About Language
Barbara Rockenbach and Aaron Ritzenberg[1]

Research-based writing lies at the heart of the mission of higher education: to discover, transform, and share ideas. As a college student, it is through writing and research that you will become an active participant in an intellectual community. Doing research in college involves not only searching for information but also digesting, analyzing, and synthesizing what you find to create new knowledge. Your most successful efforts as a college writer will report on the latest and most important ideas in a field as well as make new arguments and offer fresh insights.

It might seem daunting to be asked to contribute new ideas to a field in which you are a novice. After all, creating new knowledge seems to be the realm of experts. In this guide, we offer strategies that demystify the research and writing process, breaking down some of the fundamental steps that scholars take when they do research and make arguments. You'll see that contributing to scholarship involves strategies that can be learned and practiced.

Throughout this guide we imagine doing research and writing as engaging in a scholarly conversation. When you read academic writing, you'll see that scholars reference the studies that came before them and allude to the studies that will grow out of their research. When you think of research as engaging in a conversation, you quickly realize that scholarship always has a social aspect. Even if you like to find books in the darkest corners of the

---

1   Barbara Rockenbach, Director of Humanities & History Libraries, Columbia University and Aaron Ritzenberg, Associate Director of First-Year Writing, Columbia University.

library, even if you like to draft your essays in deep solitude, you will always be awake to the voices that helped you form your ideas and to the audience who will receive your ideas. As if in a conversation at a party, scholars mingle: They listen to others and share their most recent ideas, learning and teaching at the same time. Strong scholars, like good conversationalists, will listen and speak with an open mind, letting their own thoughts evolve as they encounter new ideas.

You might be wondering, "What does it mean to have an open mind when I'm doing research? After all, aren't I supposed to find evidence that supports my thesis?" We'll be returning to this question soon, but the quick answer is: To have an open mind when you're doing research means that you'll be involved in the research process well before you have a thesis. We realize this may be a big change from the way you think about research. The fact is, though, that scholars do research well before they know any of the arguments they'll be making in their papers. Indeed, scholars do research even before they know what specific topic they'll be addressing and what questions they'll be asking.

When scholars do research they may not know exactly what they are hunting for, but they have techniques that help them define projects, identify strong interlocutors, and ask important questions. This guide will help you move through the various kinds of research that you'll need at the different stages of your project. If writing a paper involves orchestrating a conversation within a scholarly community, there are a number of important questions you'll need to answer: How do I choose what to write about? How do I find a scholarly community? How do I orchestrate a conversation that involves this community? Whose voices should be most prominent? How do I enter the conversation? How do I use evidence to make a persuasive claim? How do I make sure that my claim is not just interesting but important?

GETTING STARTED

You have been asked to write a research paper. This might be your first research paper at the college level. Where do you start? The important thing when embarking on any kind of writing project that involves research is to find something that you are interested in learning more about. Writing and research is easier if you care about your topic. Your instructor might have given you a topic, but you can make that topic your own by finding something that appeals to you within the scope of the assignment.

Academic writing begins from a place of deep inquiry. When you are sincerely interested in a problem, researching can be a pleasure, as it will satisfy your own intellectual curiosity. More important, the intellectual problems that seem most difficult—the questions that appear to resist obvious answers—are the very problems that will often yield the most surprising and most rewarding results.

Presearching to Generate Ideas

When faced with a research project, your first instinct might be to go to Google or Wikipedia, or even to a social media site. This is not a bad instinct. In fact, Google, Wikipedia, and social media can be great places to start. Using Google, Wikipedia, and social media to help you discover a topic is what we call *presearch*—it is what you do to warm up before the more rigorous work of academic research. Academic research and writing will require you to go beyond these sites to find resources that will make the work of researching and writing both easier and more appropriate to an academic context.

Google   Let's start with Google. You use Google because you know you are going to find a simple search interface and that your search will produce many results. These results might not be completely relevant to your topic, but Google helps in the discovery phase of your work. For instance, you are asked to write about globalization and language.

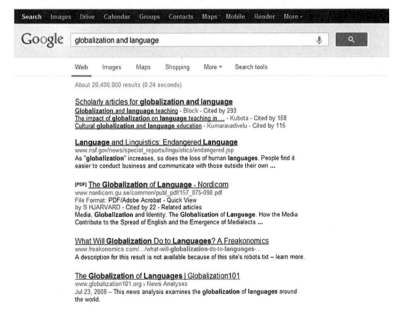

Results of a Google search for *globalization and language*.

This Google search will produce articles from many diverse sources—magazines, government sites, and corporate reports among them. It's not a bad start. Use these results to begin to hone in on a topic you are interested in pursuing. A quick look through these results might yield a more focused topic such as how globalization is affecting language and culture around the world. A particular source mentions this impact in the context of Japan, and others examine how the spread of English as a dominant language is a result of globalization.

Wikipedia A Wikipedia search on globalization and language will lead you to several articles that address both concepts. The great thing about Wikipedia is that it is an easy way to gain access to a wealth of information about thousands of topics. However, it is crucial to realize that Wikipedia itself is not an authoritative source in a scholarly context. Even though you might see Wikipedia cited in mainstream newspapers and popular magazines, academic researchers do not consider Wikipedia a reliable source and do not consult or cite it in their own research. Wikipedia itself says that "Wikipedia is not considered a credible source. . . . This is especially true considering that anyone can edit the information given at any time." For research papers in college, you should use Wikipedia only to find basic information about your topic and to point you toward scholarly sources. Wikipedia might be a great starting point for presearch, but it is not an

References

1. ^ a b Al-Rodhan, Nayef R.F. and Gérard Stoudmann. (2006, 19 June). "Definitions of Globalization: A Comprehensive Overview and a Proposed Definition." 📄
2. ^ a b Albrow, Martin and Elizabeth King (eds.) (1990). *Globalization, Knowledge and Society* London: Sage. ISBN 978-0803983243 p. 8. "...all those processes by which the peoples of the world are incorporated into a single world society."
3. ^ Carpenter, John B., 1999, "Puritan Missions as Globalization," *Fides et Historia*, 31:2, p. 103.
4. ^ Stever, H. Guyford (1972). "Science, Systems, and Society." *Journal of Cybernetics*, 2(3):1-3. doi:10.1080/01969727208542909 🔗
5. ^ a b Frank, Andre Gunder. (1998). *ReOrient: Global economy in the Asian age.* Berkeley: University of California Press. ISBN 978-0520214743
6. ^ "*Globalization and Global History* (p.127)" 📄. Retrieved 3 July 2012.
7. ^ Ritzer, George (2011). *Globalization: The Essentials.* NY: John Wiley & Sons.
8. ^ Google Books Ngram Viewer: Globalization 🔗

List of references from a Wikipedia search on globalization. Use these links to further your research.

adequate ending point for research. Use the References section at the bottom of the Wikipedia article to find other, more substantive and authoritative resources about your topic.

Using Social Media   Social media such as Facebook and Twitter can be useful in the presearch phase of your project, but you must start thinking about these tools in new ways. You may have a Facebook or Twitter account and use it to keep in touch with friends, family, and colleagues. These social networks are valuable, and you might already use them to gather information to help you make decisions in your personal life and your workplace. Although social media is not generally useful to your academic research, both Facebook and Twitter have powerful search functions that can lead you to resources and help you refine your ideas.

After you log in to Facebook, use the "Search for people, places, and things" bar at the top of the page to begin. When you type search terms into this bar, Facebook will first search your own social network. To extend beyond your own network, try adding the word "research" after your search terms. For instance, a search on Facebook for "globalization research" will lead you to a Facebook page for the Centre for Research on Globalization. The posts on the page link to current news stories on globalization, links to other similar research centers, and topics of interest in the field of globalization research. You can use these search results as a way to see part of the conversation about a particular topic. This is not necessarily the scholarly conversation we referred to at the start of this guide, but it is a social conversation that can still be useful in helping you determine what you want to focus on in the research process.

Twitter is an information network where users can post short messages (or "tweets"). Although many people use Twitter simply to update their friends ("I'm going to the mall" or "Can't believe it's snowing!"), more and more individuals and organizations use Twitter to comment on noteworthy events or link to interesting articles. You can use Twitter as a presearch tool because it aggregates links to sites, people in a field of research, and noteworthy sources. Communities, sometimes even scholarly communities, form around topics on Twitter. Users group posts together by using hashtags—words or phrases that follow the "#" sign. Users can respond to other users by using the @ sign followed by a user's Twitter name. When searching for specific individuals or organizations on Twitter, you search using their handle (such as @barackobama or @whitehouse). You will retrieve tweets that were created either by the person or organization, or tweets that mention the person or organization. When searching for a topic to find discussions, you search using the hashtag symbol, #. For instance, a search on #globalization will take you to tweets and threaded discussions on the topic of globalization.

There are two ways to search Twitter. You can use the search book in the upper right hand corner and enter either a @ or # search as described above. Once you retrieve results, you can search again by clicking on any words that are hyperlinked within your results such as #antiglobalization.

If you consider a hashtag (the # sign) as an entry point into a community, you will begin to discover a conversation around topics. For instance, a search on Twitter for #globalization leads you to YaleGlobal Online (@YaleGlobal), a community that explores globalization and the growing interconnectedness in economics, security, trade, politics, and the environment. News agencies such as Reuters are also active on Twitter, so an article from a Reuters publication will be retrieved in a search. Evaluating information and sources found in social media is similar to how you evaluate any information you encounter during the research process. And, as with Wikipedia and Google searches, this is just a starting point to help you get a sense of the spectrum of topics. This is no substitute for using library resources. Do not cite Facebook, Twitter, or Wikipedia in a research paper; use them to find more credible, authoritative sources. We'll talk about evaluating sources in the sections that follow.

Create a Concept Map

Once you have settled on a topic that you find exciting and interesting, the next step is to generate search terms, or keywords, for effective searching. Keywords are the crucial terms or phrases that signal the content of any given source. Keywords are the building blocks of your search for information. We have already seen a few basic keywords such as "globalization" and "language." One way to generate keywords is to tell a friend or classmate what you are interested in. What words are you using to describe your research project? You might not have a fully formed idea or claim, but you have a vague sense of your interest. A concept map exercise can help you generate more keywords and in many cases, narrow your topic to make it more manageable.

A concept map is a way to visualize the relationship between concepts or ideas. You can create a concept map on paper, or there are many free programs

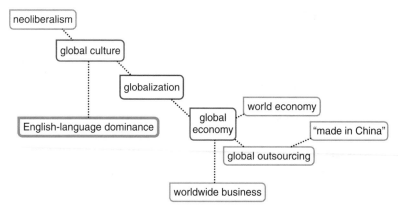

A concept map.

online that can help you do this (see, for instance, http://vue.tufts.edu/, http://wisemapping.org, or http://freeplane.sourceforge.net). There are many concept mapping applications available for mobile devices; the concept map here was created using the app SimpleMind.

Here is how you use a concept map. First, begin with a term like "globalization." Put that term in the first box. Then think of synonyms or related words to describe globalization such as "global economy," "global culture," "neoliberalism," "worldwide business," "world economy," and "global outsourcing." This brainstorming process will help you develop keywords for searching. Notice that keywords can also be short phrases.

After some practice, you'll discover that some phrases make for excellent keywords and others make for less effective search tools. The best keywords are precise enough to narrow your topic so that all of your results are relevant, but are not so specific that you might miss helpful results. Concept maps created using apps such as SimpleMind allow you to use templates, embed hyperlinks, and attach notes, among other useful functions.

Keyword Search

One of the hardest parts of writing is coming up with something to write about. Too often, we make the mistake of waiting until we have a fully formed idea before we start writing. The process of writing can actually help you discover what your idea is, and most important, what is interesting about your idea.

Keyword searches are most effective at the beginning stages of your research. They generally produce the most results and can help you determine how much has been written on your topic. You want to use keyword searches to help you achieve a manageable number of results. What is manageable? This is a key question when beginning research. Our keyword search in Google on "globalization and language" produced more than 18 million results. The same search in JSTOR.org produces more than 28,000 results. These are not manageable results sets. Let's see how we can narrow our search.

Keyword searches, in library resources or on Google, are most effective if you employ a few search strategies that will focus your results.

1. Use AND when you are combining multiple keywords. We have used this search construction previously:

Globalization AND language

The AND ensures that all your results will contain both terms, "globalization" and "language." Many search engines and databases will assume an AND search, meaning if you type.

Globalization language

The search will automatically look for both terms. However, in some cases the AND will not be assumed and "globalization language" will be treated as a phrase. This means that globalization will have to be next to the word language to return results. Worse yet, sometimes the search automatically assumes an OR. That would mean that all your results would come back with either globalization or language. This will produce a large and mostly irrelevant set of results. Therefore, use AND whenever you want two or more words to appear in a result.

2. Using OR can be very effective when you want to use several terms to describe a concept such as:

language OR speech OR communication

A search on globalization and language can be broadened to include language that is spoken, as in the case of speech, or that appears in written and spoken form, such as communication. The following search casts a broader net because results will come back with globalization and either, language, speech, or communication:

globalization AND (language OR speech OR communication)

Not all of these words will appear in each record. Note also that the parentheses set off the OR search indicating that globalization must appear in each record and then either language, speech, or communication needs to appear along with globalization.

3. Use quotation marks when looking for a phrase. For instance, if you are looking for information on language and globalization in multinational corporations you can ensure that the search results will include all of these concepts and increase the relevance by using the following search construction:

globalization AND language AND "multinational corporations"

This phrasing will return results that contain both the word globalization and the phrase "multinational corporation."

4. Use NOT to exclude terms that will make your search less relevant. You might find that a term keeps appearing in your search that is not useful. Try this:

globalization NOT politics

If you are interested in the linguistic side of this debate, getting a lot of results that discuss the politics of globalization might be distracting. By excluding the keyword politics, you will retrieve far fewer sources, and hopefully more relevant results.

Researchable Question

In a college research paper, it is important that you make an argument, not just offer a report. In high school you might have found some success by merely listing or cataloging the data and information you found; you might have offered a series of findings to show your teacher that you investigated your topic. In college, however, your readers will not be interested in data or information merely for its own sake; your readers will want to know what you make of these data and why they should care.

To satisfy the requirements of a college paper, you'll need to distinguish between a topic and a research question. You will likely begin with a topic, but it is only when you move from a topic to a question that your research will begin to feel motivated and purposeful. A topic refers only to the general subject area that you'll be investigating. A researchable question, on the other hand, points toward a specific problem in the subject area that you'll be attempting to answer by making a claim about the evidence you examine.

"Globalization and language" is a topic, but not a researchable question. It is important that you ask yourself, "What aspect of the topic is most interesting to me?" It is even more important that you ask, "What aspect of the topic is it most important that I illuminate for my audience?" Ideally, your presearch phase of the project will yield questions about globalization and language that you'd like to investigate.

A strong researchable question will not lead to an easy answer, but rather will lead you into a scholarly conversation in which there are many competing claims. For instance, the question, "What are the official languages of the United Nations?" is not a strong research question, because there is only one correct answer and thus there is no scholarly debate surrounding the topic. It is an interesting question (the answer is: Arabic, Chinese, English, French, Russian, and Spanish), but it will not lead you into a scholarly conversation.

When you are interested in finding a scholarly debate, try using the words "why" and "how" rather than "what." Instead of leading to a definitive answer, the words "why" and "how" will often lead to complex, nuanced answers for which you'll need to marshal evidence to be convincing. "Why did Arabic become an official language of the UN in 1973?" is a question that has a number of complex and competing answers that might draw from a number of different disciplines (political science, history, economics, linguistics, and geography, among others). If you can imagine scholars having an interesting debate about your researchable question, it is likely that you've picked a good one.

Once you have come up with an interesting researchable question, your first task as a researcher is to figure out how scholars are discussing your question. Many novice writers think that the first thing they should do when beginning a research project is to articulate an argument, then find sources that confirm their argument. This is not how experienced scholars work. Instead, strong writers know that they cannot possibly come up with a strong central argument until they have done sufficient research. So, instead of looking for sources that confirm a preliminary claim you might want to make, look for the scholarly conversation.

Looking at the scholarly conversation is a strong way to figure out if you've found a research question that is suitable in scope for the kind of paper you're writing. Put another way, reading the scholarly conversation can tell you if your research question is too broad or too narrow. Most novice writers begin with research questions that are overly broad. If your question is so broad that there are thousands of books and articles participating in the scholarly conversation, it's a good idea for you to focus your question so that you are asking something more specific. If, on the other hand, you are asking a research question that is so obscure that you cannot find a corresponding scholarly conversation, you will want to broaden the scope of your project by asking a slightly less specific question.

Keep in mind the metaphor of a conversation. If you walk into a room and people are talking about globalization and language, it would be out of place for you to begin immediately by making a huge, vague claim, like, "New technology affects the way that people speak to each other around the world." It would be equally out of place for you to begin immediately by making an overly specific claim, like, "Social media usage in Doha is a strong indicator of Facebook's growing strength in Qatar." Rather, you would gauge the scope of the conversation and figure out what seems like a reasonable contribution.

Your contribution to the conversation, at this point, will likely be a focused research question. This is the question you take with you to the library. In the next section, we discuss how best to make use of the library. Later, we explore how to turn your research question into an argument for your essay.

Your Campus Library

You have probably used libraries all your life, checking out books from your local public library and studying in your high school library. The difference between your previous library experiences and your college library experience is one of scale. Your college library has more stuff. It might be real stuff like books, journals, and videos, or it could be virtual stuff, like online articles, ebooks and streaming video. Your library pays a lot of money every year to buy or license content for you to use for your research. By extension, your tuition dollars are buying a lot of really good research material. Resorting to Google and Wikipedia means you are not getting all you can out of your college experience.

Not only will your college library have a much larger collection, but it will have a more up-to-date and relevant collection than your high school or community public library. Academic librarians spend considerable time acquiring research materials based on classes being taught at your institution. You might not know it, but librarians carefully monitor what courses are being taught each year and are constantly trying to find research materials appropriate to those courses and your professor's research interests. In many cases, you will find that the librarians will know about your assignment and will already have ideas about the types of sources that will make you most successful.

Get To Know Your Librarians!

The most important thing to know during the research process is that there are people to help you. Although you might not yet be in the habit of going to the library, there are still many ways in which librarians and library staff can be helpful. Most libraries now have an email or chat service set up so you can ask questions without even setting foot in a library. No question is too basic or too specific. It's a librarian's job to help you find answers, and all questions are welcome. The librarian can even help you discover the right question to ask given the task you are trying to complete.

Help can also come in the form of consultations. Librarians will often make appointments to meet one-on-one with students to offer in-depth help on a research paper or project. Chances are you will find a link on your library website for scheduling a consultation.

Among the many questions fielded by reference librarians, three stand out as the most often asked. Because librarians hear these questions with such regularity, we suggest that students ask these questions when they begin their research. You can go to the library and ask these questions in person, or you can ask vie email or online chat.

1. How Do I Find a Book Relevant to My Topic?

The answer to this question will vary from place to place, but the thing to remember is that finding a book can be either a physical process or a virtual process. Your library will have books on shelves somewhere, and the complexity of how those shelves are organized and accessed depends on factors of size, number of libraries, and the system of organization your library uses. You will find books by using your library's online catalog and carefully noting the call number and location of a book.

Your library is also increasingly likely to offer electronic books or ebooks. These books are discoverable in your library's online catalog as well. When looking at the location of a book you will frequently see a link for ebook versions. You will not find an ebook in every search, but when you do the advantage is that ebook content is searchable, making your job of finding relevant material in the book easier.

If you find one book on your topic, use it as a jumping-off point for finding more books or articles on that topic. Most books will have bibliographies either at the end of each chapter or the end of the book in which the author has compiled all the sources used. Consult these bibliographies to find other materials on your topic that will help support your claim.

Another efficient way to find more sources once you've identified a particularly authoritative and credible book is to go back to the book's listing in your library's online catalog. Once you find the book, look carefully at the record for links to subjects. By clicking on a subject link you can find other items in your library on the same subject. For instance, a search on

globalization AND language
will lead you to items with subjects such as these:

Language and culture

English language—21st century

Language and languages—study and teaching

2. What Sources Can I Use as Evidence in My Paper? There are many types of resources out there to use as you orchestrate a scholarly conversation and support your paper's argument. Books, which we discussed earlier, are great sources if you can find them on your topic, but often your research question will be something that is either too new or too specific for a book to cover. Books are very good for historical questions and overviews of large topics. For current topics, you will want to explore articles from magazines, journals, and newspapers.

Magazines or periodicals (you will hear these terms interchangeably) are published on a weekly or monthly schedule and contain articles of popular interest. These sources can cover broad topics like the news in magazines such as *Newsweek*, *Time*, and *U.S. News and World Report*. They can also be more focused for particular groups like farmers (e.g., *Dairy Farmer*) or photographers (e.g., *Creative Photography*). Articles in magazines or periodicals are by professional writers who might or might

Library catalog search for "globalization and language."

not be experts. Magazines typically are not considered scholarly and generally do not contain articles with bibliographies, endnotes, or footnotes.
This does not mean they are not good sources for your research. In fact,
there could be very good reasons to use a magazine article to help support
your argument. Magazines capture the point of view of a particular group
on a subject, like how farmers feel about increased globalization of food
production. This point of view might offer support for your claim or an op-
posing viewpoint to counter. Additionally, magazines can also highlight
aspects of a topic at a particular point in time. Comparing a *Newsweek* article from 1989 on Japan and globalization to an article on the same topic
in 2009 allows you to draw conclusions about the changing relationship
between the U.S. and Japan over that 20-year period.

Journals are intended for a scholarly audience of researchers, specialists,
or students of a particular field. Journals such as *Globalization and Health*,
Modern Language Journal, or *Anthropological Linguistics* are all examples
of scholarly journals focused on a particular field or research topic. You

might hear the term "peer-reviewed" or "refereed" in reference to scholarly journals. This means that the articles contained in a journal have been reviewed by a group of scholars in the same field before the article is published in the journal. This ensures that that the research has been vetted by a group of peers before it is published. Articles from scholarly journals can help provide some authority to your argument. By citing experts in a field you are bolstering your argument and entering into the scholarly conversation we talked about at the beginning of this guide.

Newspaper articles are found in newspapers that are generally published daily. There is a broad range of content in newspapers ranging from articles written by staff reporters, to editorials written by scholars, experts, and general readers, to reviews and commentary written by experts. Newspapers are published more frequently and locally than magazines or journals, making them excellent sources for very recent topics and events as well as those with regional significance. Newspaper articles can provide you with a point of view from a particular part of the country or world (e.g., how do Texans feel about globalization vs. New Yorkers), or a strong opinion on a topic from an expert (e.g., an economist writing an editorial on the effects of globalization on the Chinese economy).

A good argument uses evidence from a variety of sources. Do not assume you have done a good job if your paper only cites newspaper articles. You need a broad range of sources to fill out your argument. Your instructor will provide you with guidelines about the number of sources you need, but it will be up to you to find a variety of sources. Finding two to three sources in each of these categories will help you begin to build a strong argument.

3. Where Should I Look for Articles on My Topic?

The best way to locate journal, magazine, or newspaper articles is to use a database. A database is an online resource that organizes research material of a particular type or content area. For example, PsycINFO is a psychology database where you would look for journal articles (as well as other kinds of sources) in the discipline of psychology. Your library licenses or subscribes to databases on your behalf. Finding the right database for your topic will depend on what is available at your college or university because every institution has a different set of resources. Many libraries will provide subject or research guides that can help you determine what database would be best for your topic. Look for these guides on your library website, which will have a way to search databases.

Look for a section of the library website on databases, and look for a search box in that section. For instance, if you type "language" in a database search box, you might find that your library licenses a database called *MLA International Bibliography* (Modern Language Association). A search for "history" in the database search box might yield *American History and Life* or *Historical Abstracts*. In most instances, your best bet is to ask a librarian which database or databases are most relevant to your research.

When using these databases that your library provides for you, you will know that you are starting to sufficiently narrow or broaden your topic when you begin to retrieve 30 to 50 sources during a search. This kind of narrow result field will rarely occur in Google, which is one of the reasons why using library databases is preferable to Google when doing academic research. Databases will help you determine when you have begun to ask a manageable question.

When you have gotten down to 30 to 50 sources in your result list, begin to look through those results to see what aspects of your topic are being written about. Are there lots of articles on globalization, language, and China? If so, that might be a topic worth investigating because there is a lot of information for you to read. This is where you begin to discover where your voice might add to the ongoing conversation on the topic.

Using Evidence

The quality of evidence and how you deploy the evidence is ultimately what will make your claims persuasive. You might think of evidence as that which will help prove your claim. But if you look at any scholarly book or article you'll see that evidence can be used in a number of different ways. Evidence can be used to provide readers with crucial background information. It can be used to tell readers what scholars have commonly thought about a topic (although you might disagree). It can offer a theory that you use as a lens. It can offer a methodology or an approach that you would like to use. And finally, evidence can be used to back up the claim that you'll be making in your paper.

Novice researchers begin with a thesis and try to find all the evidence that will prove that their claim is valid or true. What if you come across evidence that doesn't help with the validity of your claim? A novice researcher might decide not to take this complicating evidence into account. Indeed, when you come across complicating evidence, you might be tempted to pretend you never saw it! But rather than sweeping imperfect evidence under the rug, you should figure out how to use this evidence to complicate your own ideas.

The best scholarly conversations take into account a wide array of evidence, carefully considering all sides of a topic. As you probably know, often the most fruitful and productive conversations occur not just when you are talking to people who already agree with you, but when you are fully engaging with the people who might disagree with you.

Coming across unexpected, surprising, and contradictory evidence, then, is a good thing! It will force you to make a complex, nuanced argument and will ultimately allow you to write a more persuasive paper.

Other Forms of Evidence

We've talked about finding evidence in books, magazines, journals, and newspapers. Here are a few other kinds of evidence you might want to use.

Interviews Interviews can be a powerful form of evidence, especially if the person you are interviewing is an expert in the field that you're investigating. Interviewing can be intimidating, but it might help to know that many people (even experts!) will feel flattered when you ask them for an interview. Most scholars are deeply interested in spreading knowledge, so you should feel comfortable asking a scholar for his or her ideas. Even if the scholar doesn't know the specific answer to your question, he or she might be able to point you in the right direction.

Remember, of course, to be as courteous as possible when you are planning to interview someone. This means sending a polite email that fully introduces yourself and your project before you begin asking questions. Email interviews might be convenient, but an in-person interview is best, as this allows for you and the interviewee to engage in a conversation that might take surprising and helpful turns.

It's a good idea to write down a number of questions before the interview. Make sure not just to get facts (which you can likely get somewhere else). Ask the interviewee to speculate about your topic. Remember that "why" and "how" questions often yield more interesting answers than "what" questions.

If you do conduct an in-person interview, act professionally. Be on time, dress respectfully, and show sincere interest and gratitude. Bring something to record the interview. Many reporters still use pens and a pad, as these feel unobtrusive and are very portable. Write down the interviewee's name, the date, and the location of the interview, and have your list of questions ready. Don't be afraid, of course, to veer from your questions. The best questions might be the follow-up questions that couldn't have occurred to you before the conversation began. You're likely to get the interviewee to talk freely and openly if you show real intellectual curiosity. If you're not a fast writer, it's certainly OK to ask the interviewee to pause for a moment while you take notes. Some people like to record their interviews. Just make sure that you ask permission if you choose to do this. It's always nice to send a brief thank you note or email after the interview. This would be a good time to ask any brief follow-up questions.

Images Because we live in a visual age, we tend to take images for granted. We see them in magazines, on TV, and on the Internet. We don't often think about them as critically as we think about words on a page. Yet, a critical look at an image can uncover helpful evidence for a claim. For example, if you are writing about the impact of globalization on language, you could introduce an image of a sign such as the one pictured next.

This is an image of a Coca-Cola boxcar in Haikou, Hainan, China. Although we might not be able to read the language, it is recognizable as an advertisement for Coca-Cola. This image enables you to discuss how visual

A Coca-Cola boxcar in Haikou, Hainan, China.

elements (the distinctive Coca-Cola stripe, the vertical lettering on the can, etc.) can be read like a language—a language that is increasingly global. You would also use this image as evidence for a claim that the language of branding is becoming an international or global language. Images can add depth and variety to your argument and they are generally easy to find on the Internet. Use a Google Image search or Flickr.com to find images using the same keywords you used to find books and articles. Ask your instructor for guidance on how to properly cite and acknowledge the source of any images you wish to use. If you want to present your research outside of a classroom project (e.g., publish it on a blog or share it at a community event), ask a research librarian for guidance on avoiding any potential copyright violations.

Multimedia   Like images, multimedia such as video, audio, and animations are increasingly easy to find on the Internet and can strengthen your claim. For instance, if you are working on globalization and language, you could find audio or video news clips illustrating the effects of globalization on local languages. There are several audio and video search engines available such as Vimeo (vimeo.com) or Blinkx (blinkx.com), a search engine featuring audio and video from the BBC, Reuters, and the Associated Press among others. As with images, ask your instructor for guidance on how to properly cite and acknowledge the source of any multimedia you wish to use. If you want to present your research outside of a classroom project (e.g., publish it on a blog or share it at a community event), ask a research librarian for guidance on avoiding any potential copyright violations.

Evaluating Sources

A common problem in research isn't a lack of sources, but an overload of information. Information is more accessible than ever. How many times have you done an online search and asked yourself the question: "How do I know what is good information?" Librarians can help. Evaluating online sources is more challenging than traditional sources because it is harder to make distinctions between good and bad online information than with print sources. It is easy to tell that *Newsweek* magazine is not as scholarly as an academic journal, but online everything might look the same. There are markers of credibility and authoritativeness when it comes to online information, and you can start to recognize them. We'll provide a few tips here, but be sure to ask a librarian or your professor for more guidance whenever you're uncertain about the reliability of a source.

1. **Domain**—The "domain" of a site is the last part of its URL. The domain indicates the type of website. Noting the web address can tell you a lot. An .edu site indicates that an educational organization created that content. This is no guarantee that the information is accurate, but it does suggest less bias than a .com site, which will be commercial in nature with a motive to sell you something, including ideas.

2. **Date**—Most websites include a date somewhere on the page. This date could indicate a copyright date, the date something was posted, or the date the site was last updated. These dates tell you when the content on the site was last changed or reviewed. Older sites might be outdated or contain information that is no longer relevant.

3. **Author or editor**—Does the online content indicate an author or editor? Like print materials, authority comes from the creator of the content. It is now easier than ever to investigate an author's credentials. A general Google search might lead you to a Wikipedia entry on the author, a LinkedIn page, or even an online resume. If an author is affiliated with an educational institution, try visiting the institution's website for more information.

Managing Sources

Now that you've found sources, you need to think about how you are going to keep track of the sources and prepare the bibliography that will accompany your paper. Managing your sources is called "bibliographic citation management," and you will sometimes see references to bibliographic citation management on your library's website. Don't let this complicated phrase deter you—managing your citations from the start of your research will make your life much easier during the research process and especially the night before your paper is due when you are compiling your bibliography.

EndNote and RefWorks Chances are your college library provides software, such as *EndNote* or *RefWorks*, to help you manage citations. These are two commercially available citation management software packages that are not freely available to you unless your library has paid for a license. *EndNote* or *RefWorks* enable you to organize your sources in personal libraries. These libraries help you manage your sources and create bibliographies. Both *EndNote* and *RefWorks* also enable you to insert endnotes and footnotes directly into a Microsoft Word document.

Zotero If your library does not provide *EndNote* or *RefWorks*, a freely available software called *Zotero* (Zotero.org) will help you manage your sources. *Zotero* helps you collect, organize, cite, and share your sources and it lives right in your web browser where you do your research. As you are searching Google, your library catalog, or library database, *Zotero* enables you to add a book, article, or website to a personal library with one click. As you add items to your library, *Zotero* collects both the information you need for your bibliography and any full-text content. This means that the content of journal articles and ebooks will be available to you right from your *Zotero* library.

To create a bibliography, simply select the items from your *Zotero* library you want to include, right-click and select Create Bibliography from Selected Items . . . , and choose the citation style your instructor has asked you to use for the paper. To get started, go to Zotero.org and download *Zotero* for the browser of your choice.

Taking Notes It is crucial that you take good, careful notes while you are doing your research. Not only is careful note taking necessary to avoid plagiarism, but it can also help you think through your project while you are doing research.

Many researchers used to take notes on index cards, but most people now use computers. If you're using your computer, open a new document for each source that you're considering using. The first step in taking notes is to make sure that you gather all the information you might need in your bibliography or works cited. If you're taking notes from a book, for instance, you'll need the author, the title, the place of publication, the publisher, and the year. Be sure to check the style guide assigned by your instructor to make sure you're gathering all the necessary information.

After you've recorded the bibliographic information, add one or two keywords that can help you sort this source. Next, write a one- or two-sentence summary of the source. Finally, have a section in your document that is reserved for specific places in the text that you might want to work with. When you write down a quote, remember to be extra careful that you are capturing the quote exactly as it is written, and that you enclose the quote in quotation marks. Do not use abbreviations or change the punctuation. Remember, too, to write down the exact page numbers from the source you are quoting. Being careful with small details at the beginning of your project can save you a lot of time in the long run.

WRITING ABOUT LANGUAGE

In your writing, as in your conversations, you should always be thinking about your audience. Although your most obvious audience is the instructor, most college instructors will want you to write a paper that will be interesting and illuminating for other beginning scholars in the field. Many students are unsure of what kind of knowledge they can presume of their audience. A good rule of thumb is to write not only for your instructor, but also for other students in your class and for other students in classes similar to yours. You can assume a reasonably informed audience that is curious but also skeptical.

Of course it is crucial that you keep your instructor in mind. After all, your instructor will be giving you feedback and evaluating your paper. The best way to keep your instructor in mind while you are writing is to periodically reread the assignment while you are writing. Are you answering the assignment's prompt? Are you adhering to the assignment's guidelines? Are you fulfilling the assignment's purpose? If your answer to any of these questions is uncertain, it's a good idea to ask the instructor.

From Research Question to Thesis Statement

Many students like to begin the writing process by writing an introduction. Novice writers often use an early draft of their introduction to guide the shape of their paper. Experienced scholars, however, continually return to their introduction, reshaping it and revising it as their thoughts evolve. After all, because writing is thinking, it is impossible to anticipate the full thoughts of your paper before you have written it. Many writers, in fact, only realize the actual argument they are making after they have written a draft or two of the paper. Make sure not to let your introduction trap your thinking. Think of your introduction as a guide that will help your readers down the path of discovery—a path you can only fully know after you have written your paper.

A strong introduction will welcome readers to the scholarly conversation. You'll introduce your central interlocutors and pose the question or problem that you are all interested in resolving. Most introductions contain a thesis statement, which is a sentence or two that clearly states the main argument. Some introductions, you'll notice, do not contain the argument, but merely contain the promise of a resolution to the intellectual problem.

Is Your Thesis an Argument?

So far, we've discussed a number of steps for you to take when you begin to write a research paper. We started by strategizing about ways to use presearch to find a topic and ask a researchable question, then we looked at ways to find a scholarly conversation by using your library's resources. Now we discuss a crucial step in the writing process: coming up with a thesis.

Your thesis is the central claim of your paper—the main point that you'd like to argue. You could make a number of claims throughout the paper; when you make a claim, you are offering a small argument, usually about a piece of evidence that you've found. Your thesis is your governing claim, the central argument of the whole paper. Sometimes it is difficult to know if you have written a proper thesis. Ask yourself, "Can a reasonable person disagree with my thesis statement?" If the answer is no, then you likely you have written an observation rather than an argument. For instance, the statement, "There are six official languages of the UN" is not a thesis, as this is a true fact. A reasonable person cannot disagree with this fact, so it is not an argument. The statement, "Arabic became an official language of the UN for economic reasons" is a thesis, because it is a debatable point. A reasonable person might disagree (by arguing, for instance, that "Arabic became an official language of the UN for political reasons"). Remember to keep returning to your thesis statement while you are writing. Not only will you be thus able to make sure that your writing remains on a clear path, but you'll also be able to keep refining your thesis so that it becomes clearer and more precise.

Make sure, too, that your thesis is a point of persuasion rather than one of belief or taste. "Chinese food tastes delicious" is certainly an argument you could make to your friend, but it is not an adequate thesis for an academic paper, because there is no evidence that you could provide that might persuade a reader who doesn't already agree with you.

Organization

For your paper to feel organized, readers should know where they are headed and have a reasonable idea of how they are going to get there. An introduction will offer a strong sense of organization if it:

- introduces your central intellectual problem and explains why it is important;
- suggests who will be involved in the scholarly conversation;
- indicates what kind of evidence you'll be investigating;
- offers a precise central argument.

Some readers describe well-organized papers as having a sense of flow. When readers praise a sense of flow, they mean that the argument moves easily from one sentence to the next and from one paragraph to the next. This allows your reader to follow your thoughts easily. When you begin writing a sentence, try using an idea, keyword, or phrase from the end of the previous sentence. The next sentence, then, will appear to have emerged smoothly from the previous sentence. This tip is especially important when you move between paragraphs. The beginning of a paragraph should feel like it has a clear relationship to the end of the previous paragraph.

Keep in mind, too, a sense of wholeness. A strong paragraph has a sense of flow and a sense of wholeness: Not only will you allow your reader to trace your thoughts smoothly, but you will ensure that your reader understands how all your thoughts are connected to a large, central idea. Ask yourself this question as you write a paragraph: What does this paragraph have to do with the central intellectual problem that I am investigating? If the relationship isn't clear to you, then your readers will likely be confused.

Novice writers often use the form of a five-paragraph essay. In this form, each paragraph offers an example that proves the validity of the central claim. The five-paragraph essay might have worked in high school, as it meets the minimum requirement for making an argument with evidence. You'll quickly notice, though, that experienced writers do not use the five-paragraph essay. Indeed, your college instructors will expect you to move beyond the five-paragraph essay because a five-paragraph essay relies on static examples rather than fully engaging new evidence. A strong essay will grow in complexity and nuance as the writer brings in new evidence. Rather than thinking of an essay as something that offers many examples to back up the same static idea, think of an essay as the evolution of an idea that grows ever more complex and rich as the writer engages with scholars who view the idea from various angles.

Integrating Your Research

As we have seen, doing research involves finding an intellectual community by looking for scholars who are thinking through similar problems and might be in conversation with one another. When you write your paper, you will not merely be reporting what you found; you will be orchestrating the conversation that your research has uncovered. To orchestrate a conversation involves asking a few key questions: Whose voices should be most prominent? What is the relationship between one scholar's ideas and another scholar's ideas? How do these ideas contribute to the argument that your own paper is making? Is it important that your readers hear the exact words of the conversation, or can you give them the main ideas and important points of the conversation in your own words? Your answers to these questions will determine how you go about integrating your research into your paper.

Using evidence is a way of gaining authority. Even though you might not have known much about your topic before you started researching, the way you use evidence in your paper will allow you to establish a voice that is authoritative and trustworthy. You have three basic choices to decide how best you'd like to present the information from a source: summarize, paraphrase, or quote. Let's discuss each one briefly.

Summary You should summarize a source when the source provides helpful background information for your research. Summaries do not make strong evidence, but they can be helpful if you need to chart the intellectual terrain of your project. Summaries can be an efficient way of capturing the main ideas of a source. Remember, when you are summarizing, to be fully sympathetic to the writer's point of view. Put yourself in the scholar's shoes. If you later disagree with the scholar's methods or conclusions, your disagreement will be convincing because your reader will know that you have given the scholar a fair hearing. A summary that is clearly biased is not only inaccurate and ethically suspect; it will make your writing less convincing because readers will be suspicious of your rigor.

Let's say you come across the following quote that you'd like to summarize. Here's an excerpt from *The Language Wars: A History of Proper English*, by Henry Hitchings:

> No language has spread as widely as English, and it continues to spread. Internationally the desire to learn it is insatiable. In the twenty-first century the world is becoming more urban and more middle class, and the adoption of English is a symptom of this, for increasingly English serves as the lingua franca of business and popular culture. It is dominant or at least very prominent in other areas such as shipping, diplomacy, computing, medicine and education. (300)

Consider this summary:

> In *The Language Wars*, Hitchings says that everyone wants to learn English because it is the best language in the world (300). I agree that English is the best.

If you compare this summary to what Hitchings actually said, you will see that this summary is a biased, distorted version of the actual quote. Hitchings did not make a universal claim about whether English is better or worse than other languages. Rather, he made a claim about why English is becoming so widespread in an increasingly connected world.

Now let's look at another summary, taken from the sample paper at the end of this research guide:

> According to Hitchings, English has become the go-to choice for global communications and has spread quickly as the language of commerce and ideas (300).

This is a much stronger summary than the previous example. The writer shortens Hitchings's original language, but she is fair to the writer's original meaning and intent.

Paraphrase   Paraphrasing involves putting a source's ideas into your own words. It's a good idea to paraphrase if you think you can state the idea more clearly or more directly than the original source does. Remember that if you paraphrase you need to put the entire idea into your own words. It is not enough for you to change one or two words. Indeed, if you only change a few words, you could put yourself at risk of plagiarizing.

Let's look at how we might paraphrase the Hitchings quote that we've been discussing. Consider this paraphrase:

> Internationally the desire to learn English is insatiable. In today's society, the world is becoming wealthier and more urban, and the use of English is a symptom of this (Hitchings 300).

You will notice that the writer simply replaced some of Hitchings's original language with synonyms. Even with the parenthetical citation, this is unacceptable paraphrasing. Indeed, this is a form of plagiarism, because the writer suggests that the language is his or her own, when it is in fact an only slightly modified version of Hitchings's own phrasing.

Let's see how we might paraphrase Hitchings in an academically honest way.

> Because English is used so frequently in global communications, many people around the world want to learn English as they become members of the middle class (Hitchings 300).

Here the writer has taken Hitchings's message but has used his or her own language to describe what Hitchings originally wrote. The writer offers Hitchings's ideas with fresh syntax and new vocabulary, and the writer is sure to give Hitchings credit for the idea in a parenthetical citation.

Quotation   The best way to show that you are in conversation with scholars is to quote them. Quoting involves capturing the exact wording and punctuation of a passage. Quotations make for powerful evidence, especially in humanities papers. If you come across evidence that you think will be helpful in your project, you should quote it. You might be tempted to quote only those passages that seem to agree with the claim that you are working with. But remember to write down the quotes of scholars who might not seem to agree with you. These are precisely the thoughts that will help you build a powerful scholarly conversation. Working with fresh ideas that you might not agree with can help you revise your claim to make it even more persuasive, as it will force you to take into account potential counterarguments. When your readers see that you are grappling with an intellectual problem from all sides and that you are giving all interlocutors a fair voice, they are more likely to be persuaded by your argument.

To make sure that you are properly integrating your sources into your paper, remember the acronym ICE: introduce, cite, and explain. Let's imagine that you've found an idea that you'd like to incorporate into your paper. We'll use a quote from David Harvey's *A Brief History of Neoliberalism* as an example. On page 7, you find the following quote that you'd like to use: "The assumption that individual freedoms are guaranteed by freedom of the market and of trade is a cardinal feature of neoliberal thinking, and it has long dominated the US stance towards the rest of the world."

1. The first thing you need to do is **introduce** the quote ("introduce" gives us the I in ICE). To introduce a quote, provide context so that your readers

know where it is coming from, and you must integrate the quote into your own sentence. Here are some examples of how you might do this:

> In his book *A Brief History of Neoliberalism*, David Harvey writes . . .
> One expert on the relationship between economics and politics claims . . .
> Professor of Anthropology David Harvey explains that . . .
> In a recent book by Harvey, he contends . . .

Notice that each of these introduces the quote in such a way that readers are likely to recognize it as an authoritative source.

2. The next step is to **cite** the quote (the C in ICE). Here is where you indicate the origin of the quotation so that your readers can easily look up the original source. Citing is a two-step process that varies slightly depending on the citation style that you're using. We offer an example using MLA style. The first step involves indicating the author and page number in the body of your essay. Here is an example of a parenthetical citation that gives the author and page number after the quote and before the period that ends the sentence:

> One expert on the relationship between economics and politics claims that neoliberal thinking has "long dominated the US stance towards the rest of the world" (Harvey 7).

Note that if it is already clear to readers which author you're quoting, you need only to give the page number:

> In *A Brief History of Neoliberalism*, David Harvey contends that neoliberal thinking has "long dominated the US stance towards the rest of the world" (7).

The second step of citing the quote is providing proper information in the works cited or bibliography of your paper. This list should include the complete bibliographical information of all the sources you have cited. An essay that includes the quote by David Harvey should also include the following entry in the Works Cited:

> Harvey, David. *A Brief History of Neoliberalism*. New York: Oxford UP, 2005. Print.

3. Finally, the most crucial part of integrating a quote is **explaining** it. The E in ICE is often overlooked, but a strong explanation is the most important step to involve yourself in the scholarly conversation. Here is where you will explain how you interpret the source you are citing, what aspect of the quote is most important for your readers to understand, and how the source pertains to your own project. For example:

> David Harvey writes, "The assumption that individual freedoms are guaranteed by freedom of the market and of trade is a cardinal feature of neoliberal thinking, and it has long dominated the US stance towards the rest of the world" (7). As Harvey explains, neoliberalism suggests that free markets do not limit personal freedom but actually lead to free individuals.

Or:

> David Harvey writes, "The assumption that individual freedoms are guaranteed by freedom of the market and of trade is a cardinal feature of neoliberal thinking, and it has long dominated the US stance towards the rest of the world" (7). For Harvey, before we understand the role of the United States in global politics, we must first understand the philosophy that binds personal freedom with market freedom.

Novice writers are sometimes tempted to end a paragraph with a quote that they feel is especially compelling or clear. But remember that you should never leave a quote to speak for itself (even if you love it). After all, as the orchestrator of this scholarly conversation, you need to make sure that readers are receiving exactly what you'd like them to receive from each quote. Notice, in the preceding examples, that the first explanation suggests that the writer quoting Harvey is centrally concerned with neo-liberal philosophy, whereas the second explanation suggests that the writer is centrally concerned with United States politics. The explanation, in other words, is the crucial link between your source and the main idea of your paper.

Avoiding Plagiarism

Scholarly conversations are what drive knowledge in the world. Scholars using each other's ideas in open, honest ways form the bedrock of our intellectual communities and ensure that our contributions to the world of thought are important. It is crucial, then, that all writers do their part in maintaining the integrity and trustworthiness of scholarly conversations. It is crucial that you never claim someone else's ideas as your own, and that you always are extra-careful to give the proper credit to someone else's thoughts. This is what we call responsible scholarship.

The best way to avoid plagiarism is to plan ahead and keep track with careful notes as you read your sources. Remember the advice (above) on *Zotero* and taking notes: Find the way that works best for you to keep track of what ideas are your own and what ideas come directly from the sources you are reading. Most acts of plagiarism are accidental. It is easy when you are drafting a paper to lose track of where a quote or idea came from; plan ahead and this won't happen. Here are a few tips for making sure that confusion doesn't happen to you.

1. Know what needs to be cited. You do not need to cite what is considered common knowledge such as facts (the day Lincoln was born), concepts (the earth orbits the sun), or events (the day Martin Luther King was shot). You do need to cite the ideas and words of others from the sources you are using in your paper.
2. Be conservative. If you are not sure if you should cite something, either ask your instructor or a librarian, or cite it. It is better to cite something you don't have to than not cite something you should.
3. Direct quotations from your sources need to be cited as well as anytime you paraphrase the ideas or words from your sources.
4. Finally, extensive citation not only helps you avoid plagiarism, but it also boosts your credibility and enables your reader to trace you scholarship.

Citation Styles

It is crucial that you adhere to the standards of a single citation style when you write your paper. The most common styles are MLA (Modern Language Association, generally used in the humanities), APA (American Psychological Association, generally used in the social sciences), and Chicago (*Chicago Manual of Style*). If you're not sure which style you should use, you must ask your instructor. Each style has its own guidelines regarding the format of the paper. Although proper formatting within a given style might seem arbitrary, there are important reasons behind the guidelines of each style. For instance, whereas MLA citations tend to emphasize author's names, APA citations tend to emphasize the date of publications. This distinction makes sense, especially given that MLA standards are usually followed by departments in the humanities and APA standards are usually followed by departments in the social sciences. Whereas papers in the humanities value original thinking about arguments and texts that are canonical and often old, papers in the social sciences tend to value arguments that take into account the most current thought and the latest research.

There are a number of helpful guidebooks that will tell you all the rules you need to know to follow the standards for various citation styles. If your instructor hasn't pointed you to a specific guidebook, try the following online resources:

Purdue Online Writing Lab: owl.english.purdue.edu/

Internet Public Library: www.ipl.org/div/farq/netciteFARQ.html

Modern Language Association (for MLA style): www.mla.org/style

American Psychological Association (for APA style): www.apastyle.org/

The Chicago Manual of Style Online: www.chicagomanualofstyle.org/tools_citationguide.html

SAMPLE STUDENT RESEARCH PAPER

Sarah Mich
Professor Ritzenberg
English 101
15 March 2013

Earth Goes Flat, English Goes Round

In cities across the United States, students practice Spanish, Chinese, and French to communicate with people around the world and to gain exposure to different cultures. The reverse current is even stronger: Globally, people clamor to learn English. This latter trend is fueled by recent developments in globalization, and what journalist Thomas Friedman calls "the flattening of the world," in which commerce has expanded from the hands of select countries to also include developing nations, companies, and, increasingly, individuals and small groups. English has become the go-to choice for these communications and has spread quickly as the language of commerce and ideas (Hitchings 300). But the resulting desire of millions to learn English, and become versed in Western culture, is a complicated prospect. Many see the trend as destructive, threatening languages and eroding cultures for the sake of multinational consumerism (Leonard). When done well, however, the teaching of English as a Foreign Language (EFL) need not be destructive. Focusing the discussion on how—not whether—English is taught ensures that students around the world are offered the same benefits that American students receive in their language classes: global communication skills that do not undermine their own language or culture.

To help protect other languages, EFL instruction should treat English as a complementary language, not a replacement. Teachers of Chinese students note that their students believe English is better than their native tongue, and interregional families in India often opt to speak English with their children instead of teaching multiple dialects (Traves, Sharma). But undervaluing language in this manner could have significant negative impacts on human communication. Lera Boroditsky, a linguist at Stanford, has shown that language shapes the way humans think and behave, and that the loss of language could limit human access to certain concepts and behaviors (118). A recent study by Boroditsky illustrates these findings by having participants arrange a set of cards according to a temporal progression. The scientists then study the direction in which the participants oriented the cards. English speakers arranged the cards left to right, whereas Hebrew speakers mostly arranged right to left, in the direction of Hebrew writing. A third case was conducted with the Kuuk Thaayorre, an aboriginal community in Australia that describes directions such as "left" and right" using cardinal coordinates. The researchers found that the Kuuk arranged their cards from east to west, independent of the direction in which they were seated, using "spatial orientation to construct their representations of time" (Boroditsky 123). Language thus allows us to create and articulate unique concepts that are linked with diverse cultures. EFL instruction can work to support this diversity. Classes could include information about research connecting language and thought, asking learners of a language to reflect on the ideas that they are able to express in a native tongue that do not carry over to English. Students could even be asked to complete exercises that incorporate some of their native language into English. The resulting phenomenon—in which speakers craft a "version" of English to reflect their own language, culture, and needs—has been documented in certain areas of the world and should be encouraged (Hitchings 308). The more students are asked to value the contributions of their own language and culture during EFL instruction, the more incentivized they will be to maintain multiple languages and the rich concepts and cultures associated with each.

Like their native tongues, the past experiences and desired outcomes of English language learners vary widely across the globe, and effective language instruction should respond to this diversity. In many ways, instruction already addresses local needs. The English training of Afghan youth in India offers a different model for local empowerment. As Afghanistan became the first epicenter for the military campaign against terrorist organizations in the wake of September 11th, English took root as a near-essential skill for Afghans wishing to advance in business or government (Polanki). Starting in 2011, the government began sponsoring a program to meet this need, sending 70 students to India for a rigorous 20-month training certificate in English. Students speak eagerly about the program, sharing their aptitude in English, recognizing the advantages it will give them, and promising to give back: "God-willing, when we return, we will teach the new generation English" (Polanki).

Mich   5

The Afghan government supports these efforts by giving out scholarships to students training as English teachers abroad. The program thus uses language to aid something larger than individual development, by creating a means for sustaining and scaling future language instruction and empowering its participants based on local need. Such programs thus avoid the trap described by journalist Julia Traves: "where once English facilitated the staffing of colonial offices, now it helps fill the cubicles of multinational corporations." By promoting instructional programs that respond to particular social contexts, and creating sustainable opportunities for local communities to grow, EFL instruction ensures that it does more good than harm.

It is not enough, however, for EFL instruction to honor native languages and local needs; it must also expose students to content about globalization, such that informed EFL learners will be able to make more active choices about the way they learn and use English. Many of these changes would be simple to implement. EFL students could be taught that by the end of the century, linguists predict 50 percent of world languages will no longer be spoken—including the native tongues of many EFL students—thus helping students think about the implications of learning English and make informed choices about their role in globalization (Leonard). Language instruction would also benefit from a discussion of why English serves as the language of choice for globalization. David Hill, who teaches English in Istanbul, writes that "English is global for highly dubious reasons: colonial, military and economic hegemony, first of the British, now of the US" (qtd. in Traves). He then goes on to argue, "If we are not to be imperialists then we must help our students to express themselves, not our agenda" (qtd. in Traves). Indeed, self-expression should be a key part of EFL education, and for that project it is essential that students learn about the larger system in which their language instruction operates. As English classrooms frequently serve as an EFL learner's first structured education on international issues, they are an important environment for discussions on globalization. Thus, individuals become informed members of global processes, using English to serve needs other than Western ones, and gaining the opportunity to develop autonomous thoughts about globalization.

Some might argue that such a teaching approach to EFL Instruction—one that emphasizes the value of native languages, fits the needs of its learning population, and discusses issues of globalization—is too prescriptive. True, this approach condones a certain set of values. But all teaching occurs around a value set, and this particular approach highlights the needs and contributions of the learners, not those who pushed English in the first place. The focus is thus on helping empower individuals around the world to take an active role in global and local processes. Is this approach feasible, though? It is, though it won't be easy. The industry for EFL is huge: a $7.8-billion one, with Western instructors pulling in sizable salaries (Traves). Textbook companies in the UK and US often teach Western values such as consumerism and materialism (Traves). But though the industry is a

Mich   7

behemoth, new approaches are emerging that could pressure EFL institutions and instructors into thinking critically about their teaching practices. At Glendon College in Ontario, for example, the Certificate in the Discipline of Teaching English as an International Language pays "close attention to issues of cultural sensitivity and autonomy when training teachers" (Traves). An English teacher halfway around the world offered a similar sentiment on an Internet discussion board: "I feel the need of reminding our students and young colleagues that the purpose of learning English is not for us to 'speak and act' like an English person . . . but to 'speak English' as an educated Indonesian" (Traves). Teachers thus play a key role in this transformation. By having more teachers—and the institutions and companies that train them—take an intentional and sensitive approach, EFL instruction could become a tool of widespread empowerment, not subjugation.

English, however, is here to stay—and growing. The way we teach English matters now and will have impacts both tomorrow and years down the road. If instruction is done blindly—with the same uncritical eye that led to years of colonialism on the part of England and the United States—we risk losing the talent and engagement of many around the world in solving global problems. This would be a loss to the world: We all own these problems and their solutions. But if EFL instruction is made intentional—used to complement other languages, engage the needs of its learners, and deliver content about globalization—we might have a shot at increasing communication and empowerment in a globalizing world.

Works Cited

Boroditsky, Lera. "How Does Our Language Shape the Way We Think?" *What's Next? Dispatches on the Future of Science: Original Essays from a New Generation of Scientists*. Ed. Max Brockman. New York: Vintage, 2009. 116–129. Print.

Friedman, Thomas. "It's a Flat World, After All." *New York Times Magazine*. New York Times, 3 Apr. 2005. Web. 25 Jan. 2013.

Hitchings, Henry. *The Language Wars: A History of Proper English*. New York: Farrar, 2011. Print.

Leonard, Stephen Pax. "Death by Monoculture." *University of Cambridge: Research*. University of Cambridge, 2 Sep. 2011. Web. 25 Jan. 2013.

Nadeem, Shehzad. "Accent Neutralisation and a Crisis of Identity in India's Call Centres." *The Guardian*. The Guardian, 9 Feb. 2011. Web. 25 Jan. 2013.

Polanki, Pallavi. "Operation Mind Your Language." *Open*. Open Mag., 29 May 2010. Web. 25 Jan. 2013.

Sharma, Reshma Krishnamurthy. "The New Language Landscape."*The Hindu Life & Style*. The Hindu, 12 Feb. 2012. Web. 25 Jan. 2013.

Traves, Julie. "The Church of Please and Thank You." *This Magazine*. This Magazine, March–April 2005. Web. 25 Jan. 2013.

index